Register Now for
to Your L

MW00857070

Your print purchase of *Treating the Traumatized Child,* **includes online access to the contents of your book**—increasing accessibility, portability, and searchability!

Access today at:

http://connect.springerpub.com/content/book/978-0-8261-7188-7 or scan the QR code at the right with your smartphone and enter the access code below.

3B3BRRU3

Scan here for quick access.

LS

SPRINGER PUBLISHING COMPANY
View all our products at springerpub.com

Advance Praise for *Treating the Traumatized Child: A Step-by-Step Family Systems Approach*

This book builds upon my early work and the work of others by offering a comprehensive guide to practitioners interested in facing and helping to heal trauma and manage the drama systemically with a special focus on children and adolescents. The FST model is a contribution to the fields of trauma, family sciences, and human development practice.

—**Charles R. Figley, PhD, Kurzweg Chair in Disaster Mental Health at Tulane University in New Orleans, Louisiana**

Across the globe and populations, researchers have consistently found that children recover better when their families are part of treatment, and virtually all parents of traumatized children also experience secondary if not direct trauma themselves. As the professional community becomes increasingly attuned to trauma, Dr. Sells and Souder's evidence-based treatment manual for frontline therapists is an invaluable resource for anyone working with children, adolescents, and families in any contemporary context. To date, I know of no other comprehensive approach that goes beyond treating trauma symptoms to ensuring a healthy and vibrant future for traumatized children and their families.

—**Diane Gehart, PhD, Professor, California State University, Northridge, and author of *Mastering Competencies in Family Therapy: A Practical Approach to Theory and Clinical Case Documentation***

Family therapy has lagged behind the rest of mental health in recognizing the impact of trauma on family patterns, so this book is very welcome and useful.

—**Richard C. Schwartz, PhD, Developer of the Internal Family Systems Model of psychotherapy**

Trauma forms the core for much of our work with children. Our field so dearly needs this well written book. Treating the Traumatized Child *offers a well-rounded road map for healing the trauma wounds that we so often confront. As a child psychiatrist with over 35 years of practice, I can only say I wish I had a guide like this when I was starting out. Highly recommended!*

—**Scott Shannon, MD, Author of *Mental Health for the Whole Child: Moving Young Clients From Disease & Disorder to Balance & Wellness***

As a family therapist, I was thrilled to read this work by skilled clinicians who know from personal experience that individual treatment, while helpful, is not long lasting when treating trauma, unless the family system is involved. This work provides cases that illustrate how individual techniques fail and family therapy triumphs, giving a marvelous suggestion, along with valuable tools for therapists to use to reach this very special population. Seasoned clinicians, new clinicians, and students will find this a treasure chest that will give them confidence when treating clients and their families for trauma and providing them with hope.

—**Linda Metcalf, PhD, Director of Graduate Counseling Programs, Texas Wesleyan University, Fort Worth, Texas, and author of *Marriage and Family Therapy: A Practice-Oriented Approach***

This is the book we have been waiting for. Using easy-to-understand metaphors as a way of capturing complex processes, this book provides a step-by-step road map to preparing, engaging, assessing, and intervening in a wide range of problems.

Well written . . . this book is striking in simplicity, while impressive in reach. We highly recommend this book as a valuable resource for family therapy practitioners, educators, and supervisors.

—**Laurie MacKinnon, MSW, PhD, and Kerrie James, MSW, MLitt, Insite Therapy and Consulting, Sydney, Australia**

Scott P. Sells, PhD, LCSW, LMFT, is former tenured professor of social work, Savannah State University, Savannah, Georgia, and associate professor at the University of Las Vegas, in Las Vegas, Nevada. Dr. Sells is the author of two best-selling books *Treating the Tough Adolescent: A Family-Based, Step-by-Step Guide* (1998) and *Parenting Your Out-of-Control Teenager: 7 Steps to Reestablish Authority and Reclaim Love* (2001). He has written more than 20 articles in such periodicals as *Psychotherapy Networker, Contemporary Corrections, Journal of Child and Adolescent Substance Abuse, Professional Issues in Criminal Justice, Family Process,* and *Journal of Marital and Family Therapy,* as well as chapters in the *Handbook of Family Therapy Research Methods* (1996) and *Social Workers' Desk Reference, Second Edition* (2008.) Dr. Sells has extensive experience as a keynote speaker for the American Association of Marriage and Family Therapy, the National Association of Social Workers, the Southeastern Psychological Association, and others. He was invited to be one of six expert presenters at the American Association of Marriage and Family Therapy's prestigious summer institutes as well as the world-renowned Cape Cod Institute. Dr. Sells is currently the founder and model developer of an evidence-based model known as Parenting with Love and Limits® (PLL), which is being used by both juvenile justice and child welfare departments in more than 14 states and in Europe.

Ellen Souder, MA, LPCC-S, holds a master's degree in professional counseling and is a family therapist, trainer, and public speaker. She has traveled extensively, conducting seminars and trainings for professional clinicians throughout the United States and Europe. Ms. Souder worked alongside Dr. Sells in the development of the evidence-based PLL treatment model, which encompasses the family systems trauma (FST) treatment model. Her personal childhood experience with trauma, as well as experience in providing treatment for traumatized youth and families through the years, provided unique insight in the co-authoring of this book. Ms. Souder is vice president of PLL and she has overseen the clinical implementation of PLL and the FST model in more than 50 agencies or organizations throughout the United States and Europe.

Treating the
TRAUMATIZED
CHILD
A Step-by-Step Family Systems Approach

Scott P. Sells, PhD, LCSW, LMFT
Ellen Souder, MA, LPCC-S

SPRINGER PUBLISHING COMPANY

Springer Publishing Company, LLC
11 West 42nd Street
New York, NY 10036
www.springerpub.com

Acquisitions Editor: Sheri W. Sussman
Compositor: Exeter Premedia Services Private Ltd.

ISBN: 978-0-8261-7187-0
ebook ISBN: 978-0-8261-7188-7

17 18 19 20 21 / 5 4 3 2 1

The author and the publisher of this Work have made every effort to use sources believed to be reliable to provide information that is accurate and compatible with the standards generally accepted at the time of publication. The author and publisher shall not be liable for any special, consequential, or exemplary damages resulting, in whole or in part, from the readers' use of, or reliance on, the information contained in this book. The publisher has no responsibility for the persistence or accuracy of URLs for external or third-party Internet websites referred to in this publication and does not guarantee that any content on such websites is, or will remain, accurate or appropriate.

Library of Congress Cataloging-in-Publication Data

Names: Sells, Scott P., author. | Souder, Ellen, author.
Title: Treating the traumatized child : a step-by-step family systems
    approach / Scott P. Sells and Ellen Souder.
Description: New York, NY : Springer Publishing Company, [2018] | Includes
    bibliographical references and index.
Identifiers: LCCN 2017033600| ISBN 9780826171870 | ISBN 9780826171887 (e-book)
Subjects: | MESH: Stress Disorders, Traumatic—therapy | Family
    Therapy—methods | Child | Adolescent
Classification: LCC RJ506.P66 | NLM WM 172.5 | DDC 618.92/8521—dc23
LC record available at https://lccn.loc.gov/2017033600

Contact us to receive discount rates on bulk purchases.
We can also customize our books to meet your needs.
For more information please contact: sales@springerpub.com

Printed in the United States of America.

To my friend, Jesus, who helped me change from the inside out and reminds me daily of how this book can help the mandate given within Malachi 4:5 in the Bible. And to my wife, Nancy, and my twin boys, David and Jonathan, who love me unconditionally and helped me become a better man. Finally, to Dr. Neil Schiff, whose friendship and mentorship over the many years allowed this book to be possible.
—*Scott Sells*

To my mom, Mary D. Vaughn, who lived a life that was solely devoted to service; service to her Lord and Savior Jesus Christ, service to her family, and service to everyone else she came in contact with. She taught me what it means to show grace and love to others, how to overcome obstacles without complaining, and how to find the sweet and wonderful things in life no matter the circumstance. She was and always will be the best example of a person who truly lived out everything she taught.
—*Ellen Souder*

Contents

Foreword

Treating the Traumatized Child is one of the first books of its kind to move from the perspective of the traumatized child to the child as part of the traumatized family. What is also unique is the detailed step-by-step procedures and handouts to help the therapist go from point A to point B. It took the authors 8 long years to develop, research, and create the FST model.

I first met Scott Sells at an international conference more than 13 years ago and was impressed by how easily he could take complex theoretical concepts and simplify them into easy-to-understand procedures. Later, I asked him to train our entire staff in the Netherlands on the principles of his first two books and an evidence-based model known as PLL.

Twelve years later, we are still using PLL and have even translated the curriculum into Dutch. Therefore, it is my great pleasure to write the foreword of this book. Scott Sells has brought to this book the same spirit and tenacity with which he approached his earlier work, giving the reader step-by-step procedures for working with the traumatized child.

Sells and his coauthor, Ellen Souder, give us the structure and tools we need to be active and for supporting therapists to help the family get out of painful and damaging interactions. Traumatic events that hit individuals also affect the family as a whole. We know a lot about individual trauma therapy for the child, but much less about how to use the family's power to help their child grieve and move on with their lives in the here and now. This is exemplified when the parent says something like "We want to move forward with these wounds instead of getting stuck in our past." In the same way that families need support and structure to confront their destructive patterns, professionals need support and, as the authors emphasize, "clear step-by-step procedures."

Therapists also want techniques and tools that can be used in a flexible way to fit each unique family. In this book, the step-by-step procedures, techniques, and tools are flexible enough to fit different families and cultures. Examples include the stress chart that can be used to understand one another's stress levels and the seed/tree diagram, which can help the family move away from a child-only–centered problem to one that is systemic in nature. Specific skills are highlighted, such as how to integrate safety planning, nutrition, and self-regulation, and use what are called "wound playbooks"—strategic directives to get the family unstuck and heal the child's trauma. The authors describe how to successfully engage and include the extended family, and emphasize the hidden power this contains to heal what is called complex trauma.

My own experience has reinforced for me how important it is that the therapist know how to curb emotions and protect the family from inadvertently hurting each other by asking loaded questions such as, "Why didn't you come to me for help when it happened?" The therapist must prepare for those interactions and have techniques ready to use immediately. Sells and Souder show the therapist how to do this, for example, by using statements such as "Freeze!" if the family or child starts to over-flood with emotion, as well as showing why the trauma is not healing on its own through what are known as "unhealthy undercurrents" or interactional feedback loops, which can be illustrated using a flip chart or PowerPoint.

Structure is also offered using a phased or staged approach. This means that behavioral or hybrid contracts may be used to first stabilize the child or adolescent's extreme symptoms (e.g., self-harm, suicidal ideation, depression, aggression, substance abuse) before active trauma work is initiated. In other words, prior to setting the goals of therapy, the therapist must answer the critical question of whether the evidence suggests stabilization or safety planning first and active trauma work second, or whether immediate trauma work is possible. The three rules of thumb for this important decision are outlined in Chapter 5.

After reading this book, I came to an important conclusion. The goal of the book is not to advocate for a systems approach over an individual one but to reinforce how integration of the two together can be accomplished and be more effective in the long run.

Sander van Arum is an independent expert consultant, developer, and tutor with many years of experience in working with both victims and perpetrators of domestic violence and child abuse. For many years, he was chief clinical director at De Waag, a specialized ambulatory organization for mental health care in the Netherlands. He is chief tutor at the Centrale Rinogroep, a large Dutch postgraduate training center for the mental health professions. Focus in his clinical work is on family trauma, relational violence, child abuse within the family, and family resilience.

In close collaboration with his colleague Linda Vogtländer, child psychiatrist, he developed and implemented assessment tools and treatment programs, which integrate individual and systemic approaches in working with adults and children.

He holds a Master of Science in Clinical Child, Family, and Education Studies from the University of Utrecht. He is a fully licensed all-around psychotherapist and supervisor, and chairs the forensic systems therapy section of the Dutch Association for Relational and Family Therapy.

Preface

Everywhere one turns, there seems to be another book on trauma-informed practice. But within these books, there are several missing core pieces.

Work with the traumatized child or adolescent involves individual therapy. Individually focused trauma-informed therapy models abound. Examples include but are not limited to trauma-focused cognitive therapy (TF-CBT), neurobiological trauma treatment (NTT), developmental therapy, attachment-focused therapy (AFT), dialectical behavior therapy (DBT), and eye movement desensitization reprocessing (EMDR). However, for the most part, the focus is how to treat the traumatized child through individual therapy. Moving from the perspective of the traumatized child to the child as part of a traumatized family within a systems theory framework is limited.

Additionally, traumatized children and families are lacking answers to the "Now what?" question:

> Dr. Sells, it helped to talk about our child's wounds and ours. But NOW WHAT? What do we do in the here and now to heal these wounds? In fact, the more we talk about it, the worse we feel. We want tools to move forward instead of getting stuck in our past.

Finally, frontline therapists like theory and general concepts up to a point. But after the theory, therapists want and need the "mini-steps" or detailed step-by-step procedures with a plethora of case examples. This is especially the case when it comes to navigating the complexities of treating traumatized children and their families.

Treating the Traumatized Child was written in response to these challenges. It synthesizes 8 years of research with children and their families in 15 different states (c.f., Karam, Sterrett, & Kiaer, 2017; Sells, Smith, & Rodman, 2006; Sells, Sullivan, & DeVore, 2012; Sells, Winokur-Early, & Smith, 2011; Sterrett-Hong, Karam, & Kiaer, 2017; Winokur-Early, K, Chapman, & Hand, 2013).

An early treatment failure makes an interesting backstory to the writing of this book. Our first two books, entitled *Treating the Tough Adolescent* (Sells, 2004) and *Parenting Your Out-of-Control Teenager* (Sells, 2002), provided therapists and parents with step-by-step interventions for treating children and adolescents between the ages of 10 and 18 years with extreme emotional and behavioral problems. However, outcomes showed that a percentage of children and families were relapsing after initial success with this process.

At first, we thought these relapses could be explained within the context of a first- versus second-order change. In other words, while the family was initially successful in applying new behavioral techniques (first-order change), they did not adopt changed roles or communication patterns as their "new normal" after treatment ended (second-order change). Therefore, when stressful situations occurred, the family went back to old interactional patterns and the child or adolescent relapsed. In addition, we also thought that the stabilization of a chaotic and disorganized family system would also heal the trauma within both the child and the family.

However, an early treatment failure dispelled these initial assumptions and ignited the spark for this book to be written. We call this case the **Uncorked Bottle**.

The treatment failure ironically began with a treatment success. Fifteen-year-old Allison came into therapy with extreme symptoms of aggression, disrespect, and clinical depression. After 3 months of intensive outpatient family therapy, Allison was symptom-free and ready for graduation or termination from treatment. However, this outcome suddenly changed when Allison's mom called and asked to see Dr. Sells alone. At this meeting, the mother dropped a bombshell:

> Dr. Sells, Allison continues to do well. She is no longer violent and disrespectful. And her depression has lifted. Mike and I continue to use the new tools you taught us on how to be consistent, stop button pushing, and use consistent hugs each day to foster nurturance. However, as things have gotten better with Allison, I am getting worse. I am suddenly having flashbacks and nightmares of past sexual abuse by my own father that I buried long ago. I have stopped all intimacy with my husband, and in turn, he has grown cold and is verbally abusive. I feel such shame that I will not tell him about the abuse. Mike also said that he thought we would be "home free" after Allison got better and that we could finally re-kindle our love and our marriage.
>
> And it gets worse. Allison is watching me like a hawk. Yesterday, she came to me and said, "We had a deal. You told me that if I (Allison) got better, you and dad would get better." Instead, Allison has watched me get worse and sees that I am now depressed and unhappy. Allison actually threatened to return to old ways as a way to distract me from the pain I am going through. I don't want Allison to sacrifice herself for me, but I don't know what to do or where else to turn.

The mother's bombshell revealed critical information and blind spots in our previous assumptions. While the mom and dad were moving into second-order change with Allison, unresolved trauma with Allison's mom was fueling current and new symptoms. Unchecked, Allison's relapse was inevitable.

This case represented an uncorked bottle. The mother's trauma of her past sexual abuse was not revealed during treatment and was out of her awareness. It only came to the surface after Allison metaphorically uncorked the bottle by becoming symptom-free. Without Allison in perpetual crisis to distract from the pain, her mom started having flashbacks. Her unresolved trauma rose to the surface and set off a ripple effect of conflict and family secrets in the marriage.

To make matters worse, Dr. Sells did not have a treatment model outlining how to work with the entire family when there was clear unresolved trauma. When he sought other treatment models that articulated a family systems approach to trauma work, he could find none that suited his needs. Models that did exist articulated generalized concepts but lacked clear step-by-step procedures. Dr. Sells met with Allison's mom individually to recommend a self-referral to someone in the community with skills in individual trauma treatment. However, the mother refused, citing the fact that a great deal of trust and rapport had been built through the earlier family therapy with Allison. In addition, the marriage had quickly moved to a crisis point of possible divorce. Mom stated that she did not feel strong enough to reveal the secret of the abuse to another therapist.

Based on this information, Dr. Sells agreed to see the mother on an individual basis to address the traumatic symptoms along with conjoint marital therapy. He researched, read, and applied principles from several well-known trauma-informed models that outlined individual therapy for adults. Then, after several individual sessions and a marital therapy session with the husband and wife to discuss the sexual abuse, the mother turned to Dr. Sells and asked, "Now what?"

> I have talked about my abuse on my own and now with my husband. After initially feeling better and getting an emotional release, I am starting to get worse. Re-telling the story is starting to make me worse. So my question is, "Now what?" What tools are you going to give me, my husband, and my daughter to help us move past these wounds in the present and not get stuck in the past?

Dr. Sells did not have an answer. He had plenty of family systems tools to alter stuck family interactions but nothing to alter those around trauma. More individual treatment was recommended and, while there was some initial improvement, stress remained high with little systemic change to the husband-and-wife relationship or the mother's trauma around the sexual abuse. As predicted, Allison, the daughter, soon relapsed. The husband then gave up and stopped coming to sessions. In turn, the mother lost confidence in the treatment approach and terminated therapy prematurely.

We learned much from this first-identified treatment failure around trauma. We were reminded of the saying "Necessity is the mother of all invention" (n.d.). That is, when the need for something becomes imperative, one is forced to find ways of getting or achieving it. If we were to be able to deal with similar cases of trauma in the future, we realized it was imperative that we go back to the drawing board to address three key research questions.

First:

- What were the diagnostic indicators that would indicate that trauma, or what we termed **unhealed wounds**, were key drivers of the adolescent's presenting problems or symptoms? Moreover, how should we present this information to the family from a strengths-based perspective that would not cause family members to get scared and end treatment prematurely?

Second:

- When was behavior modification useful, appropriate, and helpful, and when should family systems trauma work be initiated? (Timing is everything.)

And third:

- How do we develop a step-by-step family systems trauma model integrating the same structural–strategic family systems principles that undergirded the first two books?

We discovered that finding the answers to these questions, and developing detailed step-by-step procedures, was no easy task. Building the FST model would involve a long, 8-year trek (see Chapter 3). To begin this journey, we painstakingly replicated the grounded theory and task analysis (Sells, Smith, & Sprenkle, 1995) research methods from *Treating the Tough Adolescent* (Sells, 2004) to analyze key in-session change events from videotaped sessions with therapists using newly developed FST model interventions. We also used what are called ethnographic focus group interviews with both clients and therapists (Sells, Newfield, Smith, & Newfield, 1996; Sells, Smith, & Moon, 1996; Sells, Smith, & Newfield, 1997).

As was the case in the earlier book (Sells, 2004), this labor-intensive process yielded key moments of change as well as step-by step procedures that helped answer the original three research questions. This included the timing of when and how to implement each step with behavioral interventions to stabilize the family and the ideal timing of when to actively address child or adolescent trauma using what we called **wound playbooks** (see Chapters 5 and 6).

For those curious about the type of research process used to create this book, we direct you to Chapter 12, entitled "Process-Outcome Research and the Family-Based Model: Refining and Operationalizing Key Theoretical Concepts," in *Treating the Tough Adolescent* (cf., Sells, 2004). We chose not to replicate the chapter for this book as the process is well described elsewhere, and this book is designed as a resource for practical application, not research.

Moving from research to practice, the Family Systems Trauma (FST) model in this book is a key component of the evidence-based Parenting with Love and Limits (PLL) system of care. A traditional treatment model uses a book or manualized curriculum to teach individual therapists techniques and strategies. This book and the other books by the author (cf., Sells, 2002; 2004) accomplish this goal. In contrast, a system of care (cf., Cook & Kilmer, 2010) contains both the model curriculum *and* essential tools for outcome research and implementation to become evidence-based.

These tools include supervision fidelity measures, intensive training by model developers, and a research outcome infrastructure to measure the model's effectiveness. Both therapists and agencies often believe that treatment models and a **system of care** are one and the same. They are not. Without the system of care piece, therapists receive the techniques in a book, but lack the tools necessary to assess both model effectiveness and therapist fidelity. Without the latter, the FST treatment model and other models cannot be evidence-based.

In response to this problem, the PLL system of care was created which includes both the treatment model and the research and implementation components. This includes the manualized curriculum of the PLL-FST (Family Systems Trauma) model in this book and what is called PLL-FSS (Family Systems Stabilization; outlined in Chapter 3) and PLL-Group Therapy (Sells, 2004). It should be noted the PLL system of care includes an end-to-end service delivery model that goes beyond the written pages of this book.

The PLL system of care has been replicated and is currently used by mental health agencies and state child welfare and juvenile justice departments in 13 states and Europe. PLL is currently listed on SAMHSA's (Substance Abuse and Mental Health Services Administration) National Registry of Evidence-Based Programs (cf., www.nrepp.samhsa.gov), the OJJDP (Office of Juvenile Justice Delinquency and Prevention) Model Programs Guide (www.ojjdp.gov/mpg), and the CEBC (California Evidence-Based Clearinghouse for Child Welfare) (cf., www.cebc4cw.org).

The PLL system of care contains each of the following implementation components. For more information, please visit www.gopll.com.

- Treatment Models and Manualized Curriculum of PLL-FST (Family Systems Trauma), PLL-FSS (Family Systems Stabilization), and PLL-Group Therapy
- Five days of intensive onsite training
- Monthly supervision by PLL clinical supervisors
- Fidelity measures including submission of videotapes of PLL sessions
- 24/7 availability of a PLL clinical supervisor
- Computerized dashboard to measure outcomes in real time
- Dedicated implementation staff
- Fidelity site reviews
- Quasi-experimental research evaluations

Overview of the Book

Key concepts or themes that make this book unique and exciting to read include:

- A step-by-step road map and case examples to illustrate the clear integration of the FST model with unresolved trauma in children and adolescents, aged 10 through 18 years, and their families
- Detailed techniques within Chapters 3 through 13 that provide therapists with both the knowledge base and concrete tools they need to use the FST model with their clients
- A complementary fit between FST and more traditional individual trauma treatment methods (e.g., TF-CBT or NTT). Trauma treatment can be extremely effective when individual and family therapy are used in concert with one another
- Multiple case examples to illustrate the application and integration of the FST model

The reader is encouraged to first read and master Part I, which features three chapters that connect FST theory into practice, and then delve deeply into the actual techniques and strategies in Part II. In other words, "zoom out" before "zooming in." Otherwise, the reader runs the risk of becoming eclectic rather than integrative. The former involves being a master of techniques but using them like a bag of tricks, whereas the latter involves having a solid theoretical base with a clear understanding of when and how to best apply a particular FST technique or strategy.

We hope you find this outcome of our work from the past 8 years helpful to your practice. We built this model from the ground up—or from the families themselves. As you read this book, we hope the families' stories of pain and triumph are well represented. Finally, as an added bonus, the authors will use brief video interviews that describe interesting backstories about each chapter and key insights. To view these brief interviews please go to either www.gopll.com/trauma or www.familytrauma.org and go to "Videos." Other online resources will also be available.

REFERENCES

Cook, J. R., & Kilmer, R. P. (2010). Defining the scope of systems of care: An ecological perspective. *Evaluation and Program Planning, 33*(1), 18–20.

Karam, E. A., Sterrett, E. M., & Kiaer, L. (2017). The integration of family and group therapy as an alternative to juvenile incarceration: A quasi-experimental evaluation using Parenting with Love and Limits. *Family Process, 56*(2), 331–347. doi:10.1111/famp.12187

Necessity is the mother of all invention. (n.d.). In *Cambridge Dictionary*. Retrieved from http://dictionary.cambridge.org/dictionary/english/necessity-is-the-mother-of-invention

Sells, S. P. (2002). *Parenting your out-of-control teenager*. New York, NY: St. Martin's Press.

Sells, S. P. (2004). *Treating the tough adolescent: A step-by-step, family-based guide*. New York, NY: Guilford Press.

Sells, S. P., Newfield, N., Smith, T. E., & Newfield, S. (1996). Ethnographic research methods. In D. H. Sprenkle & S. M. Moon (Eds.), *Handbook of family therapy research methods* (pp. 25–63). New York, NY: Guilford Press.

Sells, S. P., Smith, T. E., & Moon, S. (1996). An ethnographic study of client and therapist perceptions of therapy effectiveness in a university-based training clinic. *Journal of Marital and Family Therapy, 22*(3), 321–343.

Sells, S. P., Smith, T. E., & Newfield, N. (1997). Teaching ethnographies in social work: A model course. *Journal of Social Work Education, 33*(1), 1–18.

Sells, S. P., Smith, T. E., & Rodman, J. (2006). Reducing substance abuse through Parenting with Love and Limits. *Journal of Child and Adolescent Substance Abuse, 15*, 105–115.

Sells, S. P., Smith, T. E., & Sprenkle, D. (1995). Integrating quantitative and qualitative methods: A research model. *Family Process, 34*, 199–218.

Sells, S. P., Sullivan, I., & DeVore, D. (2012). Stopping the madness: A new reentry system for juvenile corrections. *Corrections Today, 74*, 40–45.

Sells, S. P., Winokur-Early, K., & Smith, T. E. (2011). Reducing adolescent oppositional and conduct disorders: An experimental design using Parenting with Love and Limits. *Professional Issues in Criminal Justice, 6*(3), 9–30.

Sterrett-Hong, E. M., Karam, E., & Kiaer, L. (2017). Statewide implementation of Parenting with Love and Limits among youth with co-existing internalizing and externalizing functional impairments reduces return to service rates and treatment costs. *Administration and Policy in Mental Health and Mental Health Services Research, 44*(5), 792–809. doi:10.1007/s10488-016-0788-4

Winokur-Early, K., Chapman, S. F., & Hand, G. A. (2013). Family-focused juvenile reentry services: A quasi-experimental design evaluation of recidivism outcomes. *Journal of Juvenile Justice, 2*(2), 1–22.

Acknowledgments

I wish to thank several people who supported me over the years to make this 8-year journey to write this book a reality. I want to first thank Dr. Neil Schiff and Jay Haley. As a young PhD student, both Neil and Jay allowed me to do a research study with them that led to my first book, *Treating the Tough Adolescent*. And now, 17 years later, this book was birthed and it all originated from their kindness and belief in me. To my mentor, Dr. Tom Smith, who was a friend, teacher, and mentor throughout my years at Florida State and beyond. To my staff and team at PLL—Parenting with Love and Limits. They have always been there for me and together we did the impossible: created a grassroots evidence-based model outside a university setting. To my co-author, Ellen. Together, we forged new ground; this book would not be possible without her wisdom and guidance. She has always believed in me. To my father, who taught me how to become the man I am today, and my mother, who has always been in my corner.

Special thanks goes out to Sheri W. Sussman, our editor, at Springer Publishing. Her amazing patience and encouragement for this project was a true inspiration. And to the 24/7 prayer room and staff at IHOP. I spent many days and nights in the prayer room to complete this work (it was like a sauna) and always felt the love and support of the staff.

—Scott Sells

I wish to thank my husband of 37 years, Bruce Souder. Bruce has supported me over the years in everything I have done and is truly the "rock" that keeps me going. Thank you for your patience, love, and prayers … I could not have cowritten this book without you.

I also want to thank Scott Sells for our long-standing friendship and for letting me join him in this amazing journey of writing this book, and in the journey of creating the PLL model. What an amazing ride this has been and I am grateful for the "too many to count" brainstorming sessions throughout the last decade. I am a better therapist for it. And to John Burek, PLL President and CEO, and the rest of the PLL team—you all are the most amazing group of people I have ever had the privilege of working alongside. I love our "we" spirit and can't thank you all enough for your friendship and for what each of you brings to our team.

Finally, special thanks goes out to all the families who have been served through PLL and the FST model. Your courage in the midst of the storms of life and willingness to embrace new ideas and tools for positive change are nothing short of inspirational. You are our heroes and we thank you for letting us walk with you in your journey toward healing.

—Ellen Souder

A Family Systems Trauma (FST) Model Treating the Traumatized Child and Family

1

Why a Family Systems Trauma Model?

Articles and therapeutic literature over the past decade have reflected a groundswell of interest in the topic of trauma, particularly in the neurobiology of trauma and various treatment approaches (cf., Chapman, 2014; Levine & Frederick, 1997; Siegel & Solomon, 2003; van der Kolk, 2015). However, trauma treatment for the most part is individual therapy with limited to no active family participation from a systems theory perspective. Systems therapists conceptualize symptoms in terms of family interactions and prioritize family rather than the individual as the primary site of intervention.

In line with this trend, adolescent trauma treatment is primarily focused on the individual using such models as Trauma-Focused Cognitive Therapy (TF-CBT; Cohen, Mannarino, & Deblinger, 2012), Neurobiological Trauma Treatment (NTT; Chapman, 2014; Siegel, 1999; van der Kolk, 1994), Developmental Therapy (Blaustein & Kinniburgh, 2010), Attachment-Focused Therapy (AFT; Gomez-Perales, 2015; James, 1994), Dialectical Behavior Therapy (DBT; Eich, 2015), and Eye Movement Desensitization Reprocessing (EMDR; Gomez, 2012).

Two models that employ a family systems emphasis (Emotionally-Focused Therapy [EFT] and Trauma Systems Therapy [TFT]) either focus exclusively on couples using EFT (Johnson, 2002) or employ generalized family systems principles using TFT (Saxe, Ellis, & Kaplow, 2007). A standout in FST work is Figley's (1988) Family Traumatic Stress Therapy (FTST). This five-phase treatment model aims to rebuild rapport and trust among family members, promote self-disclosure, and help the family develop a healing theory. However, this model does not provide a clear road map on how to treat the troubled adolescent as the identified client with the presenting problem.

Additionally, there is a lack of research and books on how to integrate trauma-informed practice within the context of structural and strategic family therapy. This omission is important because both structural and strategic family therapy have been rated as model programs with research effectiveness for both children and adolescents in preventing and reducing substance abuse, violence, mental illness, and disruptive behaviors (Coatsworth, Santisteban, McBride, & Szapocznik, 2001; Karam, Sterrett, & Kiaer, 2016; Lambie & Rokutaini, 2002; Nickel et al., 2006; Rowe, Parker-Sloat, Schwartz, & Liddle, 2003; Santisteban et al., 2003; Scattergood, Dash, Epstein, & Adler, 1998; Sells, 2002, 2004; Springer & Orsbon, 2002; Szapocznik et al., 1989; Winokur-Early, Chapman, & Hand, 2013). This is an important gap because as James and MacKinnon (2012, p. 193) write:

> If the therapist focuses on here and now problems, for example, developing communication skills, supporting parents to be firmer and more consistent in managing a defiant child, or helping parents set behavioral consequences, and, if in fact unresolved trauma is fueling the family's difficulties, these interventions may work temporarily only to fall apart during times of stress when someone "loses it." Without an understanding of the underlying trauma, family therapists have no way to make sense of these treatment failures.

The risk for relapse is high when a structural–strategic family therapist attempts to restructure the family through behavioral consequences without also addressing the underlying trauma. It is analogous to pulling weeds (the symptoms) without addressing the roots (the underlying trauma), only to find the weeds returning again and again. This results in "first-order change," temporarily changing the roles of the family, without "second-order change," a change to the core interactional patterns and rules, keeping the family stuck (Gehart, 2013). Without second-order change, permanent change in the child or family is unlikely after treatment ends.

To address these gaps, this book on the family systems trauma (FST) model targets four areas of trauma treatment with children and adolescents aged 10 to 18 years: (a) integration of trauma and family systems theory with children; (b) answering the "Now what?" question; (c) step-by-step strategies and techniques for the frontline FST therapist; and (d) next steps that move from behavioral stabilization to active trauma treatment.

GAP 1: INTEGRATION OF TRAUMA AND FAMILY SYSTEMS THEORY WITH CHILDREN

Figley and Figley's (2009) research provided two central reasons why it is better to keep the entire family together in trauma treatment within a family systems framework. First, other family members may be traumatized by one of their members' traumatic experiences. And second, the family has the potential to be an important source of both support and validation for a traumatized member. Figley and Kiser (2013) also determined four primary ways in which a family system can be traumatized:

- *Simultaneous effects*: All members of the family are directly affected by the traumatic event, such as in natural disasters, auto accidents, or the unexpected death of a loved one.

- *Vicarious effects*: Other family members are traumatized vicariously when they learn that another family member has experienced an emotional traumatic event.

- *Chiasma traumatic stress*: Other family members are traumatized through exposure to the experience of the traumatized member.

- *Intrafamilial trauma*: Family members are traumatized by other family members, such as in cases of abuse or divorce.

We concur with these findings and believe that even though the identified patient is the traumatized child or adolescent, the immediate and extended family is also likely traumatized (secondarily). Hence, these family members not only provide support for the child but can also act as the antidote to the trauma itself. The power of the family as this antidote is limitless if they have a clear playbook, clarified roles, and dress rehearsals to practice playbook delivery. In addition, in the process of healing the child, family members heal themselves.

In alignment with these findings, Chapter 3 illustrates a five-phase FST model flowchart. After this overview, Part II, provides detailed techniques and strategies within Chapters 4 to 13 to provide the mini-steps and tools needed to incorporate the FST model into everyday practice. This level of detail was developed so that the FST model can be learned and applied even if the therapist does not have an extensive background in family systems theory, structural–strategic family therapy, or trauma-informed practice. More advanced therapists who already use a family systems paradigm will also appreciate this level of detail.

In addition, this book was written to show an integration between family systems work and more traditional individual trauma methods (e.g., TF-CBT or NTT). The goal is to demonstrate the benefits of a "both/and" approach, not "either/or." Little has been written on how this kind of integration is accomplished. Trauma treatment can be extremely effective when individual and family therapy are used in concert with one another. However, as the following case example illustrates, one treatment modality used in isolation of the other can have negative implications for the client.

Case Example

Fifteen-year-old Sally successfully completed individual Cognitive Behavioral Therapy (CBT). As a result, Sally's symptoms of post-traumatic stress disorder (PTSD)—headaches with no medical cause, nightmares, and aggression—were much improved. However, the parent–child conflict remained unchanged and was never addressed, and the mother continued to show little to no nurturance toward her daughter. This perpetuated an existing feedback loop or interactional pattern of the father continuing to take Sally's side against the mother. In turn, this pattern fueled bitter marital conflict. Sally remained hopelessly stuck in the middle of this conflict.

Over time, the positive work of the individual CBT treatment started to unravel. Each of Sally's PTSD symptoms started to worsen as the family stress remained. None of the participants (parents, Sally, or therapist) understood the family systems dynamics that ignited and maintained Sally's PTSD or underlying trauma. Due to the relapse, the parents viewed the CBT treatment as ineffective. The parents then mistakenly concluded that Sally was untreatable. The hope that Sally initially experienced after the initial CBT treatment vanished when there was no change in the family system. The parents refused further treatment and termination with Sally was premature.

Salvador Minuchin, during an interview, highlighted the potential dangers of individual trauma work without a systemic focus (using the example of attachment therapy):

Focusing so intensely on the early mother-child bond, attachment-based therapy neglects a vast range of important human influences and experiences. The entire family—not just the mother or primary caretaker—including father, siblings, grandparents, often cousins, aunts and uncles, are extremely significant in the experience of the child.

It takes us back to the heyday of psychoanalysis and denies the full familial and social reality of children's lives, as well as obscuring our understanding of the context in which they grew up. . . .

These days, therapists too often talk as if child therapy is the same thing as "trauma therapy." But, the danger of focusing so much on trauma is that you develop the view that trauma is somehow the human condition, rather than occasionally a part of it. It is always tempting to make an entire psychotherapy theory from cases of the most extreme pathology. (Sykes Wylie & Turner, 2014, pp. 14–15)

GAP 2: ANSWERING THE "NOW WHAT?" QUESTION

A second important reason for the FST model is directly related to the "Now what?" question discussed briefly in the Preface. In the early years of trauma treatment, we thought that cathartic approaches of retelling the traumatic story would be enough. However, inevitably, the child or family would request tools in the here and now to move past talk and into action. As one father stated, "Now what? After talking about our trauma, we want tools to heal our pain so that we can move past it." These same kinds of statements propelled us to take the same path that Levine and Frederick (1997, p. 38) wrote about in their classic trauma book *Waking the Tiger: Healing Trauma*:

> Contrary to popular belief, trauma can be healed. Not only can it be healed, but in many cases it can be healed without long hours of therapy; without painful reliving of memories; and without a continuing reliance on medication. We must realize that it is neither necessary nor possible to change past events. Old trauma symptoms are examples of bound-up energy and lost lessons. The past doesn't matter when we learn how to be present; every moment becomes new and creative. We have only to heal our present symptoms and proceed. A healing moment ripples forward and back, out and about.

The authors' comments of moving from "old trauma symptoms to healing present day symptoms and proceeding forward" directly mirrors the "Now what?" question. We found the answer to this question through what we call "wound playbooks." Wound playbooks are strategic directives or tasks used by the family to actively heal the unresolved trauma in the here and now. In this way, structural and strategic family therapy are integrated together. The playbook is the strategic directive used to change the stuck interactional patterns (undercurrents) and restructure the family. The following case example outlines this process.

Case Example

Sixteen-year-old Trevon was returning to the community after finishing residential treatment for the second time. In all the years of treatment, no one had included the family or inquired about events surrounding his first outbreak of aggression and running away at an early age. After careful questioning, it was revealed that Trevon's grandfather had died 2 years ago from cancer. Trevon's dad had abandoned the family when he was a child, so his grandfather was the only dad he ever knew. During the family session, it was obvious that no one in the family had grieved the loss. In addition, there was underlying conflict between the grandmother and mother who were now raising Trevon in the same house together. They appeared to blame one another for the grandfather's death with finger-pointing whenever the grandfather was discussed. The major lie that the grandmother believed was that mom going to prison for a short time broke the grandfather's heart and caused the cancer. Trevon felt caught in the middle of this conflict and felt like he had to choose sides. As a result, the home became toxic, and Trevon ran away from home constantly.

To address these issues, the FST therapist came up with a creative wound playbook that contained the strategic directive or task of a 5K cancer run in his grandfather's memory. The central reframing techniques used around the playbook were as follows: (a) If Trevon could not talk out his grief, he could sweat it out through the run, and (b) instead of running away, he could run for his grandfather. Soon everyone in the family was energized and had a clear role to play to help Trevon heal. The local YMCA director was invited to the session and he left so inspired that he agreed to come over three mornings a week to train Trevon for the race at no cost.

Figure 1.1 is a reproduction of this wound playbook.

Playbook for grief:
"Running the race" in grandpa's memory

Who:
- ➢ Trevon with mom and grandma as his "cheering section"

What:
- ➢ Trevon will run in a 5K cancer race in honor of his grandpa

When:
- ➢ Race date: July 12, 2014
- ➢ Training will begin next week on Monday, Wednesday, and Saturday mornings at 6 a.m.
- ➢ Sponsors will be obtained 2 weeks prior to the raceby mom and Trevon

Where:
- ➢ At racing location
- ➢ Training will occur at local track with YMCA director

How:
- ➢ Trevon and mom will meet with the YMCA director to outline training schedule (see preceding text)
- ➢ Trevon and grandma will get special racing t-shirt made with grandpa's picture on the front
- ➢ Mom will assist trevon in going into the community to get sponsors—all proceeds will go to the cancer society
- ➢ Trevon will work with the YMCA director to train for the race, following the training schedule they developed together (see preceding text)

Figure 1.1 Wound playbook for unhealed grief.

As illustrated in the preceding case example, the wound playbook was the strategic directive or catalyst to restructure the family by healing not only Trevon but everyone else in the family as well. All family members experienced what Figley and Kiser (2013) called "simultaneous effects" (all family members were directly impacted by grandfather's death), chiasma stress (all family members were traumatized through exposure to Trevon), and "intrafamilial trauma" (whereby stress from the trauma caused conflict between family members, such as grandmother and mom).

However, after the wound playbook, the grandmother's mood immediately went from depressed to energized and joyful when she printed t-shirts with the grandfather's picture on it. And from this place of joy, grandmother was open to forgiving her daughter (Trevon's mom). And from this healed relationship, Trevon was no longer caught in the middle and the home was no longer toxic. Mother and son also started to become close again through the common goal of the race. Trevon and his grandmother grew closer and reconciled. Trevon reported that the "Now what?" was answered. His grief was healing through the run. After the 5K run, there were still grief issues to work through (e.g., how to say goodbye). However, the playbook jump-started the process and was the catalyst to restructure the family. By clearly typing out on a wound playbook the who, what, when, where, and how, each family member's role was clarified. The family was mobilized with a clear action plan to help Trevon heal his grief and, in the process, heal themselves.

In Chapter 8, a menu of creative strategic directives is presented along with ways in which these directives can be turned into wound playbooks to restructure the family to answer the "Now what?" question and heal trauma both within the child and the family. The benefits of blending structural and strategic family therapy with the "Now what?" question are highlighted.

GAP 3: STEP-BY-STEP STRATEGIES AND TECHNIQUES FOR THE FRONTLINE THERAPIST

In Chapter 12 of Dr. Sells' book, *Treating the Tough Adolescent: A Family-Based, Step-by-Step Guide* (Sells, 2004), research revealed a lack of treatment models that outlined specific treatment components within a counseling session, which effected change (e.g., Chamberlain & Rosicky, 1995). In other words, frontline therapists did not have access to "mini-steps." These are the step-by-step procedures, techniques, and therapeutic maneuvers within a particular treatment model that create change with a client or family system. Even Pinsof and Wynne (1995), in their now classic review of all marital and family outcome research, concluded that "it was impossible to know what actually occurred in counseling [to create change]" (p. 606).

Frontline therapists often survey "who won" confirmatory studies that conclude that one treatment model is more effective than another but lack the detailed steps than created the change. These studies answer the question of whether a treatment model works but fail to answer the question "*How* does it work?" When this occurs, counseling becomes a mystical process behind closed doors whereby the therapist follows no manualized procedures or standardization of a particular model. The therapist instead becomes eclectic, using many different techniques to effect change, instead of integrative, whereby one follows the disciplined pattern of timing and step-by-step application of techniques based on theory.

Early in his career, Dr. Sells experienced this problem firsthand. His first clinical position was at an adolescent psychiatric hospital as a family therapist. During family sessions, Dr. Sells used techniques such as "sculpting," "genograms," or "reframing" (Sherman & Fredman, 1986). But he lacked the timing or step-by-step procedures for when and how to use these techniques based on theory. For example, Dr. Sells mistakenly used the technique of "intensity" with an already aggressive 13-year-old boy. Intensity is a technique that involves turning up the emotional heat in the room through voice tone, pacing, or word choice to break stuck interactional patterns (S. Minuchin & Fishman, 1981). Dr. Sells asked the mother to look her son in the eye and say in a booming voice "Cut the crap or you'll lose all of your television privileges for a month." Immediately, the boy escalated and spit in Dr. Sells' face. Dr. Sells quickly went to the book on his desk to see the next steps to take. Finding nothing, he looked helplessly at the mother and said, "I don't know what to do next!" The kid threw back his head and laughed, "I told you this guy didn't know what he was doing," and then walked out of the session. From this traumatic experience, Dr. Sells knew that any books he consulted or wrote in future had to contain step-by-step procedures that were grounded in theory to help the frontline therapist.

As a result, both of Dr. Sells' first two books, *Treating the Tough Adolescent* (Sells, 2004) and *Parenting Your Out-of-Control Teenager: 7 Steps to Reestablish Authority and Reclaim Love* (Sells, 2002), contain detailed step-by-step procedures tied to structural–strategic theory. This book follows the same blueprint. Each chapter contains detailed steps along with numerous case studies to illustrate key points. In addition, when necessary, there is even a recommended script for what to say to the family to introduce or complete each mini-step. Family therapy with a multi-stressed family is challenging even on a good day. And when one adds unresolved trauma, the complexity skyrockets. Therefore, this book was written with the frontline therapist in mind.

GAP 4: NEXT STEPS TO MOVE FROM STABILIZATION TO ACTIVE TRAUMA TREATMENT

Within Dr. Sells' first two books, *Treating the Tough Adolescent* (Sells, 2004) and *Parenting Your Out-of-Control Teenager* (Sells, 2002), a core operating principle is the integration of structural and strategic family therapy through the use of behavioral contracts and other techniques to restructure the hierarchy with the defiant teenager. The behavioral contract, like the wound playbook, acts as a catalyst to create new interactional patterns between the parent and child. However, the behavioral contracts only stabilize the extreme emotional and behavioral symptoms of the child or adolescent. The contracts *do not* actively address the unhealed wounds or trauma. It is the wound playbooks that do this job effectively. As stated earlier, behavioral stabilization without active trauma work can result in relapse and a family system stuck in first-order change. The current book was written in part to fill in the gap of active trauma treatment after stabilization.

However, it is important to note that not every child and family needs a behavioral contract prior to active wound work. As Chapters 3 and 5 outline, there are three rules of thumb to determine (a) if stabilization is needed first (using contracting) before direct trauma work, or (b) if direct wound or trauma work can happen first (using wound playbooks). In sum, Dr. Sells' first two books (behavior or family structure stabilization) serendipitously paved the way for this book (active wound or trauma work). In this way, all three books are well synchronized.

This book, however, stands on its own. Concepts and principles in the first two books can be used to bring about stabilization as well as traditional structural or strategic interventions within other books (c.f., Fishman, 2013; Gehart, 2013; Haley, 1991; Madanes, 1980; P. Minuchin, Colapinto & Minuchin, 1998; S. Minuchin & Fishman, 1981; Nichols & Davis, 2016; Umbarger, 1983). Therefore, the focus of this book is on direct wound work after stabilization, or, if it is determined that stabilization is not necessary, prior to wound or trauma treatment.

PLAN OF THE BOOK

Part I gives a complete overview of the FST model. Chapter 2 includes a description of the type of adolescent, older child, and family best served using the core principles and techniques in this book. We also describe the central tenets of structural and strategic therapy that interface with each part of this treatment model. Chapter 3 presents a flowchart diagram of the FST model that includes an overview of the motivational phone call and each of the five phases of the FST treatment model along with procedural steps and prephase or pre-session preparation steps, as follows:

Motivational phone call

Phase I: Identify Symptoms (Stressors) and Set the Goals for Therapy
Pre-Session Preparation for Phase II
Phase II: Wounds Work Introduction
Pre-Session Preparation for Phase III
Phase III: Co-create Playbooks
Pre-Session Preparation for Phase IV
Phase IV: Troubleshooting and Dress Rehearsals
Pre-Session Preparation for Phase V
Phase V: Evaluate Progress and Relapse Prevention

In Part II, the specific principles and techniques within each of the five phases of the FST model are outlined within Chapters 4 to 13. These include, but are not limited to, a specialized motivational phone call script to quickly break parent resistance, the symptom/stress chart, the seed/tree diagram technique, locating unhealthy undercurrents, techniques to create wound playbooks, feedback loop drawings, and much more. Case examples are used throughout to illustrate key points, but identifying information is changed to protect confidentiality. Special treatment issues are not included because the numerous case examples and techniques can be easily replicated across special populations (e.g., child welfare families, inner-city families, juvenile justice families) or across special treatment issues with diagnostic challenges (e.g., reactive attachment disorder [RAD], self-harm, anxiety, or depression). This is the inherent or secondary benefit of having detailed techniques, step-by-step procedures, and multiple case studies. It allows for seamless replication and touch points for special issues and populations. The authors highlight these connections whenever possible to assist the reader.

Finally, as an aid to readers, we provide a glossary of important terms used throughout the book. This provides added clarity because some terms overlap and are interrelated, while others will be used for the first time within the FST field.

GLOSSARY OF IMPORTANT TERMS

- *Undercurrents.* The core interactional patterns in the family that cause the trauma or maintain it (e.g., unforgiveness, unresolved grief, family secrets, abandonment, lack of nurturance) and result in problem symptoms in the child or family. Undercurrents are known as the core DNA or drivers of the FST model. Undercurrents can be labeled as "unhealthy," keeping the family stuck and unable to heal the underlying trauma, or "healthy," when they are altered using wound playbooks. A core belief in the FST model is that the technique or strategic directive acts like a powerful antibiotic within the playbook to activate targeted healthy undercurrents and heal the underlying trauma. In turn, surface problem symptoms in the child or adolescent (e.g., self-harm, anxiety, depression, aggression) are then eliminated or alleviated. Table 1.1 is an excerpt from the table of undercurrents in Chapter 8 (Table 8.1). The term "undercurrents" is used synonymously with the terms "feedback loops," "family dances," and "interactional patterns." Feedback loops are drawn for the family in Chapter 7 and are visual representations of both healthy and unhealthy undercurrents.

TABLE 1.1 Techniques to Create Wound Playbooks and Healthy Undercurrents

Unhealthy Undercurrents	Healthy Undercurrents	Techniques to Inject Healthy Undercurrent
Unhealed grief and loss	Grief education and resolution	☐ Balloon letters of goodbye ☐ Running the race in grandpa's memory ☐ Scrapbook of memories ☐ Opening to the future/reclaiming the past ☐ Healing the family land and heart ☐ Creating a memorial
Betrayal or abandonment	Security, forgiveness, unconditional love	☐ Fostering a pet ☐ Strengthening family connections ☐ Helping others to heal our family heart ☐ *The Fresh Prince of Bel-Air* clip

- *Trauma* and *unhealed wounds.* These terms are used synonymously with one other throughout the book. The term *unhealed wounds* was created because families seemed to better relate to it, or to the word "wound," than to the word "trauma." The use of "wounds" also appeared less threatening and made it easier to talk about associated events.

- *Stressors* and *symptoms.* These terms are used synonymously with one another in this book. As with the word "wounds," it was more natural and less threatening for the family to use the word "stressors" instead of "symptoms." For example, the parent might say, "My number one problem stressor with my child is that he is depressed." Depression also can be described as a problem symptom, but the families consistently seemed to like the word "stressor" better. From this distinction, a tool known as a stress chart is used in Chapter 5 as an assessment tool to quickly get to the core symptoms or problems with the child or adolescent.

- *Child* and *adolescent.* The terms "child" and "adolescent" are used synonymously with one another in this book. The target population (see Chapter 2) is an adolescent or older child between the ages of 10 and 18 years who has experienced one or both of the following events: (a) a traumatic event, or (b) interactional trauma for longer than 1 month, a timetable that mirrors a PTSD diagnosis.

- *Dress rehearsals* and *role-plays.* The terms "dress rehearsals" and "role-plays" are used synonymously with one another in this book. Successful practice in the delivery of wound playbooks is a core piece of the FST model within Chapter 11. The FST therapist is provided with clear procedural steps to set up and execute role-plays as well as to execute spontaneous interactions or enactments.

- *FST therapist* and *therapist.* These two terms are used synonymously with one another throughout the book.

- The *village* and *extended family.* These two terms are used synonymously with one another throughout the book. Within the FST model, a high emphasis is placed on the therapeutic benefits of engaging not only the child and family members who live under one roof but also the extended family or village. These members include, but are not limited to, grandparents, aunts, uncles, friends, pastors, neighbors, or institutions (school counselors, case managers, coworkers, etc.).

REFERENCES

Blaustein, M. E., & Kinniburgh, K. M. (2010). *Treating traumatic stress in children and adolescents: How to foster resilience through attachment, self-regulation, and competency.* New York, NY: Guilford Press.

Chamberlain, P., & Rosicky J. G. (1995). The effectiveness of family therapy in the treatment of adolescents with conduct disorders and delinquency. *Journal of Marital and Family Therapy,* 21, 441–459.

Chapman, L. (2014). *Neurobiologically informed trauma therapy with children and adolescents: Understanding mechanisms of change.* Chicago, IL: W. W. Norton.

Coatsworth, J. D., Santisteban, D. A., McBride, C. K., & Szapocznik, J. (2001). Brief strategic family therapy versus community control: Engagement, retention, and an exploration of the moderating role of adolescent symptom severity. *Family Process,* 40(3), 313–332. doi:10.1111/j.1545-5300.2001.4030100313.x

Cohen, J. A., Mannarino, A. P., & Deblinger, E. (2012). *Trauma-focused CBT for children and adolescents: Treatment applications.* New York, NY: Guilford Press.

Eich, J. (2015). *Dialectical behavior therapy skills training with adolescents workbook edition.* Eau Claire, WI: PESI Publishing & Media.

Figley, C. R. (1988). Post-traumatic family therapy. In F. M. Ochberg (Ed.), *Post-traumatic therapy and victims of violence* (pp. 83–109). New York, NY: Brunner/Mazel.

Figley, C. R., & Figley, K. R. (2009). Stemming the tide of trauma systemically: The role of family therapy. *Australian & New Zealand Journal of Family Therapy*, 173–183.

Figley, C. R., & Kiser, L. J. (2013). *Helping traumatized families*. New York, NY: Routledge.

Fishman, H. C. (2013). *You can fix your family*. Charleston, SC: Self-published via CreateSpace.

Gehart, D. R. (2013). *Mastering competencies in family therapy: A practical approach to theory and clinical case documentation*. Independence, KY: Cengage.

Gomez, A. M. (2012). *EMDR therapy and adjunct approaches with children: Complex trauma, attachment and dissociation*. New York, NY: Springer Publishing.

Gomez-Perales, N. (2015). *Attachment-Focused trauma treatment for children and adolescents: Phase-Oriented strategies for addressing complex trauma disorders*. London, UK: Routledge.

Haley, J. (1991). *Problem-solving therapy*. San Francisco, CA: Jossey-Bass.

James, B. (1994). *Handbook for treatment of attachment-trauma problems in children*. New York, NY: Simon & Schuster.

James, K., & MacKinnon, L. (2012). Integrating a trauma lens into a family therapy framework: Ten principles for family therapists. *Australian and New Zealand Journal of Family Therapy*, *33*(3), 189–209. doi:10.1017/aft.2012.25

Johnson, S. M. (2002). *Emotionally focused couple therapy with trauma survivors strengthening attachment bonds*. New York, NY: Guilford Press.

Karam, E. A., Sterrett, E. M., & Kiaer, L. (2016). The integration of family and group therapy as an alternative to juvenile incarceration: A quasi-experimental evaluation using PLL. *Family Process*, *56*(2), 331–347.

Lambie, G. W., & Rokutaini, J. (2002). A systems approach to substance abuse identification and intervention for school therapists. *Professional School Counseling*, *5*(5), 353–360.

Levine, P. A., & Frederick, A. (1997). *Waking the tiger: Healing trauma*. Berkeley, CA: North Atlantic Books.

Madanes, C. (1980). *Strategic family therapy*. San Francisco, CA: Jossey-Bass.

Minuchin, P., Colapinto, J., & Minuchin, S. (1998). *Working with families of the poor*. New York, NY: Guilford Press.

Minuchin, S., & Fishman, H. C. (1981). *Family therapy techniques*. Cambridge, MA: Harvard University Press.

Nichols, M. P., & Davis, S. (2016). *Family therapy: Concepts and methods*. Upper Saddle River, NJ: Pearson.

Nickel, M., Luley, J., Krawczyk, J., Nickel, C., Widermann, C., Lahmann, C., . . . Loew, T. (2006). Bullying girls–changes after brief strategic family therapy: A randomized, prospective, controlled trial with one-year follow-up. *Psychother Psychosom*, *75*(1), 47–55. doi:10.1159/000089226

Pinsof, W. M., & Wynne, L. C. (1995). The efficacy of marital and family therapy: An empirical overview, conclusions, and recommendations. *Journal of Marital and Family Therapy*, *21*, 585–613. doi:10.1111/j.1752-0606.1995.tb00179.x

Rowe, C. I., Parker-Sloat, B., Schwartz, S., & Liddle, H. A. (2003). Family therapy for early adolescent substance abuse. In S. Stevens & A. Morral (Eds.), *Adolescent substance abuse treatment in the United States: Exemplary models from a national evaluation study* (pp. 105–132). New York, NY: Hawthorn Press.

Santisteban, D. A., Coatsworth, J. D., Perez-Vidal, A., Kurtines, W. M., Schwartz, S. J., LaPerriere, A., & Szapocznik, J. (2003). Efficacy of brief strategic family therapy in modifying Hispanic adolescent behavior problems and substance use. *Journal of Family Psychology*, *17*(1), 121–133. doi:10.1037/0893-3200.17.1.121

Saxe, G. N., Ellis, B. H., & Kaplow, J. B. (2007). *Collaborative treatment of traumatized children and teens: The trauma systems therapy approach*. New York, NY: Guilford Press.

Scattergood, P., Dash, K., Epstein, J., & Adler, M. (1998). *Applying effective strategies to prevent or reduce substance abuse, violence, and disruptive behavior among youth*. Boston, MA: Education Development Center.

Sells, S. P. (2002). *Parenting your out-of-control teenager: 7 steps to reestablish authority and reclaim love*. New York, NY: St. Martin's Griffin.

Sells, S. P. (2004). *Treating the tough adolescent: A family-based, step-by-step guide*. New York, NY: Guilford Press.

Sherman, R., & Fredman, N. (1986). *Handbook of structured techniques in marriage and family therapy*. New York, NY: Brunner/Mazel.

Siegel, D. J. (1999). *The developing mind: How relationships and the brain interact to shape who we are*. New York, NY: Guilford Press.

Siegel, D. J., & Solomon, M. (2003). *Healing trauma attachment, mind, body and brain.* Chicago, IL: W. W. Norton.

Springer, D. W., & Orsbon, S. H., (2002). Families helping families: Implementing a multifamily therapy group with substance-abusing adolescents. *Health and Social Work, 27*(3), 204–207.

Sykes, W. M., & Turner, L. (2014). Adult attachment disorder: 3 detours to the right hemisphere for clients with adult attachment disorder. *Psychotherapy Networker,* 14–15.

Szapocznik, J., Rio, A., Murray, E., Cohen, R., Scopetta, M., Rivas-Vazquez, A, . . . Kurtines, W. (1989). Structural family versus psychodynamic child therapy for problematic Hispanic boys. *Journal of Consulting and Clinical Psychology, 57*(5), 571–578. doi:10.1037/0022-006X.57.5.571

Umbarger, C. C. (1983). *Structural family therapy.* New York, NY: Grune & Stratton.

van der Kolk, B. (1994). The body keeps the score: Memory and the evolving psychobiology of Posttraumatic Stress. *Harvard Review of Psychiatry, 1*(5), 253–265. doi:10.3109/10673229409017088

van der Kolk, B. (2015). *The body keeps the score: Brain, mind, and body in the healing of trauma.* New York, NY: Penguin Books.

Winokur Early, K., Chapman, S. F., & Hand, G. A. (2013). Family-Focused juvenile reentry services: A quasi-experimental design evaluation of recidivism outcomes. *Journal of Juvenile Justice, 2*(2), 1–22. Retrieved from http://www.journalofjuvjustice.org/JOJJ0202/article01.htm

Who Are Our Traumatized Children? Family Systems Theory Within the FST Model

In this chapter, we define the target population the family systems trauma (FST) model serves. We then outline the integration of the FST model with structural–strategic family therapy and its major assumptions. Understanding the integration of theory into practice is important. As Lewis (1971) writes:

> Every practitioner should know that their observations are not merely casual scanning; they involve a conceptually ordered search for evidence. His or her eyes are trained to help select evidence relative to some framework that can permit inferences to be drawn, order revealed, meanings surmised, and an exploratory guide for action planned. (p. 6)

Without a solid theoretical foundation, the therapist can easily get lost in the complexities, white noise, and bunny trails within the traumatized family. Good theory is the lighthouse in the storm. It helps the therapist train his or her eyes to have an ordered search for evidence relative to a structural–strategic framework, rather than eclectic casual scanning or "fly by the seat of your pants." In this case, the FST therapist can train his or her eyes and ears to quickly locate unhealthy undercurrents or feedback loops that keep the child or family stuck and unable to heal wounds on their own. From this knowledge base, the FST therapist can then custom-design wound playbooks to restructure the family and inject missing healthy undercurrents to heal trauma in the here and now.

To begin this process, the first step is to identify the target population. Next, outline the major assumptions within the FST model and then discover how these integrate into a structural–strategic theoretical framework. This is important because one does not want to build a house on sand, but on a solid foundation. Therefore, prior to outlining procedures and strategies of the FST model, we want to provide the reader with the core model assumptions and theoretical framework or the foundation of the house.

WHO ARE OUR TRAUMATIZED CHILDREN AND ADOLESCENTS?

A first step in this process is to understand what we mean by the designation **traumatized child or adolescent**, the target population for the FST Model. For the purposes of this book, an older child or adolescent between the ages of 10 and 18 years is traumatized if he or she has experienced one or both of these events: (a) a traumatic event, (b) interactional trauma (see definitions in the following text) for longer than 1 month, a timetable that mirrors a post-traumatic stress disorder

(PTSD) diagnosis. This is not an official *Diagnostic and Statistical Manual of Mental Disorders* (5th. ed.; *DSM-5*) diagnosis but one that fits with our research and one the FST treatment model uses. Behavioral symptoms often associated with these two events include acting out, substance abuse, or aggression. Commonly associated emotional symptoms include high anxiety, depression, self-harm, or suicidal ideation. Both emotional and behavioral symptoms may occur prior to the traumatic event(s), accelerate afterward, or occur as a direct result of the event(s). In this book, Chapter 5, "Phase I: Identify Symptoms (Stressors) and Set the Goals for Therapy" outlines the assessment tools used (i.e., the stress chart and seed/tree diagram) and their implications for FST treatment. In addition to the assessment of trauma events and/or interactional trauma, it is equally important for the FST therapist to assess if (a) behavioral stabilization is needed prior to active trauma or wound work and (b) the family has access to an extended family (the village).

A Traumatic Event

The first type of event is commonly known as a "traumatic event." The traumatic event is a stressful occurrence "outside the usual range of human experience, and one that would be markedly distressing to almost anyone" (American Psychiatric Association, 2013). Unusual experiences include (a) serious threats to one's life or physical integrity; (b) serious threat or harm to parents, siblings, or other close relatives or friends; (c) sudden destruction of one's home or community; (d) seeing another person who is or has recently been seriously injured or killed as the result of an accident or physical violence; or (e) the experience of repeated or extreme exposure to aversive detail(s) of the traumatic event(s). The traumatized child may also engage in traumatic reenactments of the event. This occurs when the children or adolescents incorporate aspects of the trauma into their daily lives by repeating old wounds and placing themselves at emotional risk or physical danger (Hamblen & Barnett, 2015). An example of traumatic reenactment might be an adolescent who was a victim of sexual abuse and who continues to reenact this trauma by sexually abusing others.

This traumatic event may or may not lead to a formal PTSD diagnosis that includes symptoms of intrusion (persistent nightmares, flashbacks, intrusive recollections); avoidance of traumatic stimuli (trauma-related reminders such as people or places); negative altered cognitions or mood (dissociative amnesia, distorted blame of self); and negative arousal and reactivity (sleep problems, hypervigilance, exaggerated startle response; American Psychiatric Association, 2013). The child or adolescent can still be considered traumatized without a formal PTSD diagnosis because he or she still has problem symptoms that can be directly traced to unhealed wounds that are self-assessed using the tools and techniques in Chapters 5, 6, and 7.

Interactional Trauma

"Interactional trauma" is a term coined within the FST Model. It occurs when there is constant bickering, yelling, and conflict between parent and child over many months or years. The child or adolescent may also experience secondary trauma or "chiasma stress" by constantly watching the yelling and conflict between other family members such as their parents or siblings. Constant interactional trauma results in a loss of attachment or nurturance between parent and child. In turn, this can lead to bitterness, resentment, and unforgiveness. In addition, if there is an unhealed traumatic event, the interactional trauma will prevent that event from healing within a toxic home environment of constant day-to-day conflict. A good analogy is a wound's inability to heal when it is constantly being reopened.

In sum, we define the child or adolescent between the ages of 10 and 18 years as traumatized if he or she has experienced either a traumatic event and/or interactional trauma with the associated PTSD symptoms listed previously. The timeframe is for a period of longer than 1 month, which mirrors a PTSD diagnosis. After events and timeframes are assessed, it is also important to look at the child or adolescent's point of entry and if there is access to the family's village of extended family.

Point of Entry

Children or adolescents are often first referred to therapy with symptoms commonly associated with oppositional defiant disorder or conduct disorder (i.e., disrespect, truancy, lying, threats of violence, or running away) and/or comorbidity emotional problems such as depression or anxiety. In other words, the underlying trauma may be initially buried or hidden under a firestorm of these surface problem symptoms. Often, family members can identify the traumatic event but either mistakenly believe that the child is "over it" or fail to understand the cause-and-effect relationship between the trauma's impact and the child's symptom(s).

However, the good news is that these surface symptoms can serve as an **ideal point of entry** for the FST therapist. It affords the therapist the opportunity to join with the family, build trust, and help calm the chaos. The belief of "starting where the client is" applies to the traumatized family.

Drama Equals Trauma

The drama has to be resolved first to adequately address the trauma. For example, if there is interactional trauma around extreme disrespect, it acts like a sandstorm that must be stopped before the FST therapist or family can even see the underlying wounds. The therapist represents a surgeon who has to stop the bleeding in order to see or treat the deep wounds underneath. However, once surface oppositional or conduct symptoms are addressed through behavioral contracts and other strategies, the chaos or interactional trauma calms down. In turn, from this place of relative calm and reduced drama, active wound work can begin inearnest. As stated earlier, the key will be for the FST therapist to determine if stabilization is needed prior to direct trauma or wound work (see Chapter 5) or if direct wound work can begin immediately. In addition, alongside both of these issues, comes the risk of safety. For example, FST trauma work is of limited effectiveness unless ongoing issues of safety (e.g., domestic violence, sexual abuse, drug addiction, homelessness, suicidal ideation) are assessed and addressed (see Chapter 3). Safety, like interactional trauma, represents drama, and it must be addressed first or treated in conjunction with stabilization or direct wound work.

Access to the Extended Family and Friends (the Village)

We define the **village** as people or institutions that surround and impact the immediate family in a supportive, nonsupportive, or potentially supportive way. Examples of this village include but are not limited to extended family (grandparents, aunts, uncles, cousins, etc.), friends, neighbors, and institutions like school, probation, or child welfare. Our findings suggest that FST is less effective with just the immediate family and more effective with both the family and village together in the same room. A core belief of the FST model is that even though the identified patient is the traumatized child or adolescent, the immediate family, along with parts of the village, is also secondarily traumatized. As a result, whenever possible, the village is a key change agent.

Over the past 8 years of FST model development, we have seen a stark difference between therapists who regularly use a village approach and those treating only the immediate family. We often lament that resistance to treating the entire village is not coming from the family, but rather from the therapeutic system. For example, a special commission in Texas was set up to determine top reasons why children were in foster care for extended periods of time:

> Providers often did not work with birth parents and foster or kinship care parents *simultaneously* [italics added] resulting in services delivered to the child and the family separately. (Sunset Advisory Commission, 2014, p. 20)

In other words, decreasing time to permanency would be much more likely if child welfare treatment brought foster and biological families together when possible versus continued separation. The bifurcation or silos is often far too common in mental health treatment.

This key finding reflects a core problem in the traditional delivery of therapeutic services. Trauma-informed care or therapy in general is done from a nonsystemic lens of treating the individual child or individual system (parent system or foster parent system) rather than a systematic or ecosystems focus of the traumatized child as part of a traumatized village that needs to be treated together when possible.

The most common reasons we discovered for a lack of village engagement were (a) no formal ecosystems training in graduate school; (b) fear of not knowing what to do with so many people packed into one room; (c) an easy acceptance by the therapist of family members' belief that it will not work; and/or (d) the therapist's own self-fulfilling prophesy that bringing in the village will not work.

As a result, the family and village advantage is highlighted throughout this book using case examples. It will illustrate a "road less traveled," but a road that if traveled will yield much fruit for the therapist and the child and family. Access to the village is outlined in Chapter 5.

MAJOR ASSUMPTIONS OF THE FST MODEL

Five major FST model assumptions or core beliefs are presented within this book and highlighted in this section:

1. Trauma is a systemic entity
2. Undercurrents and wound playbooks are the DNA drivers
3. Toxic seeds and undercurrents are interrelated
4. Safety first
5. Secondary trauma is equally important

After these five core assumptions are presented, the main tenets of structural–strategic theory that integrate with FST are highlighted.

Core Belief 1: Trauma Is a Systemic Entity

Unresolved traumatic memories fuel the child's emotional or behavior problems as well as family conflict. In addition, conflictual family interactions (interactional trauma) maintain or exacerbate the pain of traumatic memories. Trauma by nature is interpersonal and therefore a systemic entity (Figley & Figley, 2009). Because of this, individual trauma treatment for children or adolescents without a family focus is limited at best and detrimental at worst. The U.S. Institute of Medicine (IOM), a part of the National Academies, completed a comprehensive review of the scientific literature in the evaluation and treatment of PTSD, with significant attention on military veteran populations (IOM, 2008). The IOM report concluded that a systems approach that incorporated the interpersonal context of traumatized individuals was essential. However, almost all established treatments of PTSD largely ignored the systemic approach with little overlap between the study of families and the study of trauma. Figley (2009) concluded that most traumatologists continue to focus primarily on individuals and largely ignore families and the social support they provide.

Case Example

Eleven-year-old Tristan was placed in foster care due to neglect. The mother, Teresa, had been unable to pay the utility bills, so Tristan was temporarily placed with his aunt, Suzy.

However, the family preservation therapist assigned to the case immediately saw the dislike and lack of trust between the aunt and mother. As the tension and conflict rose between them, Tristan's problem symptoms increased dramatically. Tristan would scream every time he had to visit his mom. He then started to scratch himself and pull his hair out. The case manager ordered an immediate psychiatric evaluation. The evaluator was not trained within a systemic paradigm and so did not see anyone except Tristan and the aunt. The evaluation came back with a reactive attachment disorder (RAD) *DSM-5* diagnosis that also included a recommendation not to see the mother. The evaluator cited that Tristan had episodes of unexplained fearfulness and sadness with his mother and failed to seek or respond to comfort from her. In turn, the aunt now felt justified in her assessment of the mother as unfit, and the caseworker agreed. This separation from the mother continued for more than a year with only short supervised visits.

In the meantime, Tristan's symptoms worsened into clinical depression. In turn, Tristan was placed on a multitude of psychotropic medications that helped stabilize him but also came with side effects of dry mouth, weight gain, and insomnia.

An FST-trained therapist was then brought into the picture. She convinced the caseworker to try a systemic approach based on the solution-focused axiom "If it's not working, do something different" and the metaphor of going from symptom management "weed" work to locating key unhealthy undercurrents "root" work to quickly locate what was keeping the family stuck.

After the initial interviews with Tristan, the aunt, and the mother separately, it was clear what the unhealthy undercurrents were. These undercurrents had nothing directly to do with Tristan. He was merely caught in the crossfire:

- *Unresolved grief combined with unforgiveness*: After using the seed/tree diagram technique (see Chapter 5), the key toxic seed revealed by both aunt and mother (independent from one another) was unhealed wounds. The cause of the wound was the murder of a deeply loved brother. Both aunt and mother were still in grief 10 years later. And to make things worse, both blamed the other for his death. There was deep unforgiveness to go along with the grief, and neither party could see how Tristan was caught in the middle. The cause-and-effect relationship was out of their awareness of how the undercurrents of unresolved grief and unforgiveness (roots) caused the (weed) problem symptoms of RAD and depression.

- *Divided loyalties and divided caregivers*: Tristan stated in tears that a main reason for his problems was the feeling of being caught in the middle between two people he loved. His aunt would fill his mind with bad stories about his mom so that when he was about to visit his mom, his stress level was so high that he felt

(continued)

like screaming (and did). And when things got worse and he could no longer see his mom on a regular basis, Tristan blamed himself and became more and more depressed.

As a result of this information, the FST therapist now had a clear path to follow with clear therapy goals. Great theory leads to great practice. If the unhealthy undercurrents of unresolved grief and unforgiveness could be replaced by their healthy counterparts of grief resolution and forgiveness, the caregivers would no longer be divided and the symptoms around Tristan's trauma could be eliminated.

The FST therapist brought the mother and aunt into the room first while Tristan waited outside. To control the tension and finger-pointing, the FST therapist established clear boundaries before the session started (the therapist would yell "Freeze," and remind them there would be no yelling, no blame, etc.). The FST therapist caught the mother and aunt off guard in a good way by dramatically turning off the lights and using PowerPoint to show feedback loops (see Chapter 6). With an LCD projector, the therapist was able to show through one feedback loop at a time how the loss of their brother and resulting unforgiveness was keeping them stuck and Tristan caught in the middle. This was done in a matter-of-fact and nonblaming way.

A picture of the brother was scanned in beforehand and then dissolved into the middle of the feedback loops with the question, "If your brother was here with us would he say that it honored his memory for his sisters to have unforgiveness towards one another and in the process help contribute to the slow, emotional death of his nephew, Tristan?" In other words, the brother's murder or death inadvertently set into motion bitterness and blame between mom and aunt. The fruit of this bitterness or unhealthy undercurrent was then contributing to the "emotional" murder of another family member (Tristan) and the emotional murder or deep unforgiveness and rift between his two sisters.

This powerful reframe, combined with moving to a systems theory lens using feedback loops and undercurrents, quickly shifted the worldview of aunt and mother. To cauterize the wound, with the adults' permission, Tristan was brought in and shown the same feedback loops. He wept and confirmed to both mother and aunt that he was caught in the middle and that the interactional trauma or conflict was literally tearing him apart and killing him inside.

The intensity of the moment moved the aunt and mother to immediate tears of forgiveness and reconciliation. Both parties then met with the caseworker and, as a united front, reshowed the same feedback loops and PowerPoint display (with the FST therapist's facilitation) to connect the dots for the caseworker. The FST therapist was then able to create a wound playbook (see Chapter 8) called "Reunification Goals for Tristan" and to continue conjoint sessions with both aunt and mother as the new co-parents. To keep the session from drifting, the brother's framed picture was placed on an empty chair as a reminder of the big picture and what was at stake.

The aunt even helped mom find a job and assisted her temporarily with utilities. With these new healthy undercurrents intact (forgiveness and grief resolution), Tristan's symptoms quickly abated and he was eventually moved off the antidepressants. The need for symptom management through medication was eliminated by treating the root

(*continued*)

Case Example (*continued*)

---

causes or unhealthy undercurrent causes of Tristan's symptoms. Psychotropic mediation is often a lifesaver to quickly stabilize a chaotic family system and provide quick symptom relief to the child or adolescent. It also buys the therapist and family the time they may need to stop the bleeding long enough to get to the root causes of the unhealed wounds or trauma. However, within an FST framework, medication can be seen as part of a continuum care, not the only care.

Core Belief 2: Undercurrents and Wound Playbooks Are the DNA Drivers

As defined in the glossary (Chapter 1), and highlighted in the case example in the preceding text, unhealthy undercurrents (unforgiveness, unresolved grief, family secrets, abandonment, lack of nurturance, etc.) are the core DNA drivers of the FST model. In a nutshell, unhealthy undercurrents are synonymous with feedback loops or interactional patterns within the family and/or village, which either cause the trauma or maintain it. Over time, if these unhealthy undercurrents are not replaced with their healthy counterparts (see Table 2.1), it often results in problem symptoms (e.g., extreme behavioral problems, depression, anxiety, self-harm) for both the child and the family.

TABLE 2.1 Unhealthy and Healthy Undercurrents for the Unhealed Wound Seed

Unhealthy Undercurrents	Healthy Undercurrent Counterparts
Unresolved grief or loss	Grief education and resolution
Betrayal or abandonment	Security, forgiveness, unconditional love
Family secrets	Reveal secrets/safety issues
Physical or mental abuse	Support, courage to leave, forgiveness
Lack of forgiveness/bitterness	Forgiveness
Lack of consistent nurturance	Unconditional love, consistent nurturance
High anxiety	Safety or security
High stress	Relaxation or diversionary tactics

Wound playbooks are then used like antibiotics to fill in the missing healthy undercurrents. The core assumption here is that the family members are stuck and cannot fill in these healthy undercurrents on their own. If they could have done so on their own, they would not be in the therapist's office.

Therefore, the FST therapist takes the targeted healthy undercurrent (in this case unconditional and nurturance) and selects a strategic directive or task like an apology (see Chapter 8) and converts it into a wound playbook using a who? what? when? where? and how? framework (see Figure 2.1). From this clear plan, the family can then practice their playbook delivery through dress rehearsals/role-plays and a troubleshooting countermoves checklist or a Plan B if something goes wrong (see Chapters 10 and 11). In turn, this kind of clarity dramatically increases the family's odds that they can both implement the technique and fill in the missing healthy undercurrent.

The Jacob Family Plan to Show Michael Unconditional Love
To Inject the Healthy Undercurrents of Unconditional Love and Nurturance
To Heal the Wound Seed

Who: Michael with Mom

What:
- Mom will give at least one PTR (Positive Teen Report) daily for the next 30 straight days to Michael regardless of what his behavior (disrespectful, in bad mood, etc.) might be like that day

When:
- Mom will give at least one (maybe two) any time before 9 p.m. each day Monday-Sunday
- For next 30 straight days and then reevaluate with therapist

Where:
- At Home
- But could be in surprise location? ☺ (keeps you guessing)

How:
- Mom can deliver PTR in any number of creative and <u>playful</u> ways (see below)
    - In person—Hand it to Michael and read it aloud
    - By Mail or E-Mail
    - By Text
    - Under Michael's Pillow With A Stuffed Animal
    - In Michael's Cereal Box
    - In Michael's Backpack
    - Etc.
- Michael can accept it with thank you or not since this is an act of <u>UN</u>-conditional love by Mom
- See troubleshooting checklist on "what to do if…?" Michael rejects PTR or other possible curveballs

---

Figure 2.1 Wound playbook.

The inherent strength of the healthy undercurrent–playbook combination is that it (a) moves the trauma focus from a child-only problem to a family problem to fix together. This is called expanding the symptom; and (b) provides both the child and family with a clear plan to heal the trauma or wound in the here and now within a systemic framework. It helps the child and family move from a trauma story in the past to a healing story in the present and future.

Core Belief 3: Toxic Seeds and Undercurrents Are Interrelated

Another major assumption within the FST model is that unhealthy undercurrents and toxic seeds are interrelated. Unhealthy undercurrents cause the toxic seeds, which, in turn, maintain the unhealthy undercurrents. For example, if the parent(s) consistently cannot show any nurturance to their child, this can cause an unhealed wound seed, which then increases the lack of nurturance. In addition, if the parent cannot provide adequate food, clothing, or shelter for the family, stress will skyrocket, resulting in trauma and the toxic seed of unmet primal needs (see definitions in the following text).

All of the unhealthy undercurrents can be categorized within one of these four toxic seeds: (a) misuse of power; (b) unhealed wounds; (c) mental or physical impairment; or (d) unmet primal needs. These four seeds are classified as either stabilization or trauma seeds.

Stabilization Seed

The first seed, "misuse of power," is known as the stabilization seed. It may have nothing to do with trauma but everything to do with ineffective limit setting, oppositional or defiant behavior of the child, lack of boundaries, or lack of nurturance. Therefore, the strategic directive is a behavioral contract (clear rules and consequences to allow the parent or caregiver to reestablish lost authority by realigning hierarchy), not a wound playbook to heal direct trauma. Over time, if stabilization is not secured, the family and child can easily move into trauma (interactional trauma, unforgiveness) or one of the three seed categories listed in the following text.

In addition, the stabilization seed led to the creation of model curriculum within PLL-FSS (family systems stabilization) and in the first book *Treating the Tough Adolescent* (Sells, 2008). In short, to alleviate or eliminate a child's problem symptoms and unhealthy undercurrents associated with this seed, behavioral contracts were used. For more information on this process and the PLL system of care, please go to www.gopll.com and search "PLL-FST."

- *Misuse of power*: Unhealthy undercurrents (e.g., empty threats, caustic communication, lack of consistent discipline, role confusion, lack of consistent nurturance, dance of violence, boundary violations, different parent or marital philosophies, and lack of support village) that cause or result from one of the following outcomes:
  - ☑ Children misuse power by controlling the mood of the household through behaviors such as disrespect, violence, or running away to bully or scare their parents into handing over their authority to the child.
  - ☑ As in wolf packs, the parents or caregivers should be the pack leaders; instead, the child is the alpha male or female pack leader, on the top of the hierarchy with the parent underneath them.
  - ☑ Adults may also misuse power by becoming emotionally or physically abusive to another person in an effort to control them.

Trauma Seeds

An unhealed wound and its associated unhealthy undercurrents reflect direct trauma from a traumatic event or interactional trauma. The other two seeds (mental or physical impairment and unmet primal needs) also produce trauma but in a different way and with different unhealthy undercurrents. As a result, all three seeds are collectively grouped as trauma seeds.

- *Unhealed wounds*: Unhealthy undercurrents (e.g., unresolved grief or loss, betrayal or abandonment, family secrets, physical or mental abuse, lack of forgiveness/bitterness, lack of consistent nurturance, high anxiety, and high stress) that cause or result from one of these two outcomes:
  - ☑ *Traumatic event that does not heal on its own over time*—Common examples include a bitter divorce, being emotionally or physically abandoned by someone you trusted like a parent or friend, unhealed grief from the death of someone you really loved, and so forth.

    ☑ *Interactional trauma*—Constant tension, disrespect, or arguing between parents and kids. Over time, feelings of closeness or nurturance in the home are replaced by bitterness or unforgiveness.

- *Mental or physical impairment*: Unhealthy undercurrents (i.e., drawn-out medical illness, someone seen as a patient/mental case, chemical imbalance, brain or mental impairment, etc.) that cause or result from one of these two outcomes:

    ☑ *Chemical imbalance or mental impairment*—Occurs when there is evidence that the symptoms (depression, attention–deficit hyperactivity disorder [ADHD], violence, hyperactivity, substance abuse, etc.) are mainly caused by a chemical imbalance in the brain that can be helped by psychotropic medication but can bring about unhealthy undercurrents that can cause trauma, such as the undercurrent of being seen as incapable or as a mental case.

    ☑ *Physical impairment*—This happens when a family is going along fine and suddenly someone gets a brain injury in an accident, cancer, Alzheimer's, or a baby is born with Down's syndrome, and so forth, and the family has to stop their normal routine and lifestyle to help this person. The stress goes through the roof, and if not mitigated, can result in trauma.

- *Unmet primal needs*: Unhealthy undercurrents (i.e., Maslow's unmet hierarchy of needs, lack of attachment or bonding, lack of forgiveness/resentment, lack of connection to God/a higher power, or mind, body, and spirit unbalanced) that cause or result from one of the following:

    ☑ *Basic needs not met*—Food, clothing, shelter, feeling safe in home or neighborhood, and so forth. If these needs are not met, stress skyrockets.

    ☑ *Every human being needs emotional attachment, love, and hugs*—For example, foster children often have problems with emotional attachments and react with symptoms or stressors of out-of-control behavior, depression, or cutting.

    ☑ *Imbalance of mind, body, and soul*—For many, a lack of prayer or a lack of connection to God or a higher power leads them to a feeling of disconnection, a lack of deep peace, or great difficulty in letting go of past resentments and forgiving others. Other common symptoms include workaholism, inability to sleep, or medicating the pain with alcohol or prescription drugs.

In Chapter 5, these seed definitions are revealed to the family with an FST tool called the seed/tree diagram (see Figure 2.2). This apple tree is drawn for the family on a flip chart or shown using PowerPoint to visually illustrate the connection between the problem symptoms that one can see on the surface with the naked eye (the apples on the tree) and the root causes of the problems, which are labeled unhealthy undercurrents (the roots) that cause the toxic seeds to grow (the seeds).

    The FST therapist then explains each part of the diagram and provides a definition of each seed (without the undercurrents). Each family member is asked to vote on the top two seeds they think are producing the most problems and explain why. The FST therapist then provides his or her seed picks with reasons for the selection. Finally, the FST therapist in collaboration with the family makes the decision as to which toxic seed and which of the child's associated symptoms to address first. This seed-and-symptom combination becomes the basis for the therapy goals at the end of Phase I of the FST model. Later, the undercurrents are revealed to the family in the form of feedback loops in Phase II as the (root) cause of the toxic seeds and problem symptoms.

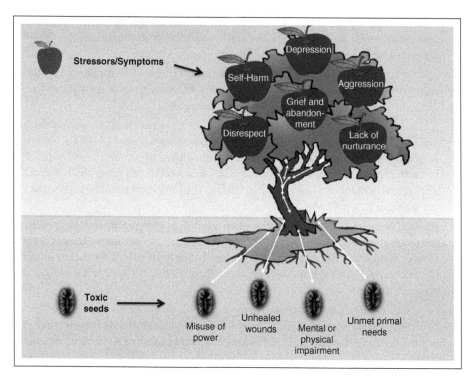

Figure 2.2 Seed/tree diagram.

Source: Adapted with permission from G. Wood, personal communication, March 23, 2017.

Core Belief 4: Safety First

Another core assumption or belief of the FST model is "safety first." The Green Cross Academy of Traumatology (1999), the International Society of Traumatic Stress Studies (ISTSS) guidelines (Cloitre et al., 2012), Dietrich (2001), and Figley (2008) presented ideal ingredients and safety guidelines for trauma-informed treatment. According to Figley and Figley (2009), "At the very minimum, trauma-informed therapy should include (a) the establishment of safety, (b) informed consent, (c) titration of exposure-related stress and (d) client self-soothing competence during and between treatment sessions" (p. 180). We subscribe to these four guidelines. Within the FST model, we highlight when each of these four guidelines are addressed within the five phases of the FST treatment model.

If these guidelines are not addressed, safety for both the child and the family can be compromised. For example, self-regulation procedures are taught to the child and family in Phase II of the FST model along with a safety risk assessment to determine if safety issues are present (see Chapter 7). As stated earlier, if there are high safety risk behaviors present, the FST therapist along with the family must lower the risk through what is called a safety playbook (see Chapter 3). Therefore, looking at the FST flowchart in Chapter 3, regardless of the decision of stabilization or direct trauma work, safety first and safety planning are continually self-assessed and addressed through all five phases of the FST model.

Core Belief 5: Secondary Trauma Is Equally Important

A final core assumption of the FST Model is that secondary trauma within the family is equally as important as primary trauma within the child or adolescent. In essence, the trauma may start with the child but then can ripple out like a pebble hitting the pond among other family members.

Therefore, the results of individual treatment with a traumatized child may not last. This is because the "whole (the family) is greater than the sum of its parts (the individual child)." This means that the benefits of individualized trauma treatment can quickly evaporate when that individual adolescent is thrust back into the same and unchanged chaotic and dysfunctional family with members who are still traumatized. An example is when the child tells the parent he has new deep breathing and coping strategies to grieve his father's murder, but the mother continues to scream at him day after day with no nurturance or support (interactional trauma) because she does not have the same coping tools. Over time, if this interactional trauma continues, the likelihood is high that the adolescent will relapse, no matter how good the individual trauma treatment.

Therefore, both primary and secondary trauma need to be treated in order to achieve a lasting impact. In turn, when both types of trauma are addressed, the risk for relapse, once treatment ends, is lowered. As stated in Chapter 1, we are looking at secondary trauma within the categories of simultaneous effects, vicarious effects, chiasma effects, or intrafamilial trauma.

STRUCTURAL–STRATEGIC FAMILY THEORY UNDERGIRDING THE FST MODEL

While undercurrents and the wound or safety playbooks are the DNA drivers, structural–strategic family therapy is the theory or the gas that powers the engine. In a nutshell, Haley maintained, "The best task is one that uses the presenting problem [of the child] to make a structural change in the family" (Haley, 1991, p. 85). In this case, the task is the strategic directive selected by the FST therapist to create a wound playbook. As stated earlier, the playbook is then the tool used by the family and the FST therapist to fill in the key missing healthy undercurrent(s) that will restructure the family and eliminate the child's presenting problems (or trauma symptoms).

For example, in the Jacobs Family Plan (see Figure 2.1), Michael's presenting problems could be anything from cutting to depression to aggression. But the key driver for these symptoms (for this particular family) was the unhealthy undercurrent of "lack of nurturance" between son and mother. Over time, this lack of nurturance can cause an unhealthy family structure of distance and conflict or even lead to an upside-down hierarchy whereby the child, not the parent, is the pack leader of the household. Therefore, to unstick these structures, the undercurrent of lack of nurturance has to be replaced by its healthy counterpart: **unconditional love and nurturance**. However, the family is stuck. The mom and Michael cannot fill in this missing healthy undercurrent on their own; if they could, they would have done so by now.

As a result, the FST therapist is needed to help with this process, and he or she uses the strategic directive or playbook to do this restructuring. This is because "directives [the wound playbook] can get people out of their ruts with *the smallest change possible*" (Gehart, 2010, p. 26). And when the directives work even a little bit, they unleash a sudden shift in emotion, insight, and behavior. And it is from this place of hope that family members rally to help their child heal the wounds, and in the process also heal themselves.

A Stuck Structure Is Formed by Unhealthy Undercurrents (Feedback Loops)

As the word "structure" implies, structural family therapists map out on paper or in their head a family's present-day structure around hierarchies, subsystems, and boundaries formed over time by utilizing feedback loops to depict the interactional patterns or unhealthy undercurrents between family members themselves and/or their environment of work, friends, school, or extended family (Minuchin, 1974). This process is illustrated in Chapter 7. After assessing the family's functioning though an undercurrent of a feedback loop lens, structural therapists aim to restructure the family. Restructuring takes the form of helping the family put into practice as the new normal any number of the healthy undercurrents listed in Table 2.1. For example, it could help family members forgive, grieve, or support one another. This restructuring is done through what are called **enactments** or techniques in which the therapist prompts the family to reenact a conflict or other interaction (Colapinto, 1991; Minuchin, 1974; Minuchin & Fishman, 1981) to bring about new and healthy undercurrents. Enactments can be done through spontaneous interaction or through planned-out role-plays (see Chapter 11).

The Gas for Structural Changes Are the Strategic Directives (Playbooks)

Just as a professional football team needs a clearly written playbook to enact new plays or formations, so does the stuck family. In other words, it is difficult if not impossible to restructure the family through enactments or role-plays without the help of a well-written wound playbook that is targeting the correct healthy undercurrent for that particular family. The strategic directives in the playbook are designed to "irritate" the system's interaction patterns to create new interactions or healthy undercurrents (Haley, 1991). These directives can be either straightforward, precisely answering who, what, where, when, and how, or indirect, using metaphors or reframes (Gehart, 2010). The following case example of 16-year-old Matt illustrates how structural and strategic theory intersects with the FST treatment model. Theory moves into practice.

Case Example

Sixteen-year-old Matt was an only child and was the pack leader of his household. When the question was asked of the family, "Who controls the mood of your household?" both parents pointed to Matt. This upside-down hierarchy caused constant interactional trauma between Matt and his parents, especially the father. A common feedback loop was the mother defending her son because she felt her husband was too hard on Matt and trying to overcompensate by not setting any limits and just be nurturing. In turn, the father, seeing that his wife was too soft with Matt, overcompensated by being too strict. In turn, Matt was able to skillfully "divide and conquer" both parents anytime he wanted. Over the years, these interactional patterns or unhealthy undercurrents resulted in the unhealthy structures listed in Table 2.2:

TABLE 2.2 Unhealthy Undercurrents and Structures

Unhealthy Undercurrents	Unhealthy Structures
Inconsistent discipline or limit setting	Lack of clear boundaries Upside-down hierarchy (child in charge) Interactional trauma (constant conflict)
Lack of nurturance (with father) Bitterness and unforgiveness (with father)	Extreme emotional distance from dad
Parents not on same page Bitterness and unforgiveness (between husband and wife)	Upside-down hierarchy Marital conflict and emotional disengagement

Matt's resulting symptoms were both extreme behavior problems (disrespect, running away, and school failure) and extreme emotional problems (depression and self-harm). In this family, constant day-to-day drama equaled trauma for both parents and child.

Because of the high drama, the FST therapist needed a quick victory to build momentum and hope. In addition, like the game of Jenga, the FST therapist needed just the right healthy undercurrents to move this stuck family toward a new structure of emotional closeness between father and son, more consistent limits with mom, and less bitterness between mom and dad, and for the parents to get on the same page.

To meet these goals, the FST therapist looked to the concept of a proper balance between a hard side of hierarchy and a soft side of hierarchy (Sells, 2004). This is a balance of parenting with love and limits. The hard side of hierarchy occurs when parents or caregivers can evoke consistent discipline with a calm voice and without empty threats. The soft side of hierarchy occurs when the parent or caregiver maintains a position of unconditional love. The caregiver communicates in words and actions that he or she may not like the misbehavior but he or she still loves the child unconditionally. The parent also refuses to hold grudges and quickly tries to repair the relationship if there are hurt feelings regardless of who is at fault. Interactional trauma is connected to an upside-down hierarchy. And the hierarchy must be corrected and realigned by the FST therapist by filling in the healthy undercurrent that is missing to ensure both a hard and soft side of hierarchy is present. Otherwise, the interactional trauma will continue.

Therefore, the unhealthy undercurrents were targeted to restructure this family and heal the trauma surrounding the emotional distance between father and son, and husband and wife. The FST therapist knew that the father had the "hard" side of hierarchy mastered but had severe deficits in the "soft" side. And based on nonverbals from previous sessions, the FST therapist could see that both Matt and the mother were starved for any kind of approval and tenderness from the father. However, both the mother and Matt had their guards up high. Therefore, the strategic directive selected also had to have with it a creative reframe and a playful delivery to lower their guards.

As a result, the FST therapist picked the straightforward directive of a "30-second hug." The father was to hug first the mother and then Matt, every morning at breakfast. The hug would be initiated by the father along with a verbalization of one thing he loved about his wife and one thing he was proud of Matt for. The delivery piece contained an indirect directive using Madanes's (1991) pretend technique of "fake it till you make it" meaning when you fake a behavior, even for a short period of time, often there is a genuine change in perspective, feeling, or behaviors.

The reframe used was that everyone's hug muscles were sore and out of practice. The person who needed the hugs was dad because his blood pressure was the highest from his frustration. Dad was like the tin man in the Wizard of Oz who needed an oil can of hugs to lower his blood pressure and get the blood flowing again. Mom would then hug dad. In turn, for both Matt and the Mom, hugs would release what are called endorphins, making them feel better and in turn the home would be less tense.

And since dad had turned to money and work to medicate his pain, he would break the hold money had by taking his wife out to dinner each Friday night if she allowed the fake-it-till-you-make-it hugs, and award to Matt either $3 a hug or $15 a week (Monday–Friday). The FST therapist knew that with Matt, he had to jump-start things with money,

(*continued*)

Case Example (*continued*)

and for the wife, the therapist needed an excuse for a date night. And for the father, the message was that family was more important than money.

As a result, the wound playbook looked like Figure 2.3.

Lowering Matt's and His Family's Blood Pressure, and Stress Plan
The Power of the Hug Prescription
To Inject the Healthy Undercurrent of Nurturance
To Heal the Wound and Misuse of Power Seeds

Who: Dad, Mom, and Matt

What:
- Dad will initiate the first hug with his wife (has to be in front of Matt) for 30 seconds. Matt will set the microwave timer. As the hug takes place, Dad will tenderly say one thing he loves or appreciates about his wife in the present or from the past.
- Mom will initiate the next hug with Dad (has to be in front of Matt) for 30 seconds. Matt will again set the microwave timer. As the hug takes place, Mom will tenderly say one thing she loves or appreciates about her husband in the present or from the past.
- After Mom, Dad will hug Matt (has to be in front of Mom) for 30 seconds. Mom will set the microwave timer. As the hug takes place, Dad will say one thing he is proud of Matt for, in the present or from the past

When:
- Before breakfast at 7:30 a.m. Monday-Friday (weekends off)
- Date night between Mom and Dad every Friday night at 6 p.m. for dinner out
- For next two straight weeks and then reevaluate with therapist

Where:
- At home in the kitchen

How:
- Dad will initiate the first hug and wife the second (see above)
- Dad will initiate the hug with Matt and before the hug, will give him the $3 in an act of faith that Matt will honor his commitment to fully participate with each hug time (give it his all). As hugs take place Dad will say one thing he is proud of about his son in the present or from the past
- See troubleshooting checklist. But remember, "everyone's hug muscles will be *sore and out of practice*," so expect everyone's muscles to be stiff and tense. This is normal.
- Everyone will initially feel weird giving hugs. This is normal. Do it anyway.

Figure 2.3 Wound playbook—using hugs to restructure the soft side of hierarchy.

To help inject this new healthy undercurrent into Matt's family, the FST therapist incorporates the core structural technique of enactments and role-plays (see Chapter 11). In the session, both husband and wife repeatedly practiced their hug delivery with Matt and each other, until this new dance became second nature.

Immediately prior to the role-plays, the FST therapist uses a tool called the troubleshooting checklist (see Chapter 10) to go through possible curveballs or Plan B countermoves for such things as "What will you do if …?" Matt is grumpy and refuses the $3 and the hug. Or "What will you do if …?" Matt's muscles get tense and he just sits there or refuses to accept dad's compliment? Each possible curveball and countermove was then role-played beforehand until mastery was achieved.

Finally, spontaneous interactions will emerge naturally in the session from these role-plays, which can turn into enactments by the therapist. For example, in Matt's family as the role-play was going on and the dad said he was proud of him, Matt got very quiet and had tears. The FST therapist quickly seized this opportunity and asked, "Matt

(continued)

Case Example (*continued*)

---

what's going on with you?" Matt replied, "Dad, this is what I wanted all these years. For you to say something you were proud of me for." The father and son then had a healing conversation where Dad was able to say that he was sorry. Later, the wife and husband had a similar healing conversation that was precipitated by the role-play. In this way, the role-plays can jump-start the enactments just as the wound playbook jump-starts the healthy undercurrents.

In sum, the "hug prescription" was the straightforward strategic directive tool used both to help restructure hierarchy and to increase emotional closeness. In turn, there was also a positive ripple effect on the marriage. The wife longed for her husband and son to have a nurturing relationship. Even through the hug was a small microchange, it had a profound effect on the wife's emotions. She started to forgive her husband and grow soft with him. In turn, the husband tried even harder to be nurturing with his son and the interactional trauma lessened even more. And the son, in turn, started to be less disrespectful and stopped running away, which, in turn, gave the wife encouragement to stand by her husband and be consistent with limits.

The hug prescription became like the Z-PAK or antibiotic used by the doctor to actively attack and cure an unseen bacterial infection. In this case, the undercurrents were not seen by the naked eye but were the drivers of Matt's symptoms. The diagram in Figure 2.4 shows the impact of using the soft side of hierarchy with a directive like the hug prescription to restructure the family. In addition, metaphorically, once hugging or nurturance becomes the new normal or operating system, it moves from antibiotic to probiotic. Hugs are now the new protective factor (a probiotic) that insulates the family from future trauma and makes them more resilient.

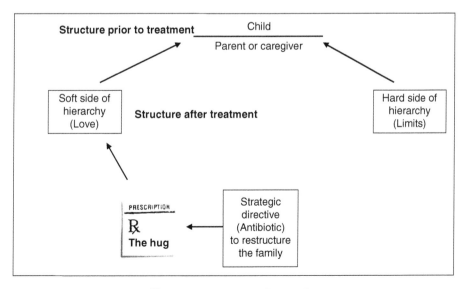

Figure 2.4 Soft side of hierarchy.

Integrating Structural and Strategic Together: The Perfect Blend

As Matt's case example illustrates, the blending or integration of both structural and strategic approaches gives the FST therapist an ideal road map and set of techniques for negotiating the twists and turns of the family maze. This is effective with both trauma and the surrounding drama of both emotional and behavioral problems in the child and other family members. Structural theory provides the FST model with such concepts as "hierarchy," "boundaries" (enmeshed or emotionally disengaged), and "enactments." In turn, the stuck or unhealthy structures show the FST therapists the need for new feedback loops or healthy undercurrents to (a) return parents to a position of authority; (b) end the drama, chaos, and interactional trauma; and (c) illustrate what strategic directives are needed for the targeted unhealthy undercurrent to directly impact the unhealed wound or trauma. Then, strategic theory gives the FST therapist "the gas" or the techniques and directives (e.g., contracting, wound playbooks, role-plays, troubleshooting, reframes, scaling) to unstick the family and make the structural changes possible. Thus, a combination of the two is an invaluable one-two punch to restructure the toughest and chronically stuck trauma cases.

The next chapter uses a zoom-out flowchart to show each of the five phases of the FST models and the timing of when and how these should be implemented. Mini-steps to accomplish each of these phases are outlined along with case examples to clarify major points. Once the zoom-out process is accomplished in the next chapter, the detailed zoom-in strategies and the techniques and strategies follow in subsequent chapters.

REFERENCES

American Psychiatric Association. (2013). *Diagnostic and statistical manual of mental disorders* (5th ed.). Arlington, VA: American Psychiatric Publishing.

Cloitre, M., Courtis, C. A., Ford, J. D., Green, B. L., Alexander, P., Briere, J., . . . Van der Hart, O. (2012). The ISTSS expert consensus treatment guidelines for complex PTSD in adults. Retrieved from https://www .istss.org/ISTSS_Main/media/Documents/ISTSS-Expert-Concesnsus-Guidelines-for-Complex-PTSD-Updated-060315.pdf

Colapinto, J. (1991). Structural family therapy. In A. Gurman & D. Kniskern (Eds.), *Handbook of family therapy* (Vol. II). New York, NY: Brunner/Mazel.

Dietrich, A. M. (2001). Risk factors in PTSD and related disorders: theoretical, treatment, and research implications. *Traumatology, 7*(1), 23–50.

Figley, C. R. (2008, October 2). *Stemming the tide of trauma systemically: The role of family therapy.* Keynote address to the Australian Family Therapy Association, Brisbane.

Figley, C. R. (2010, April 7). *Now we know much about the neurobiology of PTSD: So what?* A review of post-traumatic stress disorder: Basic science and clinical practice, edited by P. J. Shiromani, T. M. Keane, & J. E. LeDoux. *PsycCRITIQUES, 55*, Release 14, Article 6.

Figley, C. R., & Figley, K. R. (2009). Stemming the tide of traumasystemically: The role of family therapy. *Australian and New Zealand Journal of Family Therapy, 30*(3), 173–183.

Gehart, D. (2010). *Mastering competencies in family therapy: A practical approach to theory and clinical case documentation.* Pacific Grove, CA: Brooks/Cole.

Green Cross Academy of Traumatology. (1999). Standards of practice. Retrieved from http://www.greencross .org

Haley, J. (1991). *Problem-solving therapy.* San Francisco, CA: Jossey-Bass.

Hamblen, J., & Barnett, E. (2015). PTSD in children and adolescents. *PTSD: National Center for PTSD.* Retrieved from http://www.ptsd.va.gov/professional/treatment/children/ptsd_in_children_and_adolescents_overview_for_professionals.asp

Institute of Medicine. (2008). *Treatment of posttraumatic stress disorder: An assessment of the evidence.* Washington, DC: National Academies Press. doi:10.17226/11965

Lewis, H. B. (1971). *Shame and guilt in neurosis.* New York, NY: International Universities Press.

Madanes, C. (1991). *Strategic family therapy.* San Francisco, CA: Jossey-Bass.

Minuchin, S., & Fishman, H. C. (1981). *Family therapy techniques.* Cambridge, MA: Harvard University Press.

Minuchin, S. (1974). *Families and family therapy.* Cambridge, MA: Harvard University Press.

Sells, S. P. (2004). *Treating the tough adolescent: A family-based, step-by-step guide.* New York, NY: Guilford Press.

Sunset Advisory Commission. (2014, May). *Staff report.* Austin, TX: Department of State Health Services. Retrieved from https://www.sunset.texas.gov/public/uploads/files/reports/DSHS%20Staff%20Report_1.pdf

The Family Systems Trauma Model

This chapter presents a flowchart diagram of the family systems trauma (FST) model that includes an overview of the motivational phone call and all five phases of the FST treatment model along with procedural steps and prephase preparation steps:

The FST Motivational Phone Call

Phase I: Identify Symptoms (Stressors) and Set the Goals for Therapy
           Pre-session Preparation for Phase II
Phase II: Wound Work Introduction
           Pre-session Preparation for Phase III
Phase III: Co-Create Playbooks
           Pre-session Preparation for Phase IV
Phase IV: Troubleshooting and Dress Rehearsals
           Pre-session Preparation for Phase V
Phase V: Evaluate Progress and Relapse Prevention

The flowchart in this chapter and case example of Mark's family provides a dual lens capability. The FST therapist can "zoom out" (Part I) to see the big picture of the timing and sequencing of each phase and then "zoom in" to integrate detailed strategies or techniques (Part II). The zoom-in strategies are called mini-steps because they provide the FST therapist with the step-by-step procedures of how to get from point A to point B. These mini-steps are invaluable to frontline therapists who often state that therapy models provide generalized concepts but lack the necessary mini-steps to provide a clear road map. Families also benefit from the flowchart when the FST therapist replicates it as a handout and revisits it throughout the course of FST treatment. Family members frequently comment that the FST model flowchart is like a giant map at the entrance of a shopping mall with the words "You Are Here." The flowchart can both help lower anxiety and build hope as family members can track their progress through each phase of the model and see how all five phases and pre-session preparation steps synchronize together.

In addition, we have created an online resource community that will be updated regularly with short YouTube videos by Dr. Sells, new wound playbooks, and workshops in your area. Please visit www.familytrauma.com or www.gopll.com/trauma for more information.

Each phase of FST treatment can be conducted within a home-based or office setting. It will depend on the family and level of the therapist's experience, but the average length of stay to complete all five phases of family systems trauma (FST) treatment will average between six and ten 2-hour sessions or the equivalent of 12 to 20 1-hour sessions. Tune-ups or additional sessions will be used if a relapse occurs or is imminent. More advanced therapists will also move through each phase faster than those who are new to systems or structural–strategic theory.

Each of the five phases includes the symptomatic child or adolescent along with the rest of the family and the village whenever possible. Individual sessions with the child can be conducted as needed and the parent or caregiver can also be seen without the child present as needed. Clarity of when self-referrals to other complementary-fit treatment modalities are needed are highlighted in Chapters 7 and 13. As stated in Chapter 1, special treatment circumstances are highlighted through case examples.

After the FST model overview (zoom-out) is presented in this chapter, Part II (Chapters 4–13) outlines the micro-steps or specific techniques (zoom-in) within each core phase of the model. Sixteen-year-old Mark and his family illustrate each part of the FST model to demonstrate a continuity of care and see how all the phases of treatment synchronize together. The five treatment phases along with pre-session preparation steps are not intended to be rigid procedures, but instead guidelines that are systemic, yet flexible enough to adapt to novel situations.

Figure 3.1 provides the step-by-step visual zoom out road map for this chapter and beyond. The FST can copy and use this figure to keep them focused on where they are in the treatment process. Or they can copy as a handout to give to the family to show them where they are in the treatment process.

THE FST MOTIVATIONAL PHONE CALL

The main goals of the motivational phone call are to (a) lower resistance in family members prior to the first face-to-face session and (b) invite or inquire about the family's village (i.e., extended family, friends, neighbors, school, work). Jay Haley (1991) in his classic book *Problem-Solving Therapy* said it best: "For therapy to end properly, it must *begin* [italics added] properly" (p. 5). In mental health, we often fail to properly begin treatment in two ways. There is often no joining or relationship building before the first session, except for a brief phone call to set up the first appointment. As a result, family members are not warmed up to treatment through what is called a "soft start-up," and instead begin treatment under a "harsh start-up." It is also often rare to directly invite extended family members to the important first session where the goals of therapy are created. This is a tactical mistake and one that can be avoided with a good to great motivational phone call before the first session.

To accomplish these goals, there are five steps that are outlined in detail within Chapter 4. They are the following:

1. *Understand why motivational phone calls are important*: A detailed explanation of why the FST motivational phone call was developed and how it parallels some of the research by Gottman and Silver (1999) on a soft versus harsh start-up is highlighted
2. *The SPIN theory behind the FST motivational phone call*: Each of these FST motivational phone call questions were designed based on key marketing outcomes found in Neil Rackham's (1995) book *SPIN Selling*
3. *The FST motivational phone call scripts*: A detailed outline of the motivational phone call scripts for the primary caregivers, extended family or village, and the child or adolescent
4. *The stick and move technique*: How to use the specialized technique of "stick" and "move" to prevent the motivational phone call from turning into a therapy session
5. *The use of effective closing remarks*: How to become like a great trial lawyer and present succinct and well-thought-out closing remarks at the end of the phone call to motivate and inspire the parent, village, or child to action

This section provides a brief overview of these mini-steps using the case example of Mark and his family to illustrate key points.

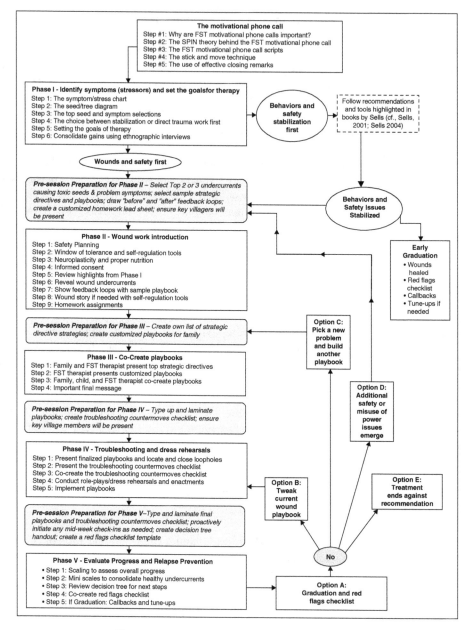

Figure 3.1 Family systems trauma (FST) model.

Case Example

Sixteen-year-old Mark was referred by his single parent mom, Ann. Two years ago, Mark was raped by a male acquaintance at a party. Mark had been too ashamed to report the incident. It was only recently that Mark revealed the rape to his mother. Before the traumatic

(continued)

Case Example (*continued*)

event, Mark was an honors student and someone without emotional or behavioral problems. However, after the abuse, Mark unsuccessfully attempted suicide twice and adopted the self-harm behavior of cutting. His grades dropped to a D average and Mark became extremely disrespectful with sudden angry outbursts toward his mother and even his teachers.

The receptionist who took the call reported that Ann was extremely agitated and angry, stating that she had already tried multiple counselors without success and that this attempt would likely be yet another failure. However, she had no choice but to keep trying.

Therefore, when the FST therapist first contacted the mother to set up an appointment, Ann answered the phone in a very terse and angry tone.

Rather than getting rattled, the FST therapist, who had the motivational phone interview script in hand, moved quickly to

Question #2: "What are some of the difficult experiences that you have had to suffer in the last year because of the problems you have been having with your teenager, Mark?" *[Estimated time of completion = 5 minutes]*. (See full script in Chapter 4.)

The mother seemed to like this question because it gave her time to vent. To avoid a long discussion that could turn into a full-blown therapy session over the phone, the FST therapist used what is called a stick and move technique. This meant that he gently interrupted and summarized what Ann stated (stick) and then went quickly on to the next topic or question (move). In this way, Ann felt heard but did not ramble.

The therapist noticed a distinct softening in Ann after he asked

Question #3: "When I get to know you better, what qualities and strengths will I come to admire about you as a [person, parent, spouse, etc.]?"

Ann stopped cold in the conversation and stated, "*None of our previous counselors have ever cared enough to ask me about my strengths let alone on a first phone call.*" Ann started to cry, stating that her strength was that she refused to give up even though she was constantly exhausted and overwhelmed.

Later in the call, the therapist got a valuable clue about why previous counseling attempts had failed, when he asked:

Question #5: "Have you seen a counselor for any of these problems before? What have other counselors missed with you? The reason I ask is that I don't want to make the same mistakes."

Ann answered that 99% of the time other counselors had only involved Mark, not the entire family. In addition, the other counselors never provided concrete tools to stop Mark's disrespect or help Ann address Mark's cutting, depression, or suicidal attempts.

As part of the motivational phone call process, the FST therapist ended the call with "closing arguments." This means that the FST therapist skillfully wove the parent's answers to the previous six motivational questions into a closing argument (like an attorney's closing arguments in front of a jury) that would motivate the parent, child, or village to attend the first session with hope and motivation (a soft start-up). In this case, the therapist ended the call with Ann using the following closing argument:

(*continued*)

Case Example (*continued*)

"Earlier in our call, you said that the quality I would come to admire about you is that you refuse to give up because you have so much love for Mark. That was important for me to know, Ann, because it is absolutely incredible that with everything you have gone through, you have not given up. Ann, you also said earlier that you wanted concrete tools from other counselors and more involvement to help solve your son, Mark's problems."

The FST therapist wrote down the statements made by the parent earlier in the call and fed them back to her within a summary format during the closing argument. This summary format is incredibly motivating to the parent because it shows that the therapist was listening and any "call to action" by the therapist is likely followed because it is prompted by the client's own words.

After the closing argument and a verbal commitment of "yes," the therapist asked permission to make a similar warm-up call, but with a different script, for Mark. The FST therapist asked the mom for the best time to call the house to reach Mark.

Finally, the therapist inquired with Ann about her village outside the immediate household (extended family, friends, schoolteachers, neighbors, etc.) who were supports to either Ann or Mark. Ann started to trust the therapist at the end of the motivational phone call and revealed that her ex-husband, Nick, her two brothers, Mitch and Hank, and her mom, Susan, were very supportive. The FST therapist asked permission to contact Mark's dad, Nick, personally and requested Ann to bring in her mom and two brothers to the first session. Ann e-mailed the therapist a signed release of information form granting permission to contact Mark's dad prior to the first session so that the motivational call to the father could take place.

Because of the FST motivational phone call, three important things took place. First, therapy began properly because the motivational phone call led to a soft start-up. Ann, Mark, and Mark's father, Nick, were softened up by the phone call and came into the first session ready for change. Second, the odds dramatically increased that the family members would show up for the first session. And third, the FST therapist was able to earn enough trust during the motivational phone call to get the extended family or village to attend the first session.

PHASE I: IDENTIFY SYMPTOMS (STRESSORS) AND SET THE GOALS FOR THERAPY

After the motivational phone call and soft start-up, Phase I begins. Phase I is the first face-to-face session that includes the child or adolescent, the immediate family, and, hopefully, the village. The main goals and objectives for Phase I are to (a) identify the child's or adolescent's problem symptom through an FST technique known as a "stress/symptom chart;" (b) use what is called a "seed/tree diagram" to illustrate the causes of the child's or adolescent's symptoms through what are called unhealthy undercurrents and four toxic seeds (i.e., misuse of power, unhealed wounds, mental or physical impairment, or unmet primal needs; see Chapter 2); (c) ask each family member to pick his or her top problem symptoms and toxic seeds that he or she wants to address with rationale; and (d) set the goals of therapy. In addition, as the flowchart in Figure 3.1 illustrates, the FST therapist must answer this critical question:

"Does the evidence in Phase I for this particular child and family suggest. . .
(A) Behavioral stabilization first (using contracting) before direct trauma work?
OR
(B) Direct wound or trauma work first (using wound playbooks)?"

If the FST therapist makes the wrong decision, the symptoms in the child or adolescent will worsen and the family will remain discouraged or hopeless, and this discouragement will likely result in a premature end to treatment. Three rules of thumb to help with this decision are outlined in detail within Chapter 5 and highlighted in the case example in this chapter.

To accomplish these goals, there are six mini-steps that are outlined in detail within Chapter 5. They are

1. *The symptom/stress chart:* Use the solution-focused scaling technique of 0% to 100% (Malinen, 2001) to help the family and FST therapist locate the top three problem symptoms of the child or adolescent that the family wants to solve to heal the trauma.
2. *The seed/tree diagram:* A visual apple tree drawing that serves as a road map for family members to discover the causes of their child's problem symptoms from the stress chart through the use of what are called undercurrents and four toxic seeds (misuse of power, unhealed wounds, mental or physical impairment, unmet primal needs).
3. *The top seed and symptom selections:* Each family member is asked to independently select the top two toxic seeds and symptoms that he or she wants to address first and explain why. The FST therapist then gives his or her picks with rationale.
4. *The choice between stabilization or direct trauma work first:* A critical tactical decision is made by the FST therapist that directly impacts the goals of therapy about which path of treatment to take first: (a) stabilize behaviors first prior to direct wound work or (b) move directly to wound or trauma work without the need for stabilization.
5. *Setting the goals of therapy:* After making the choice of stabilization or direct wound work first, the FST therapist converts their seed and symptom picks into the goals for therapy.
6. *Consolidate gains using ethnographic interviews:* The FST therapist will end Phase I with important ethnographic questions developed by Sells, Smith, and Moon (1996) such as "What was most helpful in today's session?" or "What was least helpful?" to consolidate gains made in the session or provide feedback on how to improve.

The case example of Mark and his family illustrates key concepts and techniques used in these six mini-steps.

Case Example

Returning to Mark's case, after the motivational phone call, Mark, his mom, and the village (Nick [Mark's dad]; Mitch and Hank [uncles], and Susan [grandmother]) all attended the first face-to-face session in Phase I. The FST therapist surmised that the phone calls created a soft start-up for everyone who had received the call and a harsh start-up for those who had not. The body language of Mark, Ann, and Nick (they had received the motivational call) was open and relaxed, but that of the uncles and grandmother was closed and tense (had not received the MI phone call).

(continued)

Case Example (*continued*)

The Symptom/Stress Chart

The session began with the FST therapist asking everyone the question "Would you agree that all families have stress?" Everyone nodded an affirmative "yes." The FST therapist then proceeded to a large flip chart taped to the wall and wrote the title "Stress Chart" at the top of the page with a marker and drew a scale from 0% to 100% beneath it (see Box 3.1).

BOX 3.1 Mark's Family Symptom/Stress Chart

					Stress Chart					
0%	10%	20%	30%	40%	50%	60%	70%	80%	90%	100%
0% = no stress								100% = maximum stress		

After writing out the stress chart, the FST therapist asked the question:

On a bad week, how much overall stress do you experience at home (not at work or school) out of 0% to 100%? What is the first answer that comes to mind if 0% represents no stress and 100% maximum stress?

The preceding question was slightly modified for the villagers who did not live in the immediate household:

I realize you do not live inside the house. But from the outside looking in, how much stress are you under watching what goes on with Mark and Ann, if 0% represents no stress and 100% maximum stress?

Everyone in the family and village gave a rating of 80% or higher. After each person gave an overall percentage, beginning with the adolescent Mark, the FST therapist asked everyone to break down their overall stress rating into the top three stressors. The therapist then asked each family member to go through each of his or her stressors and explain how much total stress could be eliminated if one stressor at a time could be alleviated or eliminated at a time. For example, when Mark was asked, "*Mark, if our work together in counseling was successful and your sadness lifted, how much stress out of your total 95% would be eliminated?*" Mark answered that his overall stress would be go down from 95% all the way to 35% or that there would be a 60% (95%–35%) reduction in his stress level if just his sadness lifted and nothing else (see Box 3.2).

After this part was completed, the FST therapist proactively listed common "safety stressors" that families often overlook such as threats of suicide, violence, chronic running away, drug use, and so forth (see Chapter 5 for safety handout). By normalizing safety stressors as a common occurrence, the family was more open to talk about them. It had been a family secret, but the normalization allowed the family secrets of both Mark's self-harm (cutting) and the two suicide attempts to be revealed for the first time.

(continued)

Case Example (*continued*)

The father, the uncles, and the grandmother were shocked by the revelation. The therapist then had to quickly jump in and redirect before the conversation escalated further by stating that there would be time to discuss this issue later.

The completed stress chart is illustrated in Box 3.2.

BOX 3.2 Mark's Family Completed Stress Chart

Stress Chart

								Uncles & Grandma	Dad	Mark	Mom
								X	X	X	X
0%	10%	20%	30%	40%	50%	60%	70%	80%	90%	95%	100%

Mark's Top 3 Stressors that Cause 95% Stress

#1 *"Sad all the time" (depression)—60%↓*

#2 *"Dad never around" (grief & abandonment)—70%↓*

#3 *"Grades in school" (school performance)—80%↓*

Dad's Top 3 Stressors that Cause 90% Stress

#1 *"Not connected to Mark" (lack of nurturance)—80%↓*

#2 *"Outside the loop with my ex"—60%↓ (parents not on same page)*

Uncles Top 3 Stressors that Cause 80% Stress

#1 *"Mark's sadness" (depression)—80%↓*

#2 *"Mark's outbursts and disrespect" (aggression)—70%↓*

#3 *"Dad not around" (abandonment)—85%↓*

Mom's Top 3 Stressors that Cause 100% Stress

#1 *"The abuse and trauma" (sexual abuse)— 100%↓*

#2 *"He is sad all the time" (depressed)—80%↓*

#3 *"Mark's outbursts" (aggression)—85%↓*

Grandma's Top 3 Stressors that Cause 80% Stress

#1 *"Ann's depression" (depression)—80%↓*

#2 *"Mark's sadness" (depression)—70%↓*

Safety Stressors

#1 *Mark cuts his arm (self-harm)—90%↓*

#2 *Mark's two suicide attempts (suicide)—90%↓*

The Seed/Tree Diagram

After the symptom/stress chart was complete, the FST therapist immediately drew out the seed/tree diagram and defined each seed (see Chapter 2). Mark's family seed/tree diagram is illustrated in Figure 3.2.

(*continued*)

Case Example (*continued*)

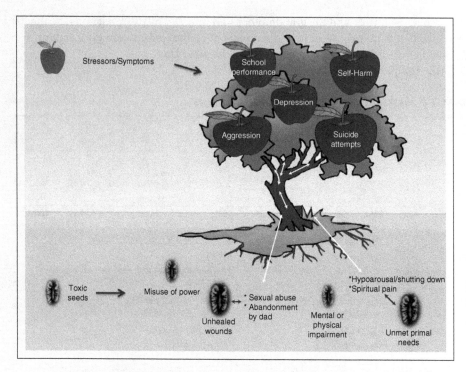

Figure 3.2 The seed/tree diagram for Mark's family.

The Top Seed and Symptom Selections

After the seed/tree diagram was created, each family and village member was asked to independently pick his or her top two seeds and problem symptom with supporting rationale. The family's answers are illustrated in Table 3.1.

TABLE 3.1 Mark's Family's Seed and Symptom Picks With Rationale

Mark's Seed Picks	Mom's Seed Picks	Dad's Seed Picks	Village's Seed Picks
#1: Unhealed wounds *Reason: Because of the rape I suffered with the kid at the party, I have never recovered. And my dad is never around.*	#1: Unhealed wounds *Reason: I agree with Mark but I am also depressed and wounded.*	#1: Unhealed wounds *Reason: I agree with Mark that it is both my not being around and the abuse.*	#1: Unhealed wounds *Reason: We agree with Mark's dad.*

(continued)

Case Example (*continued*)

TABLE 3.1 Mark's Family's Seed and Symptom Picks With Rationale (*continued*)

Mark's Seed Picks	Mom's Seed Picks	Dad's Seed Picks	Village's Seed Picks
#2: Physical impairment *Reason: Everything was going great at home and at school until the abuse. Now our whole family is different.*	#2: Unmet primal needs *Reason: Since the abuse, Mark will not let anyone near him emotionally. And his spirit, like you said, is hurting.*	#2: Unmet primal needs *Reason: I agree with Ann and want to add that my not being around has not helped matters.*	#2: Unmet primal needs *Reason: We agree with Ann too.*
Symptom Picks	**Symptom Picks**	**Symptom Picks**	**Symptom Picks**
• Depression • Grades	• Self-harm • Depression	• No more suicide threats • Depression	• Self-harm • No more suicide threats

After the family's seed and problem symptom picks were revealed, the FST therapist revealed his picks with the rationale behind them. It is these picks that would be used as the basis for the recommended goals of therapy going forward.

If the therapist's and family members' picks coincide, there is no conflict and things proceed smoothly. However, if there is disagreement, there is a potential for what is called the "battle for structure" (c.f., Carl Whitaker & Keith, 1981). This means that either the FST therapist or the family will prevail as to what the goals for therapy should be and how the problem should be defined (e.g., the child is frail and incapable vs. the child is capable but stuck in a rut). If the FST therapist loses this battle for structure by failing to convince the family of his position, therapy ends at the end of Phase I, before it begins (see Chapter 5 for guidelines and recommendations).

In this case example, there was agreement among the family as to the FST therapist's picks. They also agreed with his rationale. Even though the therapist's picks lined up perfectly with mom's picks, the therapist was able to convince the other family members that this was a good place to begin and that he was not taking mom's side over anyone else's. There was no active suicidal ideation, but just to be safe, a suicide safety plan would be put into place during the next session for relapse prevention. This safety plan satisfied both the village and the father. The FST therapist's seed and symptom picks are listed in Table 3.2.

(*continued*)

Case Example (*continued*)

TABLE 3.2 FST Therapist's Seed and Symptom Picks

FST Therapist's Seed Picks

#1: Unhealed wounds
Reason: Wound caused by the traumatic event of sexual abuse and further exacerbated by Dad and Mark's emotional distance from one another.

#2: Unmet primal needs
Reason: Mark is experiencing what is called "hypoarousal" or a normal numbing of his emotions or shutting down. He is also experiencing what is called "spiritual pain" or "pain in the heart" that happens with abuse. The spirit of the person is deeply bruised and hurt.

Symptom Picks

- Self-harm because it is a safety issue
- Depression because school grades can temporarily wait until the deep sadness and shame are lifted

---

The Choice Between Stabilization or Direct Trauma Work First

Before these goals for therapy were written, the FST therapist had to answer the question of whether the evidence suggested stabilization first or if immediate wound work was possible. To successfully make this decision, the therapist (prior to the session) studied the three rules of thumb questions outlined in Chapter 5 and highlighted in Table 3.3.

TABLE 3.3 Three Rules of Thumb to Help Decide Stabilization or Wounds First

Rule of Thumb #1: Chronicity, Bitterness, and Burnout Levels

(1) Are the behaviors extreme and happening almost every day or at least once a week? (aggression, extreme disrespect, running away, alcohol or drug use, self-harm, suicidal ideation, refusal to attend school, etc.) (2) Are the parents or caregivers extremely burnt out and overwhelmed? (3) Are the parents or caregivers extremely angry, bitter, or resentful toward their child? **Recommendation: stabilization first**

Rule of Thumb #2: Timing or Onset of the Child's Problem Symptoms

Were the problem behaviors with the child or adolescent present before the wounds occurred and simply got worse after the traumatic event *OR* did they only emerge after the trauma took place? **Recommendation: stabilization first if the former; direct wound work first if the latter**

(*continued*)

Case Example (*continued*)

TABLE 3.3 Three Rules of Thumb to Help Decide Stabilization or Wounds First (*continued*)
Rule of Thumb #3: Examine the Trauma Seeds (Wounds, Impairment, and Primal Needs)
Were the child's or adolescent's problem symptoms reported by family members and confirmed by the FST therapist as one of the three trauma seeds (unhealed wounds, mental or physical impairment, or unmet primal needs) *and not* the misuse of power seed? **Recommendation: direct trauma or wound work first**

In this case, the information gathered in Phase I clearly indicated a rule of thumb #2 decision. Mark's problem symptoms (self-harm, depression, failing grades, aggression) did not begin until *after* the traumatic event of the sexual abuse. Even the father's emotional abandonment (which occurred prior to the abuse) did not cause Mark's present-day problem symptoms. The abandonment, however, coupled with the traumatic event exacerbated Mark's symptoms. Therefore, direct and active wound work (without the need for behavioral stabilization first) was chosen as the next step. Safety planning, with regard to a suicide safety plan would be incorporated into the wound playbook using the two-track option (see Chapter 5 and the case example in Phase II).

Setting the Goals of Therapy

Once the wound work first decision was made, the final goals were written down for the family on a giant flip chart.

Goal #1:   Immediately reduce Mark's self-harm or cutting by putting into place what is called a wound playbook, a suicide safety plan, and what are called self-regulation tools beginning next session (Phases II–V) [show FST flowchart to family]

Goal #2:   Concrete tools will also be provided through a wound playbook to lessen Mark's depression and heal the underlying wounds driving his sadness and grief (Phases II–V) [show FST flowchart to family]

Mark's family was now ready to proceed to direct wound work in Phase II and bypass behavioral stabilization. Safety planning would still occur alongside direct wound work in what is called a "two-track" framework.

Consolidating Gains Using Ethnographic Interviews

The session ended on a high note with the FST therapist using what are called "ethnographic questions" developed from the Sells, Smith, and Moon (1996) research study.

(continued)

Case Example (*continued*)

The questions in the following text are asked of the family during every other session to get instant feedback of what is (a) working well or helpful in the session; (b) what is not helpful; and (c) what needs to happen in the future to make sessions more productive.

- Overall, what was most helpful in today's session?
- Overall, what was least helpful in today's session?
- What did I do or say as your therapist that was most helpful?
- What did I do or say as your therapist that was least helpful?
- What would need to happen in future sessions to make them more productive or of value to you or your family?

Mark's family seemed to enjoy these questions because it gave them a voice to comment on what they found helpful and what they did not during the session. In turn, the process seemed to consolidate or summarize the gains or forward progress they made in the session.

A common theme of what was most helpful was the experiential visuals of the stress chart and the seed/tree diagram. The mother, for example, commented on the fact "that everyone could now see each other's stressors" and this then helped drill down to specific goals. The uncles commented on the fact that the therapist's calm voice was helpful and that when things got overheated, he could keep things on track. This kind of feedback and interaction helped both end the session well and give the FST therapist clear direction of what to keep doing, adjusting, or modifying in both his style and delivery in future sessions.

If Stabilization Is Needed First

As the flowchart in Figure 3.1 illustrates, if stabilization (with or without safety planning) is needed prior to direct wound work, the child's emotional or behavioral problems are addressed using behavioral contracting. Recommended procedures to successfully implement contracting are outlined using an evidence-based model known as Parenting with Love and Limits (PLL; www.gopll.com) or through strategies in the books by Sells (cf., Sells, 2002, 2004).

If stabilization is selected, the FST therapist must clearly understand the differences between contracting, hybrids, and wound playbooks, and when to use safety playbooks and why. In short, stabilization will take place using behavioral contracting and hybrids alongside safety playbooks if needed.

Behavioral Contracting

Behavioral contracting and stabilization go together like peas and carrots. As outlined in Chapter 2, an upside-down hierarchy occurs when the child, not the parent or caregiver, is in charge of the household. The child controls the mood of the household through his or her actions and is the pack leader. As stated earlier, this process causes what we call the "Misuse of Power" seed and is part of PLL-FSS (family systems stabilization) evidence-based systems of care. Therefore, to reestablish the parents' lost authority, a straightforward behavioral contract or what we call a "hybrid" is used. A behavioral contract enables the caregiver to set consistent limits, whereas a wound playbook is used to clarify roles with step-by-step implementation of the technique selected to inject healthy undercurrents into the family system. Table 3.4 illustrates these differences using a side-by-side comparison.

TABLE 3.4 Behavioral Contracts Versus Wound Playbooks

Behavioral Contract to Restore an Upside-Down Hierarchy	Wound Playbook to Heal Unresolved Trauma
<u>**Rule:**</u> John's behavior will be considered <u>**disrespectful**</u> if he does one or more of the following: • Does not comply with adult requests the first time he is asked to do something • Argues, nags • Uses inappropriate language (profanity & phrases such as "shut up," "stupid") • Rolls eyes, sucks teeth, mimics parent **Here Are Your Choices—<u>You Have the Freedom to Choose Which One Occurs</u>** <u>**Choice #1:Reward or privilege—no instances of disrespect until bedtime**</u> ☑ Keep your cell phone and Internet the next day as long as there are no further acts of disrespect the next day or phone is not in deactivation mode (see italics below). ☑ At bedtime, we will make it a point to come up and praise you for a job well done and mark on a bonus calendar. When you achieve 7 straight days of no disrespect, you will receive a gift card. Once that milestone is achieved, when you go 14 and then 30 straight days, two more bonus items will be given (bonus items TBD). <u>**Choice #2: Consequence or loss of privilege**</u> ☑ As soon as disrespect occurs, you will be asked to put cell phone on kitchen table within 5 minutes of request and we will immediately exit to give you your space to do this. ☑ If we come back in 5 minutes and there is no cell phone on the table, it will be deactivated and you will have to pay for the reactivation fee + an extra fine for the inconvenience we had to suffer (fine $ will be earned by doing extra chores).	**Who:** • Darrell, mom, dad, grandparents, and counselor **What:** • Parents and grandparents will apologize and ask for forgiveness and then follow up with acts of kindness to put actions behind the words; counselor will facilitate process **When:** • Next Tuesday @ 6 p.m. **Where:** • At counselor's office **How:** • Counselor will show how and guide the process from start to finish • Acts of kindness will be determined and clarified after apology

TBD, to be determined.

As Table 3.4 illustrates, the contract is the strategic directive or tool the parents use to reestablish lost authority and reclaim their position as pack leaders. The unhealthy undercurrents within the misuse of power of "empty threats" and "inconsistency" are replaced (using the contract) with their healthy counterparts of "no empty threats" and "consistency" around a specific problem symptom. In Table 3.4, the problem was disrespect. In sharp contrast, strategic directives used to heal unresolved trauma or wounds are not concerned with helping parents reclaim lost authority or reverse hierarchy through the use of rules, rewards, or consequences. Instead, the goal is to clarify everyone's role to successfully implement the specific directive or answer the "who," "what," "when," "where," and "how" questions. This is done specifically to inject new and healthy undercurrents around the trauma seeds of unhealed wounds, mental or physical impairment, or unmet primal needs. In this example, it is the directive of forgiveness combined with acts of kindness to heal the wound between Darrell and his family.

Hybrids

In addition to behavioral contracts, there is something we call hybrids. Hybrids use traditional behavioral contracts to set clear limits but with a "lemon twist" of "emotional warm-ups." These are healthy undercurrents that heal wounds but do so using warm-ups such as rewards of praise, hugs, or any other form of nurturance or bonding. For example, in Chapter 2, "Matt's hug prescription" playbook was used to heal the trauma around the lack of nurturance and initiate the "soft side of hierarchy" (Sells, 2004). At the same time, the "hard side of hierarchy" was also used for consistent limit setting with clear rules and consequences. In this way, a hybrid plan is used because it contains an integration of limits to heal an upside-down hierarchy and emotional warm-ups to heal wounds and instill the soft side of hierarchy. This hybrid system is also aptly named a two-track process because two tracks (limits and emotional wound work warm-ups) are co-occurring. The two-track hybrid example in Table 3.5 shows how Matt's hug prescription is integrated with limit setting around "leaving home without permission."

TABLE 3.5 Two-Track Hybrid: Limit Setting and Wound Work Together

Behavioral Limit Setting to Restore an Upside-Down Hierarchy (Hard Side of Hierarchy)	Wound Emotional Warm-Up Playbook to Heal Unresolved Trauma (Soft Side of Hierarchy)
Leaving Home Without Permission **RULE:** Matt will be breaking the "leaving home without permission" contract if one or more of the following happen: *(Healthy undercurrents: safety & consistency)* • **Leaving the house** after mom or dad has instructed him to stay home • **Walking out of the house** and down the street when he gets angry • **Getting into the car** with someone without permission from parents • **Not coming home** at night when parents have given him permission to go out for a set period of time • **Leaving the house** during the night	**Lowering Matt's and His Family's Blood Pressure and Stress Plan** **The Power of the Hug Prescription** *To Inject the healthy undercurrent of nurturance to heal the wound and misuse of power seeds* **Who**: Dad, Mom, and Matt **What**: • Dad will initiate the first hug with his wife (has to be in front of Matt) for **30 seconds**. Matt will set the microwave timer. As the hug takes place, Dad will tenderly say one thing he loves or appreciates about his wife in the present or from the past

(continued)

TABLE 3.5 Two-Track Hybrid: Limit Setting and Wound Work Together (*continued*)

Behavioral Limit Setting to Restore an Upside-Down Hierarchy (Hard Side of Hierarchy)	Wound Emotional WarmUp Playbook to Heal Unresolved Trauma (Soft Side of Hierarchy)

CHOICES: <u>You Have the Freedom to Choose</u>
 	
<u>Choice #1— Reward or Privilege</u>
 	
• <u>**Not leaving without permission for 7 straight days**</u>
   o Go out Friday nights and will keep this privilege as long as you do not break the above rule. If you do break the rule, you have to start over and once again need 7 straight days to earn the privilege of going out Friday nights. Additionally, a new tracking phone software* on Verizon will be installed on your phone to assure us that you are where you say you are going to be. If you go somewhere else, you must get prior approval from mom or dad
 	
• <u>**Not leaving without permission for 14 straight days**</u>
   o Go out Friday <u>and</u> Saturday nights and will keep this privilege as long as you do not break the above rule. If you do break above rule, you have to start over and need 14 straight additional days to earn the privilege of going out Friday and Saturday nights. Additionally, the tracking phone software* on Verizon will be installed on your phone to assure us that you are where you say you are going to be. If you go somewhere else, you must get prior approval from mom or dad
   o *When you go 30 straight days of not leaving without permission, our trust with you skyrockets. As a result, tracking software goes to spot checking. You have earned that right and our trust*
 	
<u>Choice #2—Consequence or Loss of Privilege</u>
 	
• Loss of Friday night without 7 straight days with addition of software tracking (grounded Friday also means no friends over, no television, or electronics that night)
 	
• Loss of Saturday night without 14 straight days with addition of software tracking (grounded Saturday also means no friends over, no television, or electronics that night)
	• Mom will initiate the next hug with Dad (has to be in front of Matt) for 30 seconds. Matt will again set the microwave timer. As the hug takes place, Mom will tenderly say one thing she loves or appreciates about her husband in the present or from the past
	
	• After Mom, Dad will hug Matt (has to be in front of Mom) for 30 seconds. Mom will set the microwave timer. As the hug takes place, Dad will say one thing he is proud of Matt for, in the present or from the past
	
	When:
	• Before breakfast at 7:30 a.m. Monday–Friday (weekends off)
	• Date night between Mom and Dad every Friday night at 6 p.m. for dinner out
	• For next two straight weeks and then reevaluate with therapist
	
	Where:
	• At Home in the kitchen
	
	How:
	• Dad will initiate the first hug and wife the second (see above)
	• Dad will initiate the hug with Matt and before the hug, will give him the $3 in an act of faith that Matt will honor his commitment to fully participate with each hug time (give it his all). As hugs take place Dad will say one thing he is proud of about his son in the present or from the past
	• See troubleshooting checklist. But remember, "everyone's hug muscles will be sore and out of practice," so expect everyone's muscles to be stiff and tense. This is normal.
	• Everyone will initially feel weird giving hugs. This is normal. Do it anyway.

An additional value of two-track hybrids is that the emotional warm-ups can be parlayed into full and direct wound work later. In other words, once the family is stabilized, direct trauma work will likely be more effective. The family system is now warmed up to go into deeper wound healing as needed. For example, if Matt and his family get closer as a result of the hug prescription, the healthy undercurrent of nurturance can become the new normal in the family. Once in place, the family is now strong enough to handle direct and deeper wound work later such as the father apologizing to Matt for years of verbal abuse. In addition, direct wound work in general is much more effective because the day-to-day interactional trauma or drama around Matt's running away has ended. In sum, hybrids are the springboards for deep trauma work later.

Safety Planning

The final stabilization option is "safety planning" playbooks. As the flowchart in Chapter 3 shows, safety planning is an ongoing assessment whether the path selected is direct wound work or stabilization. As the reader would recall, during Phase I, as part of the stress/symptom chart, a safety handout was provided that listed common safety concerns a child or adolescent may face (e.g., suicide, violence, self-harm, bullying, sexual abuse). If the family confirms that one or more of the safety issues on the handout was taking place, safety concerns should be a priority when setting the goals of therapy (e.g., see the suicide safety plan for Mark in the case example). The safety concern in question is then translated into a safety playbook (see Table 3.6) that, like the hybrid, can be converted into a two-track plan that is typed and implemented side-by-side with the behavioral contract and/or wound playbook. Regardless of the path selected (wound or stabilization), the FST therapist will use a rating scale of 1 to 5 (1 = no risk; 5 = high risk; see Chapter 7) to determine if the current safety plan is working to reduce risk or if new safety concerns have emerged. It is important to note that even though the FST therapist may start with safety concerns for the child, the safety concerns can shift to safety involving the parents or the village as the case example illustrates.

TABLE 3.6 Two-Track Safety Playbook and Hybrid Stabilization

Safety Playbook	Hybrid Behavioral Contract
Who: • Leo (father), FST therapist (coordinator), Mike (Leo's best friend), Marie (mother), local pastor, Mindy and Jack (mother's best friends), and Elena (the daughter) **What:** • Leo agrees to take Marie out every Friday night instead of going out by himself in order to begin to repair their relationship. Leo will drink NO alcohol that night. *(For the first couple of weeks, to jump-start this process, Mike will come over at 6 p.m. to see Leo and Marie off/out the door together)* • If Leo goes out on Saturday, he agrees to text Mike after the first drink (while he is still sober) and again when he is on his way home (Maria will text Mike that Leo has gone out) ○ Mike will meet Leo at home and will administer a breathalyzer. If any alcohol is in Leo's system, he agrees to spend the night with Mike ○ If Leo does not call Mike, for safety reasons, Marie will lock the doors and not allow Leo entrance until Mike comes over	Elena will break no drug use rule if she does one or more of the following: • Test dirty on a randomly assigned UA (kit bought at local drug store) or refuses to take the UA when asked by either parent • Parents will test Elena randomly at least 2x per month or when they see Elena come home with red eyes, smell pot on her, or find pot in her room Rewards/Celebrations: • Every clean UA test = retain the privilege of keeping her cell phone and Internet privileges + praise and appreciation expressed by both mom and dad along with a celebration dinner • 2 consecutive clean UA tests = privilege of a sleepover with friends Consequences: If Elena tests dirty or refuses to take the UA test, the following will occur: • Mindy and Jack (mother's best friends) will sponsor two "Acts of Kindness" weekends. They will pick up Elena on Saturday at 9 a.m. for two consecutive weekends and will return Elena home at 10 a.m. Sunday morning.

(continued)

TABLE 3.6 Two-Track Safety Playbook and Hybrid Stabilization (*continued*)

Safety Playbook	Hybrid Behavioral Contract
• The next day, without shame or malice, Leo will apologize to both Marie (his wife) and Elena with the pastor and Mike present. Pastor will pray over Leo with the rest of the family. The FST therapist will also be present to help facilitate this apology • Leo will place a black mark on his wife's heart in the living room picture. After 5 Xs, Maria agrees to take Elena and leave home to stay with relatives for a minimum of 30 days. At the end of 30 days, will reevaluate with the FST therapist • If any further acts of emotional abuse exist outside of drinking on the weekends, an apology session will be called for. Marie will call Mike to arrange the meeting (if Elena sees the emotional abuse and mom does not call Mike, Elena will call Mike) • Any acts of future physical abuse will result in the police being called and charges being filed. Marie or Elena will immediately call Mike and additionally, Marie will take Elena and immediately leave to stay with relatives for a minimum of 30 days or more depending on circumstances **When:** • Each Friday or Saturday night that Leo is going out, Mike is the designated monitor until further notice • Apology sessions as needed the next day (see above) **Where:** • At the house **How:** • See the "What" section above <u>Important to Note:</u> • Each time Leo relapses, it will further break his wife's (Marie) heart, causing emotional death. It will also continue a stressful home environment that makes his daughter (Elena) continue to smoke pot to medicate her pain. This cycle is also creating risk for harder drug use later and lack of motivation to succeed in school • Each time Leo relapses, it hurts Leo's heart and causes him spiritual pain. This is because when you hurt others, you hurt yourself	Saturday will be full of helping others with acts of kindness. Acts of kindness can include visiting the elderly in local nursing homes, volunteering work at local homeless shelters, helping local neighbors with extra chores, etc. (If Elena refuses to participate in the "Acts of Kindness" activities, she must surrender her cell phone immediately or it will be deactivated and the Internet password will be changed until the next random test is 100% clean (not for 14 days until THC leaves her system) **Emotional Warm-Up Special Outings** **Who:** Elena and dad **What:** Special daughter and dad outing 1x per week **When:** Anytime on Sunday **Where:** Dad gets to decide where they go one week, then Elena decides the next week, and they continue to alternate. (**Outings cannot be going to a movie that does not provide for "face time" and conversation) **How:** Dad provides transportation to the location of their outing. If Elena refuses to go, dad will call Mike for assistance to get the outing jumpstarted <u>Important to Note:</u> • Since dad and Elena are not used to spending time together, expect the first few outings to not be fun and to feel awkward. This is normal and to be expected. Therefore, "fake it until you make it!"

(*continued*)

TABLE 3.6 Two-Track Safety Playbook and Hybrid Stabilization (*continued*)	
Safety Playbook	**Hybrid Behavioral Contract**
• Each time Leo relapses, his daughter's (Elena's) wounds fail to heal because she continues to see the father she loves hurt the mom she loves. Risk increases that she will not marry a healthy man, but instead will marry a man who will abuse her and put at risk Leo's future unborn grandchildren	

THC, tetrahydrocannabinol; UA, urine analysis.

Case Example

At the end of Phase I, safety concerns included the father's drinking and subsequent acts of emotional abuse and occasional domestic violence against the mother. In addition, it was determined that this ongoing trauma was the catalyst to 14-year-old Elena's chronic marijuana use, which also became a safety issue. Rule of thumb #2 indicated that the hierarchy was a mess long before the abuse by the father of the mother. However, the abuse created a traumatic event for Elena and a home environment so toxic that she had little reason to stop smoking pot to medicate her pain.

Therefore, a safety plan for the father and a hybrid plan for the daughter were recommended as a two-track plan of attack. The rationale was that the family had protective factors that the FST therapist could access in the form of a village that included a pastor and two sets of best friends, one for the mother and one for the father. Without these protective factors present, the FST therapist would not use a two-track plan. Instead, it would have been a one-track safety plan first prior to any stabilization in the form of a behavioral contract or hybrid second.

A tactical advantage of the two-track plan is that it could act as a fulcrum whereby one area could help strengthen the other and vice versa (nurturance between father and daughter could easily help the father want to be a better man, and drink or abuse his wife less). The father would also have better insight to know that any further abuse against his wife would neutralize the effectiveness of limit setting with his daughter and she would then have no reason to stop smoking pot to medicate her pain.

It was made clear to Elena that while she was not responsible for the father's abuse, her problem behaviors still played a role in maintaining an overall high stress level in the family.

The key reframe was "the breaking of the mother's heart." Both the father and daughter loved the mother. So the FST therapist helped the mother make it clear to both parties that if the overall risk level did not come down to a 1 or 2, her heart would literally break in two and she would die of a broken heart.

Therefore, each time the father broke the contract or the daughter tested dirty on a urine analysis (UA), the one who broke the contract had to put a black *X* on a poster of the mother's heart (with her picture on it) in the living room for all to see. After five *X*s,

(continued)

Case Example (*continued*)

the mother agreed to move out and live with her relatives with the daughter to prevent her from dying of a broken heart. If there was another act of any domestic violence by the husband, her heart would break immediately. The mother would then file domestic abuse charges with the police.

Mobilizing the village of the father's best friend, Mike, the local pastor, and the mother's best friend, Mindy, and her husband, Jack, were the game changers to unstick this family. In addition, the two-track hybrid plan in Table 3.6 contained the clarity of roles and clear step-by-step procedures to help turn around a very chaotic and disorganized family system.

Table 3.6 illustrates how a well-developed two-track hybrid and safety plan along with clarity of roles can immediately introduce healthy undercurrents to unstick the family system and heal multiple wounds at the same time. In this case example, the healthy undercurrents of accountability, forgiveness, and active community involvement helped to drop safety risk levels immediately between husband and wife of abuse and violence. Violence thrives in secrecy. Therefore, when the community is involved in a nonjudgmental way, the violence stops or decreases. The local pastor was a friend of the family and well respected by the father. Both the father and pastor connected well with the metaphor that hurting another person through words or actions (especially one's spouse) causes spiritual pain to both the person being hurt and the person doing the hurting. As a result, the pastor's prayer for the father's spirit after an act of abuse was congruent with this reframe.

In addition, the "acts of kindness" weekend and Mike, as the father's "anti-violence" sponsor, was strategic. In both cases, the daughter was hurting emotionally and so was the father. However, when Elena helped others and spent the entire day (Saturday) with healthy role models (Mindy and Jack), it jump-started her empathy chip and awakened her metaphorically out of a pot-induced coma. In addition, Mike (a natural helper), rather than the police (an artificial helper), held the father accountable and stated with love and compassion that the father was no longer alone to face his demons by himself. The emotional warm-ups of date nights with the wife and special outings between dad and daughter were further designed to change the current dance of focusing on everyone's deficits and feelings of hopelessness to focusing on strengths and nurturance.

In addition, the FST therapist found "the hook" or key reframe to motivate the family to change as a whole. That reframe was "breaking the mother's heart" with the action of putting a black X on the heart with clear consequences or implications of the mother leaving for a minimum of 30 days if five Xs appeared or immediately if there were any further acts of domestic violence.

Once the risk level moved down from a reported 5 to a reported 2 and Elena stopped marijuana, the family hierarchy was now healthy and the family environment devoid of interactional trauma. Even though this kind of cease-fire environment may be temporary, it is often long enough for the FST therapist to move into direct wound work and to get at the root causes of the pain. In Elena's case, the deep wounds began with a parent's marriage that had deteriorated over the years and ended with an upside-down hierarchy.

(continued)

Case Example (*continued*)

However, the changes the mother saw in her husband brought immediate hope. And from this hope, the FST therapist could finally facilitate deep forgiveness through the use of wound playbooks. Or if this was not possible, the written playbook would bring to the surface the need for healthy boundaries or, in this case, the mother separating or divorcing to protect her daughter if the father refused to change. In each scenario, the safety planning would unstick the family and move them forward to help Elena heal long-standing wounds one way or the other.

PRE-SESSION PREPARATION FOR PHASE II

Looking at the flowchart whether wounds are addressed immediately after Phase I or after stabilization is addressed, the next step in the FST model is pre-session preparation for Phase II. The first overall goal of this pre-session preparation is for the FST therapist to (a) select the top two or three undercurrents that are directly causing the unhealed wounds in the child or adolescent. This is known as a "clinical or working hypothesis" that can be changed or modified based on new information acquired in future sessions; (b) the second goal is to convert the problem symptom and set of undercurrents into drawings of "before" and "after" feedback loops. These predrawings will be unveiled to the family in the next face-to-face Phase II session; (c) the third goal is to closely examine wound playbook examples and then custom-build a sample wound playbook that matches the after feedback loop drawing; (d) the fourth goal is to search the Internet to predesign a homework lead sheet handout for the family; and (e) the final goal for the pre-session preparation is to call the village personally to remind or motivate them to attend the upcoming session.

It is important to note that paradigm shifts like pre-session preparation are a challenge. They represent a change to the status quo framework of "We have always done it this way before" (i.e., no formal pre-session preparation, and the 50-minute weekly session started by Freud back in 1896). The entrenchment of this mindset through decades of mental health practice is not easy to overcome either by payers or frontline therapists. This is a reality, not a criticism. However, even though FST treatment can be a brief trauma model, it is one that has no shortcuts.

Traditional therapists may not think intensely about their cases between sessions or may not do any preplanning. In sharp contrast, FST therapists conduct specific pre-session planning work. This is done tactically to both increase overall effectiveness and conduct briefer trauma treatment more successfully. Formal pre-session preparation increases the likelihood that the face-to-face sessions are more focused and more productive. Instead of going from topic to topic during a session to pinpoint a point of entry, the FST therapist, through careful preparation, has a clear goal or direction even before the session begins. In turn, what might take two to four sessions to find the right entry point, now takes only one session. In this way, good trauma treatment can be briefer, more effective because *it is more purposeful*.

To accomplish these goals, there are five mini-steps that are outlined in detail within Chapter 6. They are the following:

1. Select the top two or three undercurrents causing toxic seeds and problem symptoms: The FST therapist will closely examine what is called an undercurrent worksheet to pinpoint the top two or three unhealthy undercurrents that are causing the child's or adolescent's symptoms and closely examine their healthy counterparts, that if injected into the family, can heal the wound quickly and effectively.
2. Select sample strategic directives and playbooks: The FST therapist will go to Chapter 8 of this book or go to www.gopll.com/trauma to select a technique and a sample wound playbook template that matches up with the healthy undercurrent(s) selected in the first step and customize it for the family. This will be handed out to the family in Phase II.
3. Draw before and after feedback loops: Convert the unhealthy undercurrents into what are called before feedback loop drawings and their healthy counterparts into after feedback loop drawings that visually show the implementation of the sample wound playbook.
4. Create a customized homework lead sheet: Search the Internet to create what are called customized "homework lead sheets." This sheet will contain sample techniques and resources that the family can investigate on their own, between sessions. The family will then present their findings at the beginning of Phase III. The homework will jump-start the family to become co-owners of co-creating their own wound playbooks. The lead sheet is a handout that is given to the family at the end of Phase II.
5. Ensure key villagers will be present: Key villagers are personally contacted by the FST therapist by phone, text, or e-mail to ensure their attendance of the next session.

Case Example

Returning to Mark's case, the FST therapist pondered the question in the following text to pinpoint the top two or three unhealthy undercurrents that are causing Mark's problem symptoms of depression and self-harm. The answer to this question would then reveal the healthy undercurrents that, if injected into this family, can heal Mark's deep wounds caused by the sexual abuse, and emotional abandonment by his father. These selections would be based on the therapist's seed and problem symptom picks at the end of Phase I.

Select the Top Two or Three Undercurrents Causing the Toxic Seeds and Problem Symptoms

"What are the top two or three unhealthy undercurrents within the unhealed wound seed and unmet primal needs seed that are directly responsible for causing Mark's problems (symptoms) of depression and self-harm (cutting)?"

To answer this key question, the FST therapist closely examined the undercurrent worksheet in Table 3.7 around the seeds of unhealed wounds and unmet primal and spiritual needs (see undercurrent worksheet for all the seeds in Chapter 6).

(continued)

Case Example (*continued*)

TABLE 3.7 Undercurrent Worksheet for Unhealed Wounds and Unmet Primal Need Seeds

Unhealed Wound Seed

Unhealthy Undercurrent		Opposite Healthy Undercurrent
☐ Unresolved grief or loss	→	Grief education and resolution
☐ Betrayal or abandonmen	→	Security, forgiveness, unconditional love
☐ Family secrets	→	Reveal secrets/safety
☐ Physical or mental abuse	→	Support, courage to leave, forgive
☐ Lack of forgiveness/bitterness	→	Forgiveness
☐ Lack of consistent nurturance	→	Unconditional love, consistent nurturance
☐ High anxiety	→	Safety or security
☐ High stress	→	Relaxation or diversionary tactics

Unmet Primal or Spiritual Needs Seed

☐ Maslow's unmet hierarchy of needs	→	Fill in "missing" Maslow need
☐ Lack of attachment or bonding	→	Attachment bonds
☐ Lack of forgiveness/resentment	→	Forgiveness, prayer
☐ Lack of connection to God/higher power	→	Connecting to God or higher power
☐ Mind, body and spirit unbalanced	→	Restoring balance

By examining the worksheet in Table 3.7, the FST therapist knew that the undercurrents selected would be different based on the symptom. For example, the undercurrents causing or fueling the symptom of sexual abuse (i.e., family secrets) would likely be different than those driving or causing depression (i.e., unresolved grief). However, there are times that undercurrents can overlap. For example, depression also be caused by "family secrets" and sexual abuse can be triggered by "unresolved grief."

Therefore, the key deciding factor is context. Context is revealed from family information gathered in both the stress chart and individual family member rationale for the seed and symptom picks at the end of Phase I. For example, in Mark's family, Mark stated the following reasons why he picked the seed of unhealed wounds, *"Because of the rape I suffered with the kid at the party. I have never recovered. And my dad is never around."*

This statement provided the FST therapist with the key information he needed to select the unhealthy undercurrents of unresolved grief and "abandonment" as key drivers of the depression (see summary pick, Table 3.8). Other statements by other family members (e.g., Dad said, *"I agree with Mark that it's both my not being around and the abuse"*) support this undercurrent decision or lead to other undercurrent picks.

(*continued*)

Case Example (*continued*)

In Mark's family, the FST therapist selected the following undercurrents based on the contextual data gathered in Phase I (Table 3.8).

TABLE 3.8 FST Therapist Undercurrent Picks Causing the Child's Symptoms

Mark's Problems (Symptoms)	Top 2 or 3 Unhealthy Undercurrents Directly Causing Each Symptom	Healthy Undercurrent Counterpart
Depression	☐ Unresolved grief & loss (from unhealed wound seed) ☐ Lack of attachment (from unmet primal needs seed) ☐ Feelings of abandonment	☑ Grief healing around lost parts of childhood after the sexual abuse ☑ Reestablish attachment/ emotional bonds with dad ☑ Needs unconditional love to feel secure
Self-harm (cutting)	☐ Family secrets ☐ Unforgiveness (from unmet primal need and/or unhealed wound seeds) ☐ High anxiety (from unhealed wound seed)	☑ Reveal secrets around the abuse using self-regulation tools (Chapter 7) to counteract the hypoarousal symptoms ☑ Forgiveness of abuser or self ☑ Safety and security through body checks

After the top two or three undercurrents were selected, the FST therapist made the tactical decision of which set of unhealthy and healthy undercurrents to highlight for Mark's family. The therapist decided to focus on "reestablishing emotional bonds with dad." The reason for this selection over others was (a) it was an easy undercurrent to build a sample playbook around; (b) it was a central theme chosen by multiple family members during their seed and problem symptom selection in Phase I; and (c) it was an undercurrent that represented what we call a "quick victory" (see Chapter 8) or one that the family can accomplish quickly to build momentum rather than to begin with more difficult undercurrents first (e.g., grief resolution or forgiveness).

Select Sample Strategic Directives and Playbooks

Once this decision was made, the FST therapist looked at the possible techniques and sample wound playbooks around this healthy undercurrent. Table 3.9 is an excerpt from Table 8.17.

(*continued*)

Case Example (*continued*)

TABLE 3.9 Sample Strategic Directives for Unmet Primal Needs

Unhealthy Undercurrents	Healthy Undercurrents	Techniques to Inject Healthy Undercurrent
Lack of attachment or bonding	Attachment bonds	☑ Restoring Emotional Family Bonds ☐ Acts of Positive Communication ☐ Fostering a Pet ☐ *The Fresh Prince of Bel-Air* video clip ☐ Random Acts of Kindness ☐ Increasing Emotional Closeness

The therapist chose the technique and sample wound playbook around "restoring emotional family bonds." This sample wound playbook template was then customized by the FST therapist for what he believed would be an excellent first draft playbook for Mark's family. It is reproduced in Box 3.3.

BOX 3.3 Restoring Emotional Family Bonds: Sample Wound Playbook Template

---

Restoring Emotional Family Bonds: A Wild at Heart Weekend

To inject the healthy undercurrent of attachment and help stop Mark's depression

Mark has suffered in silence long enough. Lifting deep sadness is helped by community convey the message that Mark is not alone. Mark and his dad, Nick, have not connected emotionally for a very long time. To jump-start the process, it is recommended that Mark, Nick, (his dad) and Mark's uncles (Mitch and Hank) do a "Wild at Heart" camping weekend in the wilderness using guidelines in the book *Wild at Heart* by John Eldredge (2001). Mark and Nick are "rusty" with one another, so an all-men's weekend with Mark's uncles will help to break the ice. *We cannot change the past, but let's change the future!*

Who:

- Mark, Nick, Mitch, and Hank (Scott, the FST therapist, will facilitate a meeting with the adults (elders' "prep" meeting) before the "Wild at Heart" camping weekend)

What:

- Camping weekend trip in the wilderness
- Elders "prep" meeting with the FST therapist to determine the goals for the camping trip
- Nick, Mitch and Hank will read the *Wild at Heart* book prior to the "prep" meeting to generate talking points and goals for the camping trip

---

(*continued*)

Case Example (*continued*)

BOX 3.3 Restoring Emotional Family Bonds: Sample Wound Playbook Template (*continued*)

When:

- Elders "prep" meeting TBD
- Camping trip TBD

Where:

- Elders "prep" meeting to occur in the FST therapist's office
- Camping trip's specific location TBD

How:

- Mark and his dad (Nick) will jumpstart their "reconnection" through the camping trip with the support and assistance of Mark's uncles
- The elders "prep" meeting will occur to discuss and outline the goals for the camping trip. The adults will refer to the guidelines in the Wild at Heart book, but will also be open to the bonding that will happen naturally. (Reminder: The adults/elders will have read the book Wild at Heart before the "prep" meeting and will come to the meeting armed with comments, suggestions for goals and questions)
- The FST therapist will facilitate the discussion at the elders "prep" meeting
- Mark will be asked to come in at the end of the elders "prep" meeting to give his input on goals for the camping trip

---

TBD, to be determined.

The reason for the camping trip idea along with the *Wild at Heart* book (Eldredge, 2001) selection was twofold. First, Mark was emasculated by the rape. A camping trip adventure in the wild with campfires at night with his uncles and father might be a great transformational catalyst to reclaim lost masculinity. Second, the *Wild at Heart* book has a spiritual theme with the message that all boys want to hear, which is "You have what it takes" and "It is not your fault when others wound you." Mark likely never received these core validations from his father or any other male role model. And when coupled with the rape, the effects were devastating. Therefore, the elders' prep meeting with the FST therapist beforehand would be used to help facilitate this understanding and help them plan to look for opportunities during the camping trip whereby these crucial messages could be hammered home. Pairing these two themes together would dramatically increase the likelihood that Mark and his father would reconnect.

In addition, because there was a verbally stated safety concern at the end of Phase I, the FST therapist prepared a safety playbook around any future suicidal ideation (see safety plan in the section "Phase II: Wound Work Introduction"). If there are no safety concerns, such a playbook would not need to be prepared during this point in treatment.

(continued)

Case Example (*continued*)

Draw Before and After Feedback Loops

After the sample playbook was customized, the FST therapist predrew the following before and after feedback loops for Mark's family. These are reproduced in Figures 3.3 and 3.4.

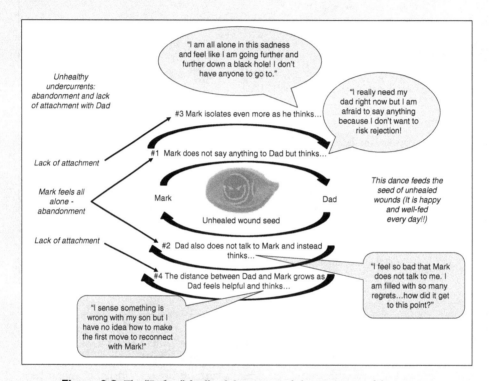

Figure 3.3 The "Before" feedback loop around the symptom of depression.

As illustrated in the before feedback loop in Figure 3.3, the arrows represent the interactional patterns or unhealthy undercurrents that keep Mark's wound of "lack of attachment" alive and well. If unaltered by using a wound playbook, there is no reason to expect that Mark and Dad will figure out how to get unstuck on their own. If they could, they would have done so by now.

Therefore, the strengths of the before feedback loop are threefold. First, the loops give the family valuable "systemic" insight. It helps move the family's worldview from a "Mark only" problem to a systemic problem. This systemic language is communicated as "dance moves" to the family. For example, the FST therapist will draw one loop and say something like "The first dance move labeled as #1 occurs when Mark does not say anything to Dad but thinks '*I really need my Dad now but I am afraid to say anything because I don't want to risk rejection.*' This then leads to #2, the second dance move which is Dad also not talking and thinking, '*I feel so bad that Mark does not talk to me. I am filled with so many regrets. . . . How did it get to this point?*'" and so forth.

(*continued*)

Case Example (*continued*)

Second, the feedback loop drawing externalizes the problem and invokes a rally cry to defeat the toxic seed of unhealed wounds. The family must work as a team against this toxic seed and pull its metaphoric feeding tube of unhealthy undercurrents.

The before feedback loop is a perfect set up for the after feedback loop drawing (Figure 3.4) or what the future might hold if the sample wound playbook (the Wild at Heart camping trip) is used like an antibiotic to replace the unhealthy undercurrents with their healthy counterparts to heal Mark's deep wounds and symptoms of depression.

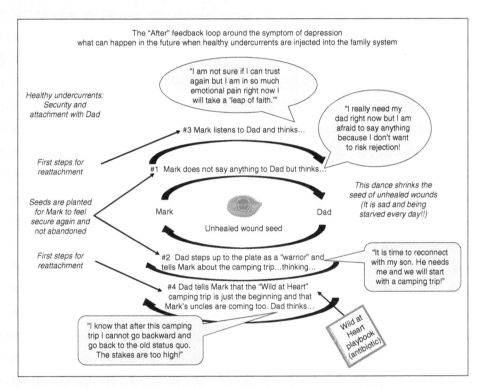

Figure 3.4 The "After" feedback loop around the symptom of depression.

It is important to note that when the FST therapist presents these drawings to the family, one dance loop at a time, so that they may disagree with some of the content. If this happens, the FST therapist can quickly correct the content in real time and the family will feel empowered because they are co-creating the feedback loops together.

The reason for the predrawing is that it gives the therapist and family a concrete point of reference to work from. Mark's family has most likely never seen feedback loops, so coming to the session with just a blank piece of paper would confuse the family even further.

(*continued*)

Case Example (*continued*)

As stated earlier, there are other undercurrents and symptoms in Mark's family at play (symptom of self-harm and undercurrents of family secrets, unforgiveness, and grief). These will be addressed later in Phases III, IV, and V. For now, the goal is to just give the family a sample or movie trailer preview of upcoming attractions to get their buy-in, increase hope, and move to an interactional or systems theory mindset.

Create a Customized Homework Lead Sheet

The next step was to Google-search the Internet to create a customized homework lead sheet.

The lead sheet would contain sample techniques and resources that Mark's family can investigate on their own between sessions. The leads would be sample techniques or tools around the key healthy undercurrents. For Mark's family the entire list would include:

- **How to grieve** techniques
- **How to restore lost attachments** techniques
- **How to talk about family secrets** techniques
- **How to forgive** techniques
- **How to do safety and security through body check** techniques

Since this list is obviously too long, the FST therapist would zero in on the two or three most likely set of techniques that fit the core healthy undercurrents as part of the original goals of therapy in Phase I.

Therefore, using this rationale, the FST therapist, with Mark's family, pinpointed lost attachments techniques and safety and security through body check techniques.

Based on this rationale, the lead sheet contained sample leads and resources for the following:

- How to restore lost attachments techniques
- How to ensure safety and security through body check techniques
- How to grieve techniques

The "how to grieve" techniques was added because even though it was likely that Mark and his family were not ready to hit this undercurrent immediately, it was the next logical one to approach after attachments and body checks. Therefore, the FST therapist wanted to "kick the tires" and see what the family might come up with and to see how energized they would be around grieving Mark's lost childhood.

Once the FST therapist had mentioned the topic areas, the next step was to search the Internet for these topics and sort through all the possible resources or techniques that emerge. Any techniques that looked comparable to the direction the therapist would move the family in Phase III and beyond would be added to the lead sheet.

(continued)

Case Example (*continued*)

This lead sheet would then be created as a handout and given to the family at the end of Phase II. Mark's family would then be asked to present their findings at the beginning of Phase III. Some or all of these techniques would then be used in the co-creation of wound playbooks, also occurring in Phase III.

The homework lead handout for Mark's family is reproduced in Box 3.4.

BOX 3.4 Sample Lead Sheet Handout Template

Homework Lead Sheet for Mark's Family

Overall Goals for This Homework Assignment

- Your family will self-discover creative techniques or strategies that will heal your wounds
- You will have input on what techniques or strategies go into your wound playbook that we create together at our next meeting
- Research shows that if you work hard to discover your own strategies, your rate of treatment success dramatically increases. Why? Because you now have "skin in the game"
- This lead sheet contains a few potential resources to jump-start the process, but please add your own
- Then next time we meet _____ (write in date and time here) I will ask you to present your techniques. If you do not come up with anything, please still come to the next session because I will have some to share. This means, even though you are signing your names below that you will try to complete the homework, sometimes things come up and get in the way. If you are unable to do this assignment, do not let it stop you from coming to the next session. No one will be upset.

Areas to Target

- Techniques to restore lost attachments
- Body check techniques to restore safety and security
- Techniques on how to resolve grief

Sample Leads for Your Family to Follow-Up On (Add your own)
Leads for possible strategies or techniques to restore lost attachments (targeted healthy undercurrents)

- ☐ Psychology Today: 5 Secrets to Love Your Child Unconditionally: When your child feels unconditionally loved, he's more likely to blossom. (Markham, March 2014)– https://www.psychologytoday.com/blog/peaceful-parents-happy-kids/201403/5-secrets-love-your-child-unconditionally

- ☐ How to Forgive Someone When It's Hard: 30 Tips to Let Go of Anger. (Deschene, 2016)–http://tinybuddha.com/blog/how-to-forgive-someone-when-its-hard-30-tips-to-let-go-of-anger

---

(*continued*)

Case Example (*continued*)

BOX 3.4 Sample Lead Sheet Handout Template (*continued*)

Leads for possible strategies or techniques to restore safety and security (targeted healthy undercurrents)

☐ Adolescent Self-Harm. (The American Association for Marriage and Family Therapy) –http://www.aamft.org/iMIS15/AAMFT/Content/consumer_updates/adolescent_self_harm.aspx

☐ WebMD Article entitled: Cutting and Self-Harm: Warning Signs and Treatment: Parents should watch for symptoms and encourage kids to get help. (Davis, 2015)– http://www.webmd.com/mental-health/features/cutting-self-harm-signs-treatment#5

Leads for possible strategies or techniques to resolve grief (targeted healthy undercurrents)

☐ We have the Right to Grieve Losses Big and Small. (Seda, 2016)–http://tinybuddha .com/blog/we-have-a-right-to-grieve-losses-big-and-small

☐ Grieve – Heal Your Inner Child. (Burney, 2013)–http://www.healyourinnerchild.com/ Grieve

Before you leave, let's answer the questions below:

• Who in the family will look for the different possible techniques or strategies?

• When or what times and days of the week will you devote to look for these strategies?

• Where will you look (on computer, library, etc.)?

• How will you summarize the information you gather to present the next week?

• What format will you present your findings in (typed up list, copies of what you find, etc.)?

Print name of each family member: _____

Signature of each family member: _____

Date _____
         Day/month/year

Ensure Key Villagers Will Be Present

Finally, the pre-session preparation work was not complete until the FST therapist personally contacted Mark's key villagers, namely, the father, uncles, and grandmother, with the mom's permission allowing the FST therapist to contact each villager. The rationale for this step is to ensure that every key village member is present when the feedback loops and sample wound playbook are presented. Wound work is difficult even in the best of circumstances but even more difficult when key extended family members are not present for the Phase II session.

PHASE II: WOUND WORK INTRODUCTION

Phase II takes place immediately following the pre-session preparation steps and is another face-to-face session following completion of Phase I. If any prior stabilization was needed, it is assumed that it was completed successfully beforehand and the family is now ready for direct wound work. If stabilization is not needed, as the flowchart in Figure 3.1 illustrates, Phase II occurs immediately after Phase I.

The five main goals for Phase II are to:

1. Conduct safety planning, window of tolerance and nutritional assessments.
2. Introduce the family systems to the inherent risks and benefits of trauma work using the FST model with informed consent.
3. Educate the family on undercurrents through the visual feedback loop drawings and a sample wound playbook.
4. Tell the wound story, if needed.
5. Provide a homework assignment lead sheet to enable family members to come up with their own tools and techniques prior to Phase III.

These five goals are combined as a prelude to get the family metaphorically prepped for direct wound work surgery within Phases III to V. Surgeons are often quoted as saying that great "pre-operative care" is more critical to the overall success of the operation than the actual surgery itself. The medical research backs up these claims (c.f., National Institute for Health and Clinical Excellence, 2008; Pritchard, 2009; Royal College of Nursing, 2005).

To accomplish these goals, there are nine mini-steps that are detailed in Chapter 7 and that are done over the course of several sessions. These mini-steps are the following:

1. *Safety planning*: Check-ins with the family using a 1 to 5 risk scale to see if any current safety issues are stabilized or any new safety concerns have emerged
2. *Window of tolerance and self-regulation tools*: An assessment of the child and family to see if there are risks for hyperarousal (fight or flight response) or hypoarousal (i.e., immobilization response) that can retraumatize the child if he or she retells the wound story. If these risks are present, self-regulation tools are taught (e.g., meditation, deep breathing, walking exercises) to counteract window of tolerance effects
3. *Neuroplasticity and proper nutrition*: How proper nutrition can feed the traumatized brain and rewire neural pathways in the brain
4. *Informed consent*: A written handout that provides the family with a list of Pros versus Cons of moving forward using the FST model
5. *Review highlights from Phase I*: Provides an overview of seeds, symptoms, and the goals of therapy from the last session as a helpful summary and to bring up to speed any new family members or village members
6. *Reveal wound undercurrents*: Show the family the undercurrent worksheet and the unhealthy and healthy undercurrents selected by the FST therapist with rationale
7. *Show feedback loops with sample playbook*: Show the family the pre-session preparation of before and after feedback loop drawings and a sample wound playbook as a preview of upcoming direct wound work in Phase III
8. *Wound story, if needed, with self-regulation tools*: Ask the child or adolescent to tell the wound story using previously provided self-regulation tools, but only if needed
9. *Homework assignments*: Provide the family with a homework lead sheet prepared during pre-session preparation that contains sample resources to help them locate their own techniques around the healthy undercurrents presented in the sixth mini-step

Case Example

Returning to Mark's case, Phase II began with the following transition statement to connect the dots to safety planning first and what was promised at the end of Phase I: A safety plan around future suicidal ideation (Mark had made two suicide attempts prior to the start of FST treatment)

Safety Planning

Before we proceed, I want to always maintain a stance of 'safety first.' This means that I want to return to what we discussed at the end of our last session. To summarize, we agreed to these goals for therapy. I have them written down on the flip chart."

Goal #1: Immediately reduce the self-harm or cutting of Mark after putting into place what is called a wound playbook, a suicide safety plan, and what are called self-regulation tools, beginning with the next session (Phases II–V) [show FST flowchart to family]

Goal #2: Concrete tools will also be provided through a wound playbook to lessen Mark's depression and heal the underlying wounds driving his sadness and grief (Phases II–V) [show FST flowchart to family]

"As everyone can see, we agreed to the need for a 'suicide safety plan' even though, Mark, you reported no thoughts of suicide in the past three months or presently. But just to confirm, Mark, is this true?"
Mark: *"Yes."*
"OK, then to be on the safe side, I want to go around the room and ask mom and Mark to assess any risks on these common signs of suicide thinking. I am asking Mark and mom because they see each other all the time. However, if any of the village wants to jump in, feel free to raise your hand."

The FST therapist used a standard suicide risk assessment tool and found that Mark's risk did not indicate immediate danger.

Nevertheless, the FST therapist passed out a suicide safety plan seen in Box 3.5 for everyone to see. To prevent Mark from getting upset, the therapist overemphasized the fact that this plan would only go into place if Mark experienced suicidal thoughts or feelings in the future with the goal of preventing another hospitalization, which Mark hated and wanted to avoid.

Please note: If the assessment had indicated risk, the above scenario would be very different. The FST therapist would hit the "pause button" on the session and move the focus of the entire session, if necessary, to troubleshooting and role-playing (see Chapter 11) and the delivery of the safety playbook.

Safety planning ended when the FST therapist reshowed the safety handout from Phase I (see Chapter 5) and double-checked to see if any of the other safety issues had emerged since the last session 2 weeks ago. The family answered no, and the therapist was ready to proceed to the next mini-step.

(continued)

Case Example (*continued*)

BOX 3.5 24-Hour Safety Watch Playbook

24-Hour Safety Watch Playbook

A 24-hour watch is exactly what it sounds like: You (mom), with the help of your village (uncles, grandmother, and father), will closely watch Mark continuously until the risk of suicide has passed. This means someone will take him to and from school, will shadow Mark wherever he goes, and will sleep in the same room. Otherwise, hospital staff at a psychiatric hospital will have to do this job for your family.

If Mark is not in school, and no one in the village can assist in this area, you must take him to work with you or take time off from work to stay at home until the danger has passed. The bottom line is that Mark cannot be left alone under any circumstances.

The house itself will also have to be suicide-proofed immediately. Throw out or place under lock and key all household chemicals, medications (including over-the-counter medicines like aspirin and Tylenol), guns, knives, and other possible weapons.

If Mark takes pills or cuts or hurts himself (beyond current surface cutting that we will address in counseling) while on the 24-hour watch or at any other time, rush him immediately to the emergency room.

Mark and Parents' Safety Agreement

I, Mark Smith, agree to the following conditions to prevent harm to myself.

If I violate any of the conditions listed below, I understand that my parents have to call the police or a psychiatric hospital for safety reasons:

1. Before I cause harm to myself in any way, shape, or form, I will talk to at least one parent or my FST therapist. If they are not available, I will wait until I can talk to them.
2. I agree to be under a 24-hour watch by my parents until I am no longer suicidal or agitated. I agree to be taken to school and picked up at the appointed time.
3. I agree that the house will be suicide-proofed with all medications, knives, and guns safely locked away, so that I will not be tempted, until the danger has passed.
4. If I feel suicidal or even think suicidal thoughts, I agree to talk with one of my parents and not stuff it inside.
5. If any of the below things happen while on the 24-hour watch, I know and accept that the police or the hospital will immediately be called:
   - Refuse to sign this safety plan
   - Leave home without permission
   - Leave school without permission or refuse to attend
   - Make any threats or acts of aggression toward self or others
   - Use drugs or alcohol
   - Refuse to stay with parents at night
   - Refuse body checks

Signatures:
Mark _____
Mom _____
Village _____

(*continued*)

Case Example (*continued*)

Window of Tolerance and Self-Regulation Tools

After the safety-planning mini-step was completed, the FST therapist was now ready to assess the window of tolerance and the need for self-regulation tools. To do a window of tolerance assessment successfully, the therapist can use a paper and pencil assessment tool such as the structured interview for disorders of extreme stress (Pelcovitz et al., 1997) and/or the handout illustrated in Chapter 7.

In Mark's family, the handout was used, and the family and Mark reported that he showed the distinct signs of hypoarousal within the areas of physical, emotional, and cognitive functioning.

Mark reported that the trauma of the rape left him feeling numb, emotionally paralyzed and shut down. He stated that he wanted to cry and feel something and that this led in part to a continued need to cut on his arms and legs. He stated that he wanted to feel something, even if it was physical pain.

Based on this self-assessment, the FST therapist introduced what are called self-regulation tools (c.f., Ogden, Minton, & Pain, 2006; van der Kolk, 2014). These are used to move a client who is either hypoaroused or hyperaroused into what is called the "optimal" or balanced window of tolerance state. This means that when Mark started to experience hypoarousal symptoms, he could use self-regulation tools to move his physical, emotional, and cognitive responses into congruency with the present. In short, the self-regulation tool selected could help Mark talk about the trauma story without shutting down. The following self-regulation tool was presented to Mark and his family based on the handout in Chapter 7. The tool was custom-fit to Mark:

Senses-Orienting Exercise

"Mark when you feel hypoarousal responses coming on, stand up and walk around the room. As you walk, focus your awareness on the movement of your legs and on your capacity to move toward and away from objects in the room. With each step, speak aloud exactly what you are doing (e.g. 'I am now moving toward the desk, I can feel my knees bending and the soles of my feet as they push into the floor, etc.'). This tool will help you to regain awareness and control of your body and counterbalance you shutting down and going numb."

Dress rehearsals or role-plays were then conducted for Mark to practice the "senses-orienting exercise." However, the timing of treatment was not right for Mark to retell his wound or trauma story. If Mark would need to tell it at all, the ideal timing would be after the feedback loop presentation at the end of the session.

However, if the role-plays revealed that Mark was completely frozen in hypoarousal and could not move forward, the FST therapist could have stopped the session and explained the need for a referral to more specialized self-regulation therapies, such as eye movement desensitization and reprocessing (EMDR; Shapiro, 1989; Shapiro & Forrest, 2004) or neurofeedback (Siegel, 1999; van der Kolk, 1994).

If this was the case, the options would be to (a) pause FST long enough for Mark to get some additional self-regulation tools; (b) use a "both/and" approach of specialized therapy and FST therapy together; or (c) proceed cautiously forward, but leave the door open to

(*continued*)

Case Example (*continued*)

circle back around to Option A if Mark started to decompensate. However, because Mark responded well to the role-plays, the decision was made to move forward. Role-plays are great if used strategically. They act like a litmus test to see if a family or child is able in the present to move forward with new feedback loops or if they are not yet ready.

Neuroplasticity and Proper Nutrition

After the role-plays were finished, the next step was to educate Mark and his family on the concept of neuroplasticity and proper nutrition, and its positive affects on trauma.

The family loved the connection and explanation of the traumatized brain and proper nutrition. Mark entered FST treatment already on an antidepressant but was suffering negative side effects of weight gain, constipation, and sleep problems. FST therapy is not designed to take the place of nutrition therapy, but to provide a complementary pathway.

Therefore, the FST therapist will use a handout questionnaire adapted from Shannon's (2014) book *Parenting the Whole Child: A Holistic Child Psychiatrist Offers Practical Wisdom on Behavior, Brain Health, Nutrition, Exercise, Family Life, Peer Relationships, School Life, Trauma, Medication, and More* (pp. 80–82) or recent dietary guidelines found at www.health.gov. Once the guidelines are presented, the FST therapist and family can (a) choose to change their diet under the guidelines suggested and/or (b) do so in consultation with a certified nutritionist. In Mark's case, the nutritional questionnaire revealed such a poor diet of sugar, lack of water, and lack of vegetables (an average score of 10; "Scoring: 8–16 = Poor diet, needs significant changes"] that a nutritionist was consulted and the dietary plan became part of the FST treatment regime (see Chapter 7).

After 3 weeks on a new diet, the change in Mark was extraordinary. The nutritional plan was focused on the following:

- Increase vegetables
- Eliminate sugar
- Increase good proteins
- Reduce bad carbohydrates and use a multivitamin

Mark had more energy, began to laugh again, was able to sleep, and his weight loss accelerated. From this brain change, Mark was much better equipped to handle the Wild at Heart camping trip with Dad and handle other future wound playbook interventions around grief and self-harm. Mark's use of antidepressants was tapered off slowly under the care of his family physician.

Informed Consent

The next step was to educate Mark and his family on "informed consent" and how it applied specifically to FST treatment going forward. The family was given a customized FST-informed consent handout (see Chapter 7) that contained the following introduction:

(continued)

Case Example (*continued*)

"This Informed Consent Form is for families who want to participate in FST (Family Systems Trauma) treatment. This Form is given now because we are about to begin active wound or trauma treatment with the introduction and completion of what are called "wound playbooks." Therefore, the optimal timing to go over this form is now to discuss both benefits and limitations of this approach to you individually and your family or village as a whole."

This Informed Consent Form has three parts:

- Part I: An Information Sheet (general information about FST treatment)
- Part II: A List of Potential Benefits and Possible Limitations
- Part III: Certificate of Consent (for signatures if you agree to take part)

"As we go through this document, there may be some terms or concepts that are not clear and need clarification. If this is the case, please ask me to stop and I will take time to explain. If you have questions at the end, please let me know."

The mother's comment was most telling after the FST therapist went through the form:

"None of you know this story. But when I called to set up the first appointment with Scott, I chewed out the receptionist and said that I was tired of therapy because it didn't work and what Mark and I had previously experienced was so unprofessional. When I said this, I meant that our previous therapy was disorganized and had no clear goals or even what to expect as next steps. However, right out of the gate, this program was completely different. From that first phone call, to the 'You Are Here' flowchart, to the stress chart, to the suicide safety plan, and to this informed consent, everything is clear and step-by-step. It gives me confidence that we are in good hands. So, 'yes' I will gladly sign this consent form. Everything up to this point has been professional so I expect this level of service to continue as we go forward."

The hour-long session was ended after the informed consent was signed. Rather than trying to rush through the next section, it was a good natural breaking point to end the session.

In Chapter 11, a good argument is made for the 2-hour sessions as the FST therapist is trying to change process, not just content. However, if a 2-hour session is not possible, this is the best breaking point to end an hour-long session.

Review Highlights from Phase I

The second session for Phase II began 1 week later. When the family arrived, they were greeted with a cleaned-up version of their stress chart, seed/tree diagram, and everyone's

(continued)

seed and symptom picks hanging side by side like a giant picture gallery at a museum. They immediately saw how far they had come in a short time. The evidence was literally visible for all to see.

Reveal Wound Undercurrents

The FST therapist then proceeded to distribute two handouts stapled together. The first page was the worksheet of all the possible undercurrents for the seeds of unhealed wounds and unmet primal needs with the therapist's markups, and the second page was the summary handout of the FST therapist's undercurrent picks specific to Mark. This customized summary handout is seen in Table 3.8.

Some therapists have commented that therapy should be more like magic. In other words, the goal is not to show the audience how the trick is performed, because the family is not able to handle too much information or too many tables and handouts. Our research and experience have shown just the opposite. Even very poor and uneducated families have an extremely high resiliency quotient (RQ) and insight quotient (IQ). Families appreciate the systematic step-by-step rationale with visuals behind every step and being included in the intricacies of how trauma work is done. In turn, family confidence and buy-in grows as FST treatment is broken down into bite-sized pieces, and provided one bite at a time.

After Mark's family received the handouts, their body language and comments indicated they were fully engaged. This is because, in our experience, people love to talk about root causes of problems and get out of a traditional focus of weed work or symptom maintenance.

After looking at the handout, the only blatant disagreement was Mark's comment that he did not need to forgive himself or the abuser because he was "over it." Rather than get into a debate, the FST therapist stated that Mark might be proved right as treatment moved forward and that these were, at best, educated guesses.

Show Feedback Loops With Sample Playbook

As the therapist drew each before feedback loop one at time from his predrawing, one could not even hear a pin drop. Everyone was fascinated to see the interactions between Mark and his dad using "thought bubbles." Comments ranged from "*I never looked at the problem this way before* " to "*I can see that this is a family problem to solve, not a 'Mark only' problem.*"

Mark also looked visibly relieved that the feedback loop was a picture that said in a thousand words: "The problem of depression and the abuse was not his to bear alone." Everyone especially liked to see where and how the unhealthy undercurrents worked as root causes to exacerbate Mark's depression.

The inherent risk of the before and after loops is that they will act as natural catalysts to increase intensity, stir up emotions, and move the child or adolescent quickly to

(*continued*)

Case Example (*continued*)

a retelling of the wound story. If this happens, the FST therapist has to make a judgment call to either (a) pause the session and facilitate an enactment with the child telling the wound story using the self-regulation tools from earlier; (b) wait until later or after all the loops and sample playbook are presented; or (c) use the stick and move technique to redirect and not have the child tell the wound story at all. Rule of thumb guidelines for this decision are presented in Chapter 7.

In Mark's case, Mark did want to tell Dad directly about his pain immediately during and after the before feedback loop. The therapist decided to allow the discussion but asked Mark to raise a finger if he started to move into hypoarousal; the therapist said that he would be looking for signs as well. The key was to allow some release from the pressure of the pain, but not too much that would scare the youth and/or family away from treatment forever. To prevent this occurrence, the FST therapist was quick to jump in to help redirect, reframe comments, and prevent blame. The discussion ended well, with the therapist asking Dad to repeat that he heard Mark say "that he missed his father."

After the before feedback loop was completed, the after feedback loop was drawn one loop at a time, with the wound playbook as the representative antibiotic or catalyst to make the change. The family liked the creativity of the Wild at Heart camping trip, and it gave everyone hope and insight into what it looked like to rally together to move forward to help heal Mark's wounds. The family was not sure they would keep the sample playbook but would discuss and think on it further between sessions. The FST therapist said that was fine and reiterated that it was a sample to get the family jump-started to here and now change.

Wound Story, if Needed, With Self-Regulation Tools

In this case, Mark had begun to tell his story as the before feedback loop was being revealed, and his body language indicated that he was emotionally drained. As a result, there was no need to push any harder at this stage of treatment.

Homework Assignments

At the end of the session, Mark and his family were given the homework lead sheet (Box 3.4).

Prior to leaving, the FST therapist facilitates answers to the logistical questions of how to successfully implement the homework assignment:

"Before you leave today, let's answer these questions by handwriting your answers:

- *Who in the family will look for the different possible techniques or strategies?*
- *Where will you look (computer, library, etc.)?*
- *How will you summarize the information you gather to present the next week?*
- *What format will you present your findings in (typed list, copies of what you find, etc.)?"*

PRE-SESSION PREPARATION FOR PHASE III

This pre-session preparation step occurs immediately after Phase II. The primary goals of this step are to (a) decide on the best strategic directives for the targeted undercurrent(s); and (b) create a customized playbook based on the particular family and technique selected.

To accomplish these goals, there are two mini-steps that are outlined in detail within Chapter 8. They are the following:

1. Create own list of strategic directive strategies: The FST therapist will look at the menu of technique options available for the specific undercurrent(s) and choose the most appropriate technique(s) or strategic directive(s) from the list (see Chapter 8 for menu of techniques) or create their own. The decision may be made by the FST therapist to recommend keeping the first sample technique and playbook from Phase II or to modify it accordingly.

2. *Create customized playbooks for family*: Based on the technique selection and sample wound playbook example, the FST therapist will customize the playbook for the particular family like the first sample wound playbook created prior to Phase II.

Case Example

With Mark's family, as discussed in the previous section, the FST therapist would recommend to the family the following with supporting rationale:

*   Stick with the camping trip weekend or something like this because (a) almost everyone in the family, including Mark, indicated that now more than ever he needed to reconnect with his dad. And being more connected with his uncles too would be an added bonus; and (b) it is optimal to address low hanging fruit or undercurrents whereby a quick victory is within reach. It appears that the other areas selected (grief, forgiveness, and talking about the wound [family secrets]) are equally important but will likely require deep tissue work. Therefore, with momentum generated from a camping trip–type activity, it is easier to go toward deep tissue work next. It is like peeling an onion. Go for the outer layers first and proceed inward, one layer at a time.

*   The body checks would be added based on the fact that it can be a safety issue in that Mark may inadvertently cut too deeply. And if done in a tender loving way, it will relieve some of the deep loneliness and isolation Mark must feel as he has to cut in secret. Again, when anxiety is reduced, it has a positive ripple effect on other wound areas such as grief, loss, and forgiveness.

The FST therapist obviously had all this in mind as early as the homework lead sheet draft. But it became more clear, concrete, and formalized after Phase II feedback loops and the family's body language and reactions to the sample wound playbook. However, it was still a working hypothesis. If the family put out new information or different

(continued)

Case Example (*continued*)

reactions to the feedback loops, the FST therapist, at this juncture of treatment, might go with one of the other undercurrents.

This process can be compared to "chumming" or "chum fishing" whereby the fisherman throws chum bait (fish parts) in the water to see if the fish are biting, particularly sharks because of their keen sense of smell (https://en.wikipedia.org/wiki/Chumming).

In the same way, the FST therapist goes in with a working hypothesis based on how the family reacts to chum fishing with feedback loops, the sample wound playbook, homework lead assignments, self-regulation role-plays, and so forth, to see where the family is biting. And then based on the bites, the therapist makes calibrated adjustments to know where to tap the right undercurrents with the right playbooks to release the healing power of the family to heal the child's or adolescent's wounds.

Create Own List of Strategic Directive Strategies

Based on the earlier information, the FST therapist already had the sample playbook for the healthy undercurrent of restoring attachments. Therefore, the only sample playbook that was needed was for the undercurrent of safety. The FST therapist then looked at the menu of techniques available for "high anxiety" (see Chapter 8) and chose the one indicated with the checked box in Table 3.10, "prayer and body checks."

TABLE 3.10 Sample Strategic Directives for Unhealed Wounds

Unhealthy Undercurrents	Healthy Undercurrents	Techniques to Inject Healthy Undercurrent
High anxiety	Safety or security	☐ The High/Low Checkup ☐ Increasing Confidence with Praise ☑ Prayer and Body Checks ☐ *The Lion King* movie clip

The prayer component was kept for this family because both the mother and Mark in the first session expressed an openness in this area. However, if they saw the sample playbook part on prayer and wanted to either remove it or modify it, this would be done.

Create Customized Playbooks for Family

The FST therapist studied the sample wound playbook for "prayer and body checks" in Box 3.6. He then took the example and sample wound playbooks and then customized a playbook for Mark and his family. Since the therapist was not sure yet who would do the body checks, mom or another village member, he left it as to be determined (TBD). This is chum fishing. By leaving this part blank, the door is open for the family to decide.

(*continued*)

Case Example (*continued*)

Please note that there are a lot of TBDs in general. This is done on purpose so that when the family gets the sample template, they can fill in their own answers, thereby co-owning the wound playbook as their own. Mark's sample playbook is reproduced in Box 3.6.

The FST therapist was now prepared and ready to head into Phase III with focus and confidence. The family is likely to be impressed, touched, and motivated by the pre-session work done by their therapist on their behalf between sessions. As Theodore Roosevelt was famously quoted as saying, *"People don't care how much you know, until they know how much you care"* (http://www.goodreads.com/quotes/34690-people-dont-care-how-much-you-know-until-they-know) This kind of going-the-extra-mile activity will help the traumatized family "care about how much you know."

BOX 3.6 Mark's Sample Wound Playbook

Sample Wound Playbook

Healing Mark's Anxiety by Bringing Safety
Body Check With Love, Prayer, and Compassion to stop Mark's Self-Harm

Who:

- Mark
- Who will do the body check for cuts & will it be one person or more? TBD (to be determined)

What:

- Body checks in the evening before bed with love and compassion (see how below)
- Prayer chain each night by whole village (mom, dad, grandmother, and uncles)—see example below

When:

- Evening before bed or morning—TBD

Where:

- In Mark's bedroom or other part of house—TBD

How: TBD but possible examples to use below

- Person doing body checks will come into room and do check
- If any cuts are found, do not censure, but hug Mark deeply and say simply, "I love you, you are not alone"
- If no cuts are found, hug Mark deeply and say, "I love you and am proud of you for resisting the temptation; I know it was not easy"
- If Mark wants to tell you about what caused the cuts, again do not censure, but use self-reflective listening. If he does not want to talk, do not ask any questions, simply leave after the hug
- Person doing the body checks can pray with Mark before checks or after the checks. Can use a prayer like one below or choose parts of the prayer below, or use your own prayer. May want to use a diary to write down the prayers to share with Mark so he sees tangible evidence of prayer

---

(*continued*)

Case Example (*continued*)

BOX 3.6 Mark's Sample Wound Playbook (*continued*)

Sample Prayer

Lord, I pray that You would surround Mark with Your hand of protection. Keep him safe from any more self-harm, accidents, diseases, drug usage, or other harmful influences. Protect him wherever he is. Keep him out of harm's way.

Lord, I pray that You would bring more healing between us and remove any lies in Mark's head and root out and eliminate core issues surrounding his self-harm wounds. I pray against his insomnia and that he would get plenty of rest so that he is completely rejuvenated when he awakens.

It is written, Let no weapon formed against my son be able to prosper (Isaiah 54: 17). Keep him at all times under the umbrella of Your protection, and deliver him from the enemy's hand so no evil comes near him. Give Your angels charge over him to keep him in all your ways (Psalm 91: 11).

I say to God "Cover my son under your wings to take refuge; His truth shall be your shield. He shall not be afraid of the terror by night, nor of the arrow that flies by day. A thousand may fall at his side, and ten thousand at your right hand; but it shall not come near Mark" (Psalm 91: 4-7).

TBD, to be determined.

PHASE III: CO-CREATE PLAYBOOKS

Phase III takes place following the pre-session preparation and is a face-to-face session with the family. The main goals and objectives for Phase III are (a) to ask the family to present their top or favorite technique (strategic directive) findings from their homework lead sheet; (b) for the FST therapist to show them their customized playbook(s) and present recommendations (from pre-session preparation) as to which undercurrents and symptoms to prioritize first, with rationale; (c) to co-create the playbook(s) together (FST therapist, child, and family); and (d) to predict relapse if the family tries to implement the playbook before troubleshooting and dress rehearsals are completed in the next session (Phase IV).

To accomplish these goals, there are four mini-steps that are outlined in detail within Chapter 9. They are the following:

1. *Family and FST therapist present top strategic directives*: The family presents their favorite techniques from their homework lead sheet and then the FST therapist presents their picks. The FST therapist takes the recommendations and sample wound playbooks of the pre-session preparation and presents these to the family for consideration. The therapist is faced with the challenge of whether to integrate parts of the family's picks into their sample wound playbook or to not use them.

2. *FST therapist presents customized playbooks*: The family and FST therapist then begin the process of co-creating their first wound playbook(s). Within this framework, the therapist makes the final decision to (a) keep the therapist's sample wound playbook as is with limited changes; (b) integrate new techniques outlined by the family during their homework presentation; or (c) scrap the therapist's sample playbook altogether and start

from scratch using one of the family's techniques. This is an important decision and is based on timing, the particular family, and a mindset of keep it simple or low hanging fruit first.

3. *Family, child, and FST therapist co-create playbooks*: Based on the earlier decision, the FST therapist and family then co-create their first wound playbook together. It is recommended to do only one or a maximum of only two playbooks at a time to avoid overwhelming them or setting the family up for failure.

4. *Important final message*: The final mini-step is to clearly convey the message of the dangers and risks of implementing the new wound playbook prior to first practicing its delivery through role-plays (dress rehearsals) and troubleshooting done during the next session (Phase IV).

Case Example

Family Presents Top Homework Technique Picks

Phase III began with Mark and his family presenting their favorite techniques from the homework lead sheet on reestablishing attachments, body checks, and grief resolution. The very act of doing the homework seemed to give them a sense of hope. This was revealed to the FST therapist by a stark change in body language and affect. In previous sessions, Mark and the family as a whole lacked energy and had a heaviness about them. In this session, the family laughed and even joked about how fun it was being like detectives on an assignment. Hank, the uncle, said it best when he stated, "*The homework acted like a homing pigeon or lighthouse to rally everyone together for Mark. We had a clear road map and we weren't going to waste this opportunity.*"

These epiphany moments are common as the family unveils its homework findings. The FST therapist really begins to see the fruit of strategic family theory on how to heal the entire family, not just the child, of trauma through individual therapy. This happens because the homework directives and other activities such as the wound playbook, completing the stress chart, locating seeds and symptoms together, and so forth, get families out of the rut with just the smallest change. As Gehart (2012) so eloquently writes:

> From the clients' perspective, directives *jolt them awake* [italics added] from their usual life patterns; generally, the clients know exactly how to shift themselves to make the necessary changes. Unlike insight in traditional psychodynamic therapy, directives create visceral "aha" moments because clients are in the midst of the action that needs to change. (p. 76)

This "aha" moment for Dad and his grief came in the midst of action to help his son. Other "aha" and exciting moments came as different family members revealed their homework findings. A few of these top findings are summarized:

Attachment findings

- The father discovered and liked the book *When Sorry Isn't Enough: Making Things Right with Those You Love* (2013) by Chapman and Thomas. His favorite technique was "letter writing." The father gave examples of how a handwritten apology to Mark might help and he could write one and give it to or read out aloud to Mark.

(continued)

Case Example (*continued*)

Grief resolution findings

- The family reported that they did not have time to do this part of the assignment even though the Internet links and books were easily accessible.
- This chum fishing was a success. It showed the FST therapist that the family was not yet ready to go down this path. Initial low hanging fruit undercurrents (e.g., attachment) had to be successfully accomplished first. The family likely knew this in their gut but were unable to express it through words so expressed it through inaction.

FST Therapist Presents Top Homework Technique Picks

The FST Therapist now had a perfect setup to reveal his technique picks. If the homework presentation by the family is enjoyable and purposeful, hope and confidence in the treatment process progresses. As a result, family members look forward to checking if their therapist's ideas match theirs. If the family forgets their homework, Phase III begins here.

The FST therapist distributes a handout (see Table 3.11) that highlights just those areas of focus being presented from the larger menu of techniques in Chapter 8. There is no need to confuse the family with undercurrents and techniques that do not apply to them at this time. Also the tables are relabeled from "Sample Strategic Directives for X Seeds" to "Sample Techniques to Help Heal Child's X Symptom." The latter is more relevant for the family.

TABLE 3.11 Sample Techniques to Help Heal Mark's Symptoms of Depression and Cutting

Unhealthy Undercurrents	Healthy Undercurrents	Techniques to Inject Healthy Undercurrent
Lack of attachment or bonding	Attachment bonds	☑ Restoring Emotional Family Bonds ☐ Acts of Positive Communication ☐ Fostering a Pet ☐ *The Fresh Prince of Bel-Air* video clip ☐ Random Acts of Kindness ☐ Increasing Emotional Closeness
Unhealthy Undercurrents	**Healthy Undercurrents**	**Techniques to Inject Healthy Undercurrent**
High anxiety	Safety or security	☐ The High/Low Checkup ☐ Increasing Confidence with Praise ☑ Prayer and Body Checks ☐ *The Lion King* movie clip

(continued)

Case Example (*continued*)

After the handout of Table 3.11 was distributed, the FST therapist quickly connected the dots of the technique of "restoring emotional bonds" to the earlier sample camping wound playbook. The only difference was that whenever possible, the FST therapist integrated the family's earlier homework ideas into this area. The following is the transcript of how this goal was accomplished:

As we revisit the sample camping playbook from last week [hold it up] let me add the following new information. I think your homework ideas could and should be integrated into this playbook. Dad, your earlier idea of a written letter was brilliant. If we decided to go with the camping template, picture a roaring fire, the stars out and you reading this letter from the heart by the light of the fire. It is dark, so Mark, you are more protected on how you want to respond and react. Or you can read the letter at the end of the trip as a capstone event. And Hank and Mitch, you might write a letter as well about how brave Mark is and present it on a different night.

And then before the camping trip, Dad, you and Mark, along with Mitch and Hank, can practice the tools in the book, How to Talk So Teens Will Listen and Listen So Teens Will Talk (Faber & Mazlish, 2010), and then imagine sitting at a stream in the woods or practicing the tools on a long hike. It can be a game changer. And then Mom, when Mark returns home from the trip, you can continue to use these tools. Mark will have practiced these tools so he will be better equipped.

The family loved this creative integration, and it served to increase their motivation to adopt this sample wound playbook.

FST Therapist Presents Recommendations and Customized Playbooks

After this discussion, the FST therapist was now ready to make a formal recommendation based on one of three possible options: Option A—keep the therapist's sample wound playbook as is with limited changes; Option B—integrate new techniques outlined by the family during their homework presentation; and Option C—scrap the therapist's sample playbook altogether and start from scratch using any of the family's techniques. As with Phase I, the final call has to be made by the FST therapist. There cannot be "too many cooks in the kitchen." Someone has to be the quarterback or leader and make the final call. Later, once treatment ends, that final call will be made by the parent as the pack leader, but for the present, the family is stuck, so it is the therapist's call. The battle for structure can again take place here and if the therapist loses, as with other key crossroads (Phase I: Set the Goals for Therapy), treatment can end here.

However, at the end of the day, the FST therapist must do something and choose an option. The family will not tolerate more weeks of "let me think about it" or indecision. Even if the option selected may not be the right one or the best one, it can still get the family to the finish line. For example, if Option C was selected and the new playbook created was not the greatest, the family is resilient and any healthy undercurrents, albeit

(*continued*)

Case Example (*continued*)

---

clumsily written, can still heal the child's wounds. At the very least, roles are still clarified, there is an actual written plan for the first time, and the family members will use role-plays and troubleshooting to practice their delivery in Phase IV.

Based on the earlier discussion, the FST therapist was able to choose and recommend the best option, Option B. The FST therapist would keep both the camping trip and cutting playbooks as the blueprint template and then integrate many of the family's homework techniques. The recommendations were formally written on a flip chart, and are reproduced in the following text:

> Recommendation #1: Keep the camping trip and "Wild at Heart" playbook but tweak it to add the earlier homework ideas of writing a letter and practicing the tools in the book: *How to Talk So Teens Will Listen and Listen So Teens Will Talk* (Faber & Mazlish, 2010).

> Recommendation #2: Use the pretend option to fill out and customize the body check playbook together today and then practice its delivery through dress rehearsals next session just to see how far it takes us. Mark can pull the plug later if he wants.

Formally writing out the recommendations in black and white was a big help to the family. They could see what they were committing to for the next action step.

Family, Child, and FST Therapist Co-Create Playbooks

The FST therapist then used the rest of the session to pull up both playbooks and go through line by line to fill in the TBD sections and integrate the family's homework ideas. It was a 2-hour session and the therapist used an HDMI cable and connected his laptop to the flat-screen television in his office so that changes could be easily made in real time. The modified playbooks are reproduced in Table 3.12. Anything added or modified during the session is indicated in a "bold and larger font."

TABLE 3.12 Co-Created Wound Playbooks

Restoring Emotional Family Bonds A "Wild At Heart" Weekend	Restoring Safety and Reducing Anxiety With Love, Prayer, and Compassion
Who: Mark, Nick, Mitch, and Hank (Scott, the FST therapist will facilitate a meeting with the adults [elders' "prep" meeting) (see below) **Keep as is**	**Who:** • Mark • Who will do the body check for cuts & will it be one person or more—TBD (to be determined) **Mom will start and if camping trip goes exceptionally well dad might pretend one evening a week (Mark's idea)**

(continued)

Case Example (*continued*)

TABLE 3.12 Co-Created Wound Playbooks (*continued*)

Restoring Emotional Family Bonds A "Wild At Heart" Weekend	Restoring Safety and Reducing Anxiety With Love, Prayer, and Compassion
What: • Camping weekend trip in the wilderness • Elders' "prep" meeting with the FST therapist to determine goals for the camping trip • Nick, Mitch and Hank will read the *Wild at Heart* book and generate talking points for the camping trip • **Add Dad's letter to read on camping trip** • **Add—Uncle's letter for camping trip** • **Add—(Mark's request) Mark's letter to Dad to read before Dad reads his letter** • **Add—Practice tools in the book *How to Talk So Teens Will Listen and Listen So Teens Will Talk* (Faber & Mazlish, 2010)** **When:** • **Elders' "prep" meeting next week at 5 p.m. in Scott's office—Mark will wait in waiting room and come in midway through to get his input** • **Camping trip three weeks from today** **Where:** • Elders' "prep" meeting to occur in the FST therapist's office **Scott's Office** • Camping trip specific location **Meet this weekend to decide where** **How: Keep as is with additions in bold** • Mark and his dad (Nick) will jumpstart their "reconnection" through the camping trip with the support and assistance of Mark's uncles • The elders' "prep" meeting will occur to discuss and outline the goals for the camping trip. The adults will refer to the guidelines in the *Wild at Heart* book, but will also be open to the bonding that will happen naturally. (Remember: the adults/elders will read the book *Wild at Heart* before the "prep" meeting and will come to the meeting armed with comments, suggestions for goals and questions • **Practice "How to Talk So Kids Will Listen Tools" at next session and more if needed** • The FST therapist will facilitate the discussion at the elders' "prep" meeting • Mark will be asked to come in **halfway through** the elders' "prep" meeting to give his input on goals for the camping trip	**What:** • Body checks in the evening before bed with love and compassion (see how below) **Keep as is** • Prayer chain each night by whole village (mom, dad, grandmother, and uncles) **Keep as is** **When:** • Evening before bed or morning—TBD **Just evening** **Where:** • In Mark's bedroom or other part of house—TBD **Guest bedroom, NOT Mark's bedroom (Mark's request)** **How:** • Person doing body checks will come into room and do check. **As of today, just a pretend check— Mark will pretend as if he has cuts and will indicate where but not actually show them** • If any cuts are found, do not censure, but **pretend to** hug Mark deeply and say, "I love You, you are not alone" • If no cuts are found, **Mom will pretend to (actually do it but in a pretend mode)** hug Mark deeply and say, "I love you and am proud of you for resisting the temptation, I know it was not easy" • Mark **(can pretend) to** tell you about what caused the cuts, again do not censure, but use self-reflective listening. If he does not want to talk, do not ask any questions, simply leave after the hug. • **Not at this time, but it is OK for the village to pray individually**

TBD, to be determined.

(*continued*)

Case Example (*continued*)

As illustrated in the playbooks in Table 3.12, what often happens is that just the act of writing the playbook together starts to generate healthy undercurrents on its own. In this case, Mark asked to write a letter to Dad and read it by the campfire first and said that "maybe" Dad could do a "pretend" body check one day in the future. In addition, Mark said it would be OK if Mom did a pretend hug after a pretend body check. Having the playbook prewritten rather than having a blank page helped enormously to keep the session on track and moving forward.

Important Final Message

After successfully co-creating the first, and in this case, also the second playbook, the family is understandably ready to implement it as soon as the session concluded. This is a huge mistake because the family has not practiced their delivery of the playbook(s) through role-plays (dress rehearsals) and troubleshooting that occurs during the next session (Phase IV). This huge mistake would be like sending a football team out on the field with a playbook but with no practice of any of the plays ahead of time. The football team would not only lose the game, but they would get slaughtered. This message was conveyed to Mark and his family. And because of the trust and rapport built up to this point, the family agreed to wait 1 more week.

PRE-SESSION PREPARATION FOR PHASE IV

This pre-session preparation step occurs immediately after Phase III. The primary goals of this preparation step are to (a) type and laminate the family's playbook(s), (b) create a customized troubleshooting checklist to present to the family at the beginning of Phase IV, and (c) ensure that the key village members will be present for the Phase IV session.

The troubleshooting checklist is the centerpiece of Phase IV like a script in a movie. The checklist sets up everything for "What will you do if?" scenarios or curveballs to be answered by what are called "countermoves" or actions or statements by the family in order to successfully address each curveball. These countermoves then become the perfect on-ramp for practicing role-plays or dress rehearsals. To understand this process, part of Mark's family's troubleshooting checklist is illustrated in Table 3.13.

The troubleshooting checklist example in Table 3.13 underscores a critical point. Imagine what would happen if the family came into Phase IV and was handed a blank checklist to fill in from scratch? Not only would it take an inordinate amount of time, but also the family members would be lost. The family is stuck and needs a prewritten troubleshooting checklist to work from, just like a prewritten wound playbook.

As a result, this pre-session preparation phase is very important to the success of Phase IV. A completed first-draft troubleshooting checklist like the one in the preceding text provides everything the family and the therapist need to be successful.

TABLE 3.13 Wound Playbook: Restoring Emotional Family Bonds—A "Wild At Heart" Weekend

Areas of the Wound Playbook to Address	Common "What Will You Do if?" Curveballs to Derail Playbook	Countermoves Actions or Statements
What: *Dad's letter is read on camping trip in front of the campfire after Mark reads his letter*	• What will you do if Mark goes into hypoarousal and shuts down or gets up and walks off into the woods late at night?	• Before we go, we need boundaries and agreement from Mark that he will not walk off into the woods. Once we get to the campground, we can establish a "safe zone" for Mark to go to if he needs to "gather himself" • During our session, we will come up with a plan with Mark's ideas to jumpstart what this could look like • Mark will be gently reminded by his uncles to use his self-regulation sensory-orienting technique to bring him back into the "optimal" window of tolerance zone • Once there, Hank or Mitch (TBD) can ask Mark to put into words what is going on through the technique of "reflective listening" [we will practice during our session] or tools from the book *How to Talk so Teens Will Listen and Listen so Teens Will Talk* (Faber & Mazlish, 2010) • If Mark still shuts down, we can try again the next morning. The important thing is to not let Mark's emotions get stuck inside him like in the past
	Other Possible Situations Not Listed • •	• •

TBD, to be determined.

To accomplish these goals, there are three mini-steps that are outlined in detail within Chapter 10. They are the following:

1. Type and laminate playbooks: Prior to Phase IV, it is important to take any edits or additions from Phase III and type them into a finalized wound playbook. In addition, if possible, laminate the finalized copy. There is something very special and professional when a family is handed a wound playbook that is laminated and spill-proof.
2. Create troubleshooting countermoves checklist: As illustrated in Mark's troubleshooting checklist example, the FST therapist takes the finalized wound playbook(s) created at the end of Phase III and produces a first-draft checklist that is presented to the family at the beginning of Phase IV. The checklist is then tweaked by the family and FST therapist and the countermoves are used as a script for the role-plays or dress rehearsals.
3. Ensure key village members will be present: As was done prior to Phase II, the FST therapist personally calls, texts, or e-mails key village members as a reminder to come to the session. Phase IV is the practice delivery phase and it is critical for the key players to be in attendance. If they cannot attend, Phase IV should be rescheduled until they can be there.

PHASE IV: TROUBLESHOOTING AND DRESS REHEARSALS

The main goals of Phase IV are to (a) look over the finalized playbooks to identify any logistical loopholes and correct these errors (e.g., intervention steps not clearly listed or incorrect date); (b) present a customized troubleshooting countermoves checklist handout to each family member prepared during pre-session preparation; (c) make any changes or adjustments in the troubleshooting checklist with the family as needed; (d) conduct role-plays/dress rehearsals or spontaneous enactments around key countermoves; (e) determine if dress rehearsals are a success or more practice is needed; and (f) implement the playbooks.

To accomplish these goals, there are five mini-steps outlined in detail within Chapter 11. These are as follows:

1. *Present finalized playbooks and locate and close loopholes*: The FST therapist passes out the typed and finalized wound playbook (hopefully laminated) and goes through it line by line with the family. Any logistical errors such as time, date, or location of the intervention or strategic directives are corrected in real time.
2. *Present the troubleshooting countermoves checklist*: The FST therapist passes out the troubleshooting countermove checklist handout. The checklist contains a first draft of the most likely loopholes (curveballs) the family might encounter when implementing their wound playbook along with possible countermoves to address the curveballs.
3. *Co-create the troubleshooting countermoves checklist*: The FST therapist and family go through the first draft of the checklist line by line and make any changes needed.
4. *Conduct role-plays/dress rehearsals and enactments*: The FST therapist uses key countermoves as an on-ramp for role-plays or spontaneous interactions or enactments between the child and family members to prompt healthy undercurrent communication.
5. *Implement playbooks*: If family members demonstrate competency in delivery of playbooks during the role-plays, the recommendation is made by the FST therapist to go forward with implementation. If not, additional sessions are recommended for further practice.

Case Example

Present Finalized Playbooks and Locate and Close Loopholes

The laminated playbook may seem like a small thing, but the family held both playbooks with a sense of pride and thanked the FST therapist for going the extra mile.

After looking through both playbooks, there was only one logistical loophole to close:

Where?

- Camping trip time: **Meet this weekend to decide where (Myers Rock Park)**

(continued)

Case Example (*continued*)

Present the troubleshooting countermoves checklist

The FST therapist then passed out a handout of the troubleshooting countermoves checklist he had put together during the pre-session preparation. He made it a point to reiterate to Mark's family that this was only a draft, like the sample wound playbook, to jump-start the process.

It is important to note that the FST therapist *will not* troubleshoot every part of the wound playbook, or the "slam dunks," but rather just the parts that are likely to challenge that particular family. The FST therapist calls certain parts slam dunks (see Chapter 11) because they are the curveballs and countermoves in the checklist that can be successfully completed by the family without the need for dress rehearsals or enactments. For example, in Mark's case, logistics of "when" and "where" the body checks or camping trip will take place is not a troubleshooting problem. It is straightforward and typed in black and white.

The real challenges in delivery or implementation will center around the "what?" and "how?" parts of the wound playbooks. For purposes of discussion, only two curveballs from Mark's family checklist are listed in Table 3.14 (for a detailed illustration of this process, see Chapter 11).

TABLE 3.14 Wound Playbook: Restoring Emotional Family Bonds—A "Wild At Heart" Weekend

Areas of the Wound Playbook to Address	Common "What Will You Do If?" Curveballs to Derail Playbook	Countermoves Actions or Statements
What: *In front of the campfire, before Dad reads his apology letter, Mark reads to his dad his own letter about how he was hurt*	• What will you do if Mark's letter is so angry and bitter that Dad shuts down and then can't read his own letter of apology?	• Need to talk this through with Dad and Mark • One option is for Dad to "not take it personally" and instead validate Mark's feelings rather than try to defend himself
	Other Possible Situations Not Listed • •	• •
What: *The elders will read the book* Wild at Heart *prior to this meeting and will come to the meeting with their questions and comments*	• What will you do if one or more of the elders (Dad, Mitch, or Hank) did not come to the meeting with the book read ahead of time?	• Postpone the meeting? • Someone will bring a bullet point summary of the book • Something else?
	Other Possible Situations Not Listed • •	• •

(*continued*)

Case Example (*continued*)

Co-create the troubleshooting countermoves checklist

As with the sample wound playbook, the FST therapist would read through each part of the checklist line by line and the family would be asked to (a) vote to keep the checklist as is with no changes; (b) add in other situations or countermoves not listed; or (c) tweak or modify specific suggestions in the script. The example in Table 3.15 illustrates these modifications in "bold and larger font."

TABLE 3.15 Modified Wound Playbook: Restoring Emotional Family Bonds—A "Wild At Heart" Weekend

Areas of the Wound Playbook to Address	Common "What Will You Do If?" Curveballs to Derail Playbook	Countermoves Actions or Statements
What: *In front of the campfire, before Dad reads his apology letter, Mark reads to his dad his own letter about how he was hurt*	• What will you do if Mark's letter is so angry and bitter that Dad shuts down and then can't read his own letter of apology? **Keep as is**	• Need to talk this through with dad and Mark **We agree with the option suggested here but need to practice it** • One option is for Dad to "not take it personally" and instead validate Mark's feelings rather than try to defend himself
	Other Possible Situations Not Listed • **Mark wants to wait for Dad to go first** • **Mark does not want to do the letter at all**	• **This would be fine with everyone** • **This would also be fine. It will be a "game time" decision**
What: *The elders will read the book* Wild at Heart *prior to this meeting and will come to the meeting with their questions and comments*	• What will you do if one or more of the elders (Dad, Mitch, or Hank) did not come to the meeting with the book read ahead of time?	• Postpone the meeting? • Someone will bring a bullet point summary of the book • Something else? **Read it soon after the meeting**
	Other Possible Situations Not Listed • **Only read a few chapters**	• **Read the remaining chapters after the meeting**

Conduct Role-Plays/Dress Rehearsals and Enactments

After the troubleshooting checklist is complete, the next step is for the FST therapist to make tactical decisions as to which countermoves to use with Mark's family as an

(*continued*)

Case Example (*continued*)

---

on-ramp to role-plays. This is done using the following eight procedural steps outlined in Chapter 11:

- **Step 1:** Eliminate Slam Dunks From Troubleshooting Checklist
- **Step 2:** Go From Easier Role-Plays to More Challenging Ones
- **Step 3:** Role-Play Introductory Statement
- **Step 4:** Clarify Roles in Role-Play (Antagonist or Protagonist)
- **Step 5:** Sidebar Open-Ended Countermoves if Needed
- **Step 6:** Storyboard Role-Plays With Verbal Walk-Throughs
- **Step 7:** Conduct Role-Plays and Segue to Enactments if Appropriate
- **Step 8:** Vote on Role-Play Performance Using a Scale of 1 to 5 (1 = need more practice and 5 = ready to implement)

In the first troubleshooting curveball of "how dad might respond if Mark's letter is bitter and angry" provides a clear setup for a role-play or dress rehearsal. The FST therapist can play the part of Mark and pretend he is reading his angry letter, while Dad pretends to respond using new feedback loops or healthy undercurrents of validating Mark's feeling without trying to defend himself or take it personally.

And if the Dad gets stuck in old patterns, the therapist can yell "freeze" and switch seats with Dad to role-model the correct or better delivery. Two or three takes can be done until Dad and the rest of the family feels that he has mastered the new delivery (see Chapter 11 on how to set up and execute a great role-play or dress rehearsal using the FST model).

In addition, the act of the role-play itself may move quickly from "pretend" to real life in a hurry. In other words, Mark and Dad or other family members could begin spontaneous interactions around long buried feelings that the role-play opened up. The FST therapist can then stop the role-play and use the moment to help facilitate healing conversations. These spontaneous conversations are called enactments (Minuchin & Fishman, 1981). How this shift takes place from role-plays to enactments and back again is outlined in Chapter 11.

However, the second curveball of "not coming to the elders' meeting prepared" is *not* a potential role-play situation, but one of simple problem solving. In this case, these are steps to take (not communication feedback loops) if and when the problem occurs. This distinction is important to understand.

In addition, the FST therapist simply does not have the time or bandwidth to role-play every countermove in Mark's checklist. Therefore, the strategy is for the therapist to make a judgment call on (a) which dress rehearsals have the highest potential to yield the most fruit regarding putting into practice a new normal of the healthy undercurrents and (b) which dress rehearsals have the highest potential level of difficulty to be successful. Sometimes these are the same, and sometimes they are different. Mark's family priority list is indicated in Table 3.16.

(*continued*)

Case Example (*continued*)

TABLE 3.16 Mark's Family's Priority List for Role-Plays/Dress Rehearsals

Dress Rehearsals That Have Highest Potential to Yield the Most Fruit	Dress Rehearsals That Have the Highest Possible Level of Difficulty
Camping Trip Playbook • Dress rehearsals around reactions to Dad's letter to read on camping trip • Dress rehearsals around reactions to uncles' letters for camping trip • Dress rehearsals around reactions to Mark's letter to Dad • Dress rehearsals around practicing tools in the book *How to Talk So Teens Will Listen and Listen So Teens Will Talk* (Faber & Mazlish, 2010)	**Camping Trip Playbook** • Dress rehearsals around practicing tools in the book *How to Talk So Teens Will Listen and Listen So Teens Will Talk* (Faber & Mazlish, 2010)
Body Checks Around Cutting • Dress rehearsals around how Mom will deliver body checks in the evening before bed with love and compassion—what does this look like? • Dress rehearsals around, if no cuts are found, Mom does not censure, but instead hugs Mark deeply and says, "I love You, you are not alone" and "I love you and am proud of you for resisting the temptation, I know it was not easy" • Dress rehearsals around Mark talking about what caused the cuts and mom using reflective listening	**Body Checks Around Cutting** • Dress rehearsals around how Mom will deliver body checks in the evening before bed with love and compassion—what does this look like? • Dress rehearsals around potential negative reactions by Mark when he pretends to say if he has cuts and where but not actually show them • Dress rehearsals around Mark talking about what caused the cuts and mom using reflective listening

Looking at Table 3.16, the rationale for "dress rehearsals that have the highest potential to yield the most fruit" was led by the decision of which dress rehearsals would have the greatest impact to inject the primary targeted healthy undercurrents. For example, with the camping trip playbook, if the apology letter by Dad went well, the potential for "attachment bonding" would skyrocket. The same would be true if the caregivers had role plays that led to the mastery of bonding or soft talk with Mark using the book *How to Talk So Teens Will Listen and Listen So Teens Will Talk* (Faber & Mazlish, 2010). However, at the same time, this new way of communicating would generate the highest level of difficulty because it was so new to the family.

Implement Playbooks

In Mark's family, the role-plays for each of the countermove scenarios averaged two to three takes each before competency was reached. To add a layer of confidence to this decision, after each role-play, the therapist asked the question: "On a scale of 1 to 5 with "1" meaning

(*continued*)

Case Example (*continued*)

---

that the parent, child, or village member lacked confidence and needs more practice and "5" meaning they demonstrate confidence and are ready to deliver the countermove, what is the first number that comes to mind?" As anticipated, the greatest level of difficulty surrounded the new and soft communication patterns between parent and child and Mark being able to talk about his feelings and pain out in the open. These role-plays led to the most impactful spontaneous enactments where for the first time, Mark was able to open up about the shame of the abuse. It happened when Mom tried to hug him in the role-play, and Mark froze.

When Mom used the soft and new communication approach of "I am right here buddy. I'm not going anywhere, we can just sit here together," Mark started to weep and said he felt dirty and that he was not "touchable." In turn, the entire village wept and inched closer to Mark until he finally let them all hug him, one at a time. This was an enactment that emerged from a simple role-play but unfroze the family system and released healing for Mark's deep wound of shame.

The total number of sessions for this family to reach competency was two 2-hour sessions or the equivalent of four 1-hour sessions.

PRE-SESSION PREPARATION FOR PHASE V

The two main goals for this final pre-session preparation work are to (a) closely examine the "decision tree checklist" to predetermine recommendation for graduation or one of the four other available options and (b) create a first draft of what is called a "red flags checklist" to predetermine the most likely early warning signs of a relapse for a particular family.

To accomplish these goals, there are four mini-steps outlined in detail within Chapter 12. These are as follows:

1. Type and laminate final playbooks and troubleshooting countermoves checklist: Any final edits are typed in the playbook and checklist and laminated, if possible. They are given to the family at the beginning of the next session.
2. Proactively initiate any midweek check-ins as needed: If it was evident during the role-plays/dress rehearsals that the family was still shaky on their delivery, it is wise to proactively make a few check-in phone calls during the week. "Shaky" is defined as the family demonstrating enough safety and stability to proceed forward, but evidenced through the role-plays would be that the delivery was still somewhat in question.
3. Create decision tree handout: During pre-session preparation, the FST therapist should study this decision tree handout closely. The therapist should reexamine all the evidence up to this point and predetermine which of the five options in the decision tree is the recommended next step for this family. One does not want to be thinking about such an important decision as the session unfolds.
4. Create a red flags checklist template: A final pre-session preparation strategy is to create a red flags checklist that is customized to the particular family being seen in the next session. Simply defined, the purpose of the red flags checklist is to (1) prevent relapse and (2) solidify positive gains.

Case Example

Create Decision Tree Handout

No midweek check-ins were needed with Mark's family because there was no evidence of shaky delivery in the dress rehearsals from Phase IV. Therefore, the FST therapist immediately proceeded to put together the FST decision tree checklist. The goal was to closely examine all the evidence from the previous four phases of FST treatment and predetermine which of the five options in the decision tree checklist is the best next step for this particular family. As part of this preparation step, the FST therapist writes private notes on his copy of the decision tree checklist that may or may not be shared with the family but are invaluable during the session to help the therapist make a recommendation with clear rationale. The family is provided the decision tree handout without the therapist's private notes.

Looking at the decision tree checklist in Table 3.17, the FST therapist, in his private notes, predicted that Option C would be the best recommendation for the family and one they would likely pick. In addition, the therapist had private notes for the other four options and it spurred his thinking around possible relapse within Option D and what to recommend to the family. Without this preparation, the therapist would not be anywhere close to prepared during the actual Phase V session and the risk for a wrong decision would increase. The therapist's private notes are indicated in bold and larger font in Table 3.17.

TABLE 3.17 Pre-session Preparation for the Decision Tree Process

Option A: **Graduation and red flags relapse prevention checklist**—Overall, your family and child self-report (and your therapist is in agreement) a 70% or higher wound playbook effectiveness on a 0% to 100% rating scale (presented at the beginning of Phase V). It is decided between you and your therapist that your child and your family are ready for graduation and to finalize your red flags relapse prevention checklist along with scheduling the first 30-day callback with your FST therapist.

Based on the information to date, I predict that Mark's family will say that their two current playbooks (camping trip and pretend body checks) are working at a rating of 90% or higher. The elders' meeting went great last week and the camping trip is now scheduled for two weeks from now. However, I predict that they will likely pick Option C below. This is because the family's confidence will have grown and they will be ready to tackle the deep tissue wounds of grief and unforgiveness with a new playbook.

Option B: **Tweak the current wound playbook**—If your wound playbook is not working at a 70% or higher effectiveness (need more practice role-plays/dress rehearsals, need more clarification, need to include key missing extended family members, etc.) a predetermined number of additional sessions is negotiated with your therapist to work through any identified barriers.

I do not think they will need help as indicated in Option B because of my predicted high rating of effectiveness. However, the father and uncles will likely need assurances on the camping trip and as the date grows closer, Mark's anxiety will likely grow and he may want to "bail." I will put this possibility in the red flags checklist but tell them to "not take 'no' for an answer."

(continued)

Case Example (*continued*)

TABLE 3.17 Pre-session Preparation for the Decision Tree Process (*continued*)

Option C: **Pick a new problem and build another playbook**—You as a family agree that although the first playbook was successful, other critical wounds still linger and remain (i.e., unresolved grief is a success but still have unforgiveness). It is also agreed that you as a family do not yet feel confident or strong enough to complete and implement a second playbook on your own. A specific number of new sessions are then negotiated with your therapist.

I think this is the option I will recommend and the one I predict the family will choose as well. Mark may be tired of therapy in general and want to stop though, so I will have to communicate that the foundational hard work has already been done and therefore, we would not need to repeat Phases I and II again. Instead, we would proceed directly to Phase III. So, the number of future sessions would likely only be four 1-hour sessions.

Option D: **Additional safety or misuse of power issues emerge**—Additional safety issues emerge or old ones resurface. Healing wounds can act as a cork in a bottle. Once the cork is removed, extreme behavioral problems may reemerge or occur for the first time with your child or teenager. They may be a temporary but, you, as the parent or caregiver, still need a behavioral or hybrid contract to weather the storm. A specific number of new sessions is then negotiated to help tweak an existing safety plan or behavioral contract or build a new one.

If the camping trip goes either exceedingly well or exceedingly poor, Mark may get worse before he gets better, meaning that too much positive change too quickly may overwhelm him. Therefore, I will want to tell everyone, including Mark, that if his anxiety suddenly skyrockets, it is normal and may actually be a good sign of healing. And, we can prepare for it, if needed, with the suicidal safety plan that is already written and waiting to be used if needed.

Option E: **Terminate against therapist's recommendation**—The therapist and your family may disagree as to next steps. Your therapist may advise you that critical work still needs to be done but one or more key family members may refuse to go any further. At this point, termination of treatment proceeds forward against your therapist's recommendation. However, the door is left open to return at any time if relapse occurs and the family agrees to then follow the therapist's recommendations.

Do not anticipate this option happening.

Create a Red Flags Checklist Template

Even though Mark's family is not likely to formally graduate FST until Option C is completed, it is still important to create a red flags checklist to prevent relapse in the interim. It can then be updated as necessary as Mark gets closer to graduation. Presently, the only area not addressed until graduation will be the need for callbacks after graduation in Part IV of the red flags checklist. Family members are asked to tape the red flags checklist to their bathroom mirror alongside their wound playbooks to review each morning as they brush their teeth. Box 3.7 is a reproduction of the red flags checklist that was created for Mark and his family.

BOX 3.7 Mark's Red Flags Checklist

Red Flags Checklist

Part I—<u>Areas of the Wound Playbook Not Followed</u>

- As the date gets closer to the camping trip, Mark's anxiety increases and he changes his mind and refuses to go.

Steps to take:

- ☑ Reassure Mark that this is normal and a good sign that his long-buried feelings are coming out of hibernation. Reinforce how important it is for him to not "bail on the trip"
- ☑ On the day of the trip, simply remind Mark that you both are committed to going and that any anxiety either of you feels will decrease naturally once you are on the road.
- ☑ If the first steps are not effective, call me, your FST therapist

- If Mark shuts down for longer than 3 days in any one week and refuses the "pretend" body checks

Steps to take:

- ☑ As promised earlier to Mark, he is using his voice and we all agreed that he could stop the "pretend" or real body checks at any time
- ☑ However, this does not mean that we stop our "feelings & hug" check-ins each evening. Mom will continue to follow her troubleshooting countermoves as rehearsed with the "feelings & hug" check-ins using her new communication tools learned in the book How to Talk So Teens Will Listen and Listen So Teens Will Talk (Faber & Mazlish, 2010)
- ☑ If Mark continues to refuse the body checks, the FST therapist will be called and we will meet together to determine the next steps
- ☑ Part II – Areas of Safety

- If Mark begins to exhibit signs of suicidal risk again (i.e. he again shows signs of the risks discussed in the risk assessment)

Steps to take:

- ☑ FST therapist is called immediately and the suicide safety watch plan will go into place immediately
- ☑ If the above happens, the parents and FST therapist will touch base daily or as needed

Part III – <u>Unhealthy Undercurrents or Trauma Symptoms Return</u>

- Mom and Dad stop communicating as parents and start to feel resentful toward one another again
- Mark starts to isolate himself again and go into hypoarousal
- Mark goes back to a junk food diet of sugar and soda
- Mom, Dad, the uncles, and/or grandmother start to "walk on eggshells" again
- The adults stop using soft talk and reflective listening tools
- Steps to take:

- ☑ Anyone in the village can call one another on any of these Part III relapse signs to discuss steps to get back on track as quickly as possible
- ☑ If these relapse signs are still happening 2 weeks later, call the FST therapist to request a session to help remove the barriers and get back on track

Part IV – <u>Date for First Callback</u>: TBD later

TBD, to be determined.

PHASE V: EVALUATE PROGRESS AND RELAPSE PREVENTION

Looking at the flowchart in Figure 3.1, the final phase in the FST treatment model shows clear "if/then" decisions within five different next action step options that coincide directly with the decision tree handout as seen in the example of Table 3.17. The goals of this final phase of treatment are to (a) begin the session with a 0% to 100% scale (0% meaning the wound playbook(s) are not working at all and 100% meaning the playbook(s) are working great 100% of the time); (b) use what are called mini scales on a scale of 1 to 5 (1= no improvement in the healthy undercurrent and 5 = a lot of improvement) within the context of before and after FST treatment; (c) pass out a decision tree checklist (devoid of FST therapist notes) handout and decide jointly with the family if ready to graduate from treatment or to choose another option; (d) pass out the first draft of the red flags checklist to prevent future relapses; and (e) define what tune-up sessions mean if graduating, and set up 30-, 60-, and 90-day callbacks.

To accomplish these goals, there are five mini-steps outlined in detail within Chapter 13. These are as follows:

1. Scaling to assess overall progress: The FST therapist uses an "overall progress" rating scale to allow each family member to rate the wound playbook's current effectiveness with rationale and how to increase its effectiveness by 10% or greater in the future. The family's overall rating is used to assess if the family is ready to graduate from FST treatment.
2. Mini scales to consolidate healthy undercurrents: The FST therapist wants to help the family to see just how far they have come in a relatively short time to instill confidence and hope. To do this, the FST therapist uses what is called a "mini scale" around the key healthy undercurrents targeted to show where the family as a whole was prior to FST treatment and the progress they made since treatment began.
3. Review decision tree for next steps: The FST therapist will distribute a handout listing the five different options or next treatment steps available to the family. The therapist will then make a recommendation by referring to the private notes created during the pre-session preparation and any new information received from the overall progress scale and mini scales.
4. Co-create red flags checklist: The FST therapist then passes out a first draft of what is called a "red flags checklist" that contains for the particular family the most likely risks for relapse and the next suggested steps to take if relapse occurs. The family is asked to make any suggested changes or modification to the red flags checklist so they are co-owners of the plan.
5. If graduating, callbacks and tune-ups scheduled: The next transition steps are clearly articulated if the child and family are ready for graduation or if one of the other four decision tree options are selected. Family members will also be shown the benefits of 30-, 60-, and 90-day callback check-ins by the FST therapist and shown the definition and use of tune-ups.

Case Example

Scaling to Assess Overall Progress

As predicted, everyone in Mark's family (Mark, Mom, Dad, uncles, and grandmother) averaged an overall rating of 90% or higher for the "restoring emotional family" bonds—a

(continued)

Case Example (*continued*)

"Wild at Heart Weekend wound playbook" and Mom and Mark rated the "healing Mark's anxiety by bringing safety body check wound playbook" lower but still high at a respectable 80% (Box 3.8). Mom and Mark were the only ones rating the body check playbook because no one else was involved in its day-to-day implementation.

BOX 3.8 FST Rating Scale of Wound Playbook's Effectiveness for Mark and his Family

Restoring Emotional Bonds—"Wild at Heart" Camping Playbook Overall Rating

							Uncles & Mark	Mom & Dad		
							X	X		
0%	10%	20%	30%	40%	50%	60%	70%	80%	90%	95%	100%

Healing Mark's Anxiety by Bringing Safety (Body Checks) Playbook Overall Rating

							Mark & Mom			
							X			
0%	10%	20%	30%	40%	50%	60%	70%	80%	90%	95%	100%

Mini Scales to Consolidate Healthy Undercurrents

After the overall progress scaling was complete, the FST therapist wanted the family to see how far they had come. Therefore, the cadence in the therapist's voice changed as he got excited. He wrote on the giant flip chart a mini scales table with the top two healthy undercurrents prior to the start of the session and covered it up with a white sheet (see Table 3.18).

TABLE 3.18 FST Mini Scales for Mark's Family to Consolidate Healthy Undercurrents

Healthy Undercurrent	Before FST	After FST (Now)
Attachment bonds		
Safety and security		

(continued)

Case Example (*continued*)

There were, of course, additional auxiliary healthy undercurrents that came to the surface through the role-plays and other sessions (i.e., safety, restoring balance, accountability, nurturance, parents getting on same page, consistency, etc.) but "attachment bonds" and "safety and security" were the two main ones for Mark and his family and listed as the goals of therapy at the end of Phase I.

After the mini scales table was revealed, the FST therapist intentionally picked the family member who would most likely continue with the enthusiasm and excitement that was starting to be generated. In addition, due to time constraints, the therapist could not call on everyone but instead wanted to get a representative sample. That excited person was Dad (his body language was popping). The following question was asked:

On a scale of 1 to 5 with "1" meaning little to no improvement in your attachment bonds before we started counseling to "5" meaning 100% positive change since counseling where do you think you started and where are you today?

The father gave a "before" rating of 1 and an "after" rating of 3 for attachment bonding, and there seemed to be a general consensus from everyone else (Table 3.19). He made the point that just the act of putting the playbook book together and meeting at Starbucks to do the homework lead worksheet was enough to move the needle significantly. This is another common theme we see with FST. The playbook itself is sometimes almost an afterthought or crutch. In reality, it is the metaphoric physical therapy portion or the role-plays, homework leads, and the act of rallying together as a family to put a step-by-step plan together with clarity of roles that is the juice or secret sauce.

TABLE 3.19 Mark's Dad's Mini Scales Rating

Healthy Undercurrent	Before FST	After FST (Now)
Attachment bonds	1 out of 5	3 out of 5

Then Mom and Mark gave their "before" and "after" ratings for Safety and Security and said more time was needed to go higher. But again, they said that the act of putting the plan together with the pretend feature was the game changer (Table 3.20).

TABLE 3.20 Mark's and Mom's Mini Scales Rating

Healthy Undercurrent	Before FST	After FST (Now)
Safety and security	1 out of 5	3 out of 5

(*continued*)

Case Example (*continued*)

Review Decision Tree for Next Steps

After the mini-scale exercise, the momentum and excitement was high, and the momentum increased further, with the adults especially, after they saw the clearly laid-out five-option decision tree handout.

As predicted, the family's general consensus was Option C and Mark had to be convinced that we would take a mini-break for 3 weeks after the camping trip and regroup for four more sessions and not full-blown therapy (see Chapter 13 for possible options and rules of thumb when there is disagreement with next step options). Mark and his family were visibly relieved when the FST therapist carefully emphasized the clear prescriptive treatment guidelines in bold font for Option C as seen in the excerpt of the decision tree handout in Table 3.21. The full decision tree handout is found in Table 13.4.

TABLE 3.21 Excerpt (Option C) From the Decision Tree Handout

Option C: Pick a New Problem and Build Another Playbook

☑ *Estimated total number of sessions:* Three to four 2-hour sessions or six to eight 1-hour sessions
- **Repeat pre-session preparation for Phase III**
- **Phase III: one 2-hour session** (two 1-hour sessions): Repeat all the steps to create a new playbook
- **Repeat pre-session preparation for Phase IV (therapist only)**
- **Phase IV: One to two 2-hour sessions** (four 1-hour sessions): Need to repeat all the steps and build a new troubleshooting countermove checklist with fresh role plays. BUT DUE TO THE FAMILY'S FAMILIARITY WITH THE PROCESS, THIS WILL TAKE LESS TIME.
- **Repeat pre-session preparation for Phase V (therapist only)**
- **Phase V: (Graduation) one 2-hour session** (two 1-hour sessions): Repeat all steps but again, due to the family's familiarity with the process, this will take less time.

**As stated for Option B, the time for these sessions may be less due to the family's familiarity with the process.

☑ *Phases in the FST model for the family to complete:* Phases III–V
☑ *Estimated Level of Difficulty:* Between a 3 and 4 (higher level of difficulty on scale of 1–5). Why? Usually at this point, the therapist is helping the family co-create a wound playbook on a more challenging problem and set of undercurrents than the first round. And they are likely building this new playbook from scratch.

Co-Create Red Flags Checklist

Surprisingly, the family only had minor edits. The biggest eye-opener was how the FST therapist predicted and normalized a "worse before it gets better" scenario in the areas of Mark's high anxiety as the camping trip got closer and realized the possible need for the suicide watch plan.

(continued)

Case Example (*continued*)

Since Mark's family was not graduating this session, the last mini-step of "graduation, callbacks, and tune-ups" was not done. The session ended with the next one scheduled 4 weeks later after the camping trip.

Postscript

It was fortunate that the FST therapist predicted the normal "fallout of change" and clear next steps in the red flags checklist because Mark tried to back out and he became suicidal again.

Nevertheless, the camping trip was a huge success. The adults and Mark reported that there was not a dry eye around the campfire. Mark did write a letter, and it was filled with anger and bitterness toward Dad. The zinger came when Mark stated, "*If you had been around when I needed a dad, maybe I would not have been raped. I blame you.*"

But the father was ready from all the dress rehearsals in Phase IV. He took his son's burden gladly and started to weep, saying, "*I am so sorry.*" Mark was flooded with emotions and wanted to run. But the uncles were right there and asked him to stay, saying, "*It's safe, you are not alone, we are right here.*"

Mark, then was able to stay with this comforting message. It was a major breakthrough.

The father then read his letter and it was filled with remorse, but held hope for the future. He asked for forgiveness, and Mark gave it. The uncles' letters the next night became the capstone event with the central messages of "What happened to Mark was not his fault" and that "he had what it takes."

However, when Mark went home and tried to sleep, the flood of emotions came rushing back. He then started to cut himself. But mom was on alert based on the red flags checklist and checked on him at night. Mark called out that he was in trouble.

What happened next was inspiring. The mother called everyone in the village and they were at the house within 15 minutes. The therapist was reached and he guided everyone through the crisis on speakerphone. The suicide watch was immediately pulled out and executed. The father and uncles slept in the room with Mark in sleeping bags for the next 3 nights in a row. The second night they said to Mark,

> "*We love you and we are like soldiers in battle with you. We will never leave a fallen comrade. We leave no one behind and that includes you Mark.*"

It was a game changer and began a positive chain reaction in Mark.

Mark stated it best,

> "*I thought I was going to go to the hospital again. My dad held me in his arms one night and said, 'I wasn't there before but I will never leave you again!' And then he actually stayed all night. I couldn't believe it. I knew right then, that I was not alone anymore and I was going to make it!*"

(*continued*)

Case Example (*continued*)

The deep tissue unhealed wounds then fell like dominos. The grief playbook was now an afterthought because it already took place, and through the intensity of the suicide watch playbook, the cutting then stopped because it no longer served any purpose. Mark could safely feel and process emotions in the "optimal zone." And this change also resulted in a lifting of the depression. The only thing left (a big one) was whether Mark could forgive the boy who raped him. This came about 8 months later, when Mark was ready.

PART II OF TREATING THE TRAUMATIZED CHILD: WHAT TO EXPECT

In sum, this chapter hopefully accomplished for the reader two important objectives. First, our vision was that this chapter would stand on its own. Deeper understanding and competency in the FST model can be enhanced if the reader "zooms out" before "zooming in." The architectural blueprints should be studied first (zoom out) before examining the nuts and bolts of the building. Second, systems theory at times can be complex as well as a huge paradigm shift. As a result, a zoom-out flowchart with an intensive case study can help accelerate the learning curve exponentially. From this flowchart and overview, it may be evident why it took eight long years to synchronize each phase of FST treatment and provide a step-by-step road map.

The reader is now ready to flip the page and zoom in to Part II. It promises to be rich like black forest cake. Therefore, take your time and read as slow or as fast as you need to. At the end of this journey (with your mind spinning, exhausted, and spent), you will have the tools to more effectively treat both the traumatized child and the traumatized family. Our traumatized children and families are in a crisis that is compounded by isolation, technology, and a lack of family and community connectedness. And the central systems theory axiom that "the whole is greater than the sum of parts" (Bertalanffy, 1968) underscores this point. Your journey awaits.

REFERENCES

American Association for Marriage and Family Therapy. (n.d.). Adolescent self-harm. Retrieved from http://www.aamft.org/iMIS15/AAMFT/Content/consumer_updates/adolescent_self_harm.aspx

Burney, R. (2013). Grieve—heal your inner child [Web log post]. Retrieved from http://www.healyourinnerchild.com/Grieve

Bertalanffy, L. V. (1968). *General system theory: Foundations, development, applications.* New York, NY: George Braziller.

Chapman, G., & Thomas, J. M. (2013). *When sorry isn't enough: Making things right with those you love.* Chicago, IL: Northfield Publishing.

Davis, J. L. (2015). Cutting and self-harm: Warning signs and treatment: Parents should watch for symptoms and encourage kids to get help. Retrieved from http://www.webmd.com/mental-health/features/cutting-self-harm-signs-treatment#5

Deschene, L. (2016). How to forgive someone when it's hard: 30 tips to let go of anger [Web log post]. Retrieved from http://tinybuddha.com/blog/how-to-forgive-someone-when-its-hard-30-tips-to-let-go-of-anger

Eldredge, J. (2001). *Wild at heart: Discovering the secret of a man's soul.* Nashville, TN: Thomas Nelson Publishers.

Faber, A., & Mazlish, E. (2010). *How to talk so teens will listen and listen so teens will talk.* New York, NY: HarperCollins.

Gehart, D. R. (2012). *Mindfulness and acceptance in couple and family therapy.* New York, NY: Guilford Press.

Gottman, J., & Silver, N. (1999). *The seven principles for making marriage work.* New York: NY: Three Rivers.

Haley, J. (1991). *Problem-solving therapy.* San Francisco. CA: Jossey-Bass.

Malinen, T. (2001). From think tank to new therapy: The process of solution-focused theory and practice development. Retrieved from http://www.tathata.fi/artik_eng/thinktank.htm

Markham, L. (2014, March). 5 secrets to love your child unconditionally: When your child feels unconditionally loved, he's more likely to blossom. *Psychology Today.* Retrieved from https://www.psychologytoday.com/blog/peaceful-parents-happy-kids/201403/5-secrets-love-your-child-unconditionally

Minuchin, S., & Fishman, H. C. (1981). *Family therapy techniques.* Cambridge, MA: Harvard University Press.

National Institute for Health and Clinical Excellence. (2008). *Surgical site infection: Prevention and treatment of surgical site infection.* London, UK: NICE.

Ogden, P., Minton, K., & Pain, C. (2006). *Trauma and the body: A sensorimotor approach to psychotherapy.* New York, NY: W. W. Norton.

Pelcovitz, D., van der Kolk, B., Roth, S., Mandel, F., Kaplan, S., & Resick, P. (1997). Development of a criteria set and a structured interview for disorders of extreme stress (SIDES). *Journal of Traumatic Stress, 10,* 3–16.

Pritchard, M. J. (2009). Identifying and assessing anxiety in pre-operative patients. *Nursing Standard, 23*(51), 35–40.

Rackham, N. (1995). *SPIN-selling.* Farnham Surrey, UK: Gower Publishing.

Royal College of Nursing. (2005). *Preoperative fasting in adults and children: An RCN guideline for the multidisciplinary team.* London: UK: Author.

Seda, L. (2016). We have the right to grieve losses big and small [Web log post]. Retrieved from http://tinybuddha.com/blog/we-have-a-right-to-grieve-losses-big-and-small

Sells, S. P. (2002). *Parenting your out-of-control teenager: 7 steps to reestablish authority and reclaim love.* New York, NY: St. Martin's Griffin.

Sells, S. P. (2004). *Treating the tough adolescent: A family-based, step-by-step guide.* New York, NY: Guilford Press.

Sells, S. P., Smith, T. E., & Moon, S. (1996). An ethnographic study of client and therapist perceptions of therapy effectiveness in a university-based training clinic. *Journal of Marital and Family Therapy, 22,* 321–342. doi:10.1111/j.1752-0606.1996.tb00209.x

Shannon, S. M. (2014). *Parenting the whole child: A holistic child psychiatrist offers practical wisdom on behavior, brain health, nutrition, exercise, family life, peer relationships, school life, trauma, medication, and more.* New York, NY: W. W. Norton.

Shapiro, F. (1989). Eye movement desensitization: A new treatment for post-traumatic stress disorder. *Journal of Behavior Therapy and Experimental Psychiatry, 20,* 211–217.

Shapiro, F., & Forrest, M. S. (2004). *EMDR: The breakthrough therapy for overcoming anxiety, stress, and trauma.* New York, NY: Basic Books.

Siegel, D. J. (1999). *The developing mind: How relationships and the brain interact to shape who we are.* New York, NY: Guilford Press.

van der Kolk, B. A. (1994). The body keeps the score: Memory and the evolving psychobiology of Posttraumatic Stress. *Harvard Review of Psychiatry, 1*(5), 253–265. doi:10.3109/10673229409017088

van der Kolk, B. A. (2014). *The body keeps the score: Brain, mind, and body in the healing of trauma.* New York, NY: Penguin Books.

Whitaker, C. A., & Keith, D. V. (1981). Symbolic–experiential family therapy. In A. S. Gurman & D. P. Kniskern (Eds.), *Handbook of family therapy* (pp. 187–224). New York, NY: Brunner/Mazel.

Specific Techniques
and Strategies

II

The FST Motivational Phone Call

Step 1: Why Are Family Systems Trauma (FST) Motivational Phone Calls Important?

Step 2: The SPIN Theory Behind the FST Motivational Phone Call

Step 3: The FST Motivational Phone Call Scripts

Step 4: The Stick and Move Technique

Step 5: The Use of Effective Closing Remarks

As the FST diagram in Chapter 3 illustrates, the FST motivational phone call occurs prior to the first face-to-face session in Phase I. Using the five key motivational interviewing (MI) principles in the following text, the FST therapist uses a 15- to 30-minute specialized motivational phone call script to increase motivation and attendance at the first session. Traditional MI principles have been available for quite some time (c.f., Miller & Rollnick, 1991). These include, but are not limited to, the following: (a) Motivation to change is elicited from the client; (b) it is the client's job, not the counselor's, to articulate and resolve ambivalence to treatment; (c) direct persuasion is not an effective method for MI interviewing; (d) readiness to change does not come naturally but is the result of the interpersonal interaction with the therapist; and (e) the therapeutic relationship resembles a partnership or collaboration (c.f., Miller, Zweben, DiClemente, & Rychtarik, 1992).

However, *unlike* traditional MI, we developed a specialized FST motivational phone call procedure that is direct and uses key strategies such as an actual script. The FST motivational phone call script questions were designed based on key marketing outcomes found in Neil Rackham's (1995) book: *SPIN Selling*. In this book, Neil Rackham conducted research studies of 35,000 actual sales phone calls to determine the central ingredients needed to motivate even the most resistant customer. The outcomes that Rackham found were both surprising and groundbreaking. They are revealed in Step #2. In sum, the steps for successfully implementing the FST motivational phone call are (a) understanding why FST motivational phone calls are important; (b) understanding the SPIN theory behind the FST motivational phone call; (c) the FST motivational phone call scripts; (d) the stick and move technique; and (e) effective closing remarks.

STEP 1: WHY ARE FST MOTIVATIONAL PHONE CALLS IMPORTANT?

There are three primary reasons why the FST motivational phone calls are important for trauma treatment of the child and the family: (a) Parent involvement is key to successful trauma treatment; (b) the value of a soft start-up versus a harsh start-up; and (c) the value of engaging the village or extended family members before treatment begins, not after.

Parent Involvement Is Key to Successful Trauma Treatment

Without the parent's active involvement, the effectiveness of FST treatment significantly diminishes. For example, according to Williams and Chang (2000), "Juveniles will return to future delinquent acts if their *parents remain unchanged* [italics added] in the areas of consistent limit setting, rebuilding emotional attachments, and improved communication" (p. 159).

In other words, without parent involvement and subsequent change, child and adolescent relapse rates are high. In addition, the parents have the power to bring the child or adolescent back to future sessions or end treatment prematurely. The implications of this statement are that the parent or caregiver must be treated with the utmost care and respect.

However, as stated in Chapter 3, there is often no joining or relationship building prior to the first session, except a phone call to set up the first appointment. The consequences for this type of poor pre-session preparation are sobering. Appointment no-shows are prevalent in treatment settings, with 29% to 42% of clients failing to begin treatment (Weisner, Mertens, Tam, & Moore, 2001) and 15% to 50% not returning for a second appointment (Festinger, Lamb, Marlowe, & Kirby, 2002; McCarty et al., 2007; Mitchell & Selmes, 2007). Let's face it, as Clark (2010) eloquently states, "You cannot treat an empty chair."

Good therapy begins with the first phone call, not just at the first face-to-face meeting (Reese, Conoley, & Brossart, 2002, 2006; Tutty, Simon, & Ludman, 2000). This is even more important when the child and family in question have experienced a traumatic experience and are hesitant to attend treatment in the first place.

In response to this challenge, we developed a specialized motivational phone call script and set of procedures within the FST model. The MI phone call has been so successful that rates of families showing up to the first appointment have increased to 80% and higher (c.f., Sells, Winokur-Early, & Smith, 2011; Sterrett-Hong, Karam, & Kiaer, 2017; Winokur-Early, Chapman, & Hand, 2013). The research outcomes indicate that a large part of this success is that the MI phone call creates what is called a soft start-up.

A Soft Versus Harsh Start-Up

Gottman and Silver (1999) noted the importance of soft start-ups in couples' therapy. Gottman could predict, with 96% accuracy, a positive or negative outcome of the conversation within the first few minutes based on whether the start-up was soft or harsh. If the conversation began with a harsh start-up (criticism, sarcasm, defensiveness, or stonewalling), it would likely end that way. However, if the conversation began with a soft start-up (appreciation, politeness, nonjudgmental), the outcome was productive, stable, and happy, even if conflict emerged later.

In parallel with Gottman's research, early in the FST model development, the FST therapists began treatment using what might be called a traditional start-up that was not soft (a phone call to simply schedule the first appointment). Within this context, burned-out and traumatized parents would often demonstrate high "no-show" rates or come to the first session with walls up and a defensive body language. However, after the FST motivational phone call, the outcomes dramatically changed. In sharp contrast, the parent or caregiver would now enter the first session more relaxed, trusting, and open to hear what the FST therapist had to say within the first 5 minutes.

The contrast between a soft and harsh start-up was even more pronounced when one parent happened to receive the FST motivational phone call, but the other did not. The parent who did not receive the FST motivational phone call came to the first session more closed off than the caregiver who did receive the call. The soft start-up benefits found in the FST model seemed to directly correlate with the findings in Gottman's couples' research.

Case Example

The FST therapist wanted to perform a personal experiment to see if the motivational phone call was a game changer in helping to jump-start the traumatized adolescent and family. With the next eight families, the therapist randomly assigned four families to Group A, the group receiving the FST motivational phone call and the other half to Group B, treatment as usual (TAU) or simply a call to set up the first face-to-face appointment. The results were dramatic. All four families in Group A showed up to the first session on time and without any no-shows. Group B had a 50% no show rate or showed up late. In addition, the body language of Group A families was mostly warm and open. In Group B, the body language was closed, or defensive with stonewalling.

But the biggest differences between the groups were in their readiness to change. In Group A, the parents came into the session more relaxed, trusting, and open. One mother said it best,

> "You [the therapist] were so warm on the phone to me and saw what was good about me as a mom. That meant the world to me because up until that point I have felt like a bad parent. But the phone call gave me hope as you laid out next steps. We have had a lot of failed counseling in the past. But this time it seemed different. You were the first counselor to call and take the time to get to know my son and me before we met. So, I was actually looking forward to our first meeting because if this counseling is anything like the first phone call, sign me up."

With this kind of soft start-up, joining and rapport building was accelerated. In turn, motivation skyrocketed and resistance to treatment lowered even before the first session began. In contrast, with a family already traumatized, a harsh start-up is costly.

The therapist, however, could not see the true benefits of the FST motivational phone call until she performed this mini experiment herself. The therapist could not bill insurance for this 15-minute phone call, but the significantly lower no-show rates and soft start-ups more than made up for this limitation.

The Value of Engaging the Village Before Treatment Begins

Finally, the FST motivational phone call has the potential to identify the key family members under the same roof as well as the extended family members or village. As stated in Chapter 2, we define the village as all members of the child's or adolescent's household under the same roof, as well as friends, neighbors, institutions like school, and the extended family that surrounds the family.

Traditional treatment often tends to focus on and treat only the individual family member who walks through the office door. Likewise, the therapist may not be formally trained in a village approach or may be unaware of its potential benefits. In addition, if there is an inquiry as to the existence of a village or a request for them to attend, it is often done using closed-ended questions that yield an immediate no from the family member being asked (e.g., "*Do you have extended family members who would attend future sessions?*").

However, chances dramatically increase that families will reveal the names of their village and of the people or institutions that are supportive and nonsupportive if the questions about the village are specific and not closed-ended:

Who are the people, friends, co-workers or institutions (school, work, etc.) outside of your immediate family that (a) give you support in raising your child or teenager [please give me their first names] and (b) are negative influences that do not provide support and may even undermine your efforts? [Please give me their first names.]

The FST motivational phone call will ask this question at the end, after the parent is warmed up and motivated. And more often than not, the parent not only reveals the key players but is open to asking them to come to the first session and/or giving permission for the FST therapist to make the same call to the targeted village members. The parent will even call the individual ahead of time, if asked, to give him or her a heads-up to prevent a cold call.

This initial effort to engage the village and get them to attend the first session is often a game changer. As outlined in Chapter 3, the initial face-to-face session contains the stress chart, the seed/tree diagram, the selection of seed and symptom picks, and setting the goals of therapy. These are very important initial goals. Therefore, imagine this first session with a single parent who is overwhelmed and depressed with her 11-year-old who sits in the corner and refuses to speak versus the same family, but with a grandmother and an aunt who bring energy and hope. Or imagine a teenager who is openly disrespectful to both parents, but who stops immediately as soon as the grandfather walks into the room. In both examples, the tone and tenor of the session will be completely different without the village present. In addition, if key villagers are not there for the first session, but come later, the FST therapist is then forced to backtrack and review the key points of the previous session(s).

Therefore, the FST motivational phone call is invaluable because, with it, the odds dramatically increase that the right people in the family and village will be present in the all-important first session, when the goals of treatment are set. Without this call, the chances are slim to none that villagers or even other family members, such as the reluctant father, will attend.

STEP 2: THE SPIN THEORY BEHIND THE FST MOTIVATIONAL PHONE CALL

The FST motivational phone call questions were designed based on key marketing outcomes found in Neil Rackham's (1995) book *SPIN Selling*. A review of these key outcomes led to the development of the FST motivational phone call scripts (Tables 4.1 and 4.2).

TABLE 4.1 Parent or Caregiver Motivational Phone Call Script	
Question #1:	Are there any other caretakers such as a father/mother, boyfriend or girlfriend, partner, housemate, etc. at home? [If yes] Do you have two phone extensions or a cell phone that has a speakerphone to allow us all to talk together? The reason I ask is that it helps to get everyone's opinion about the problem and potential solution.
Question #2:	What are some of the difficult experiences that you have had to suffer in the last year because of the problems you have been having with your child or teenager? *[Estimated time of completion = 5 minutes]*
Question #3:	When I get to know you better, what qualities and strengths will I come to admire about you as a [person, parent, spouse, etc.]? *[Estimated time of completion = 3–5 minutes]*

(continued)

TABLE 4.1 Parent or Caregiver Motivational Phone Call Script (*continued*)

Question #4:	What do you think will happen to [your teen, child, marriage, or you personally] if the problems you described earlier remain unfixed in the next three months, six months, or even a year from now? *[Estimated time of completion = 3–5 minutes]*
Question #5:	Have you seen a counselor for any of these problems before? [If yes] What have other counselors missed with you? The reason I ask is that I do not want to make the same mistakes. *[Estimated time of completion = 2–3 minutes]*
Question #6:	Do you want to fix the problem or problems you listed [list them] at a fast, medium, or slow speed? *[Estimated time of completion = 1 minute]*
Closing Remarks	
Village inquiry question	Who are the people, friends, co-workers or institutions [school, work, etc.] outside of your immediate family that (a) give you support in raising your teenager [please give me their first names] and (b) are negative influences that do not provide support and may even undermine your efforts? [Please give me their first names] *[Estimated time of completion = 3–5 minutes]*

TABLE 4.2 Child or Adolescent Motivational Phone Call Script

Question #1	What is the stress you have been under at home with your parent(s) and outside the home with friends or at school? *[Estimated time of completion = 5 minutes]*
Question #2	When I get to know you better, what qualities and strengths will I come to admire about you as a person? *[Estimated time of completion = 3–5 minutes]*
Question #3	What do you think will happen to you personally if the problems or stress you just talked about earlier does not get fixed in the next three months, six months, or even a year from now? *[Estimated time of completion = 3–5 minutes]*
Question #4	Have you seen a counselor for any of these problems before? [If yes] What have other counselors missed with you? The reason I ask is that I do not want to make the same mistakes. *[Estimated time of completion = 2–3 minutes]*
Question #5	Who inside or outside your family is a great support to you [grandparent, friend, neighbor, teacher, coach, etc.] and who is a negative influence or gives you a hard time? [Please give me their first names] *[Estimated time of completion = 3–5 minutes]*
Question #6	Do you want your parents or other adults to get off your case? What do you think needs to happen in the future to make this a reality? *[Estimated time of completion = 3–5 minutes]*

It Is More Important to Understand Than to Persuade

Rackham discovered that the most successful sales people were those who listened to clients first *before* trying to persuade them to do anything (buy a product; make a face-to-face appointment; etc.). Once the client felt understood and heard, then and only then could that person be persuaded to take any kind of action. Surprisingly, out of thousands of sales calls researched, very few salespeople used this approach. Instead, they focused on persuading.

> You never persuade clients of anything. Clients persuade themselves. Your function is to first understand the issues that matter to your clients. You have to feel their problems just the way they feel them. You have to sit on their side of the table and look at issues from their point of view. (Rackham, 1995, p. 62)

When this principle was incorporated into the FST motivational phone call, it meant understanding the client's pain and needs *before* requesting any action. Hence, the first five questions were designed to understand the parent's or adolescent's pain and needs first, before requesting the actions of (a) coming to the first FST session and (b) inviting key villagers, if needed. In Questions #2 and #4 of the parent phone call script (Box 4.1), we see prime examples of this principle of "understanding first" at play:

BOX 4.1 MI Questions #2 and #4

Question #2:	What are some of the difficult experiences that you have had to suffer in the last year because of the problems you have been having with your child or teenager? *[Estimated time of completion = 5 minutes]*
Question #4:	What do you think will happen to [your teen, child, marriage, or you personally] if the problems you described earlier remain unfixed in the next three months, six months, or even a year from now? *[Estimated time of completion = 3–5 minutes]*

MI, motivational interviewing.

Small Sales Tactics Did Not Work for Large Sales

Rackham and his staff found that in small sales (products under $200), customers did not need or even want to be understood before being persuaded. Instead, they wanted to know the benefits and features of the product or "what's in it for them" within the first 5 minutes of the call. However, in large sales (products over $200), this tactic did *not* work and only served to frustrate or even anger the customer. Instead, the customers had to first state their problem or need and then clearly see how the product being offered would solve their specific problem. If not, the sale would fail. Therefore, when creating the FST motivational phone call, we asked ourselves the following question:

> "Does asking the parent, village, or child to come into trauma treatment represent a small sale or a large sale?"

We believe that the answer is a "large sale" because of the time commitment, cost, or the fact that most people do not want to change or share their problems with a stranger. Therefore, if trauma treatment or therapy in general is a large sale commitment, is it any wonder why no-show rates or initial resistance levels are so high when a majority of therapists are likely using "small sale" motivational tactics? As Rackham (1995, p. 9) writes, "In successful large sale phone calls, it's the *buyer* [the client] who does most of the talking." Translating this into the FST phone call script means that the entire first six questions allow the client to do most of the talking rather than the therapist doing all the talking as he or she attempts to sell benefits or features (e.g., come to the first group, we have free pizza). Instead, the first six questions allow the parent or child to clearly state the problem or need and only then are benefits and features offered in the closing remarks (see Step #5). The closing remarks line up a problem, need, or strength that directly coincides with what the parent or child talked about earlier on the MI call.

Example Closing Argument for Parent or Caregiver:

Earlier in our call you said that the quality I would come to admire about you was that you will never give up on your child. That was important to know because it is absolutely incredible that with everything you have gone through, you have not given up.

I think you might like this treatment approach because I will try to build on the strengths you listed, but more importantly, help others like your child better see your strengths as well. And based on what you have said, I think your child is fortunate to have you as a parent. That being said, would you come to at least the first session to see for yourself?

The Use of a SPIN Framework

To address the challenges of a large sale, Rackham and his associates created what is called the SPIN (situation, problem, implication, need payoff) framework. This framework became the theoretical foundation of the FST motivational phone call. Table 4.3 illustrates a summary of touch points between the SPIN framework and the resulting questions used within the FST motivational phone call.

TABLE 4.3 Direct Touch Points Between SPIN and the FST MI Phone Call Script

SPIN Framework	FST Motivational Phone Call Script
S—Situation Questions According to Rackham, these questions occur when we ask the client (parents, village, or a client) for facts about their current situation. However, the research found that clients do not like too many situational questions. They are too busy and do not get a thrill out of telling the caller details about their existing situation. They want to move quickly into the problem and the solution.	When modified and adapted for the FST MI phone call script, we created Questions #1 and #2: *Question #1: Are there any other caretakers such as a father/mother, boyfriend or girlfriend, partner, housemate, etc. at home? [If yes] Do you have two phone extensions or a cell phone that has a speakerphone to allow us all to talk together? The reason I ask is that it helps to get everyone's opinion about the problem and potential solution.* *Question #2: What are some of the difficult experiences (for parents) or stressors (for children) that you have had to suffer in the last year?*

(continued)

TABLE 4.3 Direct Touch Points Between SPIN and the FST MI Phone Call Script (*continued*)

SPIN Framework	FST Motivational Phone Call Script
P—Problem Questions These are questions about the problems, difficulties, or dissatisfactions that a client is currently experiencing and that the counselor or therapist can help solve. In Rackham's research, the most experienced salespeople asked more problem questions earlier in the discussion while those less experienced asked mostly situational questions. As a result, the FST therapist must learn to be skillful in getting the client to share their pain or problems early in the phone call.	When modified and adapted for the FST MI phone call script, we created a cocktail using Questions #2, #5, and #6: *Question #2 (see above)* *Question #5: Have you seen a counselor for any of these problems before?* [If yes] *What have other counselors missed with you? The reason I ask is that I do not want to make the same mistakes.* *Question #6: Do you want to fix the problem or problems you listed* [list them] *at a fast, medium, or slow speed?*
I—Implication Questions These are questions that ask about the consequences or implications of not solving the problem. According to Rackham, these questions are the hardest to ask but the most powerful of all the other SPIN questions combined. This is because good implication questions skillfully build on the client's earlier stated problems. They create a strong need to want to look at the solutions one is offering later in the call. For example, which is more powerful for a client to say? That poor communication in their marriage is a problem or that the implication of this problem remaining unsolved will result in a painful divorce?	When modified and adapted for the FST MI phone call script, we created Question #4 *Question #4: What do you think will happen to [your teen, child, marriage, or you personally] if the problems you described earlier remain unfixed in the next three months, six months, or even a year from now?*
N—Need-Benefit Questions These are questions that ask about the value or usefulness of a proposed solution. These questions are used to get the client to tell the therapist the potential benefits that the therapist's solution would offer. These are powerful questions that "custom-fit" the benefit to the client's particular problem and allow the client to tell the therapist how the proposed solutions would be of benefit. These need-benefit questions or statements are skillfully tied into the closing remarks by the therapist after the last FST motivational phone call question is asked.	*For example, when the parent tells the FST therapist that they need concrete tools, at the end of the call, the therapist states exactly how concrete tools will be provided by the FST model and then asks the parent, villager, or child to state how this might benefit him or her.* *The therapist must learn how to ask need-benefit questions that connect to earlier statements the parent or adolescent made and then clearly communicate the benefits that are custom-fit to their stated needs.*

MI, motivational interviewing; SPIN, situation, problem, implication, need payoff.

STEP 3: THE FST MOTIVATIONAL PHONE CALL SCRIPTS

Table 4.1 provides the script to use with the parent, caregiver, or adult villager, and Table 4.2 is the modified script to use with the child or adolescent. When one is first learning, it is recommended that a timer be used, as each question has an estimated time limit. This extra level of discipline will help prevent the call from turning into a long therapy session over the phone. The goal is an ideal total time of 15 minutes and not more than 30 minutes. If it exceeds 30 minutes, the parent may feel that the problems are solved and he or she will see no reason to continue treatment.

If there are two primary caregivers (in the same home or in different homes), it is ideal to use a speaker phone or a three-way call option on your phone or call when both parents can be present. Both caregivers together provide both synergy and efficiency.

At the end of the call and after the closing remarks, the FST therapist makes a direct inquiry about the family's village (e.g., "*Who are the people, friends, coworkers, or institutions [school, work, etc.] outside of your immediate family?*"). If the call is going well, the parent will be open about the village. The FST therapist must use his or her best judgment as to who should be called, and it will be clear on the call that there are "must-have" extended family members, friends, or institutions (case manager, juvenile probation officer).

It is recommended that the FST therapist ask if he or she can contact this person or persons directly. The reason is that it is risky to rely on the parent to ask or invite the key villager to the first session. The FST therapist does not yet know the family well (one phone call) and has no idea how the invitation might be presented (e.g., "*I talked to our son's new counselor over the phone yesterday. She wants you to get off your lazy ass and be there for the first meeting*"). One does not have to use the entire parent or caregiver script but may pick certain questions (Questions #3 or #4) to break the ice.

According to the Health Insurance Portability and Accountability Act (HIPAA) Privacy Rule, the FST therapist only needs to get verbal permission from the parent to call the village:

> The provider may ask the patient's permission to share relevant information with family members or others, may tell the patient he or she plans to discuss the information and give them an opportunity to agree or object, or may infer from the circumstances, using professional judgment, that the patient does not object. (www.hhs.gov/hipaa/for-professionals/special-topics/mental-health)

The modified script in Table 4.2 can be used for the child or adolescent who is the identified problem. It is important to note, however, that the adolescent motivational phone call is a "nice to have," but that the parent or caregiver is the must-have. The parent or caregiver has the power to start or end treatment at any time and for any reason. And without parent buy-in, involvement, and change, the risk of relapse for the traumatized child is much higher. Therefore, due to time constraints of the FST therapist, if he or she has to prioritize calls, it is the parent, caregiver, or key adult villager to call first, and child or adolescent next.

STEP 4: THE STICK AND MOVE TECHNIQUE

Boxers will state that one must know how to stick and move in the ring. If they do not punch quickly and then move, they will get pummeled by their opponent. This can also happen in a therapy session when the therapist lets the client go on and on about a particular topic without interruption. For example, if the FST therapist asks Question #2, "*What are some of the difficult experiences you have had to suffer in the last year because of the problems you have been having with your child or teenager?"* and in answering this question, if the parent or caregiver goes on and on for more than 5 minutes, it can be counterproductive to therapy for two reasons. First, when the client goes on and on, there is no need to come in for a face-to-face session. It is now a full-fledged therapy session. And second, when clients go on nonstop, they may go down long bunny trails that lead to nowhere or begin to whip themselves up into an emotional frenzy. When either happens, the FST therapist loses control of the phone call.

To avoid this common problem, the following three stick and move techniques are recommended. These techniques are invaluable during the motivational phone call as well as during any future face-to-face session in each of the five FST phases of treatment (Phases I–V).

1. *Summarize quickly*
   When the client is going on and on, stick quickly with an interruption and summary of what was said and then move on to the next topic. For example, when the parent, extended family member, or child goes on and on about difficult experiences asked about in Question #2, the FST therapist can interrupt with *"Let me stop you for a second. If I am tracking you correctly, what I hear you saying is. . . . Am I close or way off?"* Stick by quickly summarizing the essence of what he or she said in one or two sentences. Then move on to the next topic. Clients enjoy this tactic because they instantly feel heard when the listener accurately summarizes what they said in just a few sentences. If the parent or adolescent goes back to being long-winded, the FST therapist continues the stick and move tactic. Eventually, the client gets the message that this is the new dance of communicating and begins to mirror the therapist.

2. *Compliments and use of names*
   Another great technique that helps the stick and move technique is compliments and the use of clients' names. For example, if the parent or adolescent goes on and on, the FST therapist can interrupt with *"Mary, what you just said was really insightful, let me stop you for a moment and see if I understood the essence of what you said before we move on"* (stick and move). Nothing is sweeter to a person than the sound of his or her name packed with a compliment right behind it. The person does not expect it and he or she is much more willing to be interrupted when treated with such respect and care. It also is great for a client who is grumpy or in a bad mood. And since the parent or adolescent does not know the therapist during the motivational phone call, compliments and the use of names is a good technique when one is about to stick and move for the first time. After rapport is established, the first stick and move technique without the compliment may be all one needs.

3. *An apology with rationale*
   A final technique is to be up-front with the parent or adolescent about the need to interrupt and its purpose. For example, you may say, *"I want to apologize ahead of time because I may need to interrupt you from time to time. When I interrupt, I am not trying to be rude. Instead, I want to cover a lot of ground in a short amount of time. Therefore, do I have your permission to interrupt, quickly summarize what I heard you say, and move on to the next topic? If so, I will simply say 'Can I stop you for a second?' and you will know what I mean."* People usually understand when one takes the time to provide the rationale with the big picture in mind. In this way, one is setting up the parameters of stick and move as the new normal at the onset of the therapeutic relationship.

In summary, after asking each FST motivational phone call question, be prepared to stick and move if necessary in order to keep the recommended time to no longer than 30 minutes. If the phone call is starting to run longer, the stick and move technique is not being used at all or is not being used properly. As with anything new, there is a normal learning curve for the proper timing and use of the stick and move techniques. At first, one might use stick and move too early or come in with the technique too late in the conversation. Practice each technique in order to feel comfortable and be able to blend the technique with one's own style and personality. And as stated earlier, each of these stick and move techniques should be used throughout the course of FST treatment.

STEP 5: THE USE OF EFFECTIVE CLOSING REMARKS

This is the single most important step within the FST motivational phone call. It mirrors the closing arguments of a great trial lawyer. Lawyers report that the jury often makes its decision based on how well or badly the closing arguments are framed and delivered. The trial itself lays the groundwork, but the closing arguments can win or lose the case. In the same way, your jury is the parent, caregiver, villager, or child. The groundwork is his or her previous answers to the six questions in the MI phone call script. Therefore, the FST therapist's closing remarks (arguments) should be linked closely to the answers. The ideal timing of the closing remarks is immediately after Question #6 and prior to the direct inquiry about the village.

After Question #6, the FST therapist will begin closing remarks to wrap things up. If everything goes well, the FST therapist will get a commitment from the parent(s) along with the adolescent to attend the first face-to-face session. Please remember to employ the SPIN "need–benefit" concept (see Table 4.3) for that particular client based on his or her answers to all six previous questions.

For example, in response to Question #5—*"Have you seen a counselor for any of these problems before? [If yes] What have other counselors missed with you?"*—the parent might state that past counselors never provided concrete tools. This would be their stated SPIN need. In response then, the SPIN benefit for this parent would be that the FST treatment model excels in providing concrete tools. This is a clear benefit to the client because the payoff is directly connected to the client's earlier stated need of "concrete tools." As a result, the parent is inherently motivated when the FST therapist's closing remarks match up with earlier stated needs.

However, the number #1 mistake new FST therapists make is to use canned or scripted closing remarks with *no* clear connection to the parent's or child's earlier words or stated explicit needs. For example, the FST therapist states, "*You will love this new FST model. It uses this awesome technique called a stress chart to instantly help you see your stress level and that of other family members.*" And the parent is thinking, "*I never mentioned that stress was a huge issue in this call. It was my daughter's depression that is my main concern. Is this counselor even listening to what I am saying?*" This is a huge tactical error and must be avoided at all costs.

As authors, we cannot think of every possible custom-fit closing remark you might employ. Therefore, the examples provided only serve to jump-start the process. They are not to be used as canned scripts. We also offer several suggestions on classic countermoves if the parent or adolescent continues to show resistance even after receiving good closing arguments. To make it easy, we have connected closing argument examples to several specific questions in the motivational phone call. Once the closing remarks process is mastered, the reader is encouraged to develop closing arguments that best fit his or her own particular style.

Examples of Closing Remarks

The first two examples connect closing remarks to strengths the parent and teen discussed in their response to Question #3 "*When I get to know you better, what qualities and strengths would I come to admire about you as a [person, parent, spouse, etc.]?*"

Example #1 Closing Remarks for Parent or Caregiver Using Responses to Question #3

Earlier in our call you said that the quality I would come to admire about you was that you will never give up on your child. That was important to know because it is absolutely incredible that with everything you have gone through, you have not given up.

I think you might like this treatment approach because I will try to build on the strengths you listed, but more importantly help others like your child better see your strengths as well. And based on what you said, I think your child is fortunate to have you as a parent. That being said, would you come to at least the first session to see for yourself?

In this example, the need–benefit connection is clear. The stated SPIN need for this parent is for recognition or even appreciation of her strengths. Therefore, the custom-fit SPIN benefit was when the FST therapist openly acknowledged the parent's strengths and stated that future sessions would help her child also see these strengths. Motivation will likely increase whenever the specific benefit offered is clearly connected to an earlier stated need.

An additional SPIN need–benefit bonus was asking the parent to agree to only the next step: "Come to the first session to see for yourself." Research calls these "micro quotas." Self-motivation and success dramatically increase when asking the person to commit only to the next small step (Ciotti, 2016). This runs counter to the temptation for both therapists and agencies to ask the parent or adolescent to commit to an entire treatment program. Therefore, having to commit only to the next step is a huge need–benefit connection and very motivating.

Example #2 Closing Remarks for Child or Adolescent Using Question #3

Earlier in our call you said that the quality I would come to admire about you was that you are smart and funny. That was important for me to know because it sounds like you have been through a lot of stressful times, but in spite of it all, you still have those strengths.

And based on what you said, I think you might like what we do. We try to help your parents see how they might have misunderstood you or even missed or overlooked the strengths you listed. The goal is to get everyone on the same page and look for the positive, not just the negative. Would you please come to the first meeting to see for yourself?

In this case, the SPIN benefit of helping the teen's parent to stop misunderstanding him and look at his strengths is stated to directly connect to the teen's SPIN need, which is "to be understood" and "to acknowledge my strengths as a person."

The third example connects closing remarks to what the parent states will happen if the problem remains unchanged in the response to Question #4: *"What do you think will happen to your teen if the problems you described earlier remain unfixed in the next three months, six months, or even a year from now?"*

Example #3 Closing Remarks for Parent or Caregiver Using Question #4

You said earlier that if things do not get better in the next few months that the odds are great that your teen will wind up in jail or even hospitalized. If that's the case, we don't have a lot of time left, it is urgent that something be done.

Therefore, based on what you said, a direct benefit to you and your family is that this treatment model attempts to get to the heart of the matter quickly. In the first session, we will get the top stressors or triggers that you said earlier in this call are causing your teen's problems [restate them here]. And without wasting time, we will get to concrete solutions quickly. Does this type of laser focused approach sound like it fits your situation, especially since you said, 'time is of the essence?'

The stated SPIN need the parent makes is that things with the child are about to get much worse if something is not done soon. Therefore, the SPIN benefit happens when the FST therapist clearly states that the first session will provide concrete solutions quickly with a clear road map of how this will happen.

This same process can be replicated in closing remarks for any of the other motivational questions. The key is for the FST therapist to listen closely for the answer that produced the most energy and passion for the client on the call. This is a good rule of thumb in determining the answers to the six questions for which the closing remarks could use the SPIN need–benefit format. One simply does not have time to offer closing remarks around each and every answer.

REFERENCES

Ciotti, G. (2016, October 30). Forget "lifehacks: Form good habits instead. Retrieved from https://www.entrepreneur.com/article/238843

Clark, H. W. (2010, November 2). *Keynote speech*. SAAS National Conference and NIATx Summit. Cincinnati, OH.

Festinger, D. S., Lamb, R. J., Marlowe, D. B., & Kirby, K. C. (2002). From telephone to office: Intake attendance as a function of appointment delay. *Addictive Behaviors, 27*(1), 131–137.

Gottman, J. M., & Silver, N. (1999). *The seven principles for making marriage work: A practical guide from the country's foremost relationship expert*. New York, NY: Harmony Publishing.

McCarty, D., Gustafson, D. H., Wisdom, J. P., Ford, J., Choi, D., Molfenter, T., . . . Cotter, F. (2007). The network for the improvement of addiction treatment (NIATx): Enhancing access and retention. *Drug and Alcohol Dependence, 88*(2–3), 138–145.

Miller, W. R., & Rollnick, S. (1991). *Motivational interviewing: Preparing people to change addictive behavior*. New York, NY: Guilford Press.

Miller, W. R., Zweben, A., DiClemente, C. C., & Rychtarik, R. G. (1992). *Motivational enhancement therapy manual: A clinical research guide for therapists treating individuals with alcohol abuse and dependence*. Project MATCH Monograph Series. Rockville, MD: National Institute on Alcohol Abuse and Alcoholism.

Mitchell, A. J., & Selmes T. A. (2007). Comparative survey of missed initial and follow-up appointments to psychiatric specialties in the United Kingdom. *Psychiatric Services, 58*(6), 868–871.

Rackham, N. (1995). *SPIN Selling*. Farnham Surrey, UK: Gower Publishing.

Reese, R. J., Conoley, C. W., & Brossart, D. F. (2002). Effectiveness of telephone counseling: A field based investigation. *Journal of Counseling Psychology, 49*, 233–242.

Reese, R. J., Conoley, C. W., & Brossart, D. F. (2006). The attractiveness of telephone counseling: An empirical investigation of client perceptions. *Journal of Counseling & Development, 84*(1), 54–60.

Sells, S, P., Winokur Early, K., & Smith, T. E. (2011). Reducing adolescent oppositional and conduct disorders: An experimental design using parenting with love and limits. *Professional Issues in Criminal Justice, 6*(3), 9–29.

Sterrett-Hong, E. M., Karam, E., & Kiaer, L. (2017). Statewide implementation of parenting with love and limits among youth with co-existing internalizing and externalizing functional impairments reduces return to service rates and treatment cost. *Administration and Policy in Mental Health and Mental Health Services Research, 44*(5), 792–809. doi:10.1007/s10488-016-0788-4

Tutty, S., Simon, G., & Ludman, E. (2000). Telephone counseling as an adjunct to antidepressant treatment in the primary care system: a pilot study. *Effective Clinical Practice, 3*, 170–178.

Weisner, C., Mertens, J., Tam, T., & Moore, C. (2001). Factors affecting the initiation of substance abuse treatment in managed care. *Addiction, 96*(5), 705–716.

Williams, R. J., & Chang, S. Y. (2000). A comprehensive and comparative review of adolescent substance abuse treatment outcome. *Clinical Psychology: Science and Practice, 7*, 138–166.

Winokur Early, K., Chapman, S., & Hand, G. (2013). Family-focused juvenile reentry services: A quasi-experimental design evaluation of recidivism outcomes. *Journal of Juvenile Justice, 2*(2), 1–22.

Phase I: Identify Symptoms (Stressors) and Set the Goals for Therapy

Step 1: The Symptom/Stress Chart

Step 2: The Seed/Tree Diagram

Step 3: The Top Seed and Symptom Selections

Step 4: The Choice Between Stabilization and Direct Trauma Work First

Step 5: Setting the Goals of Therapy

Step 6: Consolidate Gains Using Ethnographic Interviews

The flowchart in Figure 3.1 shows that Phase I begins after a soft start-up through the family systems trauma (FST) motivational phone call. It is the first face-to-face session and it will include the parent or caregiver, the child or adolescent with the identified problem, siblings, and key members of the village. The main goals and objectives of Phase I are to (a) identify the child's or adolescent's problem symptom through an FST technique known as a stress/symptom chart; (b) use what is called a seed/tree diagram to illustrate the causes of the child's or adolescent's symptoms through what are called unhealthy undercurrents and four toxic seeds (i.e., misuse of power, unhealed wounds, mental or physical impairment, or unmet primal needs); (c) ask all family members to pick their top problem symptoms and toxic seeds that they want to address with rationale; and (d) set the goals of therapy.

In addition, as the flowchart illustrates, prior to setting goals (Step 5), the FST therapist must answer the critical question: "Does the evidence gathered in Steps 1 through 3 from today's session suggest (a) stabilization first through the use of behavioral or hybrid contracts prior to direct trauma work or (b) direct trauma or wound work through the use of wound playbooks?" The answer to this question will directly impact the recommended goals of therapy at the end of Phase I. This chapter provides the three rules of thumb to assist the FST therapist in making this informed decision.

Average lengths of stay for this phase of treatment are between one and two 2-hour sessions or a minimum of two or four 1-hour sessions. As stated earlier, because the FST therapist is trying to actively change process (interactional patterns or undercurrents) instead of content (individual insight and change), sessions will take longer. As a result, the ideal session length is a 2-hour session to allow the family adequate time for education and application in the same session.

Case examples are used to illustrate the six key mini-steps in Phase I. These six mini-steps are

1. The symptom/stress chart
2. The seed/tree diagram
3. The top seed and symptom selections

4. The choice between stabilization and direct trauma work first
5. Setting the goals of therapy
6. Consolidate gains using ethnographic interviews

Outcome results that include this important Phase I system of care piece of PLL-FST (Family Systems Trauma) treatment are highlighted within the journal articles in the research section of www.gopll.com. Please visit this website for access to these articles.

PRIOR TO THE SESSION

Prior to beginning Phase I, the FST therapist should come to the session prepared with the following items:

☑ *A symptom stress chart template*: The FST therapist has a choice of either replicating the symptom/stress chart template in Box 5.1 on a flip chart or using a PowerPoint slide to show the family. An HDMI cable can be used to connect the therapist's laptop computer to either a flat-screen television or a portable LCD projector. Many families have flat-screen televisions today with an HDMI input, which can be used in the case of a home visit. Or the therapist can predraw the template on a giant flip chart that is purchased at an office supply store, which can be stuck on a blank wall in the family's home or office. It should be covered with a blank sheet of paper to hide it from view until the tool is ready to be used.

☑ *Copies of the safety stressor questionnaire handout*: The FST therapist will copy the safety stressor questionnaire from Table 5.1 to hand out to each family member. This questionnaire includes the seven common safety issues (i.e., threats or acts of violence, alcohol or drug use beyond experimentation, bullying, self-harm) found with at-risk children and adolescents.

☑ *The seed/tree diagram*: The FST therapist will replicate the same process as with the stress chart (decide between laptop and flip chart), but this time will use the seed/tree diagram in Figure 5.1.

☑ *Copies of a toxic seed definition handout*: The FST therapist will create a handout of the four toxic seed (i.e. misuse of power, unhealed wounds, mental or physical impairment, and unmet primal needs) definitions found in Chapter 2.

☑ *Copies of the village handout*: Immediately after goals are set in Step 5, the FST therapist has a golden opportunity to parlay this momentum into getting key villagers or extended family who did not attend the Phase I session to come to Phase II. However, what often happens is that family members say, "We have no village." In response, the FST therapist will have the village handout ready to help the family identify all potential villagers as well as whether they are supportive, nonsupportive, or potentially supportive.

STEP 1: THE SYMPTOM/STRESS CHART

The theoretical underpinnings and rationale for the symptom stress chart along with the step-by-step procedures needed for successful implementation are presented in the following text.

Theory and Rationale

The symptom stress chart is a modification of the scaling technique developed by DeShazer within solution-focused therapy (Malinen, 2001). It is an ideal first strategy for four reasons.

- *Treatment can begin as innocuously as possible*: If direct questions around trauma are asked too early, it will scare the family away or paralyze them with anxiety. Using the metaphor of an onion, it is better to peel back the outer layers first to get to the unhealed trauma in the center. Also, within this context, stress and problem symptoms are synonymous terms. Families talk in terms of stress and therapists talk in terms of symptoms, but they are one and the same. However, to increase joining and build rapport, it is optimal to use the family's language of "stress" instead of the more technical term of "problem symptoms."

- *All pathways to the traumatized child go through symptoms first*: Rarely, if ever, will a parent bring a traumatized child to treatment and say something like "*I don't care about my child's depression, disrespect, anxiety, self-harm, suicidal thoughts, or failing grades. Let's bypass these and get to the root cause or trauma first that is driving all these problem symptoms.*" The parent and child are in treatment primarily for one thing: emotional symptom pain relief. Therefore, the symptom stress chart is the *ideal* place to "start where the client is." Locate the stress (pain) first through the symptom stress chart, then move directly to the seed/tree diagram to help the family discover the reasons for their stress/pain (toxic seeds and unhealthy undercurrents), and then through contracts, hybrids, and wound playbooks, fix the undercurrents to heal the trauma that, if done correctly, will heal the symptoms permanently through second-order change.

- *The stress chart deflects tension away from family members*: For example, traditional therapy sessions often begin with questions such as "What is the problem?" or "Why are you here?" Although the therapist needs answers to these questions, these types of questions often initiate immediate arguing or finger-pointing. Family members then use the session as a means to unload anger or blame onto one another. In turn, the session can quickly escalate out of control. The stress chart, however, disrupts this pattern by asking everyone to look up at the wall or on the screen (not each other) and to disclose individually how stressful home life is in relation to their child and problems on a difficult week using a scale of 0% to 100% (0% = no stress; 100% = maximum stress). The technique *slows down* or bypasses the normal conflict and confrontation. The family member, loaded for bear when they first sit down, is quickly disarmed.

- *The stress chart provides an ideal segue into Step 2—The seed/tree diagram*. Immediately after the stress chart is completed, the FST therapist asks, "*Would you like to know what is causing all this stress?*" The family answers, of course, yes. In response, the therapist draws an apple tree or seed/tree diagram to discover this answer using toxic seeds and root symptom undercurrents. Therefore, the stress chart and seed/tree diagram complement one another. In turn, high rapport, momentum, and hope are quickly generated when family members walk away from a first session with clear understanding of why their child is having problems and with clear goals for therapy with next action steps outlined.

Step-by-Step Procedures and Transitional Scripts to Create the Symptom Stress Chart

As stated in Chapter 1, step-by-step procedures along with key transitional scripts are often not included within treatment books; rather, they contain generalized concepts or techniques. The frontline therapist has no clear roadmap of how to go from point A to point B and can easily get lost in the minutiae of the session. This is both dangerous and unacceptable for trauma treatment. In sharp contrast, the FST treatment model provides the frontline therapist with the step-by-step procedures needed to create and execute the symptom stress chart and other strategies in this chapter as well as the rest of the book. In sum, there are five step-by-step procedures to successfully execute the symptom stress chart technique:

1. Ask key transition question.
2. Obtain an overall stress rating from each family or village participant.
3. Convert overall stress into top three problems.
4. Locate safety stressors.
5. Discover how much each problem (stressors) will reduce the overall stress level if healed.

#1 Ask the Key Transition Question

Before jumping into therapy too quickly, Phase I begins with basic introductions and asking everyone about their hobbies and interests to settle the nerves of both the FST therapist and family. The question is asked, "*Before we get started, can I quickly go around the room and ask you about any hobbies or things you like to do?*" This question mirrors the social stage in Haley's (1991) book, *Problem-Solving Therapy*. It is also an ideal time to briefly comment on the reason why everyone was asked to come for treatment as a family, including the village.

> "I brought everyone together because I believe in the old saying: It takes a village to raise a child. Meaning that, in my experience, the family or community has the greatest potential or power to help others heal. In addition, no one can speak for someone else, so I wanted to hear everyone's own voice and opinion and not get it secondhand. Therefore, I asked everyone to come in today."

Do not ask if there are any questions after this statement. It is merely a comment to set the context. After brief socializing and setting the context, it is time to move into therapy mode.

The transition from the social stage to therapy is made using the symptom stress chart technique and begins by asking the following question:

> "*By a show of hands, how many agree with the statement, 'All Families Have Stress?'*"

This is a great transition question. Everyone's hand will be raised. When there is compliance and mutual agreement, there is less resistance.

#2 Obtain an Overall Stress Rating From Each Family or Village Participant

Following this question, the FST therapist will either go to the flip chart on the wall to reveal the stress chart (see Box 5.1) or do so from the laptop.

BOX 5.1 Symptom/Stress Chart Template

Stress Chart										
0%	10%	20%	30%	40%	50%	60%	70%	80%	90%	100%
0% = no stress								100% = maximum stress		

After the template is revealed, the FST therapist will ask the following questions that were first presented in Chapter 3:

Looking at this chart, on a bad week, how much stress do you experience regarding your worry or concern for _____name of identified problem child] in your household (not at work or school) out of 0% to 100%? What is the first answer that comes to mind if 0% represents no stress and 100% maximum stress?

This question is modified for the villagers who do not live in the immediate household as follows:

I realize you do not live inside the house. But from the outside looking in, how much stress are you under watching what goes on with _____[name of identified problem child] and_____[names of parents or caregivers] and knowing what you know, if 0% represents no stress and 100% maximum stress?

Please never forget this point. **The parents or caregivers are there for one reason: For you, the therapist, to fix their kid without having to fix themselves**. Therefore, initially, the focus must stay on the problem child or adolescent using concrete tools that the therapist suggests to fix the child or adolescent. Later, the FST therapist will, first subtly (using the seed/tree diagram) and then directly (using feedback loop drawings), expand the child's symptom to include the family. (What do you do to help your child misbehave or maintain your child's wounds?) However, until rapport and trust are built, the main or sole focus must stay on how to "fix" the child's problems. Otherwise, the likelihood is high that the parents will not return for a second session.

Because the child's problems vary, it is important to identify how much stress he or she has experienced "on a bad week." Additionally, it is important to emphasize "within the household" because the FST therapist's greatest impact is within this context. Moving outside the household leads to stressors (e.g., my job, my finances) that the therapist will be unable to help.

A final modification of the overall stress question comes in the form of a "circular" question (cf., Fleuridas, Nelson, & Rosenthal, 1986). In other words, a family member present in the session is asked to share how much stress he or she believes the missing family member (a deceased relative, an absent parent, an absent key extended family member, etc.) would state if he or she were present.

I realize that _____ is not present today (or has passed away) but if they were sitting with us today and looking at the stress chart, what overall percentage would they give for how stressed out they would be concerning _____ (name of identified problem child] if 0% represents no stress and 100% maximum stress?

This question is used for key absent members whose input would be invaluable. Because of time constraints, the FST therapist should be strategic in the choice of how many absent family or village members to inquire about. In other words, do not use a circular question for everyone who is not present.

Case Example

Twelve-year-old Max and his 6-year-old sister Jamie were removed from their home by Child Protective Services (CPS) for neglect issues. Betsy was a single parent who worked multiple jobs and was often not home. Max then had to parent his younger sister, Jamie.

(continued)

Case Example (*continued*)

Betsy stated that Max was prone to violent outbursts if he did not get his way. Max's father lived in the same town but rarely, if ever, visited.

The FST therapist was referred the case by CPS. After the referral, the therapist proceeded to use the motivational phone call to contact and speak to both Max and Betsy. And since this was a systems theory model with an emphasis on the village, the therapist conducted a motivational phone call with the foster mother, Janice. During the phone call, the FST therapist discovered the following key information:

- The mother, Betsy, was *not* unmotivated or resistant as the CPS report implied, but rather overwhelmed and not sure where to turn. She had strengths of wanting to get unstuck and do whatever it took to help her son.

- Max loved his mother very much but was unsure how to communicate his needs because he stated that "she was depressed and shut down."

- Betsy also spoke of untapped resources in her village. There was her neighbor, her pastor, and her mom and dad. She even felt that Max's dad might be willing to be involved, if contacted.

- Janice, the foster mom, was skeptical that Betsy was a capable mother but admitted that she was unsure because she had never met Betsy in person. She stated, however, she would be open to try.

The FST therapist then invited all three systems to attend the first session: the CPS caseworker, Betsy, Max, and the foster mom, Janice. This also included mom's village (her parents) and Max's dad, Mike. Since the treatment goals would be set in the first session, it was critical for everyone to be on the same page. It was like a town meeting because Betsy's support system would be there as well as Max's dad, Mike. Surprisingly, the CPS caseworker and foster parent stated that this type of town meeting almost never happened. The foster parent rarely, if ever, was in the same session with the biological family and vice versa. It was even rarer to have the absent father and the village attend a session together. But to both parties, it made perfect sense.

In addition, with Mom's verbal consent, Max's dad and Janice's villagers were also called using the motivational phone call. Because the phone call went well and they understood the need for mutual goal setting, everyone agreed to come. When asked later if they would have come with a simple invitation from the mom, everyone said no. The FST motivational phone call made everyone feel welcome and explained the purpose of a town hall goal-setting format.

Since this was a large meeting, it took place at the CPS caseworker's conference room. Janice brought Max, and the CPS caseworker drove to get mom, since she had limited transportation. Max's sister, Jamie, was not invited to this first session because she was too young. Later in the therapy process, she would be invited.

The FST therapist then asked the following transition question:

"By a show of hands, how many agree with the statement, 'All families have stress?'"

(*continued*)

Case Example (*continued*)

Everyone in the room raised their hands, including Max.

> *"Let's all look at what I call a stress chart to see how much stress each of you experiences in your household."*

As you can see on the chart, I will go around the room and ask everyone this question, beginning with Max:

> *"On a bad week, how much overall stress do you experience at home (not at work or school) out of 0% to 100%? What is the first answer that comes to mind if 0% represents no stress and 100% maximum stress?"*

And Mike, I know you do not live in the house so the question for you is:

> *"From the outside looking in, how much stress are you under watching what goes on with Max, Jamie, and their mom, Betsy, if 0% represents no stress and 100% maximum stress?"*

The grandfather was unable to attend for health reasons. Therefore, after the therapist got everyone's overall stress, he circled back around and asked the grandmother the following circular question:

> *"I realize that you husband could not be here today. But if he were, how much overall stress would he say there is—if 0% represents no stress and 100% maximum stress— from the outside looking in? When he does come in next time, it will be fun to compare his actual answer with yours."*

The grandmother liked this question. She replied that his stress would be much less than her 100% stress; she thought his stress would be around 20%. When asked why, the grandmother replied, "*I want to protect and shield him from any stress due to his poor heart condition, which everyone worries about, especially Max.*" This snippet of information was critical and might have been lost without this circular question. Later, it became clear that the grandfather's poor health was a driver of Max's anger and aggression. And when the grandfather attended a later session and was asked about the grandmother's answer, he replied, "*I hate to be protected. I know what is going on more than everyone gives me credit for. And besides it is less stressful on my heart to be in the know than be in the dark.*" This one statement was the key into opening up the Pandora's box of family secrets around protection.

The stress chart in Box 5.2 illustrates everyone's stress level on a bad week. Everyone with the exception of the grandfather and Janice, the foster mom, had an overall stress percentage of 80% or higher. Janice was only at 20% because these were the first weeks of foster care with Max and Jamie, so there were no problems yet.

BOX 5.2 Max's Family's Overall Symptom Stress Chart

					Stress Chart					
		Janice (foster mom) Grandfather				Jamie (sister)	Max	Dad	Mary (CPS)	Micah (pastor) Grandma Mom
		X				Stress b/w 50 and 90 TBD	**X**	**X**	**X**	**X**
0%	10%	20%	30%	40%	50%	60%	70%	80%	90%	100%

0% = no stress   100% = maximum stress

_____

TBD, to be determined.

#3 Convert Overall Stress Into the Top Three Problems

After obtaining the family's overall stress, the FST therapist asks each family member, starting with the identified problem child or adolescent, to identify the top three things that make up their overall stress.

> *"Now that I know your overall stress let me circle back around and ask each of you what are the top three things that make up the overall stress you just gave? Let me start with you first* [child or adolescent with problem] *and then go around the room."*

The therapist writes down the answers on the flip chart immediately underneath the scale on the same sheet and ranks the client's top three stressors. When necessary, the top three stressors are converted from what are called general complaints into concrete categories and written to the right of the client's stated complaint. For example, this process is illustrated in the following text using the top three stressors Max listed:

Max's top three stressors that make up his 80%

#1   "Mom, doesn't listen to me" (**mutual disrespect**)

#2   "Dad is never around" (**grief and abandonment**)

#3   "Mom left us in foster care" (**abandonment**)

As illustrated in this example, people naturally talk in the language of **complaints** and not concrete categories. This is normal. The problem for the FST therapist is that it is difficult to impossible to make a clear behavioral contract or wound playbook based on a complaint. For example, a wound playbook with the goal of "dad never around" makes no sense. But one that contains step-by-step procedures and clarification of family roles "to heal grief and abandonment" does make sense.

When a complaint is made, the FST therapist hits the pause button and asks the person for clarification. This is done from a curious, one-down stance. Statements to help convert a complaint to a concrete category include

- *"Max, when you say, 'Mom doesn't listen to me,' what does that look like? Or if I was a fly on the wall watching this happen, what would I see?"*

- *"Max, when you say, 'Dad was never around,' is this another way of saying that you felt abandoned or like grief over someone close to you dying?"*

- *"Max, when you say, 'Mom left us,' is this also another way of saying that you felt a little abandoned? Am I close or way off?"*

Tentatively "guessing" major categories that might fit the complaint, or saying, "What does it look like?" are great conversation starters to move from complaints to concrete categories. At other times, the client will talk about the problem as a major category ("My son is depressed" or "My daughter is violent," etc.) and there is no need for a conversion process.

It is important to note that when there is a large family (5 or more members), the FST therapist must make an important judgment call. Due to time constraints, the therapist cannot get the top three stressors from everyone and take the time to convert complaints. In addition, the family will get antsy and bored, especially the child. As a result, it is recommended that the therapist take a random sample of the most influential stakeholders (e.g., primary caregiver, problem adolescent, key extended family member). Common themes will start to emerge. Tell the family ahead of time that based on time constraints, you will only be gathering top stressors from a maximum of four to five people. Focus on the common themes that emerge.

In sum, this process looks different from a more traditional assessment session whereby the therapist uses a psychosocial questionnaire and then offers their expert *Diagnostic and Statistical Manual of Mental Disorders* (5th ed.; *DSM-5*) diagnosis at the end from a one-up, expert position. In contrast, the process of utilizing stress charts and category conversion is often more collaborative and empowers all family members to state the top problem symptoms that they want to fix or heal early on in therapy. In turn, rapport and trust is accelerated quickly between the FST therapist and the family.

Case Example

The stress chart of the top three stressors with concrete categories in Box 5.3 reveals common themes across both the immediate family and their village. They include (a) Max's threats or acts of aggression; (b) Max's grief for abandonment by his father; (c) Mom's depression and feeling overwhelmed; and (d) Max and Jamie's overall disrespect and refusal to do any chores around the house.

Due to the large number of people in the session and time constraints, once common themes kept emerging, the FST therapist did not take the time to get everyone's answers. This included the pastor, the grandfather, and foster mom. Please note how people talked about their top three stressors in terms of both concrete categories and complaints that had to be converted in real time by the therapist.

(continued)

Case Example

BOX 5.3 Max's Top Three Stress Chart With Concrete Categories

Stress Chart

									Mary (CPS)	Micah (pastor) Grandma Mom
Janice (foster mom) Grandfather **X**					Jamie (sister) Stress b/w 50 and 90 TBD		Max **X**	Dad **X**	**X**	**X**
0%	10%	20%	30%	40%	50%	60%	70%	80%	90%	100%

Max's top 3 stressors that cause 80% stress

#1   *"Doesn't listen to me"* *(mutual disrespect)*

#2   *"Dad never around"* *(grief & abandonment)*

#3   *"Mom left us in foster care"* *(abandonment)*

Mom's top 3 stressors that cause 100% stress

#1   *"Won't listen to me" (disrespect and chores)*

#2   *"I am sad and overwhelmed" (depressed)*

#3   *"Max's anger and outbursts" (aggression)*

Dad's top 3 stressors that cause 90% stress

#1   *"Not connected to my kids" (lack of nurturance)*

#2   *"Outside the loop with my ex" (parents not on same page)*

Grandma's top 3 stressors that cause 100% stress

#1   *"Daughter's depression" (depression)*

#2   *"Kids disrespect their mom" (disrespect)*

#3   *"Kids' father not around" (abandonment)*

CPS worker's top 3 stressors that cause 95% stress
#1   *"Mom's anger and lack of support" (lack of support)*
#2   *"Max's outbursts and aggression" (aggression)*
#3   *"Mom being physically present" (safety & consistency)*

CPS, Child Protective Services; TBD, to be determined.

As this part of the stress chart was being completed, the FST therapist, at times, had to apply the stick and move technique (outlined in Chapter 4) and quickly redirect. There was extreme tension between the father and the mom and the grandmother around a theme of "blame" directly related to unresolved issues from a bitter divorce and the grandmother openly taking sides with her daughter against the dad. To counter this tension, the therapist had to quickly redirect and reframe. The key was to refer to the earlier stated goal of focusing on the here and now. A town meeting with a lot of people present is not the time for deep exploration and a discussion about feelings. Instead, it is a time to problem-solve and set goals.

The FST therapist fully realized that helping the family create a plan to resolve the stress around chores would not directly address the trauma the children were suffering around grief, loss, and abandonment. However, it could indirectly help by decreasing the yelling and tension between parent and child, directly lowering interactional trauma. This in turn would help create a more peaceful and stress-free home. When this occurs, the direct treatment of trauma is much more workable. Less drama equals less trauma. Therefore, the FST therapist kept chores at the back of his mind as a possible recommended goal of treatment.

#4 Locate Safety Stressors

After the family lists their top three stressors, there is one final intermediary step. The FST therapist must make sure that there are no safety stressors that have been overlooked. It is normal and to be expected that the safety stressors are either out of the family's collective awareness or part of a family secret. To put things into perspective, Phase I is still the first session. Rapport and trust with the therapist is still new and tentative at best. However, the challenge is that the FST therapist must still obtain all the information. Otherwise, he or she cannot make an accurate assessment and proper recommendations for the goals of therapy. Therefore to address this challenge, the FST model needed a very creative solution.

A creative solution was found in the format of what we termed safety stressors with a safety stressor questionnaire handout. If family members feel nonthreatened and that the safety stressors information process was part of a normal overall assessment piece, it was readily accepted. This acceptance was aided by the fact that the safety stressors were positioned as a normal extension of the family's top three stressors.

In addition, a safety stressor handout was passed out, making it easy for family members and villagers to pick from the list. The FST therapist added these additional stressors to the stress chart with the label "Safety Stressors" (see Max's family's safety stressors in the case example in the following text). Prior to the handout, when families are asked, "Are there any safety issues?" the answer is usually no. But after the handout, the "no" often turns into a "yes." This "yes" occurs even if there are family secrets because the process is nonthreatening and normalized. The following transition statement is used as a prelude to the safety stressor discussion:

> *"Thanks everyone for giving me your top 3 stressors* [point to stress chart]. *Our next step is to figure out if there are any safety stressors. These are common and normal stressors in children or teenagers that if not addressed could cause harm to themselves or others around them. I will pass out a handout of some of the top safety stressors. I will then ask each of you to vote 'yes' or 'no.' If 'yes,' I will put it on your stress chart to address later."*

A copy of the safety stressor handout was then given to each family member. The key to whether or not a safety issue exists has to do with frequency. If the safety problem occurred, such as running away, but it only happened three times in a year, due to its infrequency, it likely would not be included on the list. However, this same behavior would be placed on the list if the family revealed that the child ran away once a week or several times a month. On the other hand, if the safety issue happens but without frequency, the family can still state that they want to put it on the list as "something to watch out for in the future."

Please note that each question in the safety stressor questionnaire does not begin with "Have you ever . . . ?" but rather, "When was the last time . . . ?" This format is done intentionally to elicit a more truthful response.

TABLE 5.1 The Safety Stressor Questionnaire

#1. Threats or Acts of Aggression
- *To the parent:* When was the last time your child/teenager was aggressive or caused property damage? How often does this occur (every day, once a week, once a month, once a year)?
- *To the child/teenager and then parent:* How often do you think you lose your temper or hurt others [people or animals] (every day, once a week, once a month, once a year)?

(continued)

TABLE 5.1 The Safety Stressor Questionnaire (*continued*)

#2. Drugs or Alcohol Beyond Experimentation
- *To the parent: When was the last time your child/teenager used drugs or alcohol?*
- *To the child/teenager and then parent:* How often do you use (every day, once a week, once a month, once a year)?

#3. Self-Harm
- *To the parent:* When was the last time your child/teenager cut or scratched himself/herself?
- *To the child/teenager:* How often do you cut or scratch yourself (every day, once a week, once a month, once a year)?

#4. Bullying
- *To the child/teenager:* When was the last time you were bullied at school or received threatening messages on Facebook, Twitter, Instagram or other social media? How often does this happen (every day, once a week, once a month, once a year)?

#5. Running Away or Leaving Home Without Permission
- *To the parent:* When was the last time your child/teenager left home without permission? How often does this happen (every day, once a week, once a month, once a year) and how long is he/she gone (hours, days, a week)?

#6. Threats or Acts of Suicide
- *To the parent:* When was the last time your child tried to hurt himself/herself or threatened to do so?
- *To the child:* When was the last time you thought about hurting yourself? (pause for answer; if positive), "How often do you have these thoughts (every day, once a week, once a month, once a year)? And do you have a plan? If yes, what does it entail?

#7. Sexting or Promiscuity
- *To the child/teenager:* When was the last time you used sexting or pornography? When was the last time you engaged in sexual behaviors with a partner? If yes, how many times a week do you engage in sexting or view pornography? How many different partners in a month or year? And how often do you use protection to prevent sexually transmitted diseases or decrease the risk of pregnancy (every time, sometimes, never)?

#8. Technology Addiction
- *To the parent:* How often does your child, on average, have an excessive use of or preoccupation with the Internet, computer, texting, video games, and so on. that impairs his or her daily life? For example, using technology over homework, technology over playing outside or seeing friends face-to-face, withdrawal symptoms (angry, irritated, depressed) if taken away, refusal to go anywhere without technology, use of technology to deal with any type of negative feelings.
- *To the child/teenager:* When I read this list off, how many apply to you? (a) You find yourself spending more and more time with phone, computer, video, or television to get the same enjoyment you used to get; (b) you feel withdrawal symptoms if you are away from technology or the Internet for any longer than a day; (c) you go directly to technology when you feel depressed or feel any negative feelings; and (d) you are constantly checking your social accounts, text messages, Facebook account, etc.

Why is the safety assessment important when it comes to the traumatized child? It is important for two main reasons. First, ongoing safety issues left unresolved will block the healing of wounds. As stated earlier, interactional trauma or drama will keep the child and family in a state of perpetual crisis. Under these conditions, it is impossible to heal wounds. For example, a parent and child in the throes of domestic violence are not going to be able to hug or forgive one another. Second, therapy cannot really begin unless safety issues are addressed first or in concert with therapy.

Once a safety issue is revealed, there is a tendency for family members to get either very excited or highly emotional, or shut down. If either situation occurs, the FST therapist must avoid going into deep history gathering or a bunny trail of feelings around the issue. This is not a time for exploration, but a time to list the stressors on the stress chart. Exploration will come later.

Case Example

After identifying the top three stressors, Max's family and village were ready to segue into the concept of safety stressors. After the FST therapist shared the list of common safety stressors, Max revealed that on occasion, he would hit his sister or hurt the dog. The therapist inquired about frequency. Max revealed that he hit the dog almost daily and his mom said he hit Jamie, his sister, at least once a week or destroyed property when angry. However, Janice, the foster mom reported that so far, the aggression or hurting pets (she did not have a pet) was not an issue at her home. However, when the therapist got to the handout section of "Bullying," Max dropped a bombshell. He revealed that three classmates were bullying him. This consisted of posted social media threats and verbal threats in the school hallway. These problems were then added to the family's stress chart under the heading safety stressors.

Safety Stressors

#1 "Hits or hurts dog in secret almost every day" (**threats or acts of aggression**)

#2 "Hits sister or destroys property weekly" (**threats or acts of aggression**)

#3 "Bullied in school by three classmates" (**bullying**)

When the safety issues of hurting the dog and the school bullying were identified, Max's parents, grandmother, and members of the village were in shock, and the situation started to get highly emotional. The therapist had to quickly use the stick and move technique, promising that he would come back to these issues at the end of the session. The therapist also had to protect the mother from the stereotypical perception of "Mom is bad" and "Foster mom is good" or "This is why it was good to remove Max and his sister from the home." A better and more helpful reframe is that stress and depression breed deep pain, and emotional pain unhealed over time turns into outward aggression toward others. So if the FST therapist can shift Janice and the caseworker away from vilification of the mother to a frame of "Let's work together to remove the root causes of stress" (unhealthy undercurrents) to support Mom, with Mom and Janice working together (ideas for wound playbook or contract, etc.), then both systems move into a collaborative rather than an adversarial stance.

Everyone was satisfied with that promise, and it allowed the FST therapist to move on to identifying how much stress reduction would take place based by the elimination of each individual stressor. These answers provide the FST therapist a compass to set the terms or goals for therapy. If it were not for the safety stressor handout, it is very unlikely that the bullying would have been revealed, and the goals of therapy would then have been skewed.

#5 How Much Will Each Problem (Stressor) Reduce the Overall Stress Level If Healed?

After obtaining the top three stressors as well as the safety stressors, the FST therapist then goes through each person's three top stressors, one at a time, and asks how much of their overall stress would be reduced if just one of the three stressors was eliminated.

To accomplish this step, the FST therapist covers up two of the three stressors and asks if just that one uncovered stressor were eliminated, how much overall stress would be reduced. This process is repeated until the person has identified a specific amount of reduction for each of the three stressors if eliminated. As with the previous steps, the therapist begins with the identified problem child or adolescent and then moves to the remaining family and/or village members listed on the stress chart.

Determining which individual stressors yield the most stress reduction is like gold for the FST therapist. Traumatized family systems are inundated with multiple symptoms and stressors, and they are often too overwhelmed to effectively prioritize which symptom to address first, second, third, and so forth. However, using this method, the family is asked to use their own inner wisdom or gut feeling to provide a road map as to which symptoms, if eliminated, will cause the largest overall stress reduction. Despite what the family members may pick as their top symptoms, the FST therapist must still make a judgment call on which symptom is most important to focus on. This is because families may underestimate the importance of an obvious stressor (i.e., unresolved grief or abandonment) or even ignore an important safety stressor altogether.

Case Example

As the stress chart in Box 5.4 illustrates, Max's family and village revealed how much each individual stressor (symptom), if eliminated, would decrease their overall stress. To get these answers, the therapist asked each family member or villager to look at one stressor at a time. For example, with mom, the FST therapist stated:

> "Mom, let's look at your top three stressor list of disrespect around chores, depression, and aggression. Like I just did with Max, let's go to one stressor at a time and cover up the rest. If I, as your coach, could only help you stop your son's disrespect, which would include chores and nothing else, just by itself, how much of your overall stress would be reduced? Let me put my finger on your overall 100% answer and move it down on the stress chart scale slowly. Tell me at which number to stop. Now remember this is just eliminating the problem of your kid's disrespect around chores. We will get to the other two in just a moment."

The mom had the therapist stop at 25%.

> "OK, great. Wow, your stress level reduction for just stopping disrespect around chores would drop from 100% all the way to 25%. That means 100% - 25% = a 75% stress reduction. Let me write 75% with a down arrow next to your stressor of disrespect around chores."

This same downward finger exercise on the stress chart would be repeated for each person to produce a visual picture of everyone's stress reduction for each individual's reported stressors as seen in Box 5.4.

(*continued*)

Case Example (*continued*)

BOX 5.4 Stress Reductions

Stress Chart

0%	10%	20%	30%	40%	50%	60%	70%	80%	90%	100%
		Janice (foster mom) Grandfather **X**			Jamie (sister) Stress b/w 50 and 90 TBD		Max **X**	Dad **X**	Mary (CPS) **X**	Micah (pastor) Grandma Mom **X**

Max's Top 3 Stressors That Cause 80% Stress

#1   *"Doesn't listen to me" (mutual disrespect) 60%↓*

#2   *"Dad never around" (grief & abandonment) 70%↓*

#3   *"Mom left us in foster care" (abandonment) 80%↓*

Dad's Top 3 Stressors That Cause 90% Stress

#1   *"Not connected to my kids" (lack of nurturance) 80%↓*

#2   *"Outside the loop with my ex" (parents not on same page) 60%↓*

CPS Worker's Top 3 Stressors That Cause 95% Stress

#1   *"Mom's feeling overwhelmed" (lack of support) 80%↓*

#2   *"Max's outbursts and aggression" (aggression) 70%↓*

#3   *"Mom being physically present" (safety & consistency) 85%↓*

Mom's Top 3 Stressors That Cause 100% Stress

#1   *"Won't listen to me" (disrespect/ chores) 75%↓*

#2   *"I am sad and overwhelmed" (depressed) 80%↓*

#3   *"Max's anger and outbursts" (aggression) 85%↓*

Grandma's Top 3 Stressors That Cause 100% Stress

#1   *"Daughter's depression" (depression) 80% ↓*

#2   *"Kids disrespect their mom" (disrespect) 70%↓*

#3   *"Kids' father not around" (abandonment) 50%↓*

Safety Stressors

#1   *Hits or hurts dog in secret (aggression) 90%↓*

#2   *Bullied by 3 kids in school (bullying) 90%↓*

#3   *Hits sister/destroys property (aggression) 80%↓*

CPS, Child Protective Services; TBD, to be determined.

One could see in the body language and family statements that all were both shocked and pleased to see the big picture and everyone else's stressors and stress levels relative to their own. The mother replied,

> "For the first time in years I feel relieved and not so alone. I feel hope. Many of my stressors were the same as others and I can see which problems we should target first. Before now, all the problems were scattered everywhere with no clear path. Now, I can see a path."

The others in the room, including Max, echoed mom's sentiments.

(*continued*)

The FST therapist will still need another piece of the puzzle to make the final recommendations on the goals for therapy and which path to take: (a) stabilization first using contracts or hybrids or (b) direct trauma or wound work first using playbooks. This final piece comes from the next two techniques: the seed/tree diagram and the family's seed and symptom picks.

STEP 2: THE SEED/TREE DIAGRAM

The seed/tree diagram strategy takes place immediately after the symptom stress chart is completed. If the stress chart takes most of the 1-hour session, the FST therapist may want to wait to introduce and complete Step 2 in the next session. The more stress charts the FST therapist completes with families, the more efficient he/she will become. After practice, Step 1 can usually be completed in 30 minutes. But when one is first learning, it will naturally take longer. The next step, Step 2, cannot be rushed because it is a key lynchpin to begin to move the family system from an individual focus paradigm to one that is systemic in nature.

Theory and Rationale

As stated earlier, both parents and extended family enter treatment with the worldview of "fix the child through individual therapy, without fixing or involving us." In essence, family members do not see the problem or solution from a systemic lens.

In response to this challenge, the seed/tree diagram was developed to move the family members to a "systems" focus. This involves the central concept of "expanding the symptom" from a "child only" problem to a "family" problem and a family solution (Gehart, 2013). For example, before the seed/tree diagram, the dad might state something like *"My #1 stressor on my stress chart is that my daughter, Amy is angry and she needs medication or individual anger management"*. However, after the seed/tree diagram, the dad will often say something like *"After seeing the tree and understanding the seed of 'unhealed wound,' I am <u>starting</u> to see that Amy's anger is more likely caused by deep wounds of resentment after we adopted a special needs child and left Amy to fend for herself. I never thought about the problem this way before. We all have to make changes, not just Amy."* In this example, the symptom has now expanded in the father's worldview from a client-centered focus to one that is systemic. The word "starting" is underlined because this systems theory insight is still in its infancy. More tools in future phases of FST treatment will be needed (i.e., feedback loops, undercurrent worksheets, wound playbooks, dress rehearsals) before this shift in thinking takes hold and overcomes decades of thinking only individual cause and effect, the default worldview for most human beings.

In sum, this kind of paradigm shift is possible when the FST therapist directly connects the family's symptoms from the stress chart to the experiential seed/tree diagram of an apple tree. The family's stressors are rewritten as symptoms and placed on the apples of the tree. The metaphor is then used that the apples are bruised and turning brown because they are symptoms of a "stressed-out" tree that one can see with the naked eye (i.e., depressed apples, aggressive apples, resentful apples, self-harm apples). Underneath the soil and unseen to the naked eye, are the root systems (unhealthy undercurrents) and toxic seeds (unmet primal needs, unhealed wounds, etc.) that are the causes of the problem symptoms/the bruised apples. Family members want to know the root causes. Therefore, when clients get the definitions of the toxic seeds in this session and the undercurrents in the next session, they begin to self-discover (like Amy's father) the systemic causes of the problem symptoms for themselves.

There are two procedures to successfully execute the seed/tree diagram technique: (1) explain the apple tree metaphor and (2) define the toxic seeds.

#1: Explain Apple Tree Metaphor

After the stress chart is completed, the FST therapist says the next step is to find out the causes of the stress using the following transition statement:

> Now that we know your stressors, let's find out what is causing your stress. To do this, I will draw an apple tree and together we will find out why these stressors [list them from flip chart] are happening to your child and family.

Draw out the apple tree like Figure 5.1 immediately below the stress chart on the same flip chart page if there is room. In this way, one can literally connect the dots between the stress chart and tree. If there isn't enough room, use a separate flip chart page and place it next to the stress chart.

Next, the FST therapist will label each apple according to the stated stressor categories from the stress chart. Use one symptom per apple. If there are too many stressors and not enough apples, just write down the most common ones or the ones that would reduce the most stress. Once the apples are labeled as shown in Figure 5.1, the therapist explains the apple tree metaphor in simple and straightforward terms using two parts: Part I and Part II.

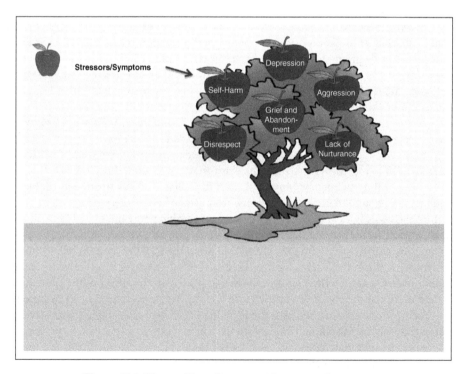

Figure 5.1 The seed/tree diagram with stressors/symptoms.

Source: Adapted with permission G. Wood, personal communication (2017, March 23).

Part I: What the Apples Represent

The FST therapist explains that the bruised apples represent their stressors on the chart and indicate a stressed-out family, just as bruised apples are evidence of a stressed-out tree. The following statement is used:

> These apples [point to them on the flip chart] represent the stressors in your family. These are also called symptoms [write label "stressors/symptoms" and then draw an arrow from that label to the apples]. Like the tree's apples, I can see your stressors or symptoms with my naked eye. If I came over to your house, I could see [name their stressors: depression, aggression, disrespect, etc.].

Look closely at everyone's body language as you explain what the apples represent. If anyone looks confused, ask that person, "*What did you hear me say?*" The metaphor is important because it segues nicely to what is often unseen or rarely talked about in the open, the root causes [undercurrents and toxic seeds] of the unhealed trauma.

Part II: What the Four Toxic Seeds Represent

The next step is to explain what the four toxic seeds represent (misuse of power, unhealed wounds, mental or physical impairment, and unmet primal needs). The therapist labels each seed in the apple tree as illustrated in Figure 5.2.

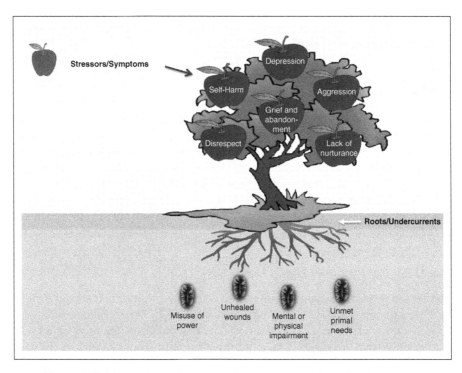

Figure 5.2 The seed/tree diagram with symptoms, seeds, and undercurrents
Source: Adapted with permission G. Wood, personal communication (2017, March 23).

After labeling each seed, the following transition statement is used:

> The stressors labeled on your apples are caused by what we call toxic or poisonous seeds deep beneath the soil that are unseen by the naked eye. [Point to seeds on diagram on flip chart.] These toxic seeds produce the poison that causes the stressors or symptoms that you just listed on the board. The roots going from the seeds up into the tree [point to flip chart] carry the poison, like veins in your arm carry the blood from your heart. These are called 'undercurrents,' and we will talk about these at our next session.

> Right now, our job is to be detectives and find out which of these four seeds is causing your stress. It may be one seed or all four. After I tell you the definition of each seed using this handout [hold up the handout], each of you will be asked to pick your top two toxic seeds.

> You will be asked to pick your seeds privately and then I will go around the room and ask each of you to tell us which seeds you picked and why. The reason this is so important is that if we find the root cause, we can solve the problem quickly.

> Any questions?

As with the apple metaphor earlier, watch the body language to make sure family members understand the metaphor. To confirm, periodically ask one family member to put into his or her own words what he or she heard you say.

These four toxic seeds are exceptionally good metaphors. Clients are intrigued when they are encouraged to self-discover the causes of their problems like detectives in their own mystery theater. Therapy, in general, is often too much talk. Therefore, breaking up the normal routine with an experiential exercise intrigues and involves the family. A picture is worth a thousand words, so clients remember the seed/tree diagram into the future.

#2 Seed Definitions

Next, the FST therapist will define each of the four seeds. The definition of each seed can be found in Chapter 2 and is not replicated here. It is recommended that the definitions be created into a handout to be passed out to the family as the FST therapist reads off each definition aloud, one seed at a time. When creating a handout for the families, do not include the unhealthy undercurrents, as this would be too much information for the families at this time. The undercurrent information will be communicated in the next phase. The therapist should pause after each seed is read to make sure there is an understanding of the definition and answer any questions before moving to the next seed.

The Use of Parallel Storytelling and Movie Scenes

It is important to speak with energy, passion, and, whenever possible, parallel storytelling when defining the four seeds. Parallel storytelling comes from the brilliant hypnotic work of the late Dr. Milton Erickson. Erickson constructed storylines that paralleled the problem a person was experiencing and offered the unconscious mind an opportunity to draw an analogy (Rosen, 1982). For example, if the family described years of parent–child conflict, when defining the unhealed wound seed, the FST therapist might say:

"I once worked with a family whose parents and children fought constantly. The household environment over the years became toxic with tension. The teenager began to run away because of the fighting. Over time, this constant fighting led to unforgiveness and resentment between parent and child. It created a wound that was never healed. We called this a form of interactional trauma because the constant fighting and tension either prevented an existing wound from healing or created a wound over time due to unforgiveness and resentment."

This story would directly parallel the story of the family in the session. The family also had constant fighting, a toxic household, and unforgiveness. However, the story about another family allowed this family to save face and gave them permission to draw on the analogy. It also made the seed definition literally jump off the page and come alive because it was relatable to that family. Parallel storytelling can be replicated for any of the four seeds, matching information gathered earlier on that family's stress chart.

If the therapist does not have a parallel story from a family he or she has worked with, he or she can create a story that fits and say, "*There was a family . . . .*" Despite the belief that each family is unique, there is a universality of shared experiences that can be drawn upon when parallel storytelling, which allows the family to save face and recognize their own circumstances more easily.

Parallel storytelling can also be creatively expanded to include movie clips. For example, the unhealed wound seed can be illustrated using a poignant scene from the movie *Antwone Fisher* in which Antwone forgives his biological mother for placing him in foster care. Other movie scenes can be used to illustrate any of the other seeds as long as they parallel the problem the family is experiencing.

Case Example

Twelve-year-old Jason was referred for symptoms of depression and bulimia. After examination of the safety stressors, it was revealed that Jason's symptoms occurred following his father's return from extended tours in Afghanistan with post-traumatic stress disorder (PTSD). William, the father, denied that his personality had dramatically transformed since the war. In order to bring the dad into awareness, parallel storytelling was used with one low-impact scene from Kevin Costner's movie *The War* (Avnet & Avnet, 1994). This clip was used to define the seed of "physical impairment" and its direct impact on Jason and the rest of the family. The father was given permission to stop the scene at any time if it created too much stress. The FST therapist set up the scene in the following manner.

> One common and toxic seed is what is called physical impairment. This occurs when a family member suffers a mental or physical impairment that can upset the family balance. For example, in one family I worked with, the father went off to war and it changed him. It wasn't the dad's fault. There was just no handbook for how to deal with the emotional stress of war. So the family had to accommodate and change to the dad's new way. It wasn't easy because they were also hurting but could not talk about it.

> I want to show you a scene from a little-known movie called The War starring Kevin Costner. In the scene entitled "Don't Come Back the Same," Stephen, played by Costner, tells his son that since returning, he has been struggling with something called post-traumatic stress disorder or PTSD. The son is visibly relieved that finally

(continued)

Case Example (*continued*)

> they are talking about bottled-up emotions. Later, the son's depression starts to lift, and the knots in his stomach start to get unknotted and he can eat and sleep again in peace. Talking with the dad openly about his PTSD was the first step to start the healing process.
>
> After the clip was shown, there were tears in everyone's eyes, especially the dad's. Normally, the therapist would want to move on to the next seed definition. However, when a movie clip is impactful in a positive way, the FST therapist must pause to allow for process.
>
> In this case, all the family members overtly stated that they also had physical impairment and that the movie characters represented them. The therapist's job was to normalize feelings and say that because this was their first session, they needed to go slow and unpack things one step at a time.
>
> The goal of today's session was to identify the seeds together, and later to introduce tools to heal the wounds. The one immediate positive outcome was that the dad stated that the discussion around the movie clip brought to his awareness the impact his PTSD was having on his family, especially his son, Jason.
>
> As a result, the father wanted individual counseling to go along with the family work. Jason was able to begin to connect his symptoms of bulimia and depression with the onset of dad's PTSD. The therapist would repeatedly return to these important anchor points from the movie throughout the course of FST treatment.

Movie clips are powerful, and they make the seed definitions come alive and the session entertaining and energized; however, they should be used judiciously. The therapist should have a menu of movie clips for each seed on their computer that can be accessed at a moment's notice. Please go to www.gopll.com/trauma or www.familytrauma.org for a suggested listing of some of our top movies for each of the four toxic seeds.

The Stabilization Seed Versus Trauma Seeds

As outlined in Chapter 2, there is an important distinction between what we call the stabilization seed (misuse of power) and trauma seeds (unhealed wounds, mental or physical impairment, unmet primal needs). As a reminder, the stabilization seed of misuse of power is defined as follows:

> Misuse of power is known as the stabilization seed because it may have nothing to do with trauma but everything to do with ineffective limit setting, oppositional or defiant behavior of the child, lack of boundaries, or lack of nurturance. Therefore, the strategic directive is a behavioral contract (clear rules and consequences to allow the parent or caregiver to reestablish lost authority by realigning hierarch), not a wound playbook to heal direct trauma.

And the trauma seeds of unhealed wounds, mental or physical impairment, and unmet primal needs are defined as follows:

> Unhealed wounds and its associated unhealthy undercurrents reflect direct trauma from a traumatic event or interactional trauma. The other two seeds (mental or physical impairment and unmet primal needs) also produce trauma but in a different way and with different unhealthy undercurrents. As a result, all three seeds are collectively grouped as trauma seeds.

These definition distinctions are important for two reasons. First, the FST therapist should be mindful of the type of seed (stabilization or trauma) all the family members select in the next mini-step and especially of the rationale they give for their selection. This is invaluable information when the FST therapist has to decide in Step 4 the path of (a) stabilization first prior to direct trauma work or (b) direct trauma or wound work first. For example, if the parent or parents both select the misuse of power seed with convincing rationale (*"My child definitely controls the mood of our household"*), then this is compelling evidence for the FST therapist to lean toward stabilization first. However, if no one picks the misuse of power seed, evidence may be just as compelling to lean toward a recommendation of direct trauma work first. The X factor is when misuse of power issues are obviously present but outside of anyone's awareness. In this case, the FST therapist must take the absence of the misuse of power seed with a grain of salt.

Second, knowing the type of seed (stabilization vs. trauma), along with the definition of the seed, is helpful for the FST therapist. Multi-stressed families with a traumatized child are intense and challenging even on a good day. These families often present so much drama and static noise that one can get lost in the fog or chaos. Therefore, knowing the type of seed and the path implications (stabilization or trauma) will be a lighthouse or road map in the storm.

Undercurrents Now or Later

It is tempting for the FST therapist to start explaining in detail the undercurrents in this phase. At times, even family members ask and want more information about the undercurrents or root system as the seeds are being explained. However, timing is everything. One does not want to overload a family with too much information too fast. Undercurrents are the main theme of Phase II of treatment, so that is the best time to discuss in depth the central DNA of FST treatment—the undercurrents.

STEP 3: THE TOP SEED AND SYMPTOM SELECTIONS

After completing the seed/tree diagram, the family and villagers are now ready to vote on their top two or three seed and symptom picks, with reasons for their selections. After the family's selections, the FST therapist will then present their seed and symptom picks with reasons for their selections. In sum, there are three procedures to successfully execute this step:

1. Use a table format to write everyone's seed and symptom selection.
2. Obtain the seed and symptom picks of the child, parents, and village first.
3. Present the FST therapist's seed and symptom picks.

Once Step 3 is completed, the therapist uses three internal rules of thumb to decide which path to recommend (stabilization or direct trauma work first; Step 4), and then will set the goals for therapy (Step 5).

Theory and Rationale

Seed and symptom picks by the child and family in some ways represent a monumental departure from traditional therapy. In traditional therapy, it is the therapist who provides the diagnosis to the client and determines the goals of therapy. However, in FST treatment, the clients are empowered to formulate their own diagnosis based on their seed and symptom selections.

This not only positions the family as the experts but also gives the FST therapist invaluable information to help make the path recommendations (Step 4) and finalize the goals of therapy (Step 5).

For example, prior to the family's seed and symptom picks, the FST therapist might think he or she knows what to recommend as both the path to take (stabilization or direct trauma work first) and goals for therapy. However, after listening to the family's seed and symptom picks, the FST therapist may change his or her own picks or refine them accordingly, and in either case, it is a true win/win collaboration and co-ownership of the diagnosis and goals of therapy.

#1 Use a Table Format to Write Family Seed and Symptom Selections

After the seeds are defined, the next step for the FST therapist to write down each family member's seed and symptom picks, using the table format illustrated in Table 5.2. Ideally, this template will already be prepared ahead of time on a flip chart page or in a Word document that is projected from the therapist's laptop.

TABLE 5.2 Template for Family Seed and Symptom Picks

Child's Seed & Symptom Picks	Parent's Seed & Symptom Picks	Villager's Seed & Symptom Picks
#1 Seed Pick_____ *Reasons:*	#1 Seed Pick_____ *Reasons:*	#1 Seed Pick_____ *Reasons:*
#2 Seed Pick_____ *Reasons:*	#2 Seed Pick_____ *Reasons:*	#2 Seed Pick_____ *Reasons:*
Top Two Problem Picks (Symptoms) • •	**Top Two Problem Picks (Symptoms)** • •	**Top Two Problem Picks (Symptoms)** • •

The following transition statement is used:

> Now that we have defined all the seeds, I will go around the room starting with _____ [name of child or adolescent] and ask each of you for your top two seed picks with your reasons for your seed picks and then for your top two problems listed on the stress chart that you want to work on first.

For sake of time, you will list your reasons for your seed picks but we will not go into detail. We will do that in our next session.

I will write your answers on the flip chart in our seed and symptom pick table. After you are finished, I will give you my seed and symptom picks with my reasons.

The seed and symptom pick table should be written on a separate flip chart page and hung next to the stress chart and the seed/tree diagram on the wall. This will help the FST therapist to visually illustrate to the family the interconnectedness of all three pieces of the puzzle (the stress chart, the seed/tree diagram, and the top two seed and symptom picks). Write the persons' names and their picks along with the reasons for their seed picks. Families are not asked to provide rationale for problem or symptom picks but only to list them. This is because of both time constraints and the fact that the rationale for symptom picks is covered in Phase II.

#2 Obtain the Seed and Symptom Picks of the Child, Parents, and Villagers First

As with other sections, the child or adolescent is asked to provide the seed and symptom picks first in order to prevent him or her from being influenced by other family members. Here is the transition statement used immediately after the introductory statement above:

[Name of child or adolescent] What were the top two toxic seeds that you picked? Tell me why you picked these seeds. And then what are the top two problems listed on the stress chart that you want to work on first? [Write answers on flip chart]

After the child has finished, the parents or older siblings give the picks, followed by key village members.

[Name of parent, older sibling. or key village member] What were the top two toxic seeds that you picked? Tell me why you picked these seeds. And then what are the top two problems listed on the stress chart that you want to work on first? [Write answers on flip chart]

Due to time constraints, if there is a large family or village (5 or more), one will not have the time to get everyone's picks. Look for common themes or the same answers that keep coming up over and over again and then stop. Always start with the immediate family first and then expand outward to the most influential villagers. It is also perfectly fine at this point in treatment for a family member to only have one pick (not two) and not have reasons for all their seed picks. It is recommended that the FST therapist seek clarification if a client gives a one-word answer by asking questions such as "*What does that look like?*", "*Can you give me one concrete example?*", or "*Can you tell me more?*" However, there is that fine line between clarification and in-depth exploration. Please keep to the former, not the latter.

Please note: The FST therapist should avoid long bunny trails and discussions on rationale surrounding seed picks. It is extremely tempting to explore in detail why the family picked a particular seed. This is *especially true* for the unhealed wound seed. Wounds by their very nature tend to be an electrifying topic for discussion. It is also usually the first time family members openly state their wounds or make a direct connection between their problems and wounds. Other family members may also be shocked or surprised to learn new information around seeds and the rationale provided for the seed pick. As a result, there is an overwhelming temptation to immediately want to know more details for both the family and therapist. This is why the transition statement is phrased as *"For sake of time, you will list your reasons for your seed picks but we will not go into detail. We will do that in our next session."* This statement is there to proactively set the parameters ahead of time.

Max's case example will illustrate how family members provide and vote on their own seed picks. Highlighted in the case example is the tension and anxiety that is released when family members talk openly about their trauma, often for the first time. As a result, the FST therapist had to be proficient in the stick and move technique (see Chapter 4) and have a highly directive style. Otherwise, emotions in Max's family would have quickly escalated out of control and the FST therapist would have lost control of the session. This is still the first or second session. Therefore, one does not want all the hard foundational work of the stress chart and seed/tree diagram to go up in smoke as the session loses focus and escalates out of control.

Case Example

Max was asked first to provide his top two seed picks with rationale. As soon as Max revealed his first seed pick of unhealed wounds, the tension rose as both his mom and his grandfather began to make heated accusations against Max's father.

Also, Max's mom became defensive when Max shared that part of his reason for picking the unhealed wound seed involved his mom "checking out," resulting in his foster care placement. The FST therapist could not passively sit back but had to immediately redirect using the stick and move technique. Otherwise, the session would have quickly escalated out of control. Max's top two seed and symptom picks are seen in Table 5.3.

TABLE 5.3 Max's (Child's) Seed and Symptom Picks
Max's Seed & Symptom Picks
#1 Seed Pick **Unhealed Wounds**
Reasons: Because of Mom not being around and her being so sad and upset all the time . . . she finally "checked out," and because of that I got put into foster care; to make matters worse, kids tease me at school; Dad also has "checked out" and I never get to see him
#2 Seed Pick **Misuse of Power**
Reasons: I agree with your story about the wolves. I hate to say it but I am the pack leader of our house because Mom has "checked out." I have to take care of my little sister. And yes, I don't treat my mom very well
Top Two Problem Picks (Symptoms) • Being bullied at school • Disrespect

Later in treatment, Max admitted that had it not been for the safety stressors, he would not have been able to reveal the "bullying." But once it was out, he was relieved to be able to put it on his list as his #1 problem pick. He also liked the misuse of power definition because of the use of wolf packs and because it allowed him an on-ramp to share his frustration over having to be a parent for his younger sister. He wanted Mom to take charge and be a mom so he could go back to being a kid again.

When other family and village members were asked about their seed and symptom picks, common themes emerged, as is the case for most family systems. The theme that cut across everyone's picks was unhealed wounds (see Table 5.4).

(continued)

Case Example (*continued*)

The grandmother had the same answer as her daughter, so her answers were not written on the flip chart. The caseworker's picks were of particular interest. She made the direct connection between the reason for removal (neglect) and the mom's depression. That insight was helpful to the FST therapist before he had to make his selection. It was also helpful that most of the adults saw Max getting bullied as an immediate safety issue that must be addressed. It makes the FST therapist's job easier when his recommendations already match the family's picks. Compliance is almost guaranteed when this one-to-one match happens.

TABLE 5.4 Parents' and Villagers' Seed and Symptom Picks

Mom's Seed & Symptom Picks	Dad's Seed & Symptom Picks	Caseworker's Seed & Symptom Picks
#1 Seed Pick **Unhealed Wounds**	#1 Seed Pick **Unhealed Wounds**	#1 Seed Pick **Mental and Physical Impairment**
Reasons: My babies are in foster care because of me. And I have been "checked out" emotionally for a long time	Reasons: My son and daughter need me and I have not been around	Reasons: Mom was overwhelmed with her depression and she shut down
#2 Seed Pick Misuse of Power	#2 Seed Pick **Unmet Primal Needs**	#2 Seed Pick **Unhealed Wounds**
Reasons: Max said it best. Because of me "checking out," he had to be the parent for everyone, including me	Reasons: Max and Jamie need those hugs you talked about and I have not been there to give them to the kids	Reasons: Max and Jamie both have been wounded by their removal from the home and Mom's depression along with Dad being out of the picture
Top Two Problem Picks (Symptoms) • Max getting bullied • Can't decide between Max's disrespect and my depression	**Top Two Problem Picks (Symptoms)** • Disrespect to his mom • My lack of connection to the kids (lack of nurturance)	**Top Two Problem Picks (Symptoms)** • Mom's depression • Max's aggression and getting bullied

It is of note that no one mentioned the grandfather's heart condition. The only time it was mentioned was during the circular questioning at the beginning of the session around the stress chart. This is a potential family secret and one the family is not ready to explore this early in treatment. The FST therapist must decide whether the timing is right to push the issue, leave it alone, or somewhere in between. As illustrated in the therapist's seed picks, the answer was somewhere in between. He mentions "grandfather's health issues" among the reasons for his unhealed wound seed pick and would return to it later after more therapeutic trust and rapport was built.

#3 FST Therapist's Seed and Symptom Picks

After the family's seed and symptom picks, it is time for the FST therapist to make his selections with supporting rationale. This is the transition statement used:

> Thank you for your seed and problem list. I will now give you my picks with my reasons why. I will then take these picks and convert them into what I call "the goals of therapy" or what we want to accomplish together to help your child or teenager and heal their wounds, as well as the rest of the family's wounds at the same time. Let's begin with my top two seed picks, and why I chose them.

Case Example:

After getting everyone's top seed and symptom picks, the FST therapist wrote his top two seed and symptom picks, with the rationale, beneath everyone's else's picks (see Table 5.5).

TABLE 5.5 FST Therapist's Seed and Symptom Picks

FST Therapist's Seed & Symptom Picks

#1 Seed Pick **Mental and Physical Impairment**

Reasons: As soon as Mom's depression hit, she shut down. After she shut down, Max felt as though he needed to take on the parent role and take care of his little sister, Jamie.

#2 Seed Pick **Unhealed Wounds**

Reasons: Everyone picked this seed and I see multiple wounds in this family. Max and his sister not seeing their dad, mom's depression and Max's worry about mom and subsequent feeling like he had to step up and take on the parental role and take care of Jamie, and being placed in foster care. Dad's wound of his "lost" kids and Mom's wounds from the divorce and feeling a lack of support. And Max not knowing how to deal with his grandfather's health issues.

#3 Seed Pick **Misuse of Power**

Reasons: Because of the wounds and Max stepping into the parental role, it is normal for a child to eventually overtake the authority and take charge of the household. Max did not do this in a mean spirited way, he just adapted to the situation. Over time, though, the lack of limits led to an imbalance of power.

Top Two Problem Picks (Symptoms) **

(1)   Safety issue to stop the bullying in school

(2)   Limit setting around any disrespect and to ensure no aggression with pets or sister

Possible Bonus: Meet with Mom and Dad to set up special outings with Dad with clear parameters to rebuild trust and in accordance with the CPS plan

**Continue with Max's case example in this chapter for underlying rationale for the selections above

---

CPS, Child Protective Services.

Connecting the Dots to Anchor FST Therapist's Seed and Symptom Picks

In a parallel process to the "closing remarks" strategy within the FST motivational phone call (see Chapter 4), the FST therapist can use a similar closing remarks strategy. As the therapist presents his seed and symptom picks, he should connect his picks and rationale directly to earlier statements made by the family, reminding them of what they said, pointing to something written on the symptom stress chart, or pointing to their own picks and rationale. This process serves to both strengthen the FST therapist's selections and allows family members to say to themselves, "*Our therapist really heard us.*" And it greatly reinforces the idea that everything in FST treatment builds on itself (from the stress chart to the seed/tree diagram, to the seed picks, to the undercurrent worksheet and feedback loops in Phase II, etc.). For example, in the FST therapist's pick of unhealed wounds in Table 5.5, the therapist could say something like

> I picked the seed of unhealed wounds for two reasons. First, everyone in your family picked it and did a fantastic job supporting this pick. I look at your stress chart [point to it] and I see what Max said about his worry for you, Mom, and the stress from going to foster care. And I see, Dad, your whopping 80% stress reduction if you could reconnect with both kids.

As with the closing remarks during the motivational interviewing (MI) phone call, the FST therapist is literally connecting the dots from what the family said earlier in the session and reinstating it to support therapist seed and symptom picks. Family members love this reinstatement process. It is recommended that the therapist carry a laser pointer with him or her. When the giant flip charts are hung side by side (stress chart, next to the seed tree diagram, next to the family seed and symptom picks), the therapist, in his closing remarks, can literally use the laser pointer to connect the dots.

Case Example

The following text contains a brief snippet of the process of making reinstatement closing remarks. In Max's family, as the therapist unveiled his seed picks, he used a laser pointer to back up his picks by pointing out what the family or villagers said earlier in the session. The therapist stood up in the room and, like a trial lawyer, had high energy and excitement as he delivered his seed and symptom picks. The family loved the emotion and enthusiasm.

> Now, that you see my seed and symptom pick answers on the board, let me use this laser pointer in my pocket to connect the dots from your stress chart and the seed/ tree diagram to your picks and my picks. Let's start with my pick of the mental and physical impairment seed pick first.
>
> As you can see, the only other person who picked this seed was the case manager, Phyllis.
>
> I am not taking sides but her pick makes sense based on the evidence.
>
> As you can see from your stress chart, grandma, mom, and Phyllis all zeroed in on mom feeling overwhelmed with a lack of support, and feeling depressed [point to each of these stressors with the laser pointer for dramatic effect].

(continued)

Case Example (*continued*)

And both mom and grandma stated that if these issues were addressed and solved it would be a whopping 80% stress reduction for you, Mom. And Max, you said if you feel more hopeful, you will naturally feel less angry. And the bonus of this happening is a stated 80% reduction noted by your caseworker if your mom's feelings of being overwhelmed with a lack of support could be fixed. Which I think would make your caseworker happy and increase reunification for mom, Max and Jamie." [Caseworker nodded yes to this inference.]

But maybe best of all, decreasing this mental and impairment seed will directly reduce your son's stress level. He will not worry about you so much, and without worry, he can use that energy to become more of a kid again. And his mom will now have the support and hope to parent Jamie, and even the strength to set limits again. And that brings me to the side benefit of also tackling the misuse of power seed. Mom's support will be like chemotherapy hitting the misuse of power seed.

The "connect the dots" closing remarks process got everyone's attention. Max looked visibly relieved and the caseworker loved how we could make her job easier. Using the FST model, the rationale for the therapist's picks continued as each pick was clearly connected back to both the stress chart and seed/tree diagram.

A Vote of "Yes" or "No"

After the FST therapist's picks and rationale are presented, the family is asked to vote "yes" or "no" using this transition statement:

Before we move on, I just wanted to pause and go around the room to ask each of you if you agree with my seed and problem picks with a simple 'yes' or 'no.' If you disagree, no problem, it will not hurt my feelings. But if you disagree, please tell me and tell me why. I want to find out why because I don't want to set the goals until we are on the same page. Does that make sense?

The FST therapist must have this litmus test before going forward to know if there will be a battle for structure or not. And the therapist does not want to recommend a path to take (stabilization or direct trauma work) or goals for therapy unless key family members are onboard. Otherwise, the family and therapist are working at cross-purposes.

The must-have and yes votes are needed from the parents or caregivers, caseworkers, or probation officers. These are the individuals who have the power to return the child or adolescent back to further treatment. The "nice-to-haves" come from the child, adolescent, and siblings. If a "no" vote comes from one of these nice-to-have individuals, it may be because they intuitively know that the family might be changed in a way that might limit their current power and authority. Another reason might be that the child or adolescent does not yet trust the therapist. Nevertheless, if the parents like the treatment, they will return, and the child's "no" can change into a "yes" later as he or she sees the positive changes in the family.

What to Do If a Battle for Structure Ensues?

With "no" votes, the FST therapist may still be faced with what is termed a battle for structure (c.f., Carl Whitaker & Keith, 1981). As the battle for structure outlined in Chapter 3 suggests, if the

FST therapist agrees with the majority of the family's seed and symptom picks, there is no battle for structure. The FST therapist and family are literally on the same page because their collective seed and symptom picks match.

However, the battle often begins if the therapist makes selections that the family did not select or if he or she appears to take sides with one person over another because their picks happen to match. In either case, to prevent or mitigate this risk, the therapist has two choices: (a) Use persuasive reframing to convince the dissenting family member, or (b) convince the dissenting family member to perform a personal experiment by going with your seed picks for a set period of time to see if positive changes occur. Both choices adhere to the premise that clients typically change through one of two methods: (a) through new insights or getting clients to "think their way into a new way of acting," or (b) getting clients to perform personal experiments or to "act their way into a new way of thinking."

Therefore, if there are disagreements on either seed or symptom picks, the FST therapist must be poised to use either persuasion or recommend personal experiments. Whenever possible, the first recommended tactic is to use persuasion. If the therapist can persuade family members to change their mind or see the same situation differently, they are brought on board immediately. However, if one has to experiment, the client is in a "wait and see" mode to see if the experiment worked or not.

The best persuasion tactics are usually in the form of good reframes. For example, a father may not list unhealed wounds or unmet primal need seeds because he is thoroughly convinced that the child's true motivation for disrespect is to be manipulative and mean-spirited. In sharp contrast, evidence from the session may indicate just the opposite. The FST therapist may see evidence that the adolescent's symptom of disrespect is due to both a dearth of parent–child nurturance and unhealed wounds from a bitter divorce. Therefore, in response, the therapist might use the following reframe:

> Dad, I can see from our picks that we agree on the stressor or problem pick of disrespect but we disagree on the seed picks that are causing your son's problem. You picked misuse of power and I picked the seeds of unhealed wounds and unmet primal needs. It is possible that you might be right; the jury is still out. But, let me share the reason for my picks. When kids are defiant, what we see on the surface as disrespect can sometimes be driven by hurt on the inside.
>
> When my parents divorced, for example, I was angry at the world. At first, my dad thought I was just manipulative, but later he saw that my disrespect was because I was wounded from the divorce and needed one-on-one time with him to help heal this wound. After that, my disrespect all but disappeared. So, I picked the wound seed because I suspect your son is not bad, but really sad.

In the example above, the sad reframe turned the father around in his thinking and gave him new insight from a different perspective. If however, the father still refused, the therapist could then quickly go to plan B with the experimentation track. Using this example, the dialogue statement might look something like the following:

> I can see by your face and your words that you still disagree. I appreciate your candor and honesty. Therefore, let me propose the following. Can we experiment with my theory or seed picks for the next 30 days? This means that in the next couple of sessions, we will co-create a wound playbook. Your son will still be accountable for any disrespect in the future, but we will approach the solutions from healing wounds first and harsher consequences or rules second. If after 30 days, we don't see measurable improvements, we can switch gears toward your seeds. We have little to lose with this experiment. It is only 30 days out of a 365-day year. So will you take a leap of faith here and try this proposed experiment?

After the FST therapist's seed and symptom picks, it is time to start to close the session with recommended goals for therapy. However, within these goals is the decision to direct the family toward either (a) stabilization first using contracts or hybrids or (b) direct trauma or wound work first using wound playbooks. The FST therapist cannot say to the family, *"Thanks for your seed picks. I now need to take a week to look at the information before I give you my recommendations and we set the goals for treatment."* The family does not want to wait. They just provided their therapist with their top reasons for their child's problems. This was hard work and the family feels vulnerable. The last thing the family wants to do is wait another week for clear next action steps. Therefore, the FST therapist must assimilate all family data received up to this point very quickly. The decision of what direction to take must occur internally and in real time as the goals for therapy are being laid out.

Three Rules of Thumb to Help Decide Stabilization or Wounds First

As stated in Table 3.3, there are three rules of thumb to make this decision more clear. The three rules are replicated from Chapter 3 in the following text but contain additional information and clarification. In addition, the timing of when to initiate PLL-FSS (family systems stabilization) versus when to initiate PLL-FST (family systems trauma) also include a systems of care framework. For example, an agency or therapist using the FST model must decide the benefits of a PLL system of care addition that includes group therapy, fidelity supervision, and outcome data to measure impact on these rules of thumb. For more information on how this intricate dance works, please visit the PLL Systems of Care model at www.gopll.com.

Rule of Thumb #1: Chronicity, Bitterness, and Burnout Levels

☐   (1) Are the child's behaviors extreme and happen almost everyday or at least once a week? (i.e., aggression, extreme disrespect, running away, alcohol or drug use, self-harm, suicidal ideation, refusal to attend school, etc.) or safety issues present such as ongoing sexual abuse, domestic violence, parent drug use, homelessness

☐   (2) Are the parents or caregivers extremely burnt out and overwhelmed?

☐   (3) Are the parents or caregivers extremely angry, bitter, or resentful toward child?

If the answer is "yes" to all three questions, the FST therapist will choose stabilization prior to direct wound work first. The reason parents often require respite in the form of stabilization first is to reduce the disorganization and chaos in the family. For example, extreme disrespect between parent and child with constant fighting causes interactional trauma. Unless this is stopped through behavioral contracting and limit setting first, the family will not be able to directly tackle the unhealed wounds. A helpful metaphor is to stop the bleeding first before one can see and remove the shrapnel.

Recommendation: stabilization first

Rule of Thumb #2: Timing or Onset of the Child's Problem Symptoms

☐   Were the problem behaviors with the child or adolescent present before the wounds first emerged and simply got worse or exacerbated after the trauma OR did they only emerge after the trauma took place?

If the former, stabilization is needed first through a behavioral contract. This is because the likelihood is high that the hierarchical structure before and after the traumatic event is still the same: The child is in charge of the household instead of the parent or caregiver. This is also referred to in the FST model as the seed of misuse of power. If the family in question has an upside-down hierarchy, the FST therapist must first restructure the hierarchy using behavioral contracts to have any chance for wound work success. However, if the child's problem symptoms only occurred after the traumatic event, then direct wound work is the best approach.

Recommendation: stabilization first if the former; direct trauma first if the latter.

Rule of Thumb #3: Examine the Trauma Seeds (Wounds, Impairment, and Primal)

☐ Were the child's or adolescent's problem symptoms reported by family members and confirmed by the FST therapist as one of the three trauma seeds (unhealed wounds, mental or physical impairment, or unmet primal needs) and not misuse of power seed?

As outlined in Chapter 2, the unhealed wound seed and its associated unhealthy undercurrents reflect a traumatized child and/or family based on a traumatic event(s) and/or interactional trauma. The other two seeds (mental or physical impairment and unmet primal needs) also produce trauma but in a different way and often with different undercurrents. As a result, all three seeds (i.e., unhealed wounds, mental or physical impairment, and unmet primal needs) are collectively grouped as trauma seeds. Therefore, direct wound work using wound playbooks is needed with any of these three trauma seeds and *not* a behavioral contract to realign hierarchy.

Recommendation: direct trauma or wound work first

In summary, based on these rules of thumb and the information collected during Phase I, the FST therapist will set the goals of therapy (Step 5). These initial goals of therapy will involve either the recommended track of behavioral stabilization first with any safety planning as needed or direct trauma wound work with any safety planning as needed. As stated in Chapter 3, safety planning and assessment will be ongoing, regardless of whether the track selected is direct wound work or behavioral stabilization.

In Chapter 3, there are multiple examples of the different types of contracts (behavioral, hybrid, two track) or playbooks (wound or two track) directly associated with stabilization or direct wound work. Therefore, these examples will not be replicated here. Once the goals of therapy are communicated to the family with the recommended path, the type of contract or playbook can be mentioned but will not be shown and explained in detail until Phase II. As the flowchart illustrates, the rest of this book focuses on direct wound work interventions. If prior stabilization work is recommended at the end of this phase (Phase I), readers are referred to Dr. Sells' first two books (c.f., Sells, 2002, 2004) for stabilization tools.

Case Example

After the FST therapist's seed and symptom picks, he had a tough decision to make regarding which path to take in Max's family. On one hand, the misuse of power seed path that would lead to a stabilization track was interesting for two reasons.

First, the mom, and, ironically, Max are the only ones who picked this seed. Yet, their rationale adds up. And it appears that the first rule of thumb also applied:

(continued)

Case Example (*continued*)

Rule of thumb #1: The information in both the stress chart and the seed and symptom picks indicated a "yes" answer to two out of the three questions in the first rule of thumb:

☑ YES—(1) Are Max's behaviors extreme and happening almost every day or at least once a week? (disrespect and aggression toward dog and sister)
☑ YES—(2) Is Max's mom extremely burned-out and overwhelmed?
☑ NO—(3) Is Mom or Dad extremely angry, bitter, or resentful toward Max or Jamie?

Because Max and Jamie are in foster care, however, both circumstances indicated by the affirmative "yes" might be on hold at the present time. At the foster care home, Janice, the foster mom, is the pack leader, not Max. And Max is not exhibiting extreme misbehaviors at the foster care home. However, Max and Jamie have only been with Janice a short time and both are likely in the "honeymoon period."

For the second rule of thumb, the information in both the stress chart and the seed and symptom picks indicated a clear "yes" answer to the first question that would indicate stabilization as well:

☑ YES—(1) Were the problem behaviors with the child or adolescent present before the wounds occurred and simply get worse after the traumatic event?
☑ NO—*Or* (2) did they only emerge after the trauma took place?

Decision Time

Based on the rule of thumb information and the fact that at least two family members picked misuse of power, the FST therapist would recommend a two-track plan of (1) safety planning for the bullying and (2) a hybrid contract for limit setting along with emotional warm-ups. This recommendation lines up with two of the therapist's seed picks of misuse of power and unhealed wounds as well as the symptom picks of bullying and limit setting. The seed pick of mental and physical impairment will be addressed both directly by recommending that mom be evaluated for the possibility of medication to treat her depression and indirectly as Mom is helped to take back her rightful parenting role with support.

Here is the rationale:

Stabilization

- *Why limit setting with Max when he is with foster mom and currently not symptomatic?* Answer: Mom needs her confidence back as a parent, which, in turn, will positively impact her depression. If some of the future sessions could include Mom, Janice (foster mom), Max, and Jamie, there can be instant synergy.

- Janice would use a behavioral contract to set clear rules around disrespect, chores, and no aggression that included a hybrid of emotional warm-ups. In turn, Mom could be the co-parent and help with ideas and role-plays, and back up Janice as another adult to show respect. As a result, the normal adversarial role between foster parent and biological parent would be replaced by cooperation and mutual respect. Max and Jamie would then not experience divided loyalties or get caught in the middle of two parent systems.

- Any contracts or tools Mom learned with Janice would be transferable or generalizable to Mom's household when reunification occurred. Afterward, if desired, Mom may still want Janice to be in the children's lives in more of a surrogate aunt-type role.

Safety Planning

- *Why was bullying addressed immediately?* While the other safety issues (aggression and cruelty to animals) were not currently happening, bullying was active.
- As a result, the FST therapist would want to contact the school with everyone's permission to set up and facilitate an "anti-bullying" plan. The meeting will include the relevant school personnel, the caseworker, Mom and the foster parent, and, possibly, Dad.
- The safety plan would be a two-track plan side-by-side with the hybrid contract.

Other Issues to Address

- Mom and the grandmother will see Mom's doctor (or specialist set up by the caseworker) to be evaluated for the possible need for medication to treat Mom's depression.
- Mom, the FST therapist, and Dad will meet together to explore parameters and baby steps toward Max and Dad reconnecting.

The FST therapist was now ready to move to Step 5 and set the goals of therapy.

Do Not Get Overwhelmed

Because of the intricacies of the case study in the preceding text, the reader may feel, "I could never think that quickly on my feet and formulate such a detailed plan of action." Please remember that for the book, one has to naturally include many details so theory and practice can become clearer. However, in real life, one may have broader brush strokes but still stay within the same general parameters. In addition, the FST model was developed so each concept builds on the other; therefore, as you move through the model, the information has slowly percolated to provide a clearer road map. Finally, practice makes perfect. In the book *Outliers: The Story of Success,* author Malcolm Gladwell (2008) says that it takes roughly 10,000 hours of practice to achieve mastery in a field. While the number may not be nearly that high, the point is that one will go faster and be more efficient the more these steps are done with more families.

In addition, increased therapist competence is a major reason why we developed the PLL System of Care with its emphasis on videotape supervision. Supervision often consists of the therapist verbally describing a case to a supervisor and where they are stuck. However, the supervisor cannot see what happened because the session was conducted behind closed doors. And the therapist may be unaware of the tactical mistakes that they are making. No supervisor actually sees the therapy session. To address this common problem, PLL-FST therapists are required to send videotapes of their work of all phases of the FST model.

Our PLL supervisors will then rate each video using an FST-VSM (Video Supervision Manual) on how closely the therapist followed the FST Model as well as their delivery. We use WebEx technology to view the edited sessions together with the therapist to highlight therapist progress and areas to strengthen. This entire videotaped supervision is labor intensive for our PLL supervisors but dramatically shortens the learning curve on achieving competence with the FST Model as well as better quality assurance. Practice makes perfect now becomes working smarter, not harder. For YouTube video clips of this process please go to www.gopll.com.

STEP 5: SETTING THE GOALS OF THERAPY

Step 5 is one of the most important steps in the entire FST treatment model. If there is open disagreement over the goals of therapy between the FST therapist and the parents or caregiver, treatment ends here before it even begins. The FST therapist must also navigate the choppy waters of assuming the role of system irritants and the normal paradox of the family communicating that they want to change but staying the same. A recommended classic family therapy book that epitomizes this challenge at this critical juncture in treatment is entitled *Fishing for Barracuda: Pragmatics of Brief Systemic Theory* by Joel Bergman (1985, p. 58). In this book, he writes:

> The first prescription [goal of therapy] given to a resistant family often contains both capturing qualities and initial strategic moves towards changing the symptom in the system. Without the capturing qualities, which reduce resistance to treatment and enable the therapist to eventually make a contract with the family to begin family therapy, there is a poor chance that they will remain in treatment long enough for change to take place.

When applying this eloquent insight by Bergman into the FST model, the capturing qualities occur when the FST therapist literally connects the dots using the family's own stress chart, seed/tree diagram, and their seed and symptom picks. The family is captured when their own ideas are interconnected with the therapist's goals. As stated earlier, in traditional treatment, the therapist asks probing diagnostic questions and comes up with a formal diagnosis. Using the FST model, however, the family is an active collaborator in the solution.

Goals of Therapy Are Written Down

After the family votes "yes" or "no" on the therapist's picks, the next step is to translate these picks into a concrete and succinct list of the goals for therapy. The following transition statement is used:

> Thank you for the vote of confidence on my seed and problem picks. I will now translate these into our goals for our work together. Here are our next action steps to solve the problems you told me on your stress chart that you want to heal with _____ [child's or adolescent's name]. I am simply going to write them out here for all to see. [Write them out.]

People do well with clear goals that are written rather than verbally stated. As the following example illustrates, the goals should not be "clinical," but written in easy-to-understand everyday language. For example, in Max's case, the following goals for therapy were clearly written out on the giant flip chart:

> **Goal #1: Immediately put an end to Max's bullying using what is called a safety playbook. With the caseworker's consent, I would like to contact the school on Max's behalf to get information on the school's policy and procedures around bullying prior to our next meeting.**
> **At our next meeting_____[date and time], I will have a first draft of an anti-bullying plan for us to tweak or modify as needed. Then after we are satisfied with the plan we can take it and meet with school officials.**

> *"Max, I can see the look of fear on your face. I will make sure to let the school know that until we all meet together, under no circumstances do we want the boys to know because it could put you in more danger. We want the boys and their parents to know only after we have a plan in place first."*

> Goal #2: Concrete tools to practice limit setting to stop future acts of disrespect or of hurting animals or Max's sister. I would like to meet with Mom and the foster mom in our next session to put a plan together. And before we finalize this plan, we will also get input from Max and his sister. Foster mom will take the lead with Mom's invaluable input and ideas.

Who should be in attendance for the next session? Everyone here today, the must-haves include Mom and Max and foster mom.

As illustrated in the example in the preceding text, the goals clearly lay out next steps in straightforward terms. And they acknowledge the reality of the present-day chain of command (CPS caseworker first, foster mom second, and Mom third). If body language from key participants indicates stress or disagreement with these goals (CPS caseworker, foster mom), others in the room are excused until the therapist has a sidebar to determine barriers to overcome. In this case, the paradigm of foster parent and biological parent working closely together is likely so new to the caseworker that she might need to process it further in a sidebar that also includes her supervisor. In addition, "Who should be in attendance for the next session?" should be openly discussed. Since the next session involves safety planning, self-regulation strategies, nutritional planning, and feedback loops, it is another session whereby the same group in Phase I should attend, as well as any key influential person who was missing. After Phase II, it is more strategic who the FST therapist invites, but Phases I and II should include the bigger village if possible.

It is important to note that it is not mandatory or even necessary to openly reveal the path (stabilization vs. trauma or wound work first) the FST therapist decides to take when goals are revealed. The path is more of an internal decision. There also should be no battle for structure at this point in the therapy process. This is because the goals are simply a direct reflection of the therapist's seed and symptom picks earlier that were voted on. If there was disagreement or a battle for structure, it should have occurred by this time.

Finally, it is a huge bonus at this point in the session to take copies of the flowchart (Figure 3.1) and tell the family "You are here" in Phase I and that in the next session we will move to Phase II to start to execute or implement these goals. The flowchart tends to give clients that big picture view and they can see progress.

The "Who?" Is Addressed Before the "What?" Question

Part of the goal-setting step is to answer the question "Who should be in attendance?" for the next FST session and beyond. After the goals are decided upon and written down, the therapist can make the following transition statement:

> *"Based on our goals and your stress chart, who do we need to come to the next meeting? [List them.] And secondly, based on what you saw today, who was not here that should be here? To make these questions super easy to answer let's take a few minutes to fill in the village handout together. As we do this, it will become clearer who should come."*

Table 5.6 can be prepared as a handout or prewritten on a flip chart page to be filled in together in the session. This handout provides an easy on-ramp to get the family to reveal (a) who the villagers are by first name to prevent the natural resistance of "I have no village," and (b) ask if that person is considered an important supporter for the child and/or family or not, and where that person lives. The location of the villager is important because depending on how significant that particular villager is, the therapist can invite that person into a session via speakerphone or through Skype if he or she lives too far away to attend a session in person.

TABLE 5.6 Village Handout		
Type of Villager	**Name**	**Supportive or Nonsupportive**
Spouse		
Boyfriend/girlfriend		
Sibling		
Grandmother		
Grandfather		
Aunt		
Uncle		
Cousin		
Best friend (for mom)		
Best friend (for dad)		
Best friend (for youth)		
Best friend (for significant other)		
Pastor		
Church members		
School workers		
Schoolteachers		
Coach		
Mentor		
Coworkers		
Neighbors		
Probation officer		
Caseworker		

In his book, *Good to Great: Why Some Companies Make the Leap... and Others Don't*, Jim Collins (2001) notes that when confronted with any problem, we should shift the decision from a "what" question ("What should we do?") to a "who" question ("Who would be the right person to take responsibility for this?"). Translated into treatment, this means that the therapist should spend time on the "who" decision. As Jim Collins (2001, p. 128) writes:

> Leaders of companies that go from good to great, start not with "where" but with "who." They start by getting the right people on the bus, the wrong people off the bus, and the right people in the right seats. And they stick with that discipline—first the people, then the direction—no matter how dire the circumstances.

The FST therapist, as the bus driver, must get the right people on the bus. Our research indicates that the FST therapist may never again have as much influence than at the conclusion of phase I, after dramatically presenting closing arguments to win the battle for structure on the seed and symptom picks and set the goals for therapy. The reason is simple. When dots are clearly connected and the family and therapist diagnose the problem together, motivation and excitement is at an all-time high. Therefore, it is recommended that as part of goal setting, strike while the iron is hot and use the simple village handout technique to get the right people on the bus and determine who should come to Phase II. If not, the FST treatment will be much less effective.

STEP 6: CONSOLIDATE GAINS USING ETHNOGRAPHIC INTERVIEWS

As stated in Chapter 3, in the Sells, Smith, and Moon (1996) study, we found that asking clients these five ethnographic interviewing questions at the end of every session was critical to overall therapeutic success:

- Overall, what was most helpful in today's session?
- Overall, what was least helpful in today's session?
- What did I do or say as your therapist that was most helpful?
- What did I do or say as your therapist that was least helpful?
- What would need to happen in future sessions to make them more productive or of value to you or your family?

In this study, when therapists were interviewed apart from their clients, they often had very different perceptions of how successful the therapy was. One therapist went so far as to say that a couple had successfully completed couples counseling. However, when the couple was interviewed, they told a completely different story. The wife stated that her pain and betrayal were never heard by the counselor and because of this, therapy was a failure.

These types of disconnected perceptions between therapist and client led this study to conclude that it is of vital importance for client feedback questions to be asked at the end of each session to ensure that both therapist and client are on the same page and moving in the same direction toward change. Otherwise, if clients perceive that their needs are not being met, therapy will derail quickly.

Brown, Dreis, and Nace (1999) found that if no improvement occurred by the third visit, it was likely that therapy was not going to improve from the client's perspective. The study also found that clients who got worse by the third visit were two times more likely to drop out of treatment than clients who reported making progress. Variables such as diagnosis, severity, family support, and type of therapy were "not . . . as important [in predicting eventual outcome] as knowing whether or not the treatment being provided [was] actually working" (Brown et al., 1999, p. 404). Other studies have documented significant improvements in both retention and outcome from treatment when therapists have access to formal, real-time feedback from clients regarding the process and outcome of therapy (Duncan & Miller, 2000; Duncan, Miller, & Sparks, 2004).

In response to this need, the Session Rating Scale (SRS; c.f., Miller, Duncan, Brown, Sorrell, & Chalk, 2006) was developed as a well-validated paper-and-pencil instrument to allow the therapist to receive real-time feedback from the clients regarding the process and outcome of therapy. The study using the SRS (Miller et al., 2006) included a large sample size of 6,424 clients who received telephonic counseling between April 1, 2002, and March 31, 2004. The study found that providing formal, ongoing feedback to therapists on how clients experienced their alliance or rapport with their therapist and progress in treatment resulted in significant improvements in both client retention and outcome.

Based on the results of the Miller et al. (2006) and Sells et al. (1996) studies, we recommend that the reader use either the five ethnographic questions in the Sells study or the SRS measure in the Miller study. If the reader decides to use the ethnographic questions, a word of caution. We found that prior to these questions being asked, the therapist had to make the client or family member feel safe with the following introductory statement:

Before we end our session today, I want to get your opinion about your experience during our meeting today. I want to ask you just a few simple questions, but before I ask these questions, I want to give a disclaimer. I want you to be as honest and candid as you want to be. I promise you that whatever you say, good or bad, you will not hurt my feelings. In fact, if there are areas to improve in or we are not going in a direction you want, that is good information because I then will have the opportunity to correct the problem and get us back on track as quickly as possible.

Without this disclaimer, we found that clients were afraid to give criticism for fear of hurting their therapist's feelings. However, after the disclaimer, clients felt safe and were willing to give honest feedback.

REFERENCES

Avnet, J. (Producer)., & Avnet, J. (Director). (1994). *The war* [Motion Picture]. United States: Island World.

Bergman, J. S. (1985). *Fishing for barracuda: Pragmatics of brief systemic therapy*. New York, NY: W. W. Norton.

Brown, J., Dreis, S., & Nace, D. K. (1999). What really makes a difference in psychotherapy outcome? Why does managed care want to know? In M. A. Hubble, B. L. Duncan, & S. D. Miller (Eds.), *The heart and soul of change: What works in therapy* (pp. 389–406). Washington, DC: American Psychological Association.

Collins, J. (2001). *Good to great: Why some companies make the leap...and others don't*. New York, NY: Random House.

Duncan, B. L., & Miller, S. D. (2000). The client's theory of change: Consulting the client in the integrative process. *Journal of Psychotherapy Integration, 10*, 169–187. doi:10.1023/A:1009448200244

Duncan, B. L., Miller, S. D., & Sparks, J. A. (2004). *The heroic client: A revolutionary way to improve effectiveness through client-directed, outcome-informed therapy*. San Francisco, CA: Jossey-Bass.

Fleuridas, C., Nelson, T. S., & Rosenthal, D. M. (1986). The evolution of circular questions: Training family therapists. *Journal of Marital and Family Therapy*, *12*, 113–127. doi:10.1111/j.1752-0606.1986.tb01629.x

Gehart, D. R. (2013). *Mastering competencies in family therapy: A practical approach to theory and clinical case documentation*. Independence, KY: Cengage.

Gladwell, M. (2008). *Outliers*. New York, NY: Little, Brown.

Haley, J. (1991). *Problem-solving therapy*. San Francisco, CA: Jossey-Bass.

Malinen, T. (2001). From thinktank to new therapy: The process of solution-focused theory and practice development. Retrieved from http://www.tathata.fi/artik_eng/thinktank.htm

Miller, S. D., Duncan, B. L., Brown, J., Sorrell, R., & Chalk, M. B. (2006). Using formal client feedback to improve retention and outcome: Making ongoing, real-time assessment feasible. *Journal of Brief Therapy*, *5*, 5–22.

Rosen, S. (1982). *My voice will go with you: The teaching tales of Milton H. Erickson*. New York, NY: W. W. Norton.

Sells, S. P. (2002). *Parenting your out-of-control teenager*. New York, NY: St. Martin's Press.

Sells, S. P. (2004). *Treating the tough adolescent: A family-based, step-by-step guide*. New York, NY: Guilford Press.

Sells, S. P., Smith, T. E., & Moon, S. (1996). An ethnographic study of client and therapist perceptions of therapy effectiveness in a university-based training clinic. *Journal of Marital and Family Therapy*, *22*, 321–342. doi:10.1111/j.1752-0606.1996.tb00209.x

Whitaker, C. A., & Keith, D. V. (1981). Symbolic-experiential family therapy. In A. S. Gurman & D. P. Kniskern (Eds.), *Handbook of family therapy* (pp. 187–224). New York, NY: Brunner/Mazel.

Pre-Session Preparation For Phase II

Step 1: Select Top Two or Three Undercurrents Causing Toxic Seed and Problem Symptoms

Step 2: Select Sample Strategic Directives and Playbooks

Step 3: Draw "Before" and "After" Feedback Loops

Step 4: Create Customized Homework Lead Sheet

Step 5: Ensure Key Villagers Will Be Present

As the family systems trauma (FST) diagram in Chapter 3 illustrates, pre-session preparation for Phase II takes place after Phase I. The exception is if stabilization is needed first. However, this chapter and the rest of the book focus on direct unhealed wound or trauma interventions. As a reminder, if prior stabilization work is needed, readers are referred to Dr. Sells' first two books (c.f., Sells, 2002, 2004) for the tools needed or the evidence-based model known as Parenting With Love and Limits (PLL; www.gopll.com). This chapter outlines the pre-session preparation steps needed prior to Phase II, the next face-to-face session with the family.

Five mini-steps accomplish the goals of this pre-session preparation. These steps are as follows:

1. Select the top two or three unhealthy undercurrents that are directly responsible for causing the toxic seed and problem symptoms identified by the family and FST therapist in Phase I.
2. Choose one set of undercurrents and one problem symptom to highlight and sketch these in what are called before and after feedback loops that are presented in Phase II.
3. Closely examine sample techniques and playbook examples in Chapter 8 and custom-build a sample playbook to match the "after" feedback loop sketch.
4. Create a customized homework lead sheet handout to give to the family in Phase II
5. Call the village members personally to remind or motivate them to attend.

STEP 1: SELECT TOP TWO OR THREE UNDERCURRENTS CAUSING TOXIC SEEDS AND PROBLEM SYMPTOMS

The first step in Phase II pre-session preparation is to decide which two or three undercurrents fit the FST therapist's seed and symptom picks at the end of Phase I. It is the therapist's picks that are selected and not the family's picks because the therapist's selections were the ones converted into the goals of therapy.

The following question is used to help the FST therapist select the correct undercurrents that match with the particular seed and symptom picks:

> What are the top two or three unhealthy undercurrents within the unhealed wound seed and/or associated seeds (mental or physical impairment, unmet primal needs) that are *directly responsible for causing* the child or adolescent's problem symptoms that were identified at the end of Phase I for this particular family?

For example, if one of the FST therapist's seed and symptom picks at the end of Phase I was unhealed wounds with the symptom of self-harm, then the therapist would use an "undercurrent worksheet" (see Table 6.1) to determine the most likely unhealthy undercurrents that are responsible for causing this problem. In one family, the key undercurrent might be "abandonment" and in another, "unforgiveness." It will all come down to context. In the family with abandonment, it might be obvious from both the stress chart and their seed and symptom picks, that it was the abandonment of the father that triggered the self-harm. While in another family with the same seed and symptom, the evidence would strongly suggest deep and long-standing resentment. In summary, the unhealthy undercurrents cannot be selected in a vacuum but rather within the body of evidence that the family presents throughout Phase I.

The key piece of the equation is the problem symptom. The problem symptom provides the best road map to the undercurrent selections. The example in Box 6.1 illustrates that 15-year-old Judith's symptom of "anxiety and panic attacks" were caused by unhealthy undercurrents that cross over both of the top two toxic seeds selected. The evidence pointed to flashbacks of previous sexual abuse from her grandfather from an unhealed wound seed combined with a lack of attachment and unmet primal need from Judith's mother.

BOX 6.1 Symptom: Road Map to the Undercurrent

Judith's Problem Symptom in Question	Top 2 or 3 Unhealthy Undercurrents Directly Causing This Symptom	Healthy Undercurrent Counterparts
Self-harm (cutting)	☐ Physical or mental abuse (from unhealed wound seed)	☑ Support and forgiveness
	☐ Lack of attachment (from unmet primal needs seed)	☑ Reestablish attachment bonds with single parent mom

In Judith's example, even though the unhealthy undercurrents are the drivers that cause and maintain the child's symptom, in this case, anxiety and panic attacks, it is the symptom (outer layer) that provides the road map to the undercurrent. Therefore, it is recommended that the FST therapist closely examine the problem symptom first and then examine all the contextual evidence from the stress chart and seed/tree diagram from Phase I.

There are three procedural steps to help the FST therapist choose the best set of undercurrents for the particular seed and symptom picks in question.

1. Synchronize the FST therapist's seed and symptom picks with the undercurrent worksheet.
2. Match the problem symptoms with the top two undercurrents.
3. Decide which symptom, seed picks, and undercurrents to highlight in the feedback loops.

Synchronize the FST Therapist's Seed and Symptom Picks With the Undercurrent Worksheet

The first step is for the FST therapist to closely examine his or her seed and symptom picks from Phase I (see Alex's case example) and then look at the undercurrent worksheet (Table 6.1) to pinpoint the top two or three undercurrents within the FST therapist's seed picks that are most likely the cause of the problem symptom in question.

TABLE 6.1 Template for Deciding What Undercurrents to Address

Decide What Undercurrents You Will Address

Check the undercurrents that relate specifically to the symptom pick you negotiated with the family to work on at the end of Phase I. These two or three undercurrents (unhealthy and corresponding healthy) will then be illustrated within the feedback loops. Only select undercurrents directly connected to the particular seed & symptom selected.

Answer this question:

"What are the top two or three unhealthy undercurrents within the seed category of _____
[seed pick] *that are directly responsible for causing the symptom of _____* [symptom pick] *for this particular family?"*

Next, from the list below, check the box of the top two or three unhealthy undercurrents that correspond with your seed and symptom picks.

Please note: The misuse of power seed is directly associated with stabilization using behavioral modification and hybrid contracts and therefore is not listed here. The clinical focus is on the creation of wound playbooks to directly affect unresolved trauma. This list only includes undercurrents directly associated with the unhealed wound and closely-associated seeds.

Unhealed Wound Seed

Unhealthy Undercurrent		Opposite Healthy Undercurrent
☐ Unresolved grief or loss	→	Grief education and resolution
☐ Betrayal or abandonment	→	Security, forgiveness, unconditional love
☐ Family secrets	→	Reveal secrets/safety
☐ Physical or mental abuse	→	Support, courage to leave, forgive
☐ Lack of forgiveness/bitterness	→	Forgiveness
☐ Lack of consistent nurturance	→	Unconditional love, consistent nurturance
☐ High anxiety	→	Safety or security
☐ High stress	→	Relaxation or diversionary tactics

Physical or Mental Impairment Seed

☐ Drawn-out medical illness	→	Education, support, stress management
☐ Someone seen as patient/mental case	→	Normality and accountability
☐ Chemical imbalance	→	Psychotropic medications
☐ Brain or mental impairment	→	Consistent structure, education, support
☐ Lack of forgiveness/resentment	→	Forgiveness
☐ Lack of consistent nurturance	→	Unconditional love, consistent nurturance

(continued)

TABLE 6.1 Template for Deciding What Undercurrents to Address (*continued*)

Unmet Primal Need Seed		
☐ Maslow's unmet hierarchy of needs	→	Fill in "missing" Maslow need
☐ Lack of attachment or bonding	→	Attachment bonds
☐ Lack of forgiveness/resentment	→	Forgiveness, prayer
☐ Lack of connection to God/higher power	→	Connecting to God or higher power
☐ Mind, body, and spirit unbalanced	→	Restoring balance

Case Example

Seventeen-year-old Alex presented problem symptoms of cutting and depression. At the end of Phase I, the FST therapist's top two seed picks were (a) unhealed wounds and (b) unmet primal needs. The target problem symptoms were depression and self-harm cutting.

The path selected was direct trauma or wound work first. The rationale was that Alex's symptoms were directly associated with the traumatic event of being sent away for an entire year involuntarily to a psychiatric hospital. Behavioral problems were currently minor and associated with the anger and resentment Alex still felt toward both of his parents. In addition, it was determined that Alex's symptoms were not due to a misuse of power seed associated with an upside-down hierarchy or other structural problems within the family. Therefore, stabilization prior to wound or trauma work was contraindicated.

To begin, the FST therapist closely examined his seed and symptom picks that were clearly written at the end of Phase I along with the reasons for the picks. The FST therapist's picks for Alex are illustrated in Table 6.2.

TABLE 6.2 FST Therapist's Seed and Symptom Picks From Phase I

FST Therapist's Seed & Symptom Picks

#1 Seed Pick **Unhealed Wounds**

Reasons: Wound caused by traumatic event of being sent to a private long-term residential center because of minor drug possession. The unforgiveness and resentment Alex feels toward his parents is intense.

#2 Seed Pick **Unmet Primal Needs**

Reasons: Alex feels all alone and no longer attached to either parent. Over the last year (since Alex came back from the hospital), he continues to isolate himself more and more and has gone to daily cutting to prevent, as Alex calls it, "from going totally numb." Over time, signs of clinical depression have dramatically increased that include insomnia, loss of interest in any sports, poor school performance, anger, sadness, and hopelessness.

(*continued*)

Case Example (*continued*)

TABLE 6.2 FST Therapist's Seed and Symptom Picks From Phase I (*continued*)

FST Therapist's Seed & Symptom Picks

Top Two Problem Picks (Symptoms)

(1)   Self-harm because it is a safety issue

(2)   Depression

After close examination, the FST therapist asked himself these two key questions:

- For Alex and his family, "What are the top two or three unhealthy undercurrents and their healthy counterparts within the *unhealed wound seed category* that are directly responsible for causing and maintaining Alex's *symptoms* of *(a) depression and (b) self-harm*?"

- For Alex and his family, "What are the top two or three unhealthy undercurrents and their healthy counterparts within the *unmet primal need seed category* that are directly responsible for causing and maintaining Alex's *symptoms* of *(a) depression and (b) self-harm*?"

To answer these key questions, the FST therapist closely examined the undercurrent worksheet in Table 6.1 around the seeds of unhealed wounds and unmet primal and spiritual needs.

Match the Problem Symptoms With the Top Two Undercurrents

The next step is to match the child's or adolescent's problem symptoms with the most likely top two undercurrents. Using Alex's case, Box 6.2 illustrates the optimal process to help maintain focus on the particular symptom in question.

BOX 6.2 FST Therapist's Undercurrent Picks Causing the Child's Symptoms

Alex's Problem Symptom in Question	Top 2 or 3 Unhealthy Undercurrents Directly Causing This Symptom	Healthy Undercurrent Counterparts
Depression	☐ Betrayal and abandonment (from unhealed wound seed)	☑ Grief healing around lost parts of childhood after sexual abuse
	☐ Lack of forgiveness (from unmet primal need and/or unhealed wounds)	☑ Reestablish attachment bonds with dad

(continued)

BOX 6.2 FST Therapist's Undercurrent Picks Causing the Child's Symptoms (*continued*)

Alex's Problem Symptom in Question	Top 2 or 3 Unhealthy Undercurrents Directly Causing This Symptom	Healthy Undercurrent Counterparts
	☐ Lack of attachment (from unmet primal needs seed)	☑ Needs unconditional love and to feel secure
Self-harm (cutting)	☐ High anxiety (unhealed wounds)	☑ Security
	☐ Lack of consistent nurturance (from unmet primal need and/or unhealed wounds)	☑ Unconditional love
	☐ Lack of attachment (unmet primal need)	☑ Reestablishing attachments
	☐ Unforgiveness (from unhealed wounds and unmet primal needs)	☑ Forgiveness

It is important to note that the undercurrents selected should be seen within the framework of a "working or clinical hypothesis." This means that new data may emerge in future sessions (e.g., family secrets) that may change the therapist's initial undercurrent selections. In our experience, this does happen; however, the stress chart combined with the safety stressors and seed/tree diagram has the proper assessment tools necessary to accurately get to the correct core undercurrent drivers after the first Phase I session. However, if new information emerges, the FST therapist must be open to changing the initial clinical hypothesis accordingly later in FST treatment.

Case Example

In Alex's family, the FST therapist selected the following undercurrents based on Alex's symptoms and the family contextual data gathered in Phase I:

The rationale for the undercurrent picks in Box 6.2 was based on connecting the dots back to key contextual family information obtained in Phase I.

☑ When Alex's father listed his seed pick of unhealed wounds, he admitted that sending his son to inpatient treatment for a year had left his son feeling betrayed and bitter. The son's body language indicated agreement with his father, confirming the undercurrent of betrayal or abandonment.

(continued)

Case Example (*continued*)

☑ Since the hospital stay, all hugs or special outings had stopped cold (more than 2 years ago and counting).

☑ Depression is often anger and unforgiveness turned inward. This description fit Alex's relationship with both parents. In turn, both parties grew emotionally distant, which only served to deepen Alex's depression.

☑ This was confirmed in later sessions when Alex described his cutting as equivalent to "a good cry."

☑ The FST therapist also selected the unhelpful undercurrent of a lack of connection to God because Dad reported that prayer and spirituality used to be a vital part of his life and he wanted to get this back and believed it would help him to reconnect with his son. The therapist's plan was to target this undercurrent in the playbook.

☑ The two core unhealthy undercurrent drivers of Alex's symptoms seemed to center around (a) loss of attachment bonding between Alex and his parents; and (b) deep resentment, a sense of betrayal, and unforgiveness by Alex toward his parents. There were ancillary undercurrents as well (i.e., high anxiety and stress that triggered cutting, lack of a spiritual connection, and lack of consistent nurturance)

☑ These core unhealthy undercurrents crossed over the seeds of both unhealed wounds and unmet primal needs.

Decide Which Symptom, Seed Picks, and Undercurrents to Highlight for Feedback Loops

The FST therapist must make an important tactical decision after the top two problem symptoms are correlated with the undercurrents. The FST therapist will not predraw feedback loops and create a sample playbook for both symptoms. Only one set of undercurrents and one symptom will be converted into before and after feedback loops.

The reason is that the primary goal in Phase II is education, not application. Phase II is a "wound work introduction," meaning that the goal is to get the family ready for change through new insight: Move the family's worldview from an individual focus to a system theory focus. This new worldview was started with the seed/tree diagram, but it will be accelerated using feedback loops combined with the sample wound playbooks. As a result, only one set of feedback loop examples and problem symptom is needed to make the point of how systems theory works.

A good rule of thumb to help this selection process is for the FST therapist to start with the end in mind. As FST treatment moves forward, the child or adolescent symptom and associated undercurrents that are likely to be a centerpiece in future sessions need to be decided. In other words, as stated earlier, the symptom and set of undercurrents representing the best chance for both quick victories and low hanging fruit for this particular family should be determined. In Alex's case, the FST therapist decided that the most likely centerpiece and low hanging fruit option concerned the problem symptom of self-harm instead of the depression. The reason is that the FST therapist felt that body checks would be an ideal catalyst to initiate positive change on multiple undercurrents with quick victories. The depression was equally important and there would still be a wound playbook on depression in future sessions. But the centerpiece for change would be the body checks.

A great metaphor is finding "grist for the mill." Just as the grist is the corn that is brought to a mill to be ground into flour, the grist to create feedback loops is an undercurrent selection in Step 1 and a sample playbook in Step 2. Both are needed to successfully sketch before and after feedback loops. The FST therapist already has the grist of the problem symptom and the targeted undercurrents. Therefore, the last remaining piece of the puzzle is the strategic directive that the FST therapist will use in the sample playbook. Once this last task is completed, the before and after feedback loops are ready to be drawn.

Examine Sample Directives and Playbooks

The first step is to closely examine sample techniques and playbooks in Chapter 8 that match with the unhealthy and healthy undercurrents for the problem symptom that will be highlighted in the feedback loops.

Case Example

In Alex's case, the targeted healthy undercurrents were security and unconditional love, forgiveness, and attachment (see Box 6.3) for the symptom of self-harm.

BOX 6.3 Alex's Symptom of Self-Harm and Corresponding Undercurrents

Alex's Problem Symptom in Question	Top 2 or 3 Unhealthy Undercurrents Directly Causing This Symptom	Healthy Undercurrents Counterparts
Self-harm (cutting)	☐ High anxiety (unhealed wounds) ☐ Lack of consistent nurturance (from unhealed wounds) ☐ Lack of attachment (unmet primal need) ☐ Unforgiveness (from unhealed wounds and unmet primal needs)	☑ Security ☑ Unconditional love ☑ Reestablishing attachments ☑ Forgiveness

The FST therapist then looked for the available techniques and wound playbooks offered in Chapter 8 for the targeted healthy undercurrents. For example, "high anxiety" (unhealthy undercurrent) and its healthy undercurrent counterpart "safety or security" had four techniques to consider. The one that most closely matched Alex's problem symptom was the technique "prayer and body checks" (Table 6.3).

(continued)

Case Example (*continued*)

TABLE 6.3 Sample Strategic Directives for the Unhealthy Undercurrent of High Anxiety Within the Unhealed Wounds Seed

Unhealthy Undercurrents	Healthy Undercurrents	Techniques to Inject Healthy Undercurrent
High anxiety	Safety or security	☐ **The High/Low Checkup** ☐ Increasing Confidence With Praise ☑ **Prayer and Body Checks** ☐ *The Lion King* movie clip

After the technique is selected, the next step is to look at the sample playbook example offered within this undercurrent category of high anxiety. In this case, the sample playbook is the "high/low checkup" (see Chapter 8).

Therefore, even though the prayer and body checks technique is not the same as the high/low checkup, the template blueprint of the latter is useful in helping the FST therapist custom-build his or her own sample wound playbook for prayer and body checks for the particular family.

This same process is replicated for the other remaining undercurrents for Alex and illustrated in Tables 6.4, 6.5, and 6.6. The techniques that the FST therapist likes for Alex's family are highlighted in **bold**. The process can be analogous to a master chef looking at a buffet of ingredient options to put together the ideal dish in a cookbook.

TABLE 6.4 Sample Strategic Directives for the Unhealthy Undercurrent of Lack of Consistent Nurturance Within the Unhealed Wounds Seed

Unhealthy Undercurrents	Healthy Undercurrents	Techniques to Inject Healthy Undercurrent
Lack of consistent nurturance	Unconditional love, consistent nurturance	☑ **30-Day Nurturing Campaign** ☐ Cups and Self-Worth ☑ **The Hug PMR (Positive Max Report) prescription** ☐ Random Acts of Kindness ☐ Helping Others Campaign ☐ *Home* movie clip

(continued)

Case Example (*continued*)

TABLE 6.5 Sample Strategic Directives for the Unhealthy Undercurrent of Lack of Attachment Within the Unmet Primal Needs Seed

Unhealthy Undercurrents	Healthy Undercurrents	Techniques to Inject Healthy Undercurrent
Lack of attachment or bonding	Attachment bonds	☑ **Restoring Emotional Family Bonds** ☐ Acts of Positive Communication ☐ Fostering a Pet ☐ *The Fresh Prince of Bel-Air* video clip ☐ Random Acts of Kindness ☐ Increasing Emotional Closeness

TABLE 6.6 Sample Strategic Directives for the Unhealthy Undercurrent of Unforgiveness Within the Unmet Primal Needs Seed

Unhealthy Undercurrents	Healthy Undercurrents	Techniques to Inject Healthy Undercurrent
Lack of forgiveness/ resentment	Forgiveness, prayer	☑ **Daily Words of Affirmation** ☐ The "Apology"—Healing the Family Heart ☐ Memory Board of Appreciation ☐ The Empty Chair ☐ *Antwone Fisher* movie clip

The next step is a *purposeful mixture*. Multiple unhealthy undercurrents as seen in the tables will be mixed together in the before feedback loops along with multiple healthy undercurrent counterparts within the after feedback loops.

For example, within Alex's illustrated before feedback loop in Figure 6.1, there are a multitude of unhealthy undercurrents between Alex and his parents. Some of the top ones include lack of attachment, lack of security, lack of nurturance, and unforgiveness. These communication interactional patterns are visually represented by feedback loops and aptly named a before feedback loop. This is because these undercurrents are happening in the present moment today and are keeping this family system stuck and unable to mobilize to help Alex heal his trauma and theirs as well.

So the before feedback loop is "before" the strategic directive or wound playbook (the antibiotic) is introduced into the system to show a chain reaction of healthy undercurrents or the "after" feedback loop. This will be a visual representation for the family of what the future can look like (a movie trailer of upcoming attractions) if the wound playbook is used and these healthy undercurrents replace the unhealthy ones and become the new normal. In turn, these healthy undercurrents will also function like good chemotherapy to shrink and destroy in this family the toxic seeds of unhealed wounds and unmet primal needs.

(continued)

Case Example (*continued*)

In summary, the FST therapist for Alex's family (same process is replicated for other cases) did the following:

- Closely examined in Chapter 8 all the available techniques (strategic directives) for the targeted "before" (unhealthy undercurrents) and "after" healthy undercurrents that he wanted to show the family using feedback loops
- Next, the therapist highlighted those techniques in **bold** that would be the ideal ingredients for his customized wound playbook to address the child's or adolescent's targeted symptom, in this case, self-harm in the form of cutting
- Like a master chef, the therapist then looked at some of the wound playbook examples available in Chapter 8 (in this case, the high/low checkup) and used it as a blueprint template to create the "Prayer and Body Check" wound playbook (see Box 6.4)
- And like a good chef, this "Prayer and Body Check" playbook mixed in techniques for these other targeted undercurrents as well:
  - ☐ **Increasing emotional closeness** (for attachment bonding)
  - ☐ **The hug prescription** (for unconditional love and consistent nurturance)
  - ☐ **Daily words of affirmation** (for forgiveness, prayer)
- Once the sample wound playbook was complete, the FST therapist had all the grist for the mill needed to sketch the best before and after feedback loops to show the family during the next session to move them quickly to an understanding of the benefits of a systems theory worldview and to inspire hope for the future.

BOX 6.4 Prayer and Body Check Wound Playbook

Prayer and Body Check Wound Playbook

To inject the healthy undercurrents of safety and security
unhealed wound seed

Who:
☑ Dad and Alex

What:
☑ Prayer by Dad: Twice a day, Dad will pray specifically for Alex's protection
☑ Body check by Dad

When:
☑ The prayer will occur each evening before bed and each morning when Alex wakes up
☑ The body check will occur each evening at 8 p.m.

Where:
☑ The prayer and body check will occur in Alex's room

(continued)

BOX 6.4 Prayer and Body Check Wound Playbook (*continued*)

How:

☑ The prayer

- Each evening before bed and in the morning, Dad, you will pray specifically for Alex's protection by praying this prayer:

Lord, I pray that You would surround Alex, my awesome son, with Your hand of protection. Keep him safe from any more self-harm, accidents, diseases, drug usage, or any other evil influences. Protect him wherever he is. Keep him out of harm's way.

Lord, I pray that You would bring more healing between us and remove any lies in Alex's mind and root out and eliminate core issues surrounding his self-harm wounds. I pray against his insomnia and that he would get plenty of rest so that he is completely rejuvenated each morning when he awakens.

It is written, "Let no weapon formed against my son be able to prosper" (Isaiah 54:17). Keep my son at all times under the umbrella of Your protection, and deliver him from the enemy's hand so that no evil can come near him. Give Your angels charge over him to keep him in all Your ways (Psalm 91:11).

I say to God, "Cover my son under Your wings to take refuge; His truth shall be your shield. Alex shall not be afraid of the terror by night, nor the arrow that flies by day. A thousand may fall at his side, and ten thousand at Your right hand; but they may not come near Alex" (Psalm 91: 4–7).

☑ The body check with unconditional love and improved communication

- Each night at 8 p.m., Dad will meet Alex in his room and do a body check for cuts

- If any cuts are found, Dad will not censure Alex but will hug him deeply and say simply, "I love you, you are not alone."

- If no cuts are found, Dad will hug him deeply and say, "I love you and am proud of you for resisting the temptation. I know it was not easy."

- If Alex wants to tell Dad about what caused the cuts, Dad, you will use reflective listening (see book below). If Alex does not want to talk, you will not ask any questions and will just leave after the hug.

- Dad will purchase and read the book *How to Talk So Teens Will Listen and Listen So Teens Will Talk* (Faber & Mazlish, 2010) by Adele Faber and Elaine Mazlish and use the recommended tools to increase your communication skills with Alex.

As Box 6.4 illustrates, the sample wound playbook and techniques selected must correspond to the targeted healthy undercurrents selected in Step 1 and the problem symptom highlighted in the feedback loops. In this case, it is Alex's symptom of self-harm in the form of cutting. The playbook itself contained a powerful cocktail of multiple healthy undercurrents (e.g., nurturance and a connection to God through prayer and hugs) to drive out, from this family, the root unhealthy undercurrents that were preventing the wound or trauma from healing. By replacing the unhealthy undercurrents with their healthy counterparts, the child's or adolescent's problem symptoms are alleviated or eliminated. No matter what the symptom is, the root causes or undercurrents are the target of change.

It is important to note that the sample wound playbook may or may not be ultimately used or adopted by the family. This decision will be made in Phase III. Therefore, in Phase II, the main goal of the sample playbook and feedback loops is to rapidly move the child and the family from what Prochaska, DiClemente, and Norcross (1994) term as a precontemplative stage of readiness (i.e., "Fix my child, I do not see that I am part of the problem or solution. It is 100% a child only problem") to the contemplative stage of readiness (i.e., "I have new insight that the solution is a family problem in which we all have to change").

In this way, a "contemplative family system" from Phase II is now poised to move into a stage of preparation in Phase III (i.e., we create a playbook and conduct as many dress rehearsals and troubleshooting activities as needed to master our delivery). From there, the family can move into the stage of action in Phase IV (we implement the playbook to actively change the child's or adolescent's problem symptom and heal the unresolved trauma). The spark that lights the fuse to move the family along Prochaska's stages of readiness for change is the feedback loops and sample wound playbook.

STEP 3: DRAW BEFORE AND AFTER FEEDBACK LOOPS

After the sample playbook is selected or modified, it is time to sketch or pre-draw both the "before" feedback loop identified in Step 1 (the unhealthy undercurrents) and the "after" feedback loop (healthy undercurrent counterparts) in Step 2. The "after" feedback loop should also illustrate the techniques (hugs, body checks, prayer, etc.) or strategic directives used within the therapist's sample wound playbook. Both the "before" and "after" feedback loops are like an artist's painting of how the family dances together around the identified child's problem symptom(s). The "before" and "after" feedback loops should be hung on the wall side by side like portraits in a museum to tell a visual story of the present and what the future holds if healthy undercurrents are deployed using wound playbooks. These predrawn feedback loops also act like cliff notes for the FST therapist. They visually summarize treatment up to this point and literally help the therapist connect the dots to focus his or her tactical thinking.

The FST therapist will then take these feedback loop sketches into the next session and use in Step 7 outlined in Chapter 7. During the next session (see Chapter 7), the therapist will re-create or re-draw these pre-session preparation "before" and "after" feedback loops one at a time for the family one loop at a time. Family members will then be invited and encouraged to confirm the accuracy of each loop and suggest any changes.

For example, it is common for a parent or adolescent to say that the basic meaning or gist of a particular loop is correct but that the actual statement or wording needs to be changed (e.g., "Your loop of 'Why do you look so sad today' needs to be changed to 'You look out of sorts'"). As each loop is drawn, the FST therapist will call the loop a dance move to make the concept of feedback loops more understandable and reflect the interactional nature of what is taking place.

Case Example

In Alex's case, the FST therapist illustrated the before and after feedback loops as seen in Figures 6.1 and 6.2.

(*continued*)

Case Example (*continued*)

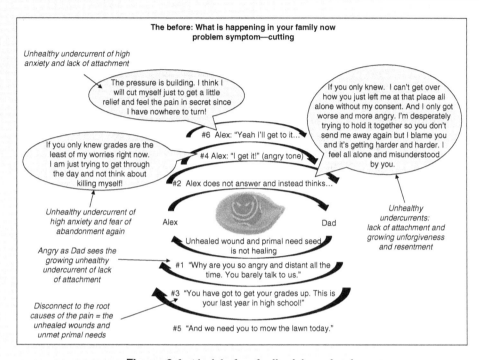

Figure 6.1 Alex's before feedback loop sketch.

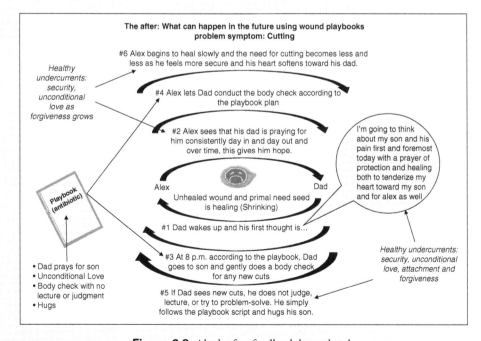

Figure 6.2 Alex's after feedback loop sketch.

(*continued*)

Case Example (*continued*)

As the feedback loops in Alex's family demonstrate, these drawing can have a powerful influence to propel family members from a precontemplative to a contemplative stage of readiness for systematic thinking.

A picture is worth a thousand words, and for chronically stuck families, the "before" and "after" feedback loops drawn side-by-side gives them hope for the future and confidence in their therapist as a change agent.

In Alex's case, also note how the after feedback loop has the actual visual representation of the wound playbook embedded within the drawing itself. Notice that the word "antibiotic" is included. This is intentional to make it easier for the family to connect the dots about the role of the intervention (the wound playbook) in changing the undercurrents. Antibiotics are used as a metaphor because family members can easily relate to visiting a doctor to get medicine to attack a virus (an unhealthy undercurrent) to jumpstart the body and enable it to fight the infection (using healthy undercurrents) and remove its source (the toxic seed) and restore the body to balance and health (unstuck system). This is also why the seed goes from looking fat and happy with a smile in the before feedback loop drawing to becoming skinny and sad when healthy undercurrents are introduced using the playbook in the after feedback loop drawing. Again, this before and after seed rendition is done intentionally to further connect the dots back to the seed/tree diagram in Phase I and further externalize the child's problem for the family to rally together to defeat the toxic seed, not just to fix the scapegoated child.

When Feedback Loop Drawings Are Not Enough

It is important to note that special circumstances may require that the FST therapist deviate from the visual illustration of the feedback loops in Step 7 of Phase II. Here are the most common reasons why and what to do if it happens:

- *Body language indicates confusion*: If multiple family members indicate by their body language that they are not understanding the process, the FST therapist will need to stop immediately to clarify or use another family member who does understand the process to explain it to the members who do not. If this still does not work, the FST therapist needs to quickly shift to the experiential sculpting strategy explained in the following text.

- *Family is agitated or in active crisis*: Before the session begins, the FST therapist senses or knows that an active crisis took place the day before or even hours prior to the session. In a state of agitation, the family is likely in no mood to sit through a feedback loop drawing presentation, no matter how engaging. For example, in one case, an hour prior to the session, the teenager took a door off its hinges and hit the mother with it. This family was in active crisis mode when the session started. The mother wanted to deal with the immediate fallout of the aggression, not feedback loops. However, the FST therapist missed these cues and continued with the feedback loop process even though the family's body language screamed to stop. In this example, the therapist needed to stop, regroup, put the drawings away for another day, and deal directly with the crisis at hand.

- *A particular family responds better with experiential activities*: Different families respond better to different modalities. In the case of the feedback loops, the family may respond better to the therapist transforming the feedback loops into a kind of sculpting activity. In this case, the FST therapist hangs the feedback loop drawings on the wall and gets different family members out of their chairs to act out the loop dances. The therapist may play the part of the child or the child can play himself while other family members play themselves. One can even ask a family member to play the part of the happy seed in the before feedback loop and the unhappy seed in the after feedback loop and speak aloud the thought bubbles (e.g., "I am so happy this family is stuck and feeding me a healthy diet of unforgiveness and bitterness every day. Yum yum!" versus "Oh, nooooo, they are getting smarter. This dad is not holding grudges anymore. No, please stop, I am starving").

One can even have a family member represent a playbook and, like a superhero, yell, "I will help save the day" as he or she swoops in and playfully attacks the unhealthy undercurrents (young kids love this role). The FST therapist moves to the role of director, sets the scene, and yells "Action!" or "Stop!" If the therapist is playful with high energy, the family will mirror this energy and start to really get into the sculpting role-play. The experiential sculpting should be a standby go-to for all FST therapists anytime the body language or energy level needs an extra playful boost or a shot in the arm to make the feedback loops literally jump off the page.

STEP 4: CREATE CUSTOMIZED HOMEWORK LEAD SHEET

After the feedback loop sketches are completed, the next step is to take the healthy undercurrents and techniques highlighted in the after feedback loops, and Google-search the Internet for additional techniques or resources. The therapist will take these resources, convert them into what is called a homework lead sheet (see Table 6.7), and present it as a handout to the family at the end of Phase II (see Chapter 7) as their homework assignment between sessions. Family members will be asked at the end of Phase II to search out techniques in between sessions on their own. However, our experience and research has shown that families will have a much better chance of successfully completing the homework if they have a Homework Lead Sheet from the therapist than having to start from scratch.

Case Example

In Alex's family, the therapist, during pre-session preparation, prepared the following homework lead sheet and handed it out to the family at the end of the next session. In the lead sheet, the FST therapist wanted the father and son to work together to find techniques for how they would enter into a difficult conversation about Alex being sent away for a year to the hospital. The therapist wanted them to specifically look for techniques around "positive communication" that would restore attachment bonds.

When the family arrived at the beginning of Phase III to present their homework findings, both father and son were smiling as they presented their creative technique. It comprised tools from the book called *Difficult Conversations: How to Discuss What Matters Most* by Stone, Patton, and Heen (1999).

(continued)

Case Example (*continued*)

Difficult conversations are inevitable, but the leaders of the Harvard Negotiation Project are here to teach you how to negotiate a pay rise, resolve a dispute or even let someone go. Arming you with the right techniques and tools in this step-by-step guide, you will learn how to manage your feelings, empathize, avoid the blame game and really listen. Difficult Conversations gives you the know-how to tackle even the most challenging exchanges.

Both father and son were so proud of themselves. Just the act of doing the homework brought them together. And the principles were so easy to utilize that they were infused directly into Alex's family's finalized wound playbook called "Forgiveness and Repairing Broken Relationships." This was the second playbook that the family and the therapist put together in Phase III that had nothing to do with self-harm but everything to do with healing Alex's second problem symptom of depression.

During the ethnographic family interview at the end of Phases II and III, when the question was asked, "*What was most helpful in today's session?*" both Dad and Alex said without hesitation it was investigating and finding strategies or techniques to help their family heal. They stated that once they understood from the feedback loops that the true enemy was not each other but those "seeds and bad undercurrents," they could rally together without finger-pointing. The lead sheet was the catalyst to action.

When creating the customized lead sheet, the key is focus. Only select one or two healthy undercurrents that are targets for the family and that fit the goals for therapy established in Phase I. In Alex's family, the core healthy targeted undercurrents were identified as reestablishing attachment and forgiveness. These were the two core drivers of the self-harm and depression symptoms. Therefore, these are the areas around which wound playbooks would be developed using specific techniques and strategies such as those contained in the *Difficult Conversations* book. Therefore, the homework lead sheet should just be focused on leads around these undercurrents. In Alex's case, these are highlighted under "Areas to Target."

Areas to Target

- How to restore lost attachments techniques
- How to forgive techniques

The FST therapist only needs to provide one or two leads per undercurrent and plug them into the homework lead sheet template as illustrated in Table 6.7. The family can then either just look up these leads or parlay them into others as well. That will be their choice. The family will then present their findings at the beginning of Phase III, and the FST therapist will decide whether to use all the family's techniques, use some and not others, or not use any of the family's techniques because of reasons that are outlined in Chapter 9.

TABLE 6.7 The Homework Lead Sheet for Alex and His Family

Homework Lead Sheet

Overall Goals for This Homework Assignment

- Your family will self-discover creative techniques or strategies that will heal your wounds.
- You will have input on what techniques or strategies go into your wound playbook that we create together at our next meeting.
- Research shows that if you work hard to discover your own strategies, your rate of treatment success dramatically increases. Why? Because you now have "skin in the game."
- This lead sheet contains a few potential resources to jump-start the process, but please add your own.
- Then next time we meet _____ (write in date and time here) I will ask you to present your top 2 or 3. If you do not come up with anything, please still come to the next session because I will have some to share. This means even though you are signing your names below that you will try to complete the homework, sometimes things come up. If you are unable to do this assignment, do not let it stop you from coming to the next session. No one will be upset.

Areas to Target

- How to "restore lost attachment" techniques
- How to "forgive" techniques

Sample Leads For Your Family to Follow-Up On (Add your own)

Leads to look up for techniques to restore "lost attachments" (targeted healthy undercurrent)

- ☐ *Rebuilding Attachments with Traumatized Children: Healing from Losses, Violence, Abuse, and Neglect* (2013) by Richard Kagan
- ☐ *How to Talk So Teens Will Listen & Listen So Teens Will Talk* (2010) by Adele Faber and Elaine Mazlish
- ☐ *Difficult Conversations: How to Discuss What Matters Most* (1999) by Douglas Stone, Bruce Patton & Sheila Heen

Leads to look up for techniques on how to "forgive" (targeted healthy undercurrent)

- ☐ *Why You Still Need to Forgive Your Parents and How To Do It With Ease and Grace* (2010) by Tipping, Holub, Jones, O'Connor, and Fontaine.
- ☐ *Forgive Your Parents, Heal Yourself: How Understanding Your Painful Family Legacy Can Transform Your Life* (1999) by Barry Grosskopf
- ☐ *Cheaper Than Therapy: How To Forgive and Overcome Anger, Anxiety, Fear and Stress* (2013) by Mykey Robinson

Before you leave, let's answer the following questions:

Who in the family will look for the different possible techniques or strategies?

-

When or what times and days of the week will you devote to look for these strategies?

-

Where will you look (on computer, library, etc.)?

-

How will you summarize the information you gather to present the next week?

-

What format will you present your findings in (typed up list, copies of what you find, etc.)?

-

Print name of each family member: _____

Signature of each family member: _____

Date _____

        Day/month/year

The final step represents one of the most underutilized activities in mental health counseling today. In our experience and research, a majority of therapists doing trauma work do not focus much attention or effort toward actively engaging the extended family or their village to participate in sessions. If the therapist does focus some effort to involve others, he or she typically relies on the parent to invite others to the sessions. The therapist does not personally call the extended family or village to invite these key villagers to the sessions. Nor does the therapist attempt to find out if there are any barriers to attendance.

This is a tactical mistake because reliance on the parent to engage the village for the therapist this early in treatment is unreliable at best. Instead, it is recommended that the FST therapist obtain a signed release at the end of Phase I for key village members and then use the adapted version of the FST motivational phone call script in Table 6.8 to introduce the reason for asking for their participation and to create a soft start-up. This is done if the FST motivational interview

---

TABLE 6.8 Motivational Phone Call Script Adapted for Use With Villagers

Village Motivational Phone Call and Check-In Script

Hello, is _____ [name of villager] there? The reason for my call is that I am the counselor who has the honor of working with _____ [name of child] and their family. After meeting with them, we all thought that you were really important to contact personally and get your insight. Did _____ [parent's name] tell you I was going to call?

[If the answer is no, say "I sincerely apologize for that."] Would you like me to try to contact ___ [parent's name] now using my 3-way call feature on my phone or would you be OK for me to give you some information now and check in with them after our call?

[If no 3-way calling option] Would you like to call them to confirm first, and I can call you back in 15 minutes or a different time? Or would you be OK for me to give you some information now and check in with them after our call?

[If yes, say "Great."] Would this be an OK time to talk now? It will only take 10 minutes.

Question #1: I am calling because _____ [name of child] is having challenges and the entire family is stressed and worried. They came to me as a counselor for help, and they told me I could call you because you were important to touch base with.

I told the family that I am old school in that we need a village to raise a child. Since they said that you were a key person to talk to, my first question is do you see that there are challenges with _____ [name of child] and if yes, what gives you concern right now?

Question #2: What do you think will happen if the concerns you listed are not fixed soon?

Question #3: If you had to guess, what are the top two things getting in the way of the family solving these problems?

Question #4: What insight or support can you give the family in the future to help fix their concerns?

Closing points: In our next meeting, we will be putting a concrete plan together to lower the family's stress and deal directly with their challenges. Based on what you said earlier, the family was right in me contacting you. Your support and insight is important to help them get unstuck.

Therefore, could you find a way to make it to the next meeting? We may not need you for another meeting but this one is critical because like I said earlier we are starting to put together a plan and more heads are better than one to solve a problem.

- Would you come?
- Are there any potential barriers that would prevent you from coming?
- Would you like a reminder call the day before?

(MI) was not done beforehand and/or new and important villagers were revealed at the end of Phase I.

As with the MI phone call, it is important, however, for the FST therapist to ask the parent or adolescent who is friendly with that particular villager to inform him or her that the therapist will be calling. Otherwise, it is a cold call and it will be more difficult to engage the villager and convince him or her to come to a session.

REFERENCES

Faber, A., & Mazlish, E. (2010). *How to talk so teens will listen and listen so teens will talk.* New York, NY: HarperCollins.

Grosskopf, B. (1999). *Forgive your parents, heal yourself: How understanding your painful family legacy can transform your life.* New York, NY: Free Press.

Kagan, R. (2013). *Rebuilding attachments with traumatized children: Healing from losses, violence, abuse, and neglect.* New York, NY: Routledge.

Prochaska, J. O., Norcross, J. C., & DiClemente, C. C. (1994). *Changing for good.* New York, NY: Avon Books.

Robinson, M. (2013). *Cheaper than therapy: How to forgive and overcome anger, anxiety, fear and stress.* Charleston, SC: CreateSpace.

Sells, S. P. (2002). *Parenting your out-of-control teenager: 7 steps to reestablish authority and reclaim love.* New York, NY: St. Martin's Griffin.

Sells, S. P. (2004). *Treating the tough adolescent: A family-based, step-by-step guide.* New York, NY: Guilford Press.

Stone, D., Patton, B., & Heen, S. (1999). *Difficult conversations: How to discuss what matters most.* New York, NY: Penguin Books.

Tipping, C., Holub, A., Jones, J., O'Connor, M., & Fontaine, B. R. (2010). *Why you still need to forgive your parents: And how you can do it with ease and grace.* Marietta, GA: Global 13 Publications.

Phase II: Wound Work Introduction

Step 1: Safety Planning

Step 2: Window of Tolerance and Self-Regulation Tools

Step 3: Neuroplasticity and Proper Nutrition

Step 4: Informed Consent

Step 5: Review Highlights of Phase I

Step 6: Reveal Wound Undercurrents

Step 7: Show Feedback Loops With Sample Playbook

Step 8: Wound Story if Needed With Self-Regulation Tools

Step 9: Homework Assignments

As the family systems trauma (FST) diagram in Chapter 3 illustrates, Phase II takes place immediately after Phase II: Pre-session Preparation has been completed. For purposes of this book, it is assumed that when Phase II: Wound Work Introduction begins, the child and family either have been stabilized first or are ready for direct trauma or wound work. In either case, this phase and those that follow outline the procedures necessary for direct trauma work. The total number of sessions needed to complete Phase II will depend both on the complexity of the case and the per-session time constraints of one hour versus two hours. Phase II can typically be completed within a duration of between one and three 2-hour sessions or two and six 1-hour sessions.

Session duration may increase when family members indicate at the onset of Phase II challenges in the areas of (a) safety planning; (b) what Siegel (1999) and Ogden, Kekuni, and Clair (2006) term as the "window of tolerance;" or (c) what Shannon (2013, 2014) calls "neuroplasticity" through proper nutrition. If the child or family indicates challenges in any of these areas, the complexity of the case can increase and so can the number of sessions. The FST model fits the recommendations of Figley and Figley (2009, p. 180) who said:

> At the very minimum, trauma-informed therapy would include (a) the establishment of safety, (b) informed consent, (c) titration of exposure-related stress (self-regulation tools) and (d) client self-soothing competence during and between treatment sessions.

These safety criteria are also drawn from the Green Cross Academy of Traumatology (1999) and the International Society of Traumatic Stress Studies (ISTSS) guidelines (e.g., Dietrich, 2001).

As a result of these recommendations, the FST model adopted these safety criteria and included them at the onset of Phase II of the FST model (e.g., safety planning, window of tolerance, proper nutrition, and informed consent). The bottom line is that the FST therapist needs to provide the child and family the tools they need to address any trauma exposure–related stress that FST treatment might inadvertently induce. In addition, family members should be briefed on the inherent treatment risks and benefits FST prior to direct wound treatment.

This chapter outlines the nine mini-steps needed to implement Phase II. These nine mini-steps are

1. Safety planning
2. Window of tolerance and self-regulation tools
3. Neuroplasticity and proper nutrition
4. Informed consent
5. Review highlights from Phase I
6. Reveal wound undercurrents
7. Show feedback loops with sample playbook
8. Wound story, if needed, with self-regulation tools
9. Homework assignments

Steps 1 to 4 can be grouped together as **Core Safety Criteria**, while Steps 5 to 9 are the **Application Steps**. Case examples are used throughout this chapter to illustrate key points.

PRIOR TO THE SESSION

Prior to beginning Phase II, the FST therapist should come to the session prepared with the following items:

☑ *Handout of self-regulation tools and proper nutritional guidelines:* Have these handouts ready to distribute if it becomes apparent in Steps 2 and 3 that there are either window of tolerance or lack of proper nutrition issues. These handouts are included in this chapter.

☑ *A copy of the informed consent:* All persons should get a copy of their own informed consent to review and sign. A sample informed consent is included in this chapter.

☑ *Undercurrent handout:* The FST therapist will be educating the family system on the top unhealthy and healthy undercurrents surrounding unhealed wounds and their associated seeds of mental or physical impairment or unmet primal needs. These undercurrents will be outlined in a handout that will be given to each family member. These undercurrents will then be illustrated as before and after feedback loops.

☑ *Three large blank flip chart pages to hang side by side or PowerPoint slides:* The therapist will use the first two blank pages to draw the before and after feedback loops. The last page will be to write the healthy and unhealthy undercurrents.

☑ *Predrawing of before and after feedback loops for the family:* The feedback loop drawings completed by the therapist in pre-session preparation should be brought to the session and used as a guide to recreate them for the family on a flip chart or using PowerPoint.

☑ *Sample playbook(s):* Bring handout of the sample playbooks that were created during pre-session preparation.

☑ *Homework lead sheet:* Bring handout of the homework lead sheet created during pre-session preparation to provide at the end of Phase II for homework.

STEP 1: SAFETY PLANNING

The FST therapist begins the session by either (a) revisiting current risk levels of safety if there was an identified safety problem during stabilization or (b) addressing safety planning for the first time. Bottom line, prior to active trauma work, the FST therapist must determine whether or not safety planning needs to be addressed and what the specific safety issues are. The actual safety playbook itself (if applicable) will be created and developed in Phase III alongside the wound playbook using a two-track process (see Chapter 3). But the actual assessment of whether safety risks exist will take place in this step.

Revisiting Old Safety and Risk Levels

If stabilization was addressed prior to direct trauma work, the FST therapist will inquire in this step if the two-track process of safety playbooks and contracts or hybrids is still effective and, specifically, if the current safety risk level is at a rating of 3 or below. As stated in Chapter 3, the FST therapist uses a risk scale of 1 to 5 (1= no risk; 5 = high risk). If the parents or child state that the risk level is currently high at 3 or above, the FST therapist is faced with an important decision:

☑ *Option A:* Postpone moving forward into active wound work within this phase of treatment (Phase III) until the risk level has dropped to lower than a 3.

☑ *Option B:* Proceed forward and monitor risk levels by including safety playbooks alongside new wound playbooks using the same two-track framework as with stabilization.

One must consider both the type of safety issue and the current structural integrity of the family. The top-ranked riskiest behavioral health issues cited by the Centers for Disease Control and Prevention (2011) are suicidal ideation, homicidal tendencies, substance addiction (not use), and ongoing aggression or domestic violence. Therefore, if current safety factors fall within these categories, the greater the need for Option A before proceeding to Option B. In addition, structural integrity means whether there is currently a healthy hierarchy in place with healthy boundaries and open communication. If the behavioral contract was effective, the family should be presently demonstrating healthy structural integrity. However, if the FST therapist assesses that structural integrity is still on shaky ground, Option A may be needed to stabilize the family further.

Case Example

Fifteen-year-old Jamal was referred to counseling for both behavioral problems and issues related to traumatic events. Behavioral problems included chronic truancy, running away from home, and disrespect. Traumatic events included witnessing several acts of domestic abuse against his mother by several different boyfriends and being part of a gang that ran guns. He also witnessed at least one murder of a best friend. In addition, Jamal was on juvenile probation for stealing a car. Stabilization was selected instead of direct wound work based on the following criteria described in the first rule of thumb: Rule of Thumb #1: chronicity, bitterness, and burnout levels. (a) Are the behaviors

(continued)

Case Example (*continued*)

extreme and happening almost every day or at least once a week? = "YES"; (b) are the parents or caregivers extremely burned-out and overwhelmed? = "YES"; and (c) are the parents or caregivers extremely angry, bitter, or resentful toward their child? = "YES." (Complete list of rules of thumb are seen in Table 3.3.)

However, to complicate matters, during the Phase I assessment, the mother revealed unmet primal needs within Maslow's hierarchy of needs: The family lacked the basic shelter needs of electricity or heat due to an inability to pay the utility bills. In addition, Jamal's teacher contacted Child Protective Services (CPS) to investigate the family for neglect. Therefore, the risk was high for child removal unless the neglect issues were addressed immediately.

As a result, it was determined that the safety risk was between 4 and 5 on a scale of 1 to 5. In other words, a two-track process, both safety and stabilization, had to occur prior to direct trauma or wound work. The initial goals of therapy would be Track 1, a safety playbook to address safety issues within Maslow's hierarchy of needs, and Track 2, a behavioral contract to stabilize the family structure to prevent expulsion from school, the probation mandate of community service (see Table 7.1).

TABLE 7.1 Round 1: Two-Track Safety Playbook and Behavioral Contract

Safety Playbook	Hybrid Behavioral Contract

Who:
• FST trained therapist (coordinator), Jamal's probation officer (JPO), local pastor, caseworker
What:
• With mom present, the FST therapist (the facilitator) will lead a "Get the Lights On" and "Bed to Sleep On" meeting
• FST therapist has pre-contacted United Way and spoken with Cynthia who directed us to the Della Lamb agency and the Low Income Home Energy Assistance Program (LIHEAP) as starting points for utility assistance
• FST therapist contacted the Salvation Army and they have donated bedding and furniture to pick up
When:
• 1st meeting on Wednesday, September 14, from 3 p.m. to 4 p.m.
• Follow-up meeting on Wednesday, September 28, from 3 p.m. to 4 p.m.
• **Where:**
• At mom's house
	For School
	• Bring log book home (see sample) with everything below
	  ◦ Your homework filled out
	  ◦ Initialed by each teacher (attended school)
	  ◦ No reports of disrespect, sleeping, getting kicked out
	• No skipping school & attend all classes
	For Probation
	• Be outside and ready for van at 5 p.m. Monday, Tuesday, Thursday
	• Attend all classes without disruption
	• Show mom attendance sheet as proof
	What Mom Does (Clarity of Her Role)
	• Mom hangs poster board on wall
	• Mom checks log book for school and probation class attendance sheet
	• If no log book or attendance sheet or not filled out or marks of disrespect = no check mark on success plan

(continued)

TABLE 7.1 Round 1: Two-Track Safety Playbook and Behavioral Contract (*continued*)

Safety Playbook	Hybrid Behavioral Contract

How:
 	
• FST Therapist will ask JPO to arrange pickup and delivery of bedroom and other furniture from the Salvation Army. JPO will go with mom's boyfriend, John, and Jamal's father to pick up the furniture. This will support mom and ease her worry, and in turn ease her depression (roles clarified)
 	
• PLL therapist will personally call the JPO on Monday, September 19 at 1 p.m. to confirm the date and time set for pickup. Then will contact the Salvation Army to coordinate time and date
 	
• PLL therapist will ask local pastor to call Della Lamb agency and LIHEAP to inquire about utility funding assistance and keep the Department of Social Services (DSS) caseworker in the communication loop (roles clarified)
 	
• PLL therapist will follow up with the pastor on Monday, September 19, to determine progress and brainstorm removing any barriers
 	
• PLL therapist will keep the caseworker in the loop throughout and mirror the Signs of Safety Plan
	• If Jamal has all checks for that day—counts as 1 day
	  ○ School Monday through Friday
	  ○ School + probation—Monday, Tuesday, and Thursday
	  ○ When Jamal gets 14 days = belt buckle
	
	What Dad Does
	• Mom lets dad know each day of success by leaving a message on his voicemail
	• Dad calls Jamal to congratulate him on Jamal's cell phone
	• Dad attends all school meetings with mom
	
	What Mike (Mother's Boyfriend) Does
	• Each day he sees mark on poster board, praises Jamal
	• Attends all school meetings with mom

Once safety and stabilization issues were addressed, Phase II: Wound Work Introduction could begin in earnest with active trauma or wound work and the creation of wound playbooks. Because stabilization had to occur prior to direct wound work, the number of 2-hour sessions doubled for Jamal's family. FST treatment was presented to the family as "Round 1" and "Round 2." The family liked this phrasing:

☑ Stabilization and safety playbooks required four to five 2-hour or eight to ten 1-hour sessions (Phases I–IV, **Round 1**: stabilization and safety two track)

☑ Wound playbooks: four to five *additional* 2-hour or eight to ten 1-hour sessions (Phases II–V [no need for another Phase I assessment], **Round 2**: wound playbooks and maintaining safety of Round 1)

Unhealed wounds were addressed in the first round using a hybrid contract with emotional warm-ups, and stabilization of safety risk levels reduced trauma. For example, looking at the safety planning playbook in Table 7.1, adequate shelter and prevention of home removal by CPS reduced both tension and drama in the entire family. In addition, the emotional warm-ups of Jamal's father praising him for going to school and attending community service introduces healthy undercurrents of nurturance.

After Round 1 was completed, Round 2 began with Phase II by revisiting both the safety plan and current risk levels. Both the CPS caseworker and the family reported a risk level of 1 that was maintained due to new furniture and restoration of lights along with a concrete plan to keep the plan going (mom now had a job with a steady income).

The FST therapist was then able to proceed as planned in Phase II with a window of tolerance assessment, nutritional analysis, informed consent, and so forth. It was determined during the nutritional analysis that Jamal was lacking in key nutrients of vegetables, vitamins, and water intake. This was an eye-opening discussion for everyone, because poor school performance was linked to lack of proper nutrition.

When the wound playbook was created in Phase III, it was important to activate resources through mom's church to help obtain donations and support to create a proper nutrition plan (Table 7.2). Therefore, the safety plan was maintained along with a two-track process of a nutritional plan and wound playbook. In this way, Round 1 and Round 2 synchronized together to parent the whole child, not just the sum of the parts.

TABLE 7.2 Round 2: Two-Track Nutritional Playbook and Wound Playbooks

Continue to Monitor Round 1 Safety Plan of "Lights On"

Maintain current risk level of a "1" or "2" through:

- Parent self-report,
- What is witnessed by FST therapist during home visits, and
- Regular check-ins with DSS caseworker

Nutritional Playbook	**Forgiveness and Reconnection Wound Playbook**
Who: • Mom, Jamal, FST therapist, mom's pastor and targeted congregation members	**Who:** • Biological dad, Jamal, FST therapist, and Mom

What:
• Used Basic Dietary Guidelines for Good Nutrition handout to assess current nutritional level. Total score = 9 which indicated that major dietary changes were recommended
• Based on the handout, the following were the areas of concern:
  ○ Insufficient water intake per day
  ○ Insufficient protein intake per day
  ○ No breakfast most days and if breakfast, only sugar cereals and fruit juice
  ○ No multivitamin
  ○ Heavy sugar intake per day
	What:
	• Forgiveness talk by Dad with Jamal
	• Reconnection through weekly special outings between Jamal and Dad
	
	When:
	• Forgiveness talk(s) over next two sessions
	• Special reconnection outings on Saturday afternoon from 12 p.m. to 2 p.m. or longer

When: • Follow Basic Dietary Guidelines for Good Nutrition handout as experiment for next 30 days to see if positive impact in school and at home	**Where:** • Forgiveness talk in therapist office or during home visit • Special outing at dad's home or in community
Where: • At Mom's house	**How:** • Forgiveness talk facilitated by FST therapist • Practice role plays with dad, therapist, and mom prior to actual talk between dad and Jamal • Special outing terms written down on paper and troubleshooting ahead of time to help ensure success.
How: • Pastor will meet with his church staff to help jump-start the family with nutritional food budget for next 30 days	

(continued)

Nutritional Playbook	Forgiveness and Reconnection Wound Playbook
• A "nutritional parent mentor" will be asked from the congregation to help mom with grocery shopping and prepare nutritious meals for the week in Tupperware containers to be served at each meal along with a multivitamin and 2-liter water bottle • FST therapist will set up a behavioral modification contract to implement new food plan that would entail consequences or loss of privileges if Jamal refuses to eat nutritious meals	

TABLE 7.2 Round 2: Two-Track Nutritional Playbook and Wound Playbooks (*continued*)

Assessing New Safety and Risk Levels

If the decision made at the end of Phase I is to proceed directly to trauma or wound work, the FST therapist will still proactively inquire about safety planning at the beginning of Phase II before proceeding to Step 2. The transition statement to use at the beginning of Phase II (if no prior stabilization was needed) is provided:

> Before going further, I want to maintain a stance of 'safety first.' This means that I want to look at your current safety risk level. At the end of our last session, we determined that your child's or teen's problems were directly the result of these unhealed wounds [state them].
>
> [**Only if applicable**] However, you mentioned some safety issues on your stress chart using our safety handout from last session (Phase I). They were [list them]. So I want to go around the room and ask each person to rate the safety issue you mentioned at our last session on a scale from 1 to 5 with "1" indicating no risk and "5" indicating high risk. If the risk is high, we will discuss how it can be lowered prior to active wound work or we will discuss how we can address healing wounds and safety at the same time.
>
> [If there were no safety issues on stress chart] Just to be on the safe side. I know you did not identify any safety concerns last session on the safety handout. However, since we met last, have any new ones emerged? Or do you feel more trust in me to say what they are now? I will go over the first session safety handout [see Safety Stressor Questionnaire in Chapter 5]. Let me know if there are any safety issues now present and, if so, I will stop and go around the room and ask you to rate it on a scale from 1 to 5 with "1" indicating no risk and "5" indicating high risk.

This transition introductory statement provides the FST therapist the road map he needs to make a thorough safety check. It is important to note that therapists sometimes make a tactical error of only going over safety issues once in the therapeutic process (assessment). The therapist may not realize that early on in treatment there is often a low level of client trust or a poor therapeutic alliance. Therefore, it is important to continue to check-in regularly regarding safety. As trust builds, more family secrets around safety are often revealed.

As a brief reminder, this first step is a risk-level safety assessment only. There is no creation of safety playbooks, if needed, until Phase III. Instead, the FST therapist will take copious notes of the safety issues involved and move into the creation of a safety playbook in Phase III as needed.

STEP 2: WINDOW OF TOLERANCE AND SELF-REGULATION TOOLS

Accurately assessing for an individual's window of tolerance is not an exact science. Window of tolerance is defined as the optimal zone of arousal whereby people can manage and thrive in everyday life and respond to whatever comes their way without being thrown off course (Siegel, 1999). Individuals who have experienced trauma, however, can easily go outside of this window of tolerance as evidenced by a vulnerability to either *hyperarousal* (i.e., unable to trust their bodily sensations, which can alert them to take appropriate action) and/or *hypoarousal* (i.e., experiencing a separation from the body such as dissociative symptoms like motor weakness, paralysis, numbness of inner body sensation; Ogden et al, 2006; van der Kolk, 2014).

As a result, if the child or parent tends to go outside the optimal zone within the window of tolerance in either direction, he or she is at risk of being retraumatized. Additionally, the child or parent may have a low threshold for relatively minor stressors, which can lead to an extreme vulnerability to traumatic triggers. In an effort to control this type of distress, clients may develop behaviors that produce immediate relief but are unhelpful and harmful in the long run. Self-harm through cutting or eating disorders are two such examples. Both give instant relief but prevent the development of healthy self-regulation alternatives.

To counteract these effects, self-regulation tools or titration control strategies (e.g., meditation, deep breathing, walking exercises) are taught (c.f., Ogden et al., 2006; Siegel, 1999). For example, if a family member or child starts to experience too much anxiety or stress (hyperarousal) as they talk about their traumatic event, the client is taught to use a self-regulation tool such as deep breathing to reduce their stress level. If not, the FST session is derailed before it begins. Self-regulation tools also include eye movement desensitization and reprocessing (EMDR) or bilateral sensory input, such as side-to-side eye movements (Shapiro, 1989; Shapiro & Forrest, 2004) and neurofeedback (Chapman, 2014; Siegel, 1999; van der Kolk, 1994).

This step outlines some of the basic self-regulation techniques that are applicable within the FST model. If family members require more intensive self-regulation strategies such as EMDR or neurofeedback, the FST therapist can refer clients to these outside professionals. Should that be necessary, FST therapy can still continue but in concert with this referred treatment. For example, a parent or a child may complete four or five individual EMDR sessions with another therapist and then have the tools necessary to continue with Phase II of the FST model. This is a prime example of using a both/and approach, synchronizing individual and family systems trauma work into one complete package.

Window of Tolerance Assessment

To begin Step 2, the following transition statement is recommended:

> Thank you for sharing any safety concerns. I wrote them down and will address these directly when we get to Phase III in our next session. In the meantime, I want to ask you some important questions around what we call your 'window of tolerance' around stress. Specifically, stress around the unhealed wounds of [list them] that we spoke about at the end of our last session. I want to make sure that if you or your child talks about your wounds in the future, everyone has the tools they need to not get retraumatized if you retell your wound story.

After this introductory statement, the FST therapist can use a formal pre- and posttest assessment to assess for window of tolerance[1] and/or use the handout in Figure 7.1.

---

[1] The *Structured Interview for Disorders of Extreme Stress* (SIDES; Pelcovitz et al., 1997). For the purposes of this book, we will not go into a detailed discussion of the use or application of this assessment. This is merely one example to jump-start the process if the reader wishes to explore for additional assessments.

Hyperarousal state		Window of tolerance optimal state		Hypoarousal state
Becoming too aroused		Natural fluctuation in arousal in response to environmental cues		Shutting down or having too little arousal
Physical signs:				
➢ Shakiness				Physical signs:
➢ Impulsivity				➢ Physical
Emotional signs:		Physical, emotional		immobilization
➢ Rage	**Extreme**	and cognitive	**Extreme**	➢ Lethargy
➢ Feeling unsafe	**◄ Stress**	responses are	**Stress ►**	➢ Passivity
➢ Defensiveness	**Reaction**	tolerable and	**Reaction**	Emotional Signs
➢ Overwhelmed		congruent with		➢ Feeling numb
Cognitive signs:		the present		➢ Feeling disconnected
➢ Racing thoughts				Cognitive signs
➢ Obsessive thoughts				➢ Scattered thoughts
➢ Intrusive imagery				➢ Inability to think clearly

Figure 7.1 Window of tolerance handout.

Using the handout in Figure 7.1, the FST therapist will first ask the parent or caregiver if he or she has seen any hyper- or hypoarousal symptoms in the child. In addition, the therapist should ask if the adults in the family also suffer from these same symptoms. After asking the parent(s), the therapist will ask the child if he or she agrees or disagrees with the parent's assessment and why, or why not? At this point, the goal is to simply find out if a problem in hyper- or hypoarousal exists. If there are no hyper- or hypoarousal symptoms, the FST therapist will proceed directly to Step 3. There is no need to go through self-regulation tools outlined in the next section.

However, one word of caution. The child or family may not yet have insight or realize they have hyper- or hypoarousal symptoms until they actually begin to retell their trauma story. In other words, a family member may say, "*I do not have these problems*" or "*I am not aware that I do.*" However, later when the story is actually told, the symptoms rapidly emerge in real time. If this happens, the FST therapist must push the pause button and retrace to this phase of treatment to provide self-regulation tools. The FST therapist will state that it is normal for hyper- or hypoarousal symptoms to be out of one's awareness until the traumatic event is relived.

Window of Tolerance: Self-Regulation Tools If Needed

If self-regulation tools are needed, the following transition statement is recommended:

Now that we know there is a risk of hyper- or hypoarousal, let's review and practice what are called basic self-regulation tools. When used properly, these self-regulation tools will help you or your child move from a hyper or hypo state to what is called an 'optimal state.' Ideally, when we are in the optimal zone, we can talk about our wounds without getting retraumatized in the process.

In addition, you will be able to use these new tools at home or at school. For example, you might be driving in your car or sitting in your school classroom tomorrow and be thinking about your old wounds. As you do this, you will be more aware of any hypo- or hyperarousal symptoms because of the insight you got today. When this happens, you can then immediately use one of your new self-regulation tools to quickly move you into the optimal zone.

After this introductory statement, the FST therapist would review some common self-regulating tools that are provided in Table 7.3. This table can be copied and passed out as a handout.

TABLE 7.3 Handout Self-Regulation Tools to Stay Within the Optimal Window of Tolerance

Techniques Using the Power of Movement

When we talk about a wound, we can be propelled into that situation, as if we are back there again. These are commonly called flashbacks and these can cause us to be retraumatized. To prevent this occurrence, we want to practice staying in the present. The strategies below can help us do this. It is recommended that you practice these regularly just as you would regularly engage in an exercise routine. This regularity will help the tools to be more effective when used to stay in the present and within the optimal window of tolerance.

☐ **Active Orienting Exercise**
When you feel yourself getting stuck in the past, immediately pause from thinking about your past trauma and look around the room (wherever you are) and find 4 objects that are the same color. Name those objects out loud. This tool will help you to slow down your automatic unhelpful response and bring you back into the window of tolerance.

☐ **Senses-Orienting Exercise**
To stop both hypo- and hyperarousal responses, stand up and walk around the room. As you walk, focus your awareness on the movement of your legs and on your capacity to move toward and away from objects in the room. With each step, speak aloud exactly what you are doing (e.g. "I am now moving toward the desk, I can feel my knees bending and the soles of my feet as they push into the floor, etc."). This tool will help you to regain awareness and control of your body and counterbalance feeling out of control.

☐ **Posture-Orienting Exercise**
Focusing on your posture can be helpful in regaining your feeling of identity and control. This exercise can be done from a sitting position or a standing position. First, focus on straightening your neck so that your head is perfectly aligned with the spine. Be sure that your chin is not jutting forward. Second, stiffen your spine so that it stretches and straightens out. Third, whether sitting or standing, position your feet directly beneath the pelvis area and push flat into the floor. The end result should feel as if you are being lifted upward by the crown of your head while keeping your feet planted firmly on the floor.

Techniques Using the Power of Breathing

When we talk about a wound, we can immediately move to hyperarousal emotions (feeling too much—feeling rage, feeling unsafe, racing thoughts, shakiness, etc.) or hypoarousal (feeling too little—feeling numb, disconnected, scattered thoughts, etc.). When this happens, we need to use the power of our breathing to get us back into the optimal state (feeling safe, able to tolerate our feelings, connected to the present, etc.). Practice these breathing exercises at home until you get really good at them and then use them whenever you feel too much or feel too little.

☐ **Simple Breathing Exercise**
Take four or five deep breaths. Breathe in through your nose and exhale through your mouth, focusing on the exhaled breath. This exercise will activate the parasympathetic nervous system and is helpful in countering the hyperarousal state. This exercise can be repeated several times.

☐ **Circle Breathing Exercise**
Inhale while raising your arms from your sides to over your head. Exhale while lowering your arms back to your sides. Repeat 5 to 10 times. This exercise is most effective if practiced regularly.

☐ **Prayer Breathing Exercise**
This exercise combines breathing and prayer with God, Jesus, the Holy Spirit, or your Higher Power. Inhale deeply and then exhale, pushing all the air out of your body. Repeat with your eyes closed as you meditate on a prayer such as *"God, I know you are with me now and I choose to think of your goodness and beauty"* or on a favorite passage such as a scripture passage from the Bible, Psalm 23:4 *"Even though I walk through the darkest valley, I will fear no evil, for you are with me; your rod and your staff, they comfort me."* This exercise can be repeated as many times as desired.

Source: Ogden, Kekuni, and Clair. (2006) and van der Kolk (2014).

The family members will be asked to closely examine Table 7.3 and then select the tools they like the best with the FST therapist's guidance. The tool(s) selected will then be practiced. The FST therapist will first role-model the correct procedure and then ask family members to mirror what they just witnessed.

It is important to limit the self-regulation selection to one or two tools. Otherwise, the therapist might overwhelm the family with too many techniques all at once. Later, after the trauma story is told, it may be necessary to incorporate other tools. Table 7.3 provides a core listing of top self-regulation tools that can used. For a more extensive list, readers are directed to other resources, especially within the field of dialectical behavior therapy (DBT; c.f., Malchiodi & Perry, 2014; Martin, Seppa, Lehtinen, & Torco, 2012; McKay, Wood, & Brantley, 2007; Ostafin, Robinson, & Meier, 2015). Additional self-regulation tools can be added to those in Table 7.3.

Case Example

During Phase I, 15-year-old Ben revealed that his unhealed wound centered around the traumatic event of being placed in foster care. He blamed his single parent mom, Mary. When he returned home more than a year later, he was filled with unforgiveness, betrayal, and resentment toward his mother. When the window of tolerance assessment was conducted, Ben stated that he had symptoms of both hyper- and hypoarousal. Whenever he thought about being in foster care (which was often), he felt instant anger and rage toward his mom, followed by his heart racing. Afterward, he went numb and felt deep hopelessness and sadness. Nighttime was the worst. He was unable to sleep because his mind raced constantly. Mary then stated that her guilt was overwhelming and this resulted in her own hypoarousal or shutting down.

Referring the self-regulation tools handout, Ben chose the following tools:

- Simple breathing exercise
- Senses-orienting exercise

Mom chose the following tools:

- Prayer breathing exercise
- Active orienting exercise

After the self-regulation tools were selected, the therapist moved into role-modeling each exercise. The therapist pretended to be Ben during the role-play and spoke out loud his negative thoughts. The FST therapist then quickly incorporated the self-regulation tools to counteract hyper- or hypoarousal to return to an optimal zone. The following is a brief transcript example of one of the demonstrated self-regulation techniques:

| FST therapist: | Ben, I am going to pretend that I am you to show you how to use the techniques you picked. After we are done, I will go to your mom and repeat the same thing with her. I am going to try to speak the thoughts in your head out loud when you think about foster care at nighttime. If I get your thoughts wrong, stop me and give me the right ones. It is |

(continued)

Case Example (*continued*)

---

	just my best guess. Then after your thoughts are stated out loud, I will counter these with the one of the self-regulation tools you just picked. Is that OK? Any questions?
Ben:	It's OK. But what if just watching you playing me starts to get me stressed out inside?
FST therapist:	Great question. If you feel that way, hold up one finger and I will stop immediately. I can still walk through the technique in words without the role-play. The same thing goes for you, Mary, when I get to you.
Ben and Mom:	[Together] That helps a lot.
FST therapist:	OK. Here is what I am going to do . . . . I am going to pretend I am lying in your bed at night and cannot sleep and my mind is racing. I am thinking over and over that "I cannot believe this has happened, I feel alone and lost, and I am so mad at my mom for abandoning me." To counter these thoughts and feelings, I am now going to get up out of bed and begin to walk around my room. As I walk, I am going to focus my awareness on the way my legs are moving and on my ability to move closer and farther away from various objects in my room. I am also going to speak aloud exactly what I am doing. [The FST therapist physically demonstrates the senses-orienting exercise, speaking aloud exactly what he is doing by saying, "I am now moving toward my dresser, I feel my feet pushing into the floor, I am now moving backward, away from my dresser," etc.]
	Ben, now that you have seen me demonstrate this tool, I want you to try it.
Ben:	Sure [Ben now gets up and mimics what the FST therapist just demonstrated]
FST Therapist:	How does that feel? The good news is that you can use this same tool not only to help you sleep but also anytime in this room when we start to talk about your pain or wounds in the future. When you start to feel overwhelmed, I want you to give me a signal by raising your right index finger. We will all patiently wait for you to use your senses-orienting exercise or the simple breathing exercise for as long as it takes until you are ready to begin again.

Ben started to immediately tear up after this reassurance. As promised, the FST therapist stopped the session to give Ben all the time he needed to regroup.

The therapist gently led Ben into "senses orienting" and quietly asked him if Mom could walk silently beside him in support. Ben was still crying but nodded, yes. Mom then walked quietly alongside Ben. After 10 minutes of walking, Ben regained his composure and they moved on to practice with Mom.

(*continued*)

Case Example (*continued*)

Later in therapy, Ben reported that Mom quietly walking beside him was a game changer. He stated,

"I was still mad, but suddenly I didn't feel alone anymore. I I knew that she had her own pain. Her pain was guilt, my pain was rage. But somewhere in the back of my mind I knew that we could heal our pain together."

STEP 3: NEUROPLASTICITY AND PROPER NUTRITION

The inclusion of Step 3 in this book can be attributed to two different sources. The first comes from the groundbreaking books by Dr. Scott Shannon (2013, 2014) entitled *Parenting the Whole Child: A Holistic Child Psychiatrist Offers Practical Wisdom on Behavior, Brain Health, Nutrition, Exercise, Family Life, Peer, Life, Trauma, Medication, and More* and *Mental Health for the Whole Child: Moving Young Clients from Disease & Disorder to Balance & Wellness.* The second source comes from the first author's wife, Nancy, and their young 8-year-old son, David. Dr. Sells' son, David, is a special needs child who was diagnosed with severe attention deficit disorder (ADD). As a result, David experienced a major traumatic event and setback when Dr. Sells and his wife, Nancy, tried to place David in a mainstream school system without any tools. In trying to find answers, Nancy stumbled upon Dr. Shannon's books. As part of the overall treatment regime, we began to pair proper nutrition with the latest research on neuroplasticity and trauma (Doidge, 2015). The results were life-changing. Proper nutrition became a foundational first step toward the long-term healing of our son's trauma. As the result of this personal experience and applying this step with other traumatized families, the nuts and bolts of neuroplasticity and nutrition are included here as a core preparation step (along with safety planning and self-regulation tools) prior to active wound work.

Research on Neuroplasticity and Nutrition

Despite the advances of nutritional therapy over the past 30 years, research studies show that there is often limited to no inclusion of nutrition as part of the mental health treatment process (Dufault et al., 2009; Geraghty, Depasquale, & Lane, 2010; Strickland, 2009; Velasquez-Manoff, 2012). In other words, many therapists move past nutrition and quickly onto psychotropic medications or other interventions (Shannon, 2014; Strickland, 2009). As a result, medicated brain change takes place before first trying nutritional brain change. Diet and nutrition can be a powerful tool to influence change in both the body and brain of a child and/or family member experiencing trauma.

In addition, the latest research shows a direct link between neuroplasticity, proper nutrition, and healing the traumatized brain (Shannon, 2014; Siegel & Solomon, 2003; van der Kolk, 2014). Neuroplasticity means that neural pathways in our brain are strengthened with repetition. One way to describe this process is that "the neurons that fire together, wire together" (Shannon, 2013, p. 33). Constant repetition of an experience leads to changes within the brain's structure and the manner in which neurons process that experience. The more consistent this experience, the stronger these neurons bond.

Traumatic experiences also form neural pathways in the brain. These pathways can be even more deeply ingrained due to shock or intensity. Therefore, when a single trigger or set of triggers occurs, the emotions associated with the trauma are revisited and the associated neural pathway further strengthened. This is why, for example, a survivor of childhood sexual abuse can still experience the trauma many years later as if it was still happening to them.

However, based on neuroplasticity research, we now know that the brain is constantly adapting and rewiring itself. Our thoughts and behaviors in the here and now influence this process. For example, if a child who experiences a lifetime of abuse and neglect enters into a new family situation of consistent love, nurturance, and caring, the brain will actually rewire itself to heal the cerebral cortex and the child will more likely in the future find positive, healthy relationships that repeat this pattern of receiving love and nurturance. In fact, a child's IQ can be raised by as much as 30 points if negative or absent stimulation is replaced with positive, nurturing stimulation (Agrawal & Gomez-Pinilla, 2012).

According to the research of Shannon and others, proper nutrition is a key ingredient or foundational first step to rewiring our neural pathways (Abenavoli, 2010; Shannon, 2013). Shannon calls this "feeding the child's brain for emotional and mental health" (Shannon, 2014, p. 69). For example, in one study, researchers followed over 3,000 teens for 3 years, monitoring their diet and mental health. These researchers found that diet quality was closely tied to mental health. Moreover, improvements in diet quality were mirrored by improvements in mental health, while decays in diet quality were associated with declining psychological functioning (Ader, Felten, & Cohen, 2000).

In summary, based on this research, safety planning and self-regulation strategies should be integrated with proper nutrition prior to direct trauma work in Phase III. The use of drug therapy can be helpful because of the speed with which it can alleviate the child's problem symptoms and provide an immediate break for the overwhelmed child and parent (Shannon, 2014). However, psychotropic medications only treat the symptoms of the core problem. Using medication alone delays treatment of the core unhealthy undercurrents that cause the child's symptoms. Therefore, combining wound playbooks with proper nutrition to bolster the neuroplasticity of the brain will work toward treating the whole child or adolescent.

It is important to note that the FST therapist is not expected to become a nutritionist in addition to doing family systems work. He or she is not qualified for such a role. Instead, the FST therapist will introduce and use a basic nutritional self-assessment, and, if needed, refer the family to a local qualified nutritionist and work in concert with the nutritionist to monitor the nutrition plan and help bring about accountability (see Table 7.4). The integration of systems therapy with proper nutrition of the traumatized brain within a holistic framework is the key goal and objective.

TABLE 7.4 Dietary Behavior Modification Contract

Our Daily Food Plan to Feed Your Brain

Healthy Breakfast
- (School days Monday through Friday): 7 a.m.
    - You may choose between oatmeal and eggs; fresh juice made with our family juicer
    - 1 liter of water
- Weekends: 1 cheat day—you pick Saturday or Sunday

When you finish a healthy breakfast, you keep the privilege of your phone, TV, video game, weekend outing with friends, and so on. Otherwise, you lose it for this day and get it back the next time you finish a healthy breakfast.

(continued)

TABLE 7.4 Dietary Behavior Modification Contract (*continued*)

Healthy Lunch
- Lunch time
  - You may choose between a salad with protein (fish or chicken) and a sandwich with a vegetable
  - 1 liter of water
- Weekends: 1 cheat day—you pick Saturday or Sunday

When you finish a healthy lunch, you keep the privilege of your phone, TV, video game, weekend outing with friends, etc. Otherwise, you lose it for this day and get it back the next time you finish a complete lunch.

Healthy Dinner
- (School days Monday through Friday): 6 p.m.—Weekends on your own
  - I will prepare a nutritious dinner that will vary but will include a variety of fish, chicken, vegetables, and meat
  - Another liter of water
- Weekends: 1 cheat day—you pick Saturday or Sunday

When you finish a healthy dinner, you keep the privilege of your phone, TV, video game, weekend outing, and so on. Otherwise, you lose it for this day and get it back the next time you finish a complete lunch.

Snacks Between Meals
- Fruit, nuts, yogurt
- No soda, cookies, or candy

*Please note: One different privilege can be assigned to each different meal. For example, smartphone retention to breakfast, video game to lunch, and early bedtime to dinner

Nutritional Self-Assessment

To begin this step, the following transition statement is used:

> The last preparation step before we move into wound work is an assessment of proper diet and nutrition. The reason for this is that the latest research shows a direct link between proper nutrition and healing the effects of trauma or emotional wounds.

> In the old days, science told us that our brains stopped growing. In other words, once we had a bad or traumatic experience it would be in our brains forever and unable to heal. But new research shows that this is not the case. We have in our brains something called 'neuroplasticity.' This means that the 200 billion neurons in our brain are constantly being *rewired* based on our present-day experiences. Therefore, if you had years of abuse and neglect but then it was suddenly replaced by love and caring, your brain could literally rewire itself with these new emotions to heal old wounds. So when we create wound playbooks together in the next session, they will literally help you and your child to begin to rewire the neurons in your brain in a positive way.

> However, every brain, just like every car, needs proper gasoline. If you put diesel gasoline in a car that needs unleaded, the car will break down. In the same way, if you feed your brain with processed sugar, bad carbs, and not enough water or vitamins, you literally starve it to death. Our brain needs the right "gasoline" to rewire itself properly. Therefore, before we move into rewiring through the wound playbooks, we must first make sure you have the proper "gasoline in the tank" to feed both your body and your brain.

> Let me pause here and ask each member to comment on or ask questions about what I just said.

This introductory statement will elicit rich conversation and debate. It will range from wholehearted argument to denial or defensiveness. In America, since the typical diet is so high in sugar and saturated fat, teenagers will often vehemently resist such a change in diet, and so might the parents. Poor nutrition is now the standard American diet. Therefore, family members may agree in theory, but when it comes to actual change, a battle for structure between the therapist and family may ensue. In fact, the discussion may even lead to premature termination, especially if the FST therapist asks that a family of overweight adults change their diet in support of their child who is asked to change their diet.

After the introductory discussion of the pros and cons of proper nutrition, the FST therapist will use the Basic Dietary Guidelines Handout (Table 7.5) to assess for proper nutrition. The questions for this handout were adapted from the section entitled "Dr. Shannon's Basic Dietary Guidelines for All Children" in his book *Parenting the Whole Child* (Shannon, 2013, pp. 80–82). The FST therapist may choose to use the guidelines provided in Table 7.5 or create his or her own (another useful resource for the most recent dietary guidelines is found at www.health.gov).

TABLE 7.5 Basic Dietary Guidelines for Good Nutrition to Feed and Rewire Your Brain

According to Dr. Scott Shannon's research and book entitled *Parenting the Whole Child* (Shannon, 2014) there are 6 key ingredients to brain growth:

1. Water
2. Protein
3. Energy (fat and carbohydrates)
4. Vitamins (fat and water soluble)
5. Minerals
6. Trace elements

Therefore, on a scale of 1 to 5 (1 = not following each guideline at all; 5 = following each guideline almost 100% of the time) rate yourself on how well you are currently following each guideline. Do the list for your child first and then for yourself as the parent.

#1- On a scale of 1–5	How well is your child hydrated? Does he or she drink 2 to 3 liters of water every day? *Please note: even slight dehydration makes the effective absorption of all other nutrients much more difficult*
#2- On a scale of 1–5	Does your child eat enough protein? (e.g., does he or she eat at least two servings a day of chicken, fish, tofu, eggs, or meat?)
#3- On a scale of 1–5	Does your child get an intake of good oils? (e.g., do you use olive oil or canola oil? Do you use butter instead of margarine, and in moderation?)
#4- On a scale of 1–5	Do you serve your child a minimum of two or three servings a week of fresh fish such as salmon, cod, or herring?
#5- On a scale of 1–5	Do you serve your child a minimum of 2 servings of vegetables, cooked or raw, per day?
#6- On a scale of 1–5	How often does your child eat a healthy breakfast to start the day; things like oatmeal, fruits, or eggs rather than sugar cereals or donuts?
#7- On a scale of 1–5	How often does your child take a multivitamin?
#8- On a scale of 1–5	How often does your child limit intake of processed sugar each day? (e.g., candy, cakes, and even juices.) Occasional treats are okay, but they shouldn't be part of a child's daily diet.

Scoring:

   8 to 16 = Poor diet, needs significant changes

   17 to 24 = Average diet, needs some modifications

   Above 25 = Good to great diet

You should also ask, "How many days a week does your child get at least eight hours of sleep per night? (Catching up on the weekends does not count.) Less than 5 out of 7 days indicates your child is not getting sufficient sleep."

After the handout questionnaire is passed out to each member, the FST therapist asks every family member, including the child, to rate the child in each area on a scale of 1 to 5 (1 = not following the dietary guideline at all; 5 = following the guideline almost 100% of the time). An average is quickly calculated for an overall score. The questionnaire is focused on the child or adolescent with the identified problem. Then, depending on the case, the therapist can repeat the same set of guidelines for siblings and/or parents. It will depend on whether the therapist wants to expand the child's symptom around the issue of diet to include the entire family or just focus on the individual child.

Nutritional Application

After the assessment is complete, the decision is made on whether a referral to a nutritionist is needed. A good rule of thumb is to consider whether the child has any specific medical issues (such as diabetes) and/or has scores rated as needing significant changes (8–16 = Poor diet, needs significant changes) on Table 7.5 . If the answer is "yes" to either question, a referral to a nutritionist is recommended. If the decision is made by the family to move forward on improving the child's nutrition, the FST therapist must find out whether other family members will also agree to improving their diet. However, as the case example in the following text illustrates, the therapist must carefully consider the benefits of correlating the child's accountability to adhering to the diet with the parents' or siblings' success in changing their diet.

As stated earlier, the likelihood that the child or teen will be compliant or enthusiastic with dietary changes is very low. Instead, just as with discipline, children are typically not mature enough developmentally to know what is in their best interest. This may need to be openly stated to the parent, preferably without the child or adolescent present. Therefore, as with discipline, the therapist might need to use some form of a dietary behavioral modification contract as illustrated in Table 7.4. The reason is that when parents must take charge, it moves into a hierarchy issue with the need for clear and concretely defined limits that are tied to rewards and consequences. In the example in Table 7.4, privileges that the child receives or takes for granted are tied to eating what is served. For younger children, the easiest privilege to tie to eating what is served is bedtime or the use of electronics or television. For adolescents, this can be modified to the privilege of seeing friends or going out on a Friday and/or Saturday night. These privileges are either given or taken away. This easy-to-follow and straightforward nutritional approach can help remove any power struggles.

Case Example

Fourteen-year-old Michael was extremely overweight and depressed. When he began treatment, he was being treated with an antidepressant. At the time, he was also being relentlessly teased and bullied by other kids in his school. This day-to-day bullying and trauma became a vicious cycle of overeating to self-regulate his stress and then becoming depressed from overeating, only to lead to more overeating later. A dietary assessment also revealed an average sleep pattern of only 4 hours per night. Michael overate with a steady diet of chips, soda, cookies, and ice cream to stuff his frustrations and numb his feelings.

(continued)

Case Example (*continued*)

If this was not bad enough, Michael was feeling the horrible side-effects from his medication, which included low energy and a dry mouth. He had been in individual treatment for over a year with no real progress. Family therapy had never been tried.

It was discovered that beginning around age 4 years, Michael's diet had a severe lack of vitamins, minerals, and, most of all, protein. In addition, the high-sugar, high-carbohydrate diet made him overweight. Therefore, to rewire Michael's brain, he needed a diet that would keep his blood sugar levels stable, nourish his growing brain with protein, and improve his mood and energy levels. Therefore, the nutritional plan focused on:

- Addressing the severe protein deficiency
- Increasing intake of vegetables
- Decreasing sugar intake
- Reducing bad carbohydrates and using a good multivitamin

At first, the parents had to tie Michael's love of his computer and his tablet to eating properly. Many role-plays and troubleshooting techniques had to be done to counter the effects of the parents' guilt and habit of giving into Michael's bad eating. The parents had to tape a sign to the refrigerator that said, "Every time we give in and feed Michael unhealthy food we are hurting his brain! We have a 30 day commitment." The written contract provided them with the step-by-step guide they needed.

Within just 3 weeks, the change in Michael was nothing short of a miracle. He had more energy, looked his parents in the eye, and had already started to lose weight. And, as he felt better, he made more friends and even started to participate in sports. The wound playbook then focused on increasing nurturance between parent and child and on finding forgiveness toward the kids who had bullied him for so many years.

Please note. After the nutrition step is completed, the FST therapist may want to end the session and begin the next session with Step 4. Variables impacting this decision include whether it is only a 1-hour session and the length of time each section takes. For example, if the family does not indicate hypo- or hyperarousal problems, the therapist can proceed directly to Step 3 or vice versa.

STEP 4: INFORMED CONSENT

Another guideline for safety planning based on the ISTSS guidelines (Dietrich, 2001) is "informed consent." This guideline is adhered to in Phase II when the FST therapist reviews with the family what is called the Surgeon General's warning. This review provides the family with a list of pros and cons of moving forward to heal wounds using the FST model. To drive this point home, the FST therapist can bring into the session an actual cigarette packet to show each family member what is meant metaphorically and experientially by a Surgeon General's warning. The parallel connection is made when the FST therapist states: "As the Surgeon General's warning on a cigarette packet points out the risks of smoking, there are also risks in doing active wound work. However, unlike cigarettes there are many benefits in wound work that we will go through together."

In addition to safety planning, there are other key reasons for informed consent. First, it builds confidence and hope when the therapist normalizes that as buried hurts are brought to the surface, one might get worse before getting better. Second, informed consent concretely defines both pros and cons up-front. When this is done, clients feel a sense of empowerment and choice. Finally, if done correctly, informed consent can be used as a paradoxical "restraining change" intervention. Restraint, or the directive to go slow, is a strategic intervention that carries a paradoxical flavor (Haley, 1991). When therapists restrain or instruct family members to go slow, by carefully considering the pros and cons in the informed consent, they ask the family not to change too fast and instead to take the change slowly. This puts the family in a double bind in that if the family goes forward and positive change happens, they are better prepared for any setbacks ahead of time and are fully-informed that these relapses are normal. In either case, the change process is "immunized" against setbacks.

FST Informed Consent

To begin this step, the following transition statement is recommended:

> Now that the foundation has been laid down with safety planning, window of tolerance, and proper nutrition, it is time to go over what is called 'informed consent' or a Surgeon General's warning. I brought along this cigarette package to illustrate this. As you can see on the package [pass it around] there is a Surgeon General's warning that gives the cigarette user an informed consent or warning if you decide to smoke the cigarettes.
>
> In the same way, I want to pass out a handout that outlines the pros and any potential cons of our doing wound work together. After reading these key points and asking questions, you all will have a choice to go forward or to end treatment today.
>
> This informed consent is not meant to scare you or deter you from going forward. Quite the opposite. My hope is that with eyes wide open you will be even more confident to go forward because you will be better prepared for setbacks ahead of time.

Once this statement is made, it is time to pass out the FST informed consent. A sample is illustrated in Table 7.6 and can be fully adopted or adapted as needed. The sample is based on the recommended language by the WHO Ethics Review Committee (WHO, 2014).

TABLE 7.6 FST Informed Consent Template

Your Agency Letterhead

This informed consent form is for families who want to participate in FST (family systems trauma) treatment. This form is given now because we are about to begin active wound or trauma treatment with the introduction and completion of what are called "wound playbooks." Therefore, the optimal timing to go over this form is now, to discuss both benefits and limitations of this approach for you individually and your family or village as a whole.

PART I: Introduction and Overall Purpose of FST Treatment

FST treatment was built to work with the entire family, not just your child or teen. This is because we believe that there is power in families to help heal one another. When one person in the family experiences a wound or traumatic event, everyone hurts. The FST treatment model was developed based on outcomes that your child can heal better and faster if everyone helps and changes.

Type of Intervention

☑ FST treatment was built on the belief that optimal change can happen best in the here and now. This means while we can learn from the past, we cannot change the past. But we can change the future. Therefore, we will talk about past hurts but then focus on the "Now what?" What tools do we need in the here and now to heal our wounds and those of our child so we do not stay stuck in our pain? To answer this question, we will be creating together what are called wound playbooks (see sample playbook).

(continued)

TABLE 7.6 FST Informed Consent Template (*continued*)

☑ As your therapist, I will actively help, give advice, and facilitate the creation of your playbook. You and your child will be active participants and together we will create your playbook.

☑ After we create the playbook or playbooks, we will practice their delivery through role-plays or dress rehearsals and troubleshoot any potential "What will you do if x, y, or z goes wrong?" ahead of time. We will then put the playbooks into action and afterward come together to evaluate how well it went and troubleshoot any problems in implementation. If there are problems, we will work together to tweak the playbook accordingly.

☑ After you complete the FST treatment, we will do "tune-ups." This means that if you or your child relapses, which is normal, we can meet, as needed, for one or two sessions at most to get back on track as quickly as possible.

PART II: List of Benefits and Limitations

Like many other trauma-focused treatments, FST treatment does not presently have clinical trials to determine its effectiveness. However, painstaking effort has gone into developing this model through research studies that show good outcomes on key components of the FST treatment model (c.f., Karam, Sterrett, & Kiaer, 2015; Sells, Winokur-Early, & Smith 2011; Winokur-Early, Chapman, & Hand, 2013).

Potential Benefits

☑ **Step-by-Step Procedures:** The FST treatment model provides your FST therapist with written step-by-step procedures. Many treatment models provide general concepts but no step-by-step procedures. These step-by-step procedures benefit you and your family because your therapist has a clear road map to follow and treatment that is standardized and based on good research outcomes.

☑ **The Whole Family and Village are Involved:** Traditional trauma treatment has mostly involved just the individual child, without active participation from the entire family or the extended family or village. FST treatment is one of the first models ever to involve your entire family in helping heal your and your child's wounds.

☑ **Skills and Playbooks:** As illustrated in the playbook sample, you will leave FST treatment with written and concrete playbooks with clear tools and skills in the here and now to heal your and your child's wounds that have not healed on their own.

☑ **An Active Coach to Help Guide the Process:** You are not alone. As your therapist, I will function like a fitness coach to help guide the process and step in if there are relapses or setbacks. Wound work is hard, especially if you have to go it alone. Now you will have a professional coach to support you throughout. Therefore, if you back away now, you will have to go it alone.

Potential Limitations

• **It is Likely to Get Worse Before It Gets Better:** Your child's present-day problems may initially get worse before they get better because we are uncorking or reopening old and unhealed wounds. This is initially scary. The good news is that having a coach (FST therapist) and a written playbook dramatically increases the odds that becoming worse is temporary on the way to permanent healing. You should expect the first 30 days to be the toughest. After 30 days, things usually turn around and get better.

• **Talking About Wounds May Initially Reopen Them:** Discussing unhealed wounds can cause one to become retraumatized just by talking about them and cause hypo or hyper reactions. This is why we built in self-regulation tools, nutrition, and safety planning into the FST treatment model.

• **The "Walking Wounded" State Is Challenged:** Currently, you or your child might be in what is called a "walking wounded" state. This means that you currently have coping strategies (alcohol, prescription painkillers, self-harm, etc.) that don't heal the wound but just help you get through the day. Using FST treatment, we try to provide better coping strategies (self-regulation tools, playbooks, etc.) and get you to a place where the wound is permanently healed. But in the meantime, your stress may increase as these unhelpful coping strategies are addressed.

• **Other Unanticipated Areas May Be Impacted:** When we throw a pebble in a pond, it creates ripples outward. In the same way, as we treat your child, other areas may be impacted as well. For example, if your child suddenly gets better after years and years of you taking care of him or her, it may shine the light on other problems that have been ignored until now. For example, parents may now face marital problems that had been ignored or other sibling resentments over the long-standing focus on the problem child while they felt ignored, or even parents asking themselves, "What is my new identify now that my child no longer needs me?"

(continued)

TABLE 7.6 FST Informed Consent Template (*continued*)

PART III: Certificate of Consent

Your participation in FST treatment is entirely voluntary. It is your choice whether to participate or not. If you choose not to participate, we will refer you to other treatment options. If you begin FST treatment and change your mind later, you can stop participating at any time even if you agree to participate today.

Typical Duration

From this point forward (not counting your assessment period previously), FST treatment typically takes place over the next three months with an average of six to eight 2-hour sessions. After graduation we will follow up with you by phone at least once a month for the next 90 days to assess for any relapse. If relapse occurs, we will recommend what we call "tune-ups." These are one to several sessions to address relapse and get back on track as quickly as possible. Tune-ups are also voluntary.

Confidentiality

All counseling content is confidential. This means that no information is released to individuals outside the counseling service without signed consent. Exceptions to this rule include threats of harm toward oneself or another person or court subpoena for records.

I have read the foregoing information, or it has been read to me. I have had the opportunity to ask questions about it and any questions that I have asked have been answered to my satisfaction. I consent voluntarily to participate in FST treatment.

Print name of each family member _____

Signature of each family member _____

Date _____

               Day/month/year

FST informed consent can be given either in Phase I or at this stage of treatment. The rationale for this timetable is that it signals the beginning of active wound work. Phase I was the assessment phase and Phases II through V are the active treatment or intervention phases. Because of this fact, Phase II is an optimal time to introduce informed consent. It also has the added strategic benefit of restraining a family system from changing before the therapist requires active change. The rationale for this timing is clarified within the first paragraph of the form:

> This form is given now because we are about to begin active wound or trauma treatment with the introduction and completion of what are called "wound playbooks." Therefore, the optimal timing to go over this form is now to discuss both benefits and limitations of this approach for you individually and for your family or village as a whole.

The FST therapist's agency may have its own standard internal informed consent form. If this is the case, it is perfectly fine to have the family sign both forms and explain that one is specific to the FST treatment and the other is for the agency or private practice in general.

STEP 5: REVIEW HIGHLIGHTS OF PHASE I

A review of the highlights of Phase I after Step 4 is needed for two reasons. First, there may be new villagers present or key core family members who were not present in Phase I. Therefore, they will need to be brought up to speed on key concepts such as the stress chart, the seed/tree diagram, and the goals of therapy. Without this prior knowledge, those absent will be lost, and lost clients are often angry and/or resistant. Second, the review of highlights presents a perfect segue to the next steps of wound undercurrents, feedback loops, sample wound playbooks, the wound story, and homework assignment. Therefore, this step is an ideal way to refocus the session on active preparation for active wound work.

Prior to the session, the FST therapist should rehang on the wall the stress chart and seed/tree diagram from Phase I. These charts can be rewritten neatly on new flip chart paper or translated into a nice clean PowerPoint slide and projected onto the wall using an LCD projector through a flat-screen television using an HDMI cord. The dramatic effect of a projected image will both entertain and grab the family's attention, especially the child or adolescent who loves technology. It is critically important to either cover the flip chart exhibits or not turn on the projector or television until ready for this step. Otherwise, the family will be distracted.

Once the overview is complete, the FST therapist is now set to show the fruits of the labor of the pre-session preparation and reveal the core undercurrents that are preventing healing from taking place.

STEP 6: REVEAL WOUND UNDERCURRENTS

This is an important step in the FST model for two reasons. First, the FST therapist is using a psychoeducational format to educate the family members on the relationship between seeds and the core drivers, or the undercurrents. It has been our experience that good therapy always combines psychoeducation and treatment into one continuum of care. Second, the undercurrent discussion continues to help expand the symptom from a child focus to a family systems focus and externalizes the problem (c.f., White & Epston, 1990). The focus now becomes one of fixing the unhealthy undercurrents using wound playbooks rather than on the child as the sole problem that must be fixed.

For purposes of continuity and clarity, the case example of 17-year-old Alex and his family from the pre-session preparation step in Chapter 6 is be used in this chapter. Other case examples are included as needed.

Introduction to the Unhealed Wound Undercurrent Concept

Please use the following introductory transition statement:

> The first thing I want to show you is a handout that lists what we call "undercurrents." They represent the secret sauce or the reason why the wounds you mentioned [name the wounds] or other seeds like unmet primal needs or mental or physical impairment are not healing on their own. These undercurrents are directly responsible for causing your child's problems. We call these "undercurrents" because they are actually the underlying root causes of the problem and are difficult to see with the naked eye.

> Let me pass out the undercurrent worksheet based on your seed picks from our first session. I will show you the undercurrents that I think are causing the problems and then we can discuss whether or not you agree with my picks.

Have the undercurrent worksheets for the seed picks readily available to pass out to each family and village member present (see Chapter 6). Younger children of 8 years or below can be excused to the waiting room at this point in treatment, or the FST therapist or parent can be ready to explain the undercurrents with concrete examples. The therapist will read aloud and explain each undercurrent. This will also provide clarification for literacy challenges. It is important to reiterate at this phase in treatment that only the seeds of unhealed wounds, mental and physical impairment, and unmet primal needs are the focus. The misuse of power seed is excluded because it is closely associated with an upside-down hierarchy between parent and child. If a hierarchy problem existed, it would have already been addressed through stabilization previous to this phase of treatment. The focus in this phase is active wound work through the unhealed wound seed and its associated seeds.

Undercurrent Education

Alex's case example is used to successfully execute this step and provides an example for the reader of the proper process and timing for this step. Mirror the same process and timing with your cases. The FST therapist will pass out the undercurrent handout that corresponds with the seed picks from Phase I.

Case Example

During pre-session preparation for Phase II, Alex's FST therapist chose the unhealthy undercurrents of high anxiety, due to the betrayal or abandonment, and lack of forgiveness/bitterness as the top two drivers of the unhealed wound seed, and lack of attachment and connection to God as the drivers for the unmet primal need seed, and checked them off in the undercurrent worksheet as illustrated in the sample in Box 7.1.

BOX 7.1 Alex's Undercurrent Handout

Seeds = Unhealed Wounds & Unmet Primal Needs

Symptoms = Cutting/Depression

Unhealed Wound Seed

- ☐ Unresolved grief or loss: **grief education and resolution**
- ☑ Betrayal or abandonment: **security, forgiveness, unconditional love**
- ☐ Family secrets: **reveal secrets/safety**
- ☐ Physical or mental abuse: **support, courage to leave, forgive**
- ☑ Lack of forgiveness/bitterness: **forgiveness**
- ☐ Lack of consistent nurturance: **unconditional love, consistent nurturance**
- ☑ High anxiety: **safety or security**
- ☐ High stress: **relaxation or diversionary tactics**

Unmet Primal Needs Seed

- ☐ Maslow's unmet hierarchy of needs: fill in "missing" Maslow need
- ☑ Lack of attachment or bonding: attachment bonds
- ☐ Lack of forgiveness/resentment: forgiveness, prayer
- ☑ Lack of connection to God or higher power: connecting to God or higher power
- ☐ Mind, body and spirit unbalanced: **restoring balance**

(continued)

Case Example (*continued*)

The connection to God was selected because prayer and spirituality was a cultural mainstay of the parents. Therefore, if this piece could be incorporated into the therapy process while respecting Alex's belief system, it would be a win/win for both parents and child. In addition, a meta-analysis of research studies on prayer concluded positive correlations between prayer and healing depression, anxiety, and self-harm in both children and adults (Koenig, 2009).

The unhealthy undercurrents illustrated in Box 7.1 were the root causes of Alex's self-harm behaviors of cutting and depression. It was unclear at this point in treatment which specific undercurrent matched up one-to-one with a particular symptom, but this one-to-one match was not necessary for successful treatment because there were likely parts of all the undercurrents that contributed in some way to Alex's symptoms. Therefore, both sets of unhealthy undercurrents were connected to both symptoms (depression and cutting). In some cases, the lumping together of symptoms with both sets of undercurrents is common. In other cases, one undercurrent clearly causes one problem symptom and another undercurrent causes another. It depends on the case.

After the big picture set of undercurrents was presented, the therapist further refined the process by visually connecting them to Alex's symptoms of both depression and cutting as illustrated in Box 7.2.

BOX 7.2 Alex's Problem Symptoms and Connected Undercurrents

Unhealed Wound Seed		
Problem Symptom(s) in Question	**Unhealthy Undercurrents Causing Alex's Problems**	**Healthy Undercurrents Needed to Heal (antibiotic or Z-Pak)**
Depression and cutting	☐ Betrayal with high anxiety ☐ Sense of abandonment	• Forgiveness • Feeling secure • Unconditional love
	☐ Lack of forgiveness ☐ Feeling resentment or bitterness	• Forgiveness • No longer feeling resentful
Related Unmet Primal Need Seed		
Problem Symptom(s) in Question	**Unhealthy Undercurrents Causing Alex's Problems**	**Healthy Undercurrents Needed to Heal (antibiotic or Z-Pak)**
Depression and cutting	☐ Lack of attachment ☐ Lack of a connection to God or a higher power	• Needing attachment (examples: hugs each day, special outings, humor, and playfulness between parent and child) • Connection to God or a higher power (example: prayer)

(*continued*)

Case Example (*continued*)

After the handouts (Box 7.1 and Box 7.2) were provided to each family member (mom, dad, and Alex), the FST therapist went on to discuss the definition of each unhealthy undercurrent and its healthy counterpart (in bold in Table 7.1) as well as the rationale for these selections over others.

STEP 7: SHOW FEEDBACK LOOPS WITH SAMPLE PLAYBOOK

After the undercurrent handouts are explained, unhealthy undercurrents are translated into before feedback loops (what is happening in the family now) and the healthy undercurrents translated into after feedback loops (what can happen in the future when strategic wound playbooks are used to restructure the family). In addition, the after feedback loops and a sample playbook are used together to show family members the direct connection between healthy undercurrents and strategic directives. Each of these items is created beforehand using the pre-session preparation strategies outlined in Chapter 6. Use feedback loop drawings unless the family needs experiential sculpting (see Chapter 6: "When Feedback Loop Drawings Are Not Enough").

Most families are surprised by this experiential step, especially those who have only experienced traditional talk therapy. Many family members liken this process to seeing a portrait of their family hanging in a museum or a movie trailer of a dance together. For most, it will be the first time they see systems theory in practical terms and can appreciate its inherent benefits. Children and adolescents are also visibly relieved and often suddenly become cooperative. This is because for the first time they can see how the FST treatment model will remove them from the scapegoat role by shifting the responsibility to the entire family. The previous undercurrent handout sets up the feedback loop step beautifully. It is like putting a golf ball on the tee.

Introductory Transition Statement and Feedback Loop Templates

Please use the following introductory transition statement:

> Now, I will take both the unhealthy and healthy undercurrents we just went over and convert them into what we call "feedback loops." In between sessions, I spent time drawing these feedback loops [hold up your sheet of paper with your "before" and "after" feedback loops]. These are my best guess on how you communicate and talk to each other when _____ [state child's name] is having the problem of _____ [state problem symptom that will be highlighted in drawings].
>
> I will draw each loop one at a time on the flip chart [or show one loop at a time on my PowerPoint]. After I draw each loop, I will pause and ask you if it is accurate or if I should change it. Remember it is my best guess. My first drawing is called a "before" feedback loop, or what I think is happening in your family right now to keep you stuck in solving _____ [child's symptom].
>
> After we see the "before" feedback loops, I will show you my best guess on what I call "after" feedback loops or what can happen in the future using playbooks. These are like movie trailers of upcoming attractions or what the future can look like if we eliminate the unhealthy undercurrents and replace them with their healthy opposites [name them]. Let's begin.

Please note, it helps the process go more smoothly if you prepare your templates for the before and after feedback loops on the flip chart prior to the session (see Figures 7.2 and 7.3 for Alex's family). The therapist should cover the templates with a blank sheet of paper until they are ready to be revealed. As the before feedback loop template in Figure 7.2 illustrates, the names of the family members involved in the interaction are already written on the template, along with the title "The Before: What Is Happening in Your Family Now." The problem symptom(s) that the loop represents should be listed at the top with the unhealthy undercurrents listed on the side.

The after feedback loop template is similar to the before template with the same family members listed. But now the title is "The After: What Can Happen in the Future Using Wound Playbooks," and the healthy undercurrent counterparts are listed on the side. Also as seen in Figure 7.3, the after feedback loop should clearly illustrate the strategic intervention of a playbook.

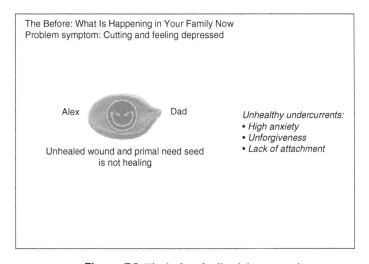

Figure 7.2 The before feedback loop template.

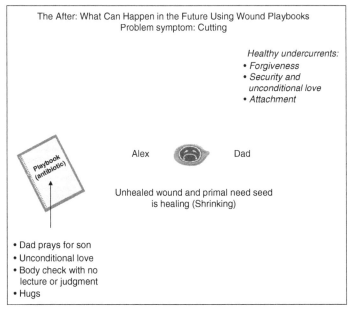

Figure 7.3 The after feedback loop template.

Feedback Loop and Playbook Application

Alex's case example illustrates the successful execution of this step and provides an example for the reader of the proper process and timing for this step. Please mirror the same process and timing with your cases. The FST therapist will proceed to the flip chart template on the wall or use the PowerPoint slide (armed with the predrawing sheet) to construct both before and after feedback loops, one loop at a time.

It is also important to note that when drawing the after feedback loop, the therapist also has in hand the sample wound playbook to illustrate specific techniques within the playbook. As stated in Chapter 6, "Pre-session Preparation," the after feedback loop healthy undercurrents must be directly connected to the interventions proposed in the sample wound playbook. For example, in Alex's after feedback loop template in Figure 7.3, the healthy undercurrents of forgiveness, security and unconditional love, and attachment are not going to suddenly appear on their own by osmosis. The family is a stuck system and would not be in therapy if they could insert these healthy undercurrents by themselves. Instead, it is the strategic directives in the form of the wound playbook that inject these healthy undercurrents into the family to restructure them to heal the toxic seed(s) and eliminate the problem symptoms. This is why this process is affectionately called "structural–strategic family therapy on steroids."

Therefore, as the FST therapist draws the after feedback loop, he or she can hold up and even pass out the sample playbook created during pre-session preparation to drive home the point of how these healthy undercurrents would be introduced into the family in future sessions. If the sample playbook is shown as a handout, it is critical that before it is shown, the therapist emphasize that the playbook is only a sample that they must return before the session ends. Otherwise, the family may take it home and use it prematurely without having the needed role-plays and troubleshooting in Phase III. Therefore, the point must be emphasized again and again by the FST therapist that this is a *sample* playbook only. The playbook is shared at this point in treatment solely for the purpose of connecting theory to practice.

It is important for the FST therapist to be forewarned that some families may actually object to the sample playbook with comments such as "*This seems too easy*," "*This playbook would not work for us*," or "*I don't get this*." If this happens, the therapist will simply reiterate the point that this playbook is only a sample to illustrate in a specific way that healthy undercurrents can be brought back into the family. Then the therapist will move on to avoid getting caught up in this bunny trail of debate.

Case Example

Both the before and after feedback loops were presented to Alex's family. The FST therapist used PowerPoint and an HDMI cable to connect his laptop to the family's flat-screen television.

The feedback loops were preloaded into the therapist's laptop from the pre-session preparation. The PowerPoint was then put into presentation mode so that each time the therapist clicked on the "page down key," one loop at a time came into view in the form of an arrow followed by the statement and/or a cognitive thought bubble.

(continued)

Case Example (*continued*)

Before Feedback Loop

After the entire before feedback loop was shown (Figure 7.4), the therapist paused and asked the family if the statements and thought bubbles were accurate, and if not, which wording or thought bubble needed correction. The therapist then simply deleted the incorrect words and made changes in real time. This is done easily if the feedback loops are drawn on the flip chart. It can also be done easily in PowerPoint by taking the PowerPoint off presentation mode to quickly edit the wording and then selecting presentation mode once again.

Please note: The therapist may also choose to elicit client feedback or suggested changes while each step in the loop is being revealed rather than waiting until the end of the feedback loop presentation. The tactical advantage of waiting until all the loops are presented is to give family members the big picture first. This helps the family zoom out before they need to zoom in with changes to the actual wording or thought bubbles.

FST therapist:	Dad, what are your overall reactions to the "before" feedback loop and are there any changes to make?
Dad:	It's eye opening to see how we all dance together as you said. It is not just Alex. All of us have to change. I think you are right when you pointed out that our focus should not be on Alex's grades and the yard work. It's the wounds and primal needs that should be our focus. As far as changes to make. . . just the first loop. We don't ever say, "Why are you so angry and you barely talk to us." We don't say anything at all these days because my wife and I walk on eggshells around Alex. We are so scared to set him off and make things worse.
FST therapist:	Alright. So, what if I write a thought bubble that states something like "I am so scared to say the wrong thing but Alex is in so much pain we don't know what to do." And then Alex might respond with something like "I can see they don't know what to do, yet they are not even talking to me about this pain."
Dad:	That fits

There are times when the client cannot give you the exact words, just a general description. When this happens, the therapist has to actively step in and make guesses. More times than not, the guesses will be close to accurate. If not, the client is then better able to correct the therapist because he or she now have something concrete to work with.

After Feedback Loops

After the before loop was shown, the FST therapist shifted gears to the after feedback loops (Figure 7.5). In this case, the family had no suggested changes to the after feedback loops but were instantly energized by the sample wound playbook (see Chapter 6 for the sample wound playbook).

After seeing how step-by-step the playbook was written, Alex's father wanted to adopt it with only minor changes and start using it immediately. However, the FST therapist

(*continued*)

Case Example (*continued*)

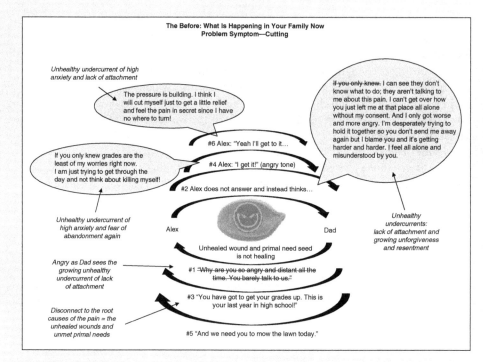

Figure 7.4 The before feedback loop.

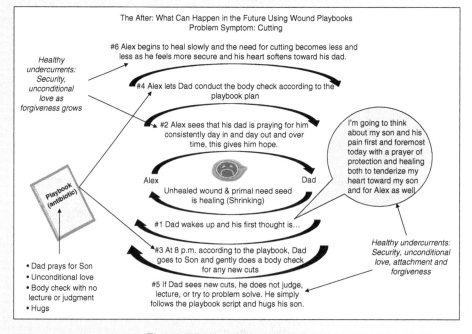

Figure 7.5 The after feedback loop.

(*continued*)

Case Example (*continued*)

had to be caring but assertive in controlling the family's expectations and reinforcing the necessity to wait for Phase III to ensure success using dress rehearsals and troubleshooting. A premature application of the playbook would most likely end in failure. The following brief transcript illustrates how the therapist took back control of the session.

FST therapist:	What are your reactions as you see the after feedback loop and the sample wound playbook that goes along with the after loops? Are there any changes you want made? Let me start with you, Dad, this time.
Dad:	No changes in the "after" loop drawing, you captured our family perfectly. I liked how concrete it was and how it gave me a movie trailer of how we can get unstuck as a family. We have been to a lot of therapy as you know and this is the first time I see a step-by-step plan with clear reasoning behind it to heal not just Alex's wounds but all of ours.
FST therapist:	Thank you for these kind words
Dad:	[Holding up sample playbook] So, here is the thing. I like this playbook so much that I want to use it unchanged and start as soon as we leave here.
Alex:	[Shakes his head "no"]
FST therapist:	You don't know how much I appreciate your enthusiasm. You are a great dad. I work with other families and I have to beg them to try the playbook but you are ready to go. But we have to wait just a little longer with just one to two more sessions. Here's why. Timing is everything. During those sessions we will do something called dress rehearsals like they do before opening night on Broadway. This means practicing the timing and delivery of the plan through role-plays. And we will troubleshoot possible loopholes in the plan ahead of time. Like what you will do if Alex does not want you to do a body check on a certain day because he is tired.
Alex:	Or how about not at all?
FST Therapist:	Thanks Alex. Or not at all. In fact, our research shows that if the playbook is launched before role-plays and troubleshooting are completed the plan fails almost 100% of the time. Like a great dish taken out of the oven too early. You all have come too far to not wait just a little longer.
Dad:	OK, we will wait.

Wound Stories and the Before Feedback Loop

It is important to note that the before feedback loop can open up an optimal window of opportunity to discuss the wound story for both children and adults. The self-regulation tools will have already been implemented in Phase II. Therefore, if the family is ready, the FST therapist has the green light to "strike while the iron is hot" and discuss the wound story. The only exception is if the therapist senses that the child or adult is experiencing "flooding," that is, the new input of the feedback loop and the wound story together is overwhelming the parent or child, and/or that the self-regulation strategies are not working. In either case, the FST therapist must be ready to jump in and stop the process. It is perfectly acceptable to say something like,

> This is a lot to take in all at once. I know your wound story goes hand in hand with the before feedback loop. But I can see your struggle. Let's take a break right now and come back to it. Let's go on to the after feedback loop and afterward we will circle back around and I will ask about your story. If we have time we can do it later today or in our next session.

In this way, the therapist is still in the role of facilitator and mediates in real time how much intensity is too much, based on the particular case and family member.

If the wound story does take place after the before feedback loop, the therapist must not feel the pressure to squeeze in the after feedback loop discussion in the same session. Instead, there is a natural break point after the wound discussion to end treatment for the day and begin the next session with the after feedback loop discussion and continue on to the next progression of steps in the FST model.

STEP 8: THE WOUND STORY, IF NEEDED, WITH SELF-REGULATION TOOLS

The FST therapist must make a judgment call whether it is therapeutic (based on the particular case) to ask the child or family member to retell the wound or trauma story, either following the before feedback loop or at this point in treatment. A *New York Times* (Carey, 2009) article cited the potential downsides or even harmful effects of catharsis:

> Some researchers say that the common psychological wisdom about crying—crying as a healthy catharsis—is incomplete and misleading. Having a "good cry" can and usually does allow people to recover some mental balance after a loss.

In addition, traumatology research studies have cited that there are inherent risks in retelling the trauma story (Bride, Radey, & Figley, 2007; Briere & Scott, 2006; Greenwald, 2005; Lance & Gyamera, 2002; McCann & Pearlman, 1990). In a nutshell, the brain keeps traumatic memories away from us for a very good reason, and it is not always healthy to try to just break apart these protective structures.

In addition, the theoretical underpinnings of the FST model are structural-strategic with an emphasis on the here and now and the use of strategic directives (wound playbooks) to alter the family system's old interaction patterns to create new ones (undercurrents). Therefore, the insight into the past is much less important than action and change in the present and future. Instead, directives are used to get the child or family unstuck with the smallest change possible because they jolt them away from their usual life patterns. For example, one adolescent was quoted as saying,

> *"When this therapy gave my dad the tools in the playbook to actually apologize and mean it, I didn't have to keep reliving the past and keep talking about it. Talk did nothing to heal me. It was action and my dad apologizing that allowed me to get unstuck and move past the pain."*

This quote epitomizes the "now what?" question that traumatized families want answered: "*We talked about our pain but 'now what' do we do in the here and now to heal and move past it?*"

As a result, the wound or trauma story is not a necessary requirement for positive change using the FST treatment model. Instead, the wound story can serve more as a joining or rapport-building strategy. The child or parent may want to talk about past hurts and their story to elicit therapist understanding and trust building. In addition, the wound story is a potentially great opportunity for strategic reframing, correcting false assumptions, or revealing family secrets.

Overall Goals for the Wound Story Using FST Treatment

The overall goals for the wound story using the FST model are threefold. First, do not evoke the story just because it is the natural thing to do in trauma-informed practice. Be as least intrusive as possible and go for the simplest solution first, not the most complex. Allow the wound playbooks to be the catalysts to heal undercurrents or family interaction patterns in the here and now. In fact, when the present is healed, the past heals on its own.

Second, if the family wants to tell their story, let them, but utilize self-regulation tools as needed. Avoid long in-depth storytelling. Instead, listen with a third ear to capture opportunities to reframe, and correct false assumptions. This means actively stopping the child or parent from going on and on once there is sufficient information to locate the key unhealthy undercurrents. Stopping the child or parent from going too deep into the trauma story also decreases the risk for retraumatization.

Finally, it is important to embrace the "If it ain't broke, don't fix it" mindset of solution-focused therapy (de Shazer & Dolan, 2007). This means that if the child or parent is doing well at this point in FST treatment (e.g., fully engaged, cooperative, and energized and hopeful from the feedback loops and sample playbook), there is no reason to risk further destabilizing the family or retraumatizing them.

Wound Story Transition Statement

If the decision is to move forward with the wound story, the following transition statement is recommended:

> After looking at the feedback loops, I want to take a moment and offer each of you the opportunity to share more about the wound story you briefly shared during our first session after the seed/tree diagram. I will go around the room and you can say "pass" if you don't want to share. But if you say "pass" now just know that you can share your wound story later in treatment. And if I see you getting stressed, I will bring back to your attention the self-regulation tools we went over earlier. Any questions? [Pause.]

Telling the Wound Story Verbally

After this transition statement, the FST therapist has two choices to help the child or family member tell the wound story. The first choice is to simply go around the room and let each person tell his or her part of the wound story if the person wants to, with the therapist actively poised to suggest self-regulation tools as needed. Look for body language that is either open or closed while telling the story from the individual's perspective. It is recommended to talk to the person with open body language first. It will set a positive tone for everyone else to follow.

Telling the Wound Story Experientially

Another way the family can retell the wound story is by using an experiential technique called "arrow in the heart" strategy. This strategy was developed by Rujon Morrison (personal communication, January 10, 2017) and helps family members connect their wound story to what are called "strongholds." These are core cognitive distortions or lies that the child or other family members believe about themselves that can be directly traced back to the traumatic event, wound, or arrow in the heart. These cognitive distortions can be integrated within an unhealthy undercurrent interactional framework to provide an excellent anchor point for FST treatment.

The "arrow in the heart" strategy technique uses the prop of an arrow that can be purchased at an archery or sporting goods store. For safety reasons, the steel tip should be removed. According to Morrison (2017), the arrow represents the wound or traumatic event that is plunged into the heart of a person. The arrow is both mentally and spiritually charged. Mentally, the arrow metaphorically contains within it poisonous strongholds (see Figure 7.6; shame, performance, blame, or approval addiction) that if not removed and dispelled as lies, will eventually lead to serious problem symptoms (e.g., chronic depression, substance abuse, self-harm, anxiety disorder). In addition, these strongholds cause spiritual pain. The arrow can kill the heart of a person and damage the spirit. As a result, the wounds caused by the arrow create a war between the head (stronghold) and the heart (spirit).

To convey these powerful messages and make sharing safe, it is recommended that the FST therapist begin by using self-disclosure. He or she shares about a time he or she was wounded (see the following case example). As the therapist talks about the wound, he or she picks up the arrow and physically puts it into his or her own heart. The therapist can even write the actual stronghold wounds ("I am damaged," "I do not deserve to be loved," "I cannot change," etc.) on small yellow Post-it notes and stick them right on the arrow itself or use Figure 7.6 as a handout.

Strongholds	Core false beliefs	Negative consequences or Problem symptoms
SHAME	• "I am damaged" • "I will never be good enough" • "I am worthless" • "I am what I am and cannot change" • "I do not deserve to be loved"	• Fear of exposure and unworthiness • Depression • Isolation, withdrawal • Hopelessness • Worried/anxious mind • Self-sabotage • Despising appearance • Passivity and self-pity
PERFORMANCE TRAP	• "My value and worth depend on what I do and my performance" • "I must do it all myself, I am alone" • "I am what I do" • "I have to do more and more to feel good"	• Fear of failure • Workaholism • Angry • Controlling • High risk for anxiety, constant worry • Eating disorders • Substance abuse
BLAME GAME	• "It is everyone else's fault when things go wrong" • "Those who fail deserve to be punished or unloved" • "The world is an unsafe place" • "I must hurt others before they can hurt me first"	• Fear of punishment • Problems with authority or oppositional defiance • Pride and narcissism • Perfectionism • Black- and white-thinking • Difficulty with responsibility
APPROVAL ADDICTION	• "I must be accepted by others to feel good about myself" • "I have to please others at any cost" • "I need to rescue others" • "I need to be needed"	• Fear of rejection & abandonment • Codependency • Overly sensitive to criticism • Withdrawal from others to avoid disapproval • Depression

Figure 7.6 Strongholds handout. (*continued*)

Figure 7.6 (*continued*) Strongholds handout.

The FST therapist will then go on to explain the implications both physically and spiritually, to the family, if the arrow is not removed as well as the ongoing war between the head and the heart. The therapist uses Figure 7.6 as a handout to explain.

The therapist ends the self-disclosure by describing how the wound playbook and the healthy undercurrents can help pull out the arrow and bring healing to the strongholds in the here and now. For example, in the following case example, the healthy undercurrent of "forgiveness" and "reconnection to God" were the key catalysts to heal the stronghold of "shame." After the therapist self-discloses and role-models the process, he or she hands over the arrow to the first family

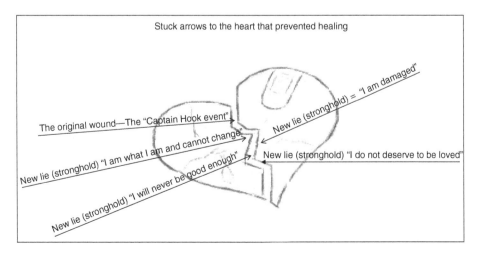

Figure 7.7 Arrows to the heart.

member who wants to disclose. No one is forced to use this strategy. However, most family members will do so after the therapist role-models first and creates a safe environment.

If the FST therapist does not want to self-disclose, he or she can explain the technique and either talk about Figures 7.6 and 7.7 and/or ask if anyone wants to retell the wound story using the arrow. However, the strategy is not as effective without self-disclosure role modeling first.

Case Example

The first author, Scott, begins the arrow in the heart strategy by self-disclosing his own wound story. Taking the arrow in his hand, he states the following:

Let me show you what happened to me as a result of my wound. It lasted until I was 45 years old. You can see in the handout [Figure 7.7]. I have labeled this arrow the 'Captain Hook event.' At the tender age of 12 years, this arrow was shot into my heart and it was lodged in there for 33 long years. I have what is called cerebral palsy in my left hand. At 12 years of age I got the courage to ask for the first time ever if a girl, Mary, would 'go steady' or be my girlfriend. She said 'yes.' But the next day someone told her about the cerebral palsy and she told me that she would not date me because in her words, 'I was a cripple.' To make matters worse, Mary then asked her girlfriends to join her in the teasing. For two straight weeks, Mary and her girlfriends went up and down the hallway saying, 'Look, I am like Scott. I am Captain Hook' with their left hands curled up in a hooklike position. This traumatic event as you can imagine shot a huge arrow to my heart [take arrow and put into heart].

As a result, of this arrow, my wounds did not heal on their own. In fact, over time, the poison from this arrow got into my bloodstream and traveled to my mind. The arrow and the wound created what is called a 'stronghold' or a lie that I believed to be true. And that lie negatively impacted how I lived day to day. The stronghold was called 'shame.'

Looking at the next handout [Figure 7.6] there are four primary stronghold categories or areas in which lies take hold. They are shame, blame, performance, and/ or addiction.

As the handout illustrates, my core false beliefs around the stronghold of 'shame' were:

- "I am damaged"
- "I will never be good enough"
- "I am worthless"
- "I am what I am and cannot change"
- "I do not deserve to be loved"

I honestly believed in these lies. As a result, I turned to drugs to medicate my pain and felt hopeless. Any time a woman started to love me, the stronghold of shame kicked in and I rejected them before they had a chance to reject me. And to top it all off, I became a workaholic. Because of my shame, I threw myself into my performance, believing that all my worth was based on how well I performed.

It wasn't until I was 45 years of age that I had a family use a wound playbook–like intervention to help me inject the undercurrents of forgiveness and reconnecting with God to finally remove this poisoned arrow from my heart. Once I got to these root causes and exposed the lie, my symptoms went away and I am now happily married with two wonderful children. The lesson from my story is that it is never too late to heal wounds.

In the books *Head to Heart* (McGee & Morrison, 1997) and *The Search for Significance: Seeing Your True Worth Through God's Eyes* (McGee, 2014), these authors describe the direct head and heart connection to the wound and the birth of a stronghold. There is even a weeklong retreat called Healing for the Nations (www.healingforthenations.org) that parents and older adolescents can attend for further intensive study and counseling in the areas of both strongholds and unhealed trauma.

STEP 9: HOMEWORK ASSIGNMENT

The final step of Phase II involves handing the family the homework lead sheet that was customized for the family during pre-session preparation. As outlined in Chapter 6, the handout contains Internet, book, or article leads around specific techniques for the family's targeted healthy undercurrents and goals for therapy. For example, if the targeted healthy undercurrent is forgiveness, family members will take the leads on the homework sheet provided to investigate possible strategies or techniques around this area. Family findings will then be presented at the beginning of Phase III and, whenever possible, included within the new wound playbook.

Please use the following transition statement when introducing this last step:

As we end today's session, I have a handout that was prepared before today's session. This is your homework assignment to take home. Let me pass it out. This is what we call a "homework lead sheet." As you can see, this sheet contains several Internet sites, books, or articles for you to look up and investigate prior to our next session. These are based on the healthy undercurrents that we just went over together within the sample playbook. You are encouraged to take these leads and find more. If you don't have a computer at home, please use the one at your local library to locate additional articles or resources.

At the beginning of our next session, I will ask you to list the top 2 to 3 interventions or techniques you found and why you like them. I will then give you some of the interventions I found as well. We will then decide together which ones will be used for your wound playbooks that we will create in our next session.

Let's review your lead sheet together so I can answer any questions you might have.

Please use the homework lead template presented in Chapter 6 (p. 151). It is important to note that the FST therapist must also emphasize the following point in the goals section of the homework lead sheet:

If you do not come up with anything, please still come to the next session because I will have some ideas to share. This means even though you are signing your names below that you will do everything you can to complete the homework, sometimes things come up. If you are unable to do the assignment, do not let it stop you from coming to the next session. No one will be upset.

If this point is not emphasized, the family will likely feel shame if they fail to complete their homework and show up for the next session empty-handed.

The logistical questions within the lead sheet that outline the details of each action step greatly increase the odds that the homework will be completed. Therefore, while the ultimate goal is for the family to complete the homework, it is not a must-have. The FST therapist will still come to the session prepared with sample interventions and playbooks to move forward.

REFERENCES

Abenavoli, L. (2010). Brain hypoperfusion and neurological symptoms in celiac disease. *Movement Disorders, 25*(6), 792–793.

Ader, R., Felten, D., & Cohen, N. C. (2000). *Psycho-neuro-immunology* (3rd ed.). New York, NY: Academic Press.

Agrawal, R., & Gomez-Pinilla, F. (2012). Metabolic syndrome in the brain: Deficiency in omega-3 fatty acid exacerbates dysfunctions in insulin receptor signaling and cognition. *Journal of Physiology, 12,* 2485–2499.

Bride, E., Radey, M., & Figley, C. (2007). Measuring compassion fatigue. *Clinical Social Work, 35,* 155–163.

Briere, J., & Scott, C. (2006). *Principles of trauma therapy.* Thousand Oaks, CA: Sage.

Carey, B. (2009, February 2). The muddled tracks of all those tears. *The New York Times.* Retrieved from http://www.nytimes.com/2009/02/03/health/03mind.html

Centers for Disease Control and Prevention. (2011). *Youth risk behavior surveillance system: 2011 national overview.* Retrieved from https://archive.org/details/ERIC_ED532746

Chapman, L. (2014). *Neurobiologically informed trauma therapy with children and adolescents: Understanding mechanisms of change.* Chicago, IL: W. W. Norton.

de Shazer, S., & Dolan, Y. (2007). *More than miracles: The state of the art of solution-focused brief therapy.* Philadelphia, PA: Haworth Press.

Dietrich, A. M. (2001). Risk factors in PTSD and related disorders: Theoretical, treatment, and research implications. *Traumatology, 7*(1), 23–50.

Doidge, N. (2015). *The brain's way of healing.* New York, NY: Viking.

Dufault, R., Schnoll, R., Lukiw, W. J., Leblanc, B., Cornett, C., Patrick, L., . . . Crider, R. (2009). Mercury exposure, nutritional deficiencies, and metabolic disruptions may affect learning in children. *Behavioral Brain Function, 5,* 44. doi:10.1186/1744-9081-5-44

Figley, C., & Figley, K. (2009). Stemming the tide of trauma systemically: The role of family therapy. *Australian and New Zealand Journal of Family Therapy, 30*(3), 173–183.

Geraghty, M. E., Depasquale, G. M., & Lane, A. E. (2010). Nutritional intake and therapies in autism: A spectrum of what we know, part 1. *Infant, Child, and Adolescent Nutrition, 2*(1), 62–69.

Green Cross Academy of Traumatology. (1999). Standards of practice. Retrieved from http://greencross.org

Greenwald, R. (2005). *Child trauma handbook.* New York, NY: Taylor & Francis.

Haley, J. (1991). *Problem-solving therapy.* San Francisco, CA: Jossey-Bass.

Karam, E. A., Sterrett, E. M., & Kiaer, L. (2015). The integration of family and group therapy as an alternative to juvenile incarceration: A quasi-experimental evaluation using parenting with love and limits. *Family Process, 56,* 331–347. doi:10.1111/famp.12187

Koenig, H. G. (2009). Research on religion, spirituality, and mental health: A review. *Canadian Journal of Psychiatry, 54,* 283–291.

Lance, J., & Gyamera, J. (2002). Existential family trauma therapy. *Contemporary Family Therapy, 24*(2), 243–255.

Malchiodi, C., & Perry, B. (2014). *Creative interventions with traumatized children* (2nd ed.). New York, NY: Guilford Press.

Martin, M., Seppa, M., Lehtinen, P., & Torco, T. (2012). *Breathing as a tool for self-regulation and self-reflection.* New York, NY: Karnac Books

McCann, I., & Pearlman, L. (1990). Vicarious traumatization: A framework for understanding tile psychological effects of working with victims. *Journal of Traumatic Stress, 3*(1), 131–149.

McGee, R. S. (2014). *The search for significance: Seeing your true worth through God's eyes.* Eugene, OR: Harvest House Publishers.

McGee, R. S., & Morrison, R. (1997). *From Head to Heart.* Ventura, CA: Vine Books.

McKay, M., Wood, J., & Brantley, J. (2007). *The dialectical behavior therapy skills workbook: Practical DBT exercises for learning mindfulness, interpersonal effectiveness, emotion regulation, and distress tolerance.* New York, NY: New Harbinger Publications.

Ogden, P., Kekuni, M., & Clair, P. (2006). *Trauma and the body: A sensorimotor approach to psychotherapy.* New York, NY: W. W. Norton.

Ostafin, B., Robinson, M., & Meier, B. (2015). *Handbook of mindfulness and self-regulation.* New York, NY: Springer-Verlag.

Pelcovitz, D., van der Kolk, B., Roth, S., Mandel, F., Kaplan, S., & Resick, P. (1997). Development of a criteria set and a structured interview for disorders of extreme stress (SIDES). *Journal of Traumatic Stress, 10,* 3–16.

Sells, S. P., Winokur-Early, K., & Smith, T. E. (2011). Reducing adolescent oppositional and conduct disorders: An experimental design using parenting with love and limits. *Professional Issues in Criminal Justice, 6*(3), 9–30.

Shannon, S. M. (2013). *Mental health for the whole child: Moving young clients from disease & disorder to balance & wellness.* New York, NY: W. W. Norton.

Shannon, S. M. (2014). *Parenting the whole child. A holistic child psychiatrist offers practical wisdom on behavior, brain health, nutrition, exercise, family life, peer relationships, school life, trauma, medication, and more.* New York, NY: W. W. Norton.

Shapiro, F. (1989). Efficacy of the eye movement desensitization procedure in the treatment of traumatic memories. *Journal of Traumatic Stress, 2*(2), 199–223.

Shapiro, F., & Forrest, M. (2004). *EMDR: The breakthrough therapy for anxiety, stress and trauma.* New York, NY: Basic Books

Siegel, D. J. (1999). *The developing mind: How relationships and the brain interact to shape who we are.* New York, NY: Guilford Press.

Siegel, D. J., & Solomon, M. (2003). *Healing trauma attachment, mind, body and brain.* Chicago, IL: W. W. Norton.

Strickland, E. (2009). *Eating for autism: The 10-step nutrition plan to help treat your child's autism, Asperger's, or ADHD* (pp. 61–71, 84–85). Boston, MA: Da Capo.

van der Kolk, B. A. (1994). The body keeps the score: Memory and the evolving psychobiology of posttraumatic stress. *Harvard Review of Psychiatry, 1*(5), 253–265. doi:10.3109/10673229409017088

van der Kolk, B. A. (2014). *The body keeps the score: Brain, mind, and body in the healing of trauma.* New York, NY: Viking.

Velasquez-Manoff, M. (2012). *An epidemic of absence: A new way of understanding allergies and autoimmune diseases* (pp. 214–241). New York, NY: Scribner.

White, M., & Epston, D. (1990). *Narrative means to therapeutic ends.* New York, NY: W. W. Norton.

World Health Organization. (2014). Informed Consent Form Templates. Retrieved from http://www.who.int/rpc/research_ethics/informed_consent/en

Winokur-Early, K., Chapman, S. F., & Hand, G. A. (2013). Family-focused juvenile reentry services: A quasi-experimental design evaluation of recidivism outcomes. *Journal of Juvenile Justice, 2*(2), 1–22.

Pre-Session Preparation for Phase III

Step 1: Create Own List of Strategic Directive Strategies

Step 2: Create Customized Playbooks for the Family

The family systems trauma (FST) flowchart in Chapter 3 indicates that this pre-session preparation step occurs immediately after Phase II. The primary goals of this step are to (a) decide on the best strategic directives for the targeted undercurrent(s); and (b) create customized playbooks based on the particular family and goals of therapy.

We list all the techniques like a buffet menu but only provide one technique and playbook example per undercurrent category. The reason is that this is not a book of techniques, but an end-to-end model of practice. For a listing of the other playbook examples and descriptions of techniques, we refer the reader to www.gopll.com/trauma. New techniques are added periodically to this website. Readers are also encouraged to develop their own playbooks and techniques within the application parameters outlined in this book. Our list of techniques is not an all-encompassing list but instead provides a core foundation of structural strategic practice.

This pre-session preparation step is complete once the FST therapist chooses the technique or directive and creates the associated customized playbook. The FST therapist is now ready to present the playbook to the family during the next session in Phase III. There are two pre-session mini-steps to accomplish these goals. They are as follows: (a) Create own list of strategic directive strategies, and (b) create customized playbooks for the family.

STEP 1: CREATE OWN LIST OF STRATEGIC DIRECTIVE STRATEGIES

As outlined in Chapter 7, while family members are completing their homework assignment lead sheet of locating strategic directives, the FST therapist is engaging in a similar parallel process during this pre-session preparation. These combined efforts yield abundant fruit because they elicit a true collaboration between the FST therapist and the client system. It also engenders hope when the family members attend Phase III and see their homework efforts alongside their therapist's. This is especially true because in traditional therapy, it is often the therapist providing interventions from a one-up expert position. In this framework, the FST therapist retains expert status, but now the client system is also an active participant in the change process. When a child or parent experiences trauma, this sense of empowerment is essential because a traumatic event often induces powerlessness.

Rationale

The FST therapist first used the tables and playbook examples in this chapter when the first sample wound playbook was created during Chapter 6 pre-session preparation. However, at this stage of treatment, it is about refinement, adjustments, and/or the introduction of new wound playbooks. This is due to the fact that the FST therapist will decide (a) if he or she will keep or discard the sample wound playbook presented in Phase II; (b) if kept, how the sample wound playbook will be refined or modified further in this step; and/or (c) if additional wound playbooks will be created to address additional undercurrents and problem symptoms.

This decision will impact how one navigates this step. For example, if the FST therapist decides to go into Phase III only with the sample wound playbook from Phase II, this step can be bypassed. The FST therapist already has the techniques needed from when he or she first examined these tables in Chapter 6. Therefore, the therapist can then proceed directly to Step 2 in this chapter to further refine or tweak the sample wound playbook based on any new information obtained in the last session.

However, this step is needed if it is decided after Phase II that the sample playbook will not be used or the family can handle the implementation of two wound playbooks simultaneously (the sample wound playbook and a new one). As a quick reminder, the goals of therapy from Phase I are a direct reflection of the FST therapist and family's "top two" seed and problem symptom picks. Therefore, there are almost always at least a minimum of two child or adolescent problem symptoms to eliminate at any one time. However, the overriding issue is not to overwhelm a traumatized child or family with too much change, too fast. In addition, there may be ongoing safety issues to mitigate. If safety is an issue, one wound playbook is all that one family should handle at a time. This decision tree process is discussed in greater detail within Step 2 of this chapter.

Case Example

Fourteen-year-old Jackie came into treatment after being diagnosed with bulimia. To make matters worse, Jackie's mom, Janice, was diagnosed with clinical depression and was emotionally unavailable a majority of the time. Jackie had been to inpatient treatment three times but each time relapsed within 6 months of returning home.

It was learned from the seed/tree diagram that Jackie's father, Jerry, had mysteriously left home over a year ago and had not been in contact with the family since. Jackie and her dad were extremely close and she openly blamed herself for her dad's departure. Even though the mother continued to tell Jackie that she was not to blame, it was obvious that Jackie did not believe her.

At the end of Phase I, the mother and daughter selected the seeds of unhealed wounds and unmet primal needs. The FST therapist agreed with their seed and symptom picks. It was also suggested that Jackie's problem symptom of bulimia might have root causes associated with Dad's abandonment, grief, and Mom literally shutting down and becoming depressed. Therefore, direct wound work without the need for prior stabilization first was recommended.

During the pre-session preparation prior to Phase II, the FST therapist looked at the table of techniques in this chapter and chose the undercurrents of unresolved grief for unhealed wounds and lack of attachment for unmet primal needs. The therapist chose to use the sample playbook of "How to Restore Family Bonds" and customize it for Jackie's

(continued)

Case Example (*continued*)

family. The therapist also predrew the before and after feedback loops around the seed of unmet primal needs and the undercurrent of a lack of attachment between Mom and Jackie. The unhealed wound seed and undercurrent of unresolved grief could also have been used. However, the attachment seed was selected because it was something that could be more easily addressed in the here and now.

However, in the midst of Phase II, new information suddenly emerged. The feedback loops acted as an emotional catalyst to bring to the surface the hidden unhealthy undercurrent of family secrets. As Mom read out aloud the "how to restore family bonds" playbook, she started crying. Janice said the problem was not a lack of attachment, but her guilt.

The FST therapist asked Mom to use the self-regulation tool of deep breathing to center herself and then asked the daughter to leave the room. The therapist sensed (and rightly so) a big family secret coming and knew that Jackie would not yet be able to handle it. After Jackie left, Janice leveled with the therapist and said that the secret was that she had had an affair with her ex-husband's best friend. And it was this affair that caused Jackie's dad to leave and not the current story that he just left for no reason.

Using the undercurrent handout, the therapist was successful in pointing out to Janice the unhealed wound of family secrets and its harmful implications. As a result, the mother agreed that the secret should be told but only with the therapist's help. The therapist promised that between sessions, he would create a playbook with tools on how to share family secrets. At the beginning of next session, the FST therapist and Mom would meet together without the daughter to role-play how to talk through the secret process.

Jackie was then brought back in before the session ended and told by both therapist and Mom that she was excused because Mom had wounds of her own that were suddenly brought to the surface because of the feedback loops. As a result, the FST therapist would need to come up with tools between sessions and help Mom with these new tools at the beginning of the next session.

As this case example illustrates, the FST therapist went into Phase II with one set of assumptions and a sample wound playbook but emerged with a new set of undercurrents and a new direction. In this case, the family secret of the affair created a lie that was severely impacting both mother and daughter. And unless this secret was addressed and removed, the other undercurrents of grief and attachment would be blocked from restoration. Therefore, using this pre-session preparation step, the FST therapist would closely examine the possible techniques offered and select one as a template to customize.

Procedures to Select Techniques (Strategic Directives) to Heal Wounds

The techniques in this section are divided into three categories: (a) techniques for unhealed wounds, (b) techniques for mental or physical impairments, and (c) techniques for unmet primal needs. Techniques are the same as strategic directives and are designed to inject targeted healthy undercurrents into the family to replace the unhealthy ones. As stated earlier, this step provides an illustrated playbook example associated with each undercurrent category. Additional playbooks can be viewed at www.gopll.com/trauma or www.familytrauma.org.

For each technique listed, the authors provide the following framework:

- *Rationale*—why the technique is recommended for a particular healthy undercurrent
- *Procedure*—the procedural steps to create the playbook
- *Sample playbook*—one playbook example for each healthy undercurrent category (i.e., grief education, security, reveal secrets, etc.)

Each technique will follow this format. It is important to note that even though there is only one sample per category, the process that created the sample can be replicated with any of the other techniques listed.

Once the technique is selected, the final step (Step 2) is to convert the technique or strategic directive selected into a customized playbook. This conversion process is outlined in the next section.

An Overlay X-Factor to Consider: The Child's or Adolescent's Love Language

There is an X factor to consider when choosing from the multiple technique options offered in this chapter. The X factor is the particular child's or adolescent's "love language." This concept was first made popular in Chapman's (2004) book *The 5 Love Languages: The Secret to Love that Lasts* for couples, and it evolved to the spin-off book for children entitled *The 5 Love Languages of Children: The Secret to Loving Children Effectively* (Chapman and Campbell, 2016).

The basic premise is simple, yet insightful. Every child or adolescent (like all people) has a special way of bonding to another person. According to Chapman and Campbell (2016), there are five ways children connect with others. They are through words of affirmation, quality time, receiving gifts, acts of service, and/physical touch:

1. *Words of affirmation*: For some children and adolescents, they like to use words to affirm other people and be affirmed themselves (e.g., "I am proud of you"). Words hold real value, and negative or insulting comments cut very deep and will not be easily forgiven.
2. *Quality time*: Some children and adolescents respond best when their parents and others give them their undivided attention. As they get older, this quality time is found in conversations, bedtime stories, or backyard sports. The activity is not important; it is the time together. Unlike the words of affirmation, talk is cheap, and it is quality time that they need to feel satisfied and comforted.
3. *Receiving gifts*: For some children and adolescents, receiving a tangible gift makes them feel extremely loved. This does not necessarily mean that they are materialistic, but a meaningful or thoughtful present makes them feel appreciated.
4. *Acts of service*: For some children and adolescents, actions speak louder than words. They want help from their parents, and they want to help others any way possible. Lending a helping hand shows you really care. They do not deal well with broken promises.
5. *Physical touch*: Nothing speaks more deeply than appropriate touch for some children and adolescents. Everyday hugging or some kind of physical connection is needed, such as a simple touch on the arm or a pat on the back. Therefore, any instance of physical abuse is devastating.

The implications for FST treatment are that different personalities respond differently to each of the five areas listed. For example, if a particular child's or adolescent's identified love language is *acts of service,* then the techniques (e.g., "running the race in grandpa's memory," "building a memorial," "random acts of kindness") that match this language will likely accelerate the wound-healing process. Other techniques will also work, but those that mirror the child's love language can potentially have the greatest impact.

Therefore, prior to a final technique selection, the FST therapist can ask himself or herself this question:

"Based on what I know to date from observing this child or adolescent in session, what do I think are his or her top one or two love languages and does the technique selected match the language(s)?"

If the therapist is not sure how to answer this question, he or she can ask the parent or caregiver to complete a love language quiz online at these two websites www.5lovelanguages.com/profile/teens/ or www.5lovelanguages.com/profile/children and provide the results prior to this step.

In addition, during Phase III, if the FST therapist knows the love language of the child or has a fairly good idea, he or she can connect the dots to the technique selected and its match to one or more of the five love languages. This is motivating for the parents and exciting that their therapist took the time to go the extra mile.

In summary, the cross-referencing of the love languages with the FST techniques in this chapter is not a must-have. Instead, it is a nice-to-have. It represents a fit between technique and the individual child's personality. In turn, this fit can accelerate the overall healing process.

RECOMMENDED TECHNIQUES TO HEAL THE UNHEALED WOUND SEED

TABLE 8.1 Sample Strategic Directives for Unhealed Wounds

Unhealthy Undercurrents	Healthy Undercurrents	Techniques to Inject Healthy Undercurrent
Unhealed grief and loss	Grief education and resolution	☑ Balloon Letters of Goodbye ☐ Running the Race in Grandpa's Memory ☐ Scrapbook of Memories ☐ Opening to the Future/Reclaiming the Past ☐ Healing the Family Land & Heart ☐ Creating a Memorial
Betrayal or abandonment	Security, forgiveness, unconditional love	☑ Fostering a Pet ☐ Strengthening Family Connections ☐ Helping Others to Heal our Family Heart ☐ *The Fresh Prince of Bel-Air* clip
Family secrets	Reveal secrets/safety	☑ A message from the movie *Ordinary People* ☐ Externalizing the Secret—the Garbage Bag ☐ Love and Protection Watch ☐ Difficult Conversations ☐ *Frozen* movie clip
Physical or mental abuse	Support, courage to leave, forgive	☑ The Heart Transplant ☐ The Nonviolence Pledge ☐ The Empty Chair ☐ *Matilda* movie clip

(continued)

TABLE 8.1 Sample Strategic Directives for Unhealed Wounds (*continued*)

Unhealthy Undercurrents	Healthy Undercurrents	Techniques to Inject Healthy Undercurrent
Lack of forgiveness/ bitterness	Forgiveness	☑ The "Apology"—Healing the Family Heart ☐ Memory Board of Appreciation ☐ *Antwone Fisher* movie clip ☐ Family Sculpture—*Enactment*
Lack of consistent nurturance	Unconditional love, consistent nurturance	☑ 30-Day Nurturing Campaign ☐ Cups and Self-Worth ☐ The Hug Prescription ☐ Random Acts of Kindness ☐ Helping Others Campaign ☐ *Home* movie clip
High anxiety	Safety or security	☑ The High/Low Checkup ☐ Increasing Confidence with Praise ☐ Prayer and Body Checks ☐ *The Lion King* movie clip
High stress	Relaxation or diversionary tactics	☑ My Life "De-Stressing" Plan ☐ The Creative Outlet ☐ The Communication Pen

Technique Highlighted: Balloon Letters of Goodbye

TABLE 8.2 Sample Strategic Directive for Unhealed Wounds

Unhealed Wound Seed		
Unhealthy Undercurrents	**Healthy Undercurrents**	**Techniques to Inject Healthy Undercurrent**
Unhealed grief and loss	Grief education and resolution	☑ Balloon Letters of Goodbye

Rationale

The playbook "Balloon Letters of Goodbye" in Box 8.1 provides an opportunity for the family to change the family structure and sequences of behavior that have prevented healing from the loss of a loved one. Often, families who have experienced the death of a loved one are left floundering as they see everything around them changing. Over time, they may settle into unhelpful sequences of behavior as they struggle to cope with their chronic feelings of overwhelming sadness, anger, irritability, or even a withdrawal from normal routines. One of the most helpful activities to break these unhelpful sequences of behavior is to design and engage in a ritual. Rituals direct the family to interact in purposeful ways that symbolize more than the ritual itself. Rather, a ritual serves to bring the family together around their loss and allows them to focus on something outside of themselves. This process combats the paralysis and isolation that is a common unhelpful response to grief and organizes the family around an activity, thus allowing them to express their grief in a productive manner.

Procedure

The FST therapist introduces the playbook by educating the family on the purpose of the activity, that is, to help them eliminate the unhealthy undercurrent of unresolved grief and loss. The playbook provides the family with an activity to organize around, and through the process, to honor the memory of their lost loved one. To jump-start the playbook, the FST therapist will explain to the family the purpose of a ritual and how it helps them to express their grief in a productive manner. The "balloon letters of goodbye" ritual in the playbook example can be adopted by the family or they can research for a different ritual, using the playbook as a guide for the types of details that must be outlined.

Sample Wound Playbook

BOX 8.1 Playbook Example: The Balloon Letters of Goodbye

The Balloon Letters of Goodbye

To Heal the Undercurrent of Unresolved Grief and Loss
Unhealed Wound Seed

Who:
- 12-year old Sally and her mom

What:
- Sally will say goodbye and begin to grieve the loss of her father who died suddenly in a car accident

When:
- Sally and her mom will visit the gravesite together next Saturday between 9 a.m. and 12 p.m. and use the balloon letter technique to say goodbye

Where:
- Shady Pines Cemetery

How:
- Sally and her mom each create a goodbye card. They will write out all the things they miss about their dad or husband and say goodbye. They will begin the card in the therapist's office and/or take it home to complete it.
- After the card is completed the following steps will occur:
  o The therapist will meet with the family at the cemetery and ask Sally and her mom to read their letter aloud.
  o Sally and her mom will then tie the cards to a helium-filled balloon and release it so it will float up to heaven.
  o As the balloon floats away to "heaven" the therapist will facilitate asking the following questions:
    1. Therapist prompts mom to ask Sally, "What are you feeling right now as the balloon floats up?"
    2. Therapist then asks Mom, "How can you keep Dad's memory alive?"
    3. Therapist then asks Mom and Sally, "How important is it to you to keep your husband's/Dad's memory alive?"
    4. Therapist then asks Mom and Sally, "How can you work together to keep his memory alive?"
- Mom and Sally's answer to question #4 may make up the content of a second playbook to keep his memory alive.

Technique Highlighted: Fostering a Pet

TABLE 8.3 Sample Strategic Directive for Unhealed Wounds

Unhealed Wound Seed		
Unhealthy Undercurrents	**Healthy Undercurrents**	**Techniques to Inject Healthy Undercurrent**
Betrayal or abandonment	Security, forgiveness, and unconditional love	☑ Fostering a Pet

Rationale

The purpose of this playbook is to replace the unhealthy undercurrent of betrayal or abandonment with the healthy undercurrents of security, forgiveness, and unconditional love by providing the youth with the opportunity to care for a pet. There are many mental health benefits to spending time with animals. In fact, increasing research supports the premise that working with animals can help children increase socialization, decrease feelings of isolation and alienation, overcome emotional disorders, and reduce loneliness (Walsh, 2009). Families who would benefit from this playbook are those whose child has been adopted, been in the foster care system, or experienced abandonment by a significant adult in life.

Procedure

Before introducing this playbook (Box 8.2), the FST therapist must ensure that there are no barriers that would prevent the family from fostering a pet in their home. Such barriers could include a family member's allergy toward the animal, insufficient space in the home or an inadequate location of the home, or a severe phobia of a specific animal. Once the family decides to move forward with this playbook, the first step will be to move the family into contemplation about the benefits of fostering animals. Once a family is in contemplation about the benefits, their motivation will increase and they will be ready to take the necessary steps to begin to foster their pet.

Sample Wound Playbook

BOX 8.2 Playbook Example: Fostering a Pet

Fostering a Pet

To Inject the Healthy Undercurrents of Security, Forgiveness, & Unconditional Love
Unhealed Wound Seed

Who: Michael with the supporters—his mom, biological dad, and cousin James
What:
- Michael and his supporters will research together on the Internet the benefits of fostering shelter animals
- Michael and his mom and dad will go together to the local animal shelter to fill out an application to become a pet foster parent
- Once a pet is selected, Michael and his supporters will research for appropriate pet caretaking needs

---

(continued)

BOX 8.2 Playbook Example: Fostering a Pet (*continued*)

When:
- Michael and his supporters will meet Friday night, November 11, for Mom's homemade tacos and will then go to the public library to research on the Internet for information on fostering a pet
- Plan to have the application completed to foster a pet by December 1 (Mom agrees to be the designated foster since Michael is a minor; however, Michael will be the primary caretaker)
- Goal is to get custody of first foster pet by January 1

Where:
- Research will occur at the public library
- Will apply to foster a pet at the local animal shelter

How:
- Possible Internet sites to research together on fostering a pet:
  - www.petfinder.com
  - www.paws.org
  - www.supportdogs.org
- Mom and Dad will go with Michael to submit application to foster a pet
- Dad will assist Michael in researching for the appropriate pet caretaking needs and will supply all the needed supplies (food bowls, collar, leash, etc.)
- James will go with Michael and his mom and dad on the day to pick up their foster pet and will assist Michael in walking and playing with the pet

---

Technique Highlighted: A Message From the Movie *Ordinary People*

TABLE 8.4 Sample Strategic Directive for Unhealed Wounds

Unhealed Wound Seed		
Unhealthy Undercurrents	**Healthy Undercurrents**	**Techniques to Inject Healthy Undercurrent**
Family secrets	Reveal secrets/safety	☑ A message from the movie *Ordinary People*

Rationale

The purpose of this playbook (Box 8.3) is to eliminate the unhealthy undercurrent of family secrets. This is done by raising the family's awareness of the destructiveness of family secrets by increasing emotional intensity high enough that the family's secrets begin to come out. By watching the clip from the movie *Ordinary People*, the goal is for the family to learn how to do a much better job of revealing secrets than the characters in the movie. This playbook is recommended for families who are currently maintaining secrets, or even better, those families who want to gain insight into how and why family secrets are so destructive and to brainstorm ways on how they can safely reveal secrets. This playbook intervention also can help a family normalize shame or fear barriers to revealing secrets.

Procedure

The FST therapist will show Scene 1:04 (1 hour and 4 minutes into the movie) to 1:11 (1 hour and 11 minutes into the movie) from the film *Ordinary People* in the office or during a home visit. Before the scene is shown, the therapist instructs the family members what to watch out for:

- Watch what happens after Mom reveals to her husband in front of the son, the secret that "Conrad secretly quit the swim team," and how the secret opens up the unhealthy undercurrents of Mom's unforgiveness toward her son
- Watch the shift in Conrad when he finally figures out this undercurrent and forgives Mom
- And watch how Conrad starts to feel calm, safe, and at peace again
- As you watch each part, ask yourself privately these questions and be ready to answer them in our post-clip discussion: (a) What can I do to help our family safely reveal or talk about our secrets in a much better way than Conrad's family did? (b) If we did a great job of talking about our secrets with our therapist, in what ways will it help our family heal? (c) Who will benefit the most and why? (d) Is the timing good to talk about the family secrets now? Why or Why not?

After these discussion questions are asked and answered, the family may be ready in the moment to reveal their secrets, with the FST therapist as a facilitator of the process. The movie clip will be the catalyst for an enactment around family secrets that is done safely within a solution-focused framework.

Sample Wound Playbook

BOX 8.3 Playbook Example: A Message From the Movie *Ordinary People*

A Message From the Movie *Ordinary People*

To Inject the Healthy Undercurrents of Safety and Peace of Mind
Unhealed Wound Seed

Who:
- Conrad (the adolescent), Beth (mom), Calvin (dad), and Conrad's therapist (Dr. Berger)

What:
- Scene in movie: 1:04–1:11 Watch this selected clip from the movie *Ordinary People*, starring Mary Tyler Moore, Donald Sutherland, and Timothy Hutton
- Watch what happens after Mom reveals to husband in front of son the secret that "Conrad secretly quit the swim team" and how the secret opens up the unhealthy undercurrents of Mom's unforgiveness toward her son
- Watch the shift in Conrad when he finally figures out this undercurrent and forgives Mom
- And how Conrad starts to feel calm and safe and at peace again

When:
- Next Thursday during your family therapy session

Where:
- In the FST therapist's office

How:
- Watch scene in movie: 1:04–1:11 and then discuss
- Discuss what action steps are now needed to reveal your family secrets in a better way than Conrad's family did and the positive things that can happen in your family as a result of revealing long-buried secrets

---

Technique Highlighted: The "Empty Chair"

TABLE 8.5 Sample Strategic Directive for Unhealed Wounds		
Unhealed Wound Seed		
Unhealthy Undercurrents	**Healthy Undercurrents**	**Techniques to Inject Healthy Undercurrent**
Physical or mental abuse	Support, courage to leave, forgive	☑ The Empty Chair

Rationale

The purpose of this playbook (Box 8.5) is to heal wounds related to the unhealthy undercurrents of physical or mental abuse. Victims of physical or mental abuse often do not recognize the destructive power of harboring unforgiveness in their hearts. Additionally, they may have wrong perceptions of what forgiveness is and what it is not. For example, many victims of abuse believe that if they forgive their abuser, they are condoning what the abuser did. Victims may also believe that if they forgive that person, it means that they must now reconcile with their abuser and feel comfortable in their presence. The "Empty Chair" playbook is used not only to educate the victim and family on what forgiveness means and what it does not mean, but also to help them to identify any false beliefs they may have adopted about themselves as a result of the abuse and to work together to replace them with the truth.

Procedure

The FST therapist begins this session by discussing with the family what forgiveness is and what it is not, using the forgiveness definition in Box 8.4. This important step will allow the therapist to ensure that the family does not have any common misperceptions about forgiveness before beginning the "Empty Chair" exercise.

BOX 8.4 Forgiveness Definition

Forgiveness Definition	
What Forgiveness is NOT	**What Forgiveness IS**
• *Forgiveness does NOT excuse or say the perpetrator's behavior is Okay.* It does not attempt to explain away the perpetrator's behavior by pointing to extenuating circumstances. • *Forgiveness does NOT deny the wrong acts of the perpetrator.* In fact, true forgiveness can only be offered after you have come to terms with reality . . . when you can admit, "This person actually did or said this to me." • *Forgiveness does NOT mean that you must pardon what the perpetrator did or justify it in any way.*	• *Forgiveness IS a choice, not a feeling.* It is a conscious decision that you will no longer dwell on the wrong that was done to you and that you will develop a lifestyle of not filing wrongs away in your mental computer to be reviewed again and again. • *Forgiveness is a letting go of bitterness.* Bitterness is an inward condition characterized by an excessive desire for vengeance that comes from deep resentment. Bitterness shows itself in various ways such as losing your temper frequently, irritability, obsession with getting even, depression, or a constant negative perspective. Letting go of

(continued)

BOX 8.4 Forgiveness Definition (*continued*)

Forgiveness Definition	
What Forgiveness is NOT	**What Forgiveness IS**
• **Forgiveness does NOT mean that the victim must reconcile with the perpetrator.** *Reconciliation requires the participation of two people and the person you are forgiving may not be able to or want to see or talk to you. Additionally some things can never be the same and you may not desire to have a relationship with the person you forgive.* • **Forgiveness does NOT erase memories.** *It is a demonstration of great grace when you are fully aware of what occurred and you still choose to forgive.*	*bitterness is painful because it hurts when you kiss revenge goodbye. But the reward is an open invitation to joy and peace.* • **Forgiveness takes place in the heart of the forgiver and requires nothing on the part of the offender.** • **Forgiveness includes forgiving yourself.** *There is no lasting joy in forgiveness if it does not include forgiving yourself. One of the most painful feelings in the world is guilt and forgiveness is worthless to you emotionally if you do not forgive yourself.*

Source: Enright and Coyle (1998).

After discussing the true definition of forgiveness, the FST therapist will then provide paper and pen to the victim in the family to list the specific offenses done by the perpetrator, along with the messages that the victim perceived about himself from the actions or attitudes of the perpetrator. Once the list is completed, the FST therapist positions two chairs facing each other and invites the victim to sit in one chair. The FST therapist then invites the victim to speak aloud what he has written on his paper. After the victim has read his list of offenses and messages received from the perpetrator about himself, the victim is instructed to state aloud, "I forgive you, the debt is now cancelled, you owe me nothing and I release you from further payment for the injuries to me."

After the Empty Chair exercise concludes, the FST therapist helps the family identify a plan for coping with any future hurts. They are also encouraged to symbolize this moment of forgiveness by ceremoniously burning the list of offenses and burying the ashes.

Sample Wound Playbook

BOX 8.5 Playbook Example: The Empty Chair

The "Empty Chair"

To Heal the Undercurrent of Physical or Mental Abuse
Unhealed Wound Seed

Who:
- Jeremy; Grandma and Grandpa; and FST therapist

What:
- Jeremy will write out, on paper, the specific offenses done to him by his abusive biological father.
- Along with the specific offenses done by his father, he will also write down the messages that he perceived about himself from the actions or attitudes of his father and the feelings or beliefs related to his self-image.
- Using his imagination, Jeremy (looking at the symbolic chair) will call his father by name, telling him specifically what he did to cause him pain and the messages he received (feelings/beliefs).

(continued)

BOX 8.5 Playbook Example: The Empty Chair (*continued*)

- Jeremy will state, "I forgive you, the debt is now cancelled, you owe me nothing, and I release you from further payment for the injuries to me."
- At the end of the session, Jeremy will discuss the fears of future hurts from remembering more past offences or facing new offenses (relapse prevention).
- The written list is burned as a family ceremony after the session.

When:
- Friday, November 20, at 6:00 p.m.

Where:
- In the home

How:
- Grandparents will provide notebook for Jeremy to write in during session.
- Grandmother will provide "stuffed person" to sit in the "empty chair."
- Jeremy will select his own "soothing" music to listen to during the writing time.

Technique Highlighted: The "Apology—Healing the Family Heart"

TABLE 8.6 Sample Strategic Directive for Unhealed Wounds

Unhealed Wound Seed		
Unhealthy Undercurrents	**Healthy Undercurrents**	**Techniques to Inject Healthy Undercurrent**
Lack of forgiveness/ bitterness	Forgiveness	☑ The "Apology"—Healing the Family Heart

Rationale

The purpose of this playbook (Box 8.6) is to heal wounds related to the unhealthy undercurrents of unforgiveness and bitterness. The difference between the "Empty Chair" playbook and the "Apology" playbook is that the empty chair forgiveness exercise is an opportunity for a family member to extend forgiveness to someone not present. However, the **apology** exercise provides an opportunity for family members who have hurt another to express their sorrow directly to that person.

Procedure

The FST therapist begins this session by discussing with the family what forgiveness is and what it is not, using the forgiveness definition in Box 8.4 with the "Empty Chair" playbook. Once the FST therapist is assured that the family does not have any common misperceptions about forgiveness, the FST therapist meets individually with each family member who is going to participate in the apology exercise to help him or her carefully write out the apology to ensure that no new wounds occur during the exercise. Each person apologizing must fully communicate his or her sorrow for the pain the other person has experienced.

Once the apology is written, the FST therapist outlines the process for the apology exercise. The person apologizing (offender) is asked to get on his or her knees in front of the victim and express sorrow for the pain the person's actions caused the victim. The physical act of publicly getting on one's knees demonstrates full repentance in front of the whole family and the fact that the victim was a victim and bears no responsibility for the pain caused.

After the apologies are made, the FST therapist helps the family write out the lies that may "creep" back into their family system and erode the work done to heal the unhealthy undercurrent of unforgiveness. The entire family contributes to creating the list of lies and the family is asked to post the list of lies in a visible location in the home to serve as a reminder of the apologies made and the untruths that can bring unforgiveness back into the family system.

Sample Wound Playbook

BOX 8.6 Playbook Example: — "The Apology" — Healing the Family Heart

---

"The Apology": Healing the Family Heart

To Heal the Undercurrent of Unforgiveness
Unhealed Wound Seed

Who:
- Mom and Austin

What:
- Mom will apologize to Austin for the pain caused by her loss of control and subsequent abuse.
- Austin will apologize to Mom for his misbehavior and for his own aggression designed to inflict pain on Mom.

When:
- Monday, October 19, 6:00 p.m.

Where:
- At home with the FST therapist and Austin's grandparents.

How:
- Mom will work with the FST therapist to write her script to ensure that she communicates her sorrow for her son's pain and her love for Austin.
- Austin will work with the FST therapist to write his script to ensure that he communicates his sorrow for his aggression and for the pain he caused to his mom by his own aggression.
- Both will create a "Lie Monster" to post in their house to serve as a reminder of the "truths" of who they each are.

Mom: …

Mom: If Austin misbehaves, he has not forgiven me

Mom: I must be a bad mother

Mom: I can't control my emotions…

Austin: …

Austin: when I mess up, it proves that I am really bad

Austin: I really am a "bad kid"

Austin: Mom will not really change

Technique Highlighted: 30-Day Nurturing Campaign

TABLE 8.7 Sample Strategic Directive for Unhealed Wounds		
Unhealed Wound Seed		
Unhealthy Undercurrents	**Healthy Undercurrents**	**Techniques to Inject Healthy Undercurrent**
Lack of consistent nurturance	Unconditional love, consistent nurturance	☑ 30-Day Nurturing Campaign

Rationale

The purpose of this playbook is to heal wounds related to the unhealthy undercurrent of a lack of consistent nurturance. Families may lack a consistent flow of unconditional nurturance for various reasons. Nurturance may be deficient due to crises that have consumed the family system, leaving little to no time for healthy nurturing among the family. Youth may have a history of not receiving consistent nurturance due to placement outside the home. Or, the family may have withdrawn from each other due to their wounds. Whatever the cause, it has long been believed that when one helps others, it not only benefits the person assisted but also the helper. In fact, Stephen Post (2011) states in his book *The Hidden Gifts of Helping: How the Power of Giving, Compassion, and Hope Can Get Us Through Hard Times,*

> Giving help to others measurably reduces the giver's stress; improves health and well-being in surprising and powerful ways; renews our optimism about what is possible; helps us connect to family, friends, place, and lots of amazing people; allows the deep, profound joy of our humanity to flow through us and out into the world; and improves our sense of self-worth.

This premise undergirds the 30-Day Nurturing Campaign playbook; that is, as the family does random acts of kindness for each other, they will receive dual benefits from both giving and receiving.

Procedure

The FST therapist's first task before this playbook can be implemented is to educate the family on the benefits of helping others. Stephen Post's book *The Hidden Gifts of Helping* is a good resource for helping to educate the family regarding such benefits. After the family agrees to the benefits of helping others, the FST therapist will help them outline the details of their playbook and ensure that everything they choose to add to their playbook is feasible for the family. The playbook example in Box 8.7 outlines such details that are needed for successful implementation.

Sample Wound Playbook

BOX 8.7 Playbook Example: "30-Day Nurture Thyself & Others" Campaign

"30 Day Nurture Thyself & Others" Campaign
To Inject the Healthy Undercurrents of Unconditional Love and Nurturance *Unhealed Wound Seed* Who: • Mom and Alexis • Ginger and Aunt Lisa are the "accountability" monitors

(continued)

BOX 8.7 Playbook Example: "30-Day Nurture Thyself & Others" Campaign (*continued*)

What:
- Mom and Alexis will work together to identify 30 specific activities that they will each do to nurture either one another or someone else.
- Mom and Alexis will enter their 30 specific activities on the calendar so that they can hold each other accountable.
- Everyone will meet each Sunday evening to discuss how the week's nurturing activities went.

When:
- The first activity will begin on Monday, August 8, and the final, 30th activity will occur on September 16, 2011 (Mom and Alexis will not do an activity on Saturday and Sunday of each week).

Where:
- Dependent upon the activity

How:
- Mom and Alexis will coordinate their activities so that if they need to leave the house to do their activity, either Mom will drive Alexis or Aunt Lisa or Ginger will provide transportation.

Technique Highlighted: The High/Low Checkups

TABLE 8.8 Sample Strategic Directive for Unhealed Wounds

Unhealed Wound Seed		
Unhealthy Undercurrents	**Healthy Undercurrents**	**Techniques to Inject Healthy Undercurrent**
High anxiety	Safety or security	☑ The High/Low Checkup

Rationale

Children or adults who have experienced trauma or witnessed a traumatic event often develop symptoms of anxiety characterized by nervousness, difficulty sleeping, and withdrawal and avoidance behaviors. The purpose of this playbook is to mitigate the symptoms of withdrawal and avoidance by providing a mechanism for the family to come together regularly and share with one another.

Procedure

The first step in the development of this playbook (Box 8.8) is for the FST therapist to educate the family on the purpose of this playbook, which is to bring the family together regularly so symptoms of withdrawal or avoidance are neutralized. Additionally, this playbook gives the adult caregivers the opportunity to open lines of communication with their child that may have closed over time as a result of the trauma. To ensure that the family fully understands how the "high–low checkup" works, the FST therapist should demonstrate the process in the session by sharing his own high–low experience from the previous day and then have the family practice sharing theirs.

Sample Wound Playbook

BOX 8.8 Playbook Example: The High ☺ Low ☹ Checkup

The High ☺ Low ☹ Checkup

To Inject the Healthy Undercurrents of Safety and Security
Unhealed Wound Seed

Who:

☑   Jenny, Mom, and Grandma

What:

☑   Once a day, Jenny will sit down with her mom and grandma for their High/Low Checkup
☑   Each person will share the worst thing of the day (low) and the best thing of the day (high)
☑   Each person will say one nice thing about someone else (it can be about each other or someone else they came in contact with that day)

When:

☑   The High/Low Checkup will occur daily before bedtime

Where:

☑   The High/Low Checkup will occur at the kitchen table

How:

☑   Mom will take the lead and share first, and by her modeling, will ensure that each person shares the low BEFORE sharing the high
☑   Mom and Grandma will provide a snack each night for Jenny to be shared by everyone during the High/Low share time
☑   Before Jenny goes to bed each night, Mom will say, "I love you, and goodnight" and will tuck Jenny into her bed

---

Technique Highlighted: My Life "De-Stressing" Plan

TABLE 8.9 Sample Strategic Directive for Unhealed Wounds

Unhealed Wound Seed		
Unhealthy Undercurrents	**Healthy Undercurrents**	**Techniques to Inject Healthy Undercurrent**
High stress	Relaxation or diversionary tactics	☑ My Life "De-Stressing" Plan

Rationale

Stress is something that everyone experiences from time to time. In fact, it can be said that stress is a normal part of living and is even needed for healthy functioning. It is the stress hormone, cortisol, that when secreted, allows human beings to have the necessary energy needed to get up and perform their normal daily tasks. However, when someone lives in a state of chronic high stress, problems begin to emerge. These problems could be physical in nature, such as hypertension, headaches, or insomnia, to name a few, and/or they could be psychological or emotional in nature, with symptoms such as difficulty thinking clearly, problems with memory recall, or problems with emotional regulation, to name a few.

The purpose of the playbook is to heal wounds related to the unhealthy undercurrent of high stress by helping the family create a plan to prevent or lessen physical, psychological, and/or emotional problems associated with high stress.

Procedure

The FST therapist will assist the family member experiencing high stress to identify, in writing, the specific difficulties associated with his or her high stress (e.g., problems with memory, racing thoughts, insomnia). Then, using the playbook example in Box 8.9, the FST therapist will assist the entire family to select several or all of the mini-strategies within the playbook to help the individual "de-stress." The family's playbook is typed and presented to the family at the end of the session with a clear date to begin implementing the playbook. If the family wishes for people to play a role on the playbook and the person or persons are not present in the session, it is imperative that the person or persons come to the next meeting to confirm involvement and fine-tune the role.

Sample Wound Playbook

BOX 8.9 Playbook Example: My Life "De-Stressing" Plan

My Life "De-Stressing" Plan

To Heal the Unhealthy Undercurrent of High Stress
Unhealed Wound Seed

I will do the following each day so that I can prevent difficulties in the following areas: thinking clearly, remembering things, managing stress, managing my feelings and frustrations (i.e., yelling, screaming), sleeping restfully, "shutting down," and avoidance of talking about important things.

Who:
- ☑ John and his support system—Aunt Kathy, Pastor John, Rick (YMCA worker), Michael (biological dad), Ms. Daly (teacher), mom

What:
- ☑ Talk to one person in his support system each day (Monday through Saturday)
- ☑ Do 25 sit-ups each morning before leaving the house
- ☑ Take "me time" in my room if I feel like I am struggling to manage my emotions in the moment ("me time" is 15 minutes of alone time in his room)
- ☑ Add two positive notes about myself each day to my "self-worth" jar to be read aloud by someone in my support system each Sunday (additional positive things can be added by anyone in John's support system at any time)
- ☑ John and his entire support system will meet together for 4 weeks on Sunday evening to review both the week and John's self-worth jar

When:
- ☑ For his "talk" with his support person:
  - o John will make sure he has called/talked to his support person each day before he goes to bed at night
  - o John will make sure he communicates to his mom who he spoke with for that day on the same day of his talk
- ☑ Sit-ups
  - o John will make sure he does his sit-ups in the morning before leaving the house for that day. If he is staying home that day, he will do his sit-ups before lunch
- ☑ Self-worth jar
  - o John will add two positive notes about himself daily before going to bed (Mom can give John one reminder)

(continued)

BOX 8.9 Playbook Example: My Life "De-Stressing" Plan (*continued*)

How:
- ☑ John's mom will keep track of each check-in call John does and with who each day on a calendar hanging on the kitchen refrigerator
- ☑ John agrees to not call the same person more than 2 days in a row
- ☑ Mom will keep a supply of note paper next to the "self-worth" jar
- ☑ Mom will agree to honor John's request for "me time" but John agrees to return to Mom after 15 minutes to resume the conversation

RECOMMENDED TECHNIQUES TO HEAL THE PHYSICAL OR MENTAL IMPAIRMENT SEED

TABLE 8.10 Sample Strategic Directives for Mental or Physical Impairment

Unhealthy Undercurrents	Healthy Undercurrents	Techniques to Inject Healthy Undercurrent
Drawn-out medical illness	Education, support, stress management	☑ Our Stress Management Plan ☐ Education/Resource Plan ☐ The Creative Outlet
Someone seen as patient/mental case	Normality and accountability	☑ My Health & Wellness Agreement ☐ Family Support Plan ☐ *The Super Nanny* video clip ☐ *The Miracle Worker* movie clip
Chemical imbalance	Psychotropic medications	☑ Medication Compliance Plan ☐ Medical Evaluation Plan ☐ Village Support Plan
Brain or mental impairment	Consistent structure, education, support	☑ Daily Hygiene Plan ☐ Self-Care Plan ☐ Education/Resource Plan
Lack of forgiveness/ resentment	Forgiveness	☑ Memory Board of Appreciation ☐ The "Apology"—Healing the Family Heart ☐ The Empty Chair ☐ *The Horse Whisperer* movie clip
Lack of consistent nurturance	Unconditional love, consistence nurturance	☑ The Hug Prescription ☐ Random Acts of Kindness ☐ 30-Day Nurturing Campaign ☐ Cups and Self-Worth

Technique Highlighted: Our Stress Management Plan

TABLE 8.11 Sample Strategic Directive for a Mental or Physical Impairment

Mental or Physical Impairment Seed		
Unhealthy Undercurrents	**Healthy Undercurrents**	**Techniques to Inject Healthy Undercurrent**
Drawn-out medical illness	Education, support, stress management	☑ Our Stress Management Plan

Rationale

This playbook is recommended for families with a family member who has a long-standing mental or physical impairment. Living with a family member with a mental or physical impairment automatically brings challenges and stress to the family system. Often, the family spends so much time caring for the family member with the impairment that their own needs are relegated to the side, if attended to at all. Other family relationships may suffer as the family system becomes unbalanced with all the attention being directed toward the member with the impairment, at the expense of everyone else. This imbalance creates wounds in the hearts of the unimpaired family members. The playbook is designed to heal such wounds in the hearts of the two parents who have put their own marital and relational needs aside as they focused on their son and his mental impairment.

Procedure

Before beginning to develop this playbook, the FST therapist should meet with the parents alone to help them understand why it is important to first take care of themselves and their marriage. Information on this topic is widely available by searching the Internet for the impact of mental or physical illness on families. This can be done together in the FST therapist's office or in the family's home if they have Internet access. Once the need for self-care is discussed, the FST therapist should share the playbook example of a "Stress Management Plan" in Box 8.10 with the couple so that they can customize their own "stress management plan" by adopting some or all of the activities outlined in the playbook example.

Depending on the severity of the mental or physical impairment of the family member, the parents may need to involve someone else, either an extended family member, like in the playbook example, or a willing friend to step in to stay with the impaired family member so that the couple can consistently engage in their selected activities. Just as with the previous playbook found in Box 8.9, another meeting may be necessary to bring the helper on board with his or her role.

Sample Wound Playbook

BOX 8.10 Playbook Example: Our Stress Management Plan

Our Stress Management Plan

To Inject the Healthy Undercurrent of Stress Management
Mental or Physical Impairment Seed

Who:
- John's mom (Carol) and dad (Jim), with Kathy's (Carol's sister's) assistance when needed

(continued)

BOX 8.10 Playbook Example: Our Stress Management Plan (*continued*)

What:
- Carol and Jim will engage in one exercise activity daily (6 out of 7 days each week) to manage their stress and spend time together

When:
- During the workweek, Carol and Jim will do their activity before going to bed each night; on Saturday and Sunday, they will do their activity before noon

How:
- Carol and Jim will take turns choosing their activity each morning before leaving their bedroom
- Each activity will be noted on the monthly calendar for tracking purposes
- Carol and Jim will commit to not choosing the same activity more than two consecutive days
- During the physical activity, Carol and Jim will commit to NOT discussing John or his behavior
- Carol's sister will come to stay with John if the activity requires that Jim and Carol need to leave the house
- The activity list below can be added to as long as the activity is a cardiovascular exercise
- Once Carol and Jim have done 20 consecutive activities together, they will treat themselves to a dinner out, just the two of them (Kathy will stay with John)

Activities List:

1. Walk together for one mile (if inclement weather, walk at the mall)
2. Dance together for 30 minutes to upbeat music
3. Weed the neighborhood garden together for 30 minutes
4. Go "line dancing" together
5. Do 10 specific cardiovascular exercises together (research for effective and appropriate cardiovascular exercises on the Internet)

Technique Highlighted: My Health and Wellness Agreement

TABLE 8.12 Sample Strategic Directive for a Mental or Physical Impairment

Mental or Physical Impairment Seed		
Unhealthy Undercurrents	**Healthy Undercurrents**	**Techniques to Inject Healthy Undercurrent**
Someone seen as patient/ mental case	Normality and accountability	☑ My Health & Wellness Agreement

Rationale

Families coping with a family member with a mental or physical impairment are invariably faced with the reality of deciding which behaviors related to the impairment are within the patient's control and which are not. This decision is not always black and white and usually not without complications. Education on the impairment is critical to making these decisions and should be a precursor to this playbook. Once the family is educated on the impairment, outlining specific behaviors for which the individual with the impairment will be accountable is an important component that decreases the overall family stress that comes with the impairment. The purpose of this playbook is to eliminate the unhealthy undercurrent of a family member with diabetes being seen as a patient with little to no accountability or healthy boundaries.

Procedure

The playbook example in Box 8.11 is based on a youth's needs to manage his diabetes. It is imperative that the playbook be customized to meet the needs of the youth or family member with diabetes in the session. In order for the FST therapist to NOT operate outside of the scope of practice, the FST therapist must obtain a release of information from the parents and youth in order to communicate with the youth's medical doctor to ensure that the playbook is in conformity with all medical directives for that particular youth. Once the FST therapist has the particulars of the youth's medical needs, the therapist, youth, and family should meet to outline the youth's accountability agreement, using the template provided in Box 8.11.

Sample Wound Playbook

BOX 8.11 Playbook Example: My Health & Wellness Agreement

My Health & Wellness Agreement

To Inject the Healthy Undercurrent of Normality and Accountability

Who:
- ☑ Jesse, Mom, Grandma

What:
- ☑ Jesse will check his blood sugar levels regularly 4 times per day
- ☑ Jesse will take his insulin as required
- ☑ Jesse will eat three meals a day

When:
- ☑ Jesse will check his blood sugar levels 10 minutes before breakfast, lunch, dinner, and bedtime
- ☑ Jesse will take his insulin 10 minutes before meals and snacks (except when eating out)

How:
- ☑ Mom will make sure that Jesse has his meter to monitor his blood sugar daily and will praise Jesse each time he checks his levels and takes his insulin
- ☑ Mom and/or Grandma will give Jesse a gentle reminder if he forgets to check sugar levels or take his insulin
- ☑ Grandma and Mom will prepare all meals and ensure that the meals meet Jesse's dietary recommendations and are at the proper time (breakfast between 8 and 9 a.m.; lunch between 11 a.m. and 1 p.m.; dinner between 5 and 7 p.m.)
- ☑ Grandma and Mom will both sign and give to Jesse a positive teen report that points out the times he successfully checked his blood sugar level and/or took his insulin—they will give this positive teen report to Jesse each night before bedtime as their way of encouraging him to continue on
- ☑ For each successful week (Sunday–Friday) of Jesse checking his blood sugar levels and taking his insulin, Jesse, Mom, and Grandma will participate in a family fun activity on Friday or Saturday (Jesse gets to choose the activity and this list can be added to with Mom's approval)

(continued)

BOX 8.11 Playbook Example: My Health & Wellness Agreement (*continued*)

Family Fun Activities
1. Play Charades together
2. Go on a scavenger hunt at the park
3. Have an "upside picnic" in the backyard where each person selects one "whacky" food item for the picnic (food items must meet the dietary recommendations for Jesse's diabetes)
4. Go fishing at the lake (Grandma will buy the bait)
5. Fly a kite together
6. Play Monopoly
7. Rent a movie and watch together (must be G or PG rated)
8. Go to the library together

Technique Highlighted: Medication Compliance Plan

TABLE 8.13 Sample Strategic Directive for a Mental or Physical Impairment

Mental or Physical Impairment Seed		
Unhealthy Undercurrents	**Healthy Undercurrents**	**Techniques to Inject Healthy Undercurrent**
Chemical imbalance	Psychotropic medications	☑ Medication Compliance Plan

Rationale

Families are often frustrated when a family member does not take medication as prescribed by the doctor. These frustrations can lead to interactional wounds as the families fight and argue incessantly about the medication noncompliance. This playbook is designed to heal the wounds related to the medication noncompliance by clearly outlining a process to improve compliance and bring back into the family system opportunities for nurturance and connection.

Procedure

Similar to the "My Health and Wellness Agreement" in Box 8.11, the FST therapist needs to obtain a release of information from the parents and youth in order to communicate with the youth's medical doctor to ensure that any "medication compliance plan" is in conformity with the medical directives for that particular youth. Once the FST therapist has the particulars of the youth's medication compliance directives, the therapist, youth, and family should meet to outline the youth's compliance accountability plan, using the template provided in the playbook example in Box 8.12.

Sample Wound Playbook

BOX 8.12 Playbook Example: Medication Compliance Plan

Medication Compliance Plan

To Manage the Unhealthy Undercurrent of Chemical Imbalance

Who:
- The FST therapist, case manager, Mom, and youth

What:
- Taking medications as prescribed by doctor to help with symptoms of anxiety

When:
- Take medications with breakfast and dinner—before 8 a.m. and between 7 and 8 p.m.

Where:
- In the dining room at home

How:
- Youth will set a reminder on his cell phone for the morning dose and the night dosage.
- Youth will send a one-line message to Mom as soon as dosage is taken saying: "Meds taken."
- If Mom does not get the text message 15 minutes after the designated time, she will text youth a reminder.
- Mom will check the bottle of medication at nighttime to ensure that the dose was taken.
- Mom will then place a check mark on the calendar on the refrigerator for successful completion of task.
- If youth forgets a dose, he will wait for the next scheduled dose. MUST text Mom to inform her.
- If youth has taken all his meds at the correct times Sunday to Friday as evidenced by the calendar on the refrigerator—Mom will treat youth to his favorite dessert on Friday night or rent a movie for him (must be approved by youth).
- Both FST therapist and case manager will check in with Mom and youth, respectively, midweek to troubleshoot any hurdles and/or praise for compliance with plan.

Technique Highlighted: Daily Hygiene Plan

TABLE 8.14 Sample Strategic Directive for a Mental or Physical Impairment

Mental or Physical Impairment Seed		
Unhealthy Undercurrents	**Healthy Undercurrents**	**Techniques to Inject Healthy Undercurrent**
Brain or mental impairment	Consistent structure, education and support	☑ Daily Hygiene Plan

Rationale

This playbook is designed to heal wounds related to a brain or mental impairment in a family member. Families attempting to cope with a family member with a brain or mental impairment are often frustrated by the lack of basic self-care on the part of the individual with the impairment. This frustration typically leads to chronic arguments and interactional wounds within the family system. This playbook outlines a "daily hygiene plan" to provide a youth and his family with a consistent and written guide for self-care to eliminate the chronic arguments that take an enormous toll on the family.

Procedure

The first step for the FST therapist is to find out what the family desires for the self-care of the individual with the impairment. It is important that the impaired individual also be present in the session and, if able to, share his or her desires for self-care. Once agreement is reached on the self-care goals, the template in the playbook example for the "Daily Hygiene Plan" in Box 8.13 is customized for the family.

Sample Wound Playbook

BOX 8.13 Playbook Example: Daily Hygiene Plan

Daily Hygiene Plan

To Inject the Healthy Undercurrent of Structure, Education and Support

Who:
- Mom, youth, Aunt Kathy, John (Big Brother/mentor)

What:
- Shower or take a bath using soap/body wash, shampoo and conditioner. Youth can have one "day off" per week on Saturday or Sunday.
- Brush teeth twice daily, once in the morning and once before bed. Youth will brush his teeth in front of an adult to get credit for it.
- Put on clean clothes each morning, including undergarments.
- Brush hair: before school on school days; when he gets up on weekends; before he leaves the house; by 10 a.m. during summer holidays

When:
- This routine must be completed EVERY DAY (other than off days as specified).

Where:
- All of these activities must be completed at home—in youth's bedroom and youth's bathroom

How:
- Mom will be present when youth starts brushing his teeth
- For the first week, Mom will assist by placing clean clothes and undergarments on the dresser in youth's bedroom every night before bed
- Mom, with youth, will put a smiley face on the daily activity log for each completed activity (use log on next page)
- Aunt Kathy will text youth once per day with words of encouragement (mom will read the text aloud for youth from her cell phone)
- John will take youth on a special outing once each weekend for 1 hour
- Mom and Aunt Kathy will take youth to see a movie at the Dollar Theater on Sunday to demonstrate their love and support for youth. If he is compliant with his daily routine for that week, Aunt Kathy will buy him his favorite movie theater snack

---

(continued)

BOX 8.13 Playbook Example: Daily Hygiene Plan (*continued*)

Daily Hygiene Activity Log							
Week	Activity	Monday	Tuesday	Wednesday	Thursday	Friday	Saturday
Week 1	Proper shower or bath						
	Brush teeth 2x						
	Dressed in clothes laid out						
	Hair brushed						
Week 2	Proper shower or bath						
	Brush teeth 2x						
	Dressed in clothes laid out						
	Hair brushed						
Week 3	Proper shower or bath						
	Brush teeth 2x						
	Dressed in clothes laid out						
	Hair brushed						
Week 4	Proper shower or bath						
	Brush teeth 2x						
	Dressed in clothes laid out						
	Hair brushed						

Technique Highlighted: Memory Board of Appreciation

TABLE 8.15 Sample Strategic Directive for a Mental or Physical Impairment		
Mental or Physical Impairment Seed		
Unhealthy Undercurrents	**Healthy Undercurrents**	**Techniques to Inject Healthy Undercurrent**
Lack of forgiveness/ resentment	Forgiveness	☑ Memory Board of Appreciation

Rationale

The purpose of this playbook is to heal wounds related to the unhealthy undercurrent of unforgiveness or resentment around the mental or physical impairment seed. As families struggle to cope with a family member with the mental or physical impairment, they also struggle to cope with feelings of disappointment, frustration, helplessness, and even anger. These feelings are a normal response to the fact that their lives are different from the normalcy that they would like to experience and that they see in other families without a member with a mental or physical impairment. Unfortunately, these feelings, if left unchecked, can lead to bitterness and resentment. This playbook is designed to provide a fun activity that will focus the family once again on positive qualities that can be appreciated in one another. The premise is that by focusing on positive qualities that the person with the impairment has and hearing the person point out qualities that he or she appreciates in another, this process will lessen resentment or bitterness and bring forgiveness back into the family system.

Procedure

The first step is to decide which family members should be involved in the implementation of this playbook. The FST therapist should recommend that all those in the family who have negative feelings toward the impaired family member participate along with the person impaired. The playbook example in Box 8.14 provides an outline that can be adopted by the family or customized to better suit their circumstances.

Sample Wound Playbook

BOX 8.14 Playbook Example: Memory Board of Appreciation to Maintain Forgiveness

---

Memory Board of Appreciation to Maintain Forgiveness

To Inject the Healthy Undercurrent of Forgiveness

Who:
- Mom and Austin
- Uncle John and Aunt Sue are the "accountability" monitors.

(continued)

BOX 8.14 Playbook Example: Memory Board of Appreciation to Maintain Forgiveness (*continued*)

What:
- Mom and Austin will shop together for materials needed for the Memory Board of Appreciation.
- Uncle John and Aunt Sue will provide the money needed.
- The Memory Board of Appreciation is created over time and shared with the accountability monitors.
- Items that can go on the memory board include special pictures documenting something you appreciate about the other person, a note of a funny or special memory about the other person, a poem written to the other person, etc.

When:
- Every Saturday morning at 11 a.m., Mom and Austin, together, will add a minimum of two items each, to the memory board.
- At weekly Sunday dinners, Mom and Austin will present the updated memory board to Uncle John and Aunt Sue.
- Memory board will be created/maintained for the next four weeks and when completed, will be proudly hung in the living room as a special picture.

Where:
- The memory board will be proudly displayed in the dining room during the next four weeks as it is being created.
- The weekly Saturday morning updates will occur in the kitchen at the kitchen table.

How:
- Mom and Aunt Sue will make sure to maintain adequate supplies for the board (tape, paper, magazines for cutouts that can be selected to represent positive qualities of the other person, writing supplies, coloring supplies, stickers, etc.)
- Initial supplies will be purchased next Saturday. Aunt Sue will go with mom and Austin to the craft store.

Technique Highlighted: The Hug Prescription

TABLE 8.16 Sample Strategic Directive for a Mental or Physical Impairment

Mental or Physical Impairment Seed		
Unhealthy Undercurrents	**Healthy Undercurrents**	**Techniques to Inject Healthy Undercurrent**
Lack of consistent nurturance	Unconditional love and consistent nurturance	☑ The Hug Prescription

Rationale

The purpose of this wound playbook is to bring back physical touch to the relationships in a family with a member who has a mental or physical impairment. Often, when a family member has a mental or physical impairment, over time, the family moves away from any or all nurturing activities, including hugs. To heal wounds related to the unhealthy undercurrent of a lack of consistent nurturance that develops, this playbook provides a hug prescription to reintegrate healthy physical touch back into the family system.

Procedure

Asking the family to Google the Internet for the benefits of hugs on overall mental health is a good first step toward the creation of this playbook. The family and FST therapist will then discuss these benefits together in order to move everyone in the family into understanding the importance of reintegrating hugs into their relationships with one another. The playbook example of "The Hug Prescription" in Box 8.15 can be adopted by the family or customized to better suit their circumstances. It is important, however, that "the hug prescription" be detailed and include when the hugs are to take place and how long each hug will be. These details are crucial in order to successfully inject the healthy undercurrent of nurturance back into the family system.

Sample Wound Playbook

BOX 8.15 Playbook Example: The Hug Prescription

The Hug Prescription

To Inject the Healthy Undercurrent of Nurturance

Who:
- Joshua and Mom and Dad

What:
- Joshua and his mom and dad will hug daily according to the prescription.

When:
- This agreement will begin immediately after the dress rehearsal session, scheduled for Monday, November 9, at 6 p.m.

Where:
- The dress rehearsal session will take place at home and the subsequent hugs will only occur in the privacy of the home with no other people around.

How:
Hug Prescription Instructions
- 6 a.m.—hug by Dad (long hug 10 seconds or more on knees)
- 3 p.m.—hug by Mom then hug by Dad
- 5:40 p.m.—hug by Mom (long hug 10 seconds or more on knees)
- 8:30 p.m.—hug by Dad, long hug 10 seconds or more on knees)

Other Parent Responsibilities
- Dad will give Mom a hug and say "way to go" once during the day and once at the end of day for encouragement.
- Secret signs = kisses on cheek by both parents when needed

RECOMMENDED TECHNIQUES TO HEAL THE UNMET PRIMAL NEED SEED

TABLE 8.17 Sample Strategic Directives for Unmet Primal Needs

Unhealthy Undercurrents	Healthy Undercurrents	Techniques to Inject Healthy Undercurrent
Maslow's unmet hierarchy of needs	Fill in "missing" Maslow need	☑ Finding Safety and Security ☐ The "Helping Hands" Campaign ☐ Daily Words of Affirmation
Lack of attachment or bonding	Attachment bonds	☑ Restoring Emotional Family Bonds ☐ Acts of Positive Communication ☐ Fostering a Pet ☐ *The Fresh Prince of Bel-Air* video clip ☐ Random Acts of Kindness ☐ Increasing Emotional Closeness
Lack of forgiveness/ resentment	Forgiveness, prayer	☑ Daily Words of Affirmation ☐ The "Apology"—Healing the Family Heart ☐ Memory Board of Appreciation ☐ The Empty Chair ☐ *Antwone Fisher* movie clip
Lack of connection to God or higher power	Connection to God or higher power	☑ Connecting to God Through Service ☐ Spiritual Growth for Our Family ☐ Connecting to God Through Prayer
Mind, body and spirit unbalanced	Restoring balance	☑ Our Family "Life Balance" Plan ☐ My Balance Wheel ☐ Reclaiming Family Traditions

Technique Highlighted: Finding Safety and Security

TABLE 8.18 Sample Strategic Directive for an Unmet Primal Need

Mental or Physical Impairment Seed		
Unhealthy Undercurrents	**Healthy Undercurrents**	**Techniques to Inject Healthy Undercurrent**
Maslow's unmet hierarchy of needs	Fill in "missing" Maslow need	☑ Finding Safety and Security

Rationale

The purpose of the playbook found in Box 8.16 is to heal wounds related to Maslow's unmet need for security and safety. This playbook accomplishes this in two ways: (a) It surrounds the youth with supportive people who have a clear role as they each invest in the youth's life; and (b) it provides a focus for the youth in which he serves others, shifting his focus to a bigger mission outside of himself.

Procedure

It is important that a strong group of supporters for the youth attend the session to create this playbook and that all agree to play a role as outlined within the playbook. Additionally, the FST therapist should come to the session having already made some preliminary inquiries into the homeless shelters that are willing to host a youth volunteer. If the FST therapist wishes to utilize this playbook for a youth who does not have an interest in drawing or artwork, the family needs to explore alternative ways to document the youth's volunteer work. Some additional methods for documentation include journaling about each work experience, creating a scrapbook depicting something significant about each work experience, or filling a jar with a short entry of the best part of each work experience.

Sample Wound Playbook

BOX 8.16 Playbook Example: Finding Safety and Security through Volunteer Work

---

"Finding Safety and Security through Volunteer Work"

To Heal the Unhealthy Undercurrent of Maslow's Unmet Need for Safety and Security

Who:
- Vincent, Mom, Cheyla, Wally, Rosa, and Omar
- Wally will hold Vincent accountable for completing this project and Wally will take Vincent to dinner to celebrate its completion.

What:
- Vincent will volunteer for 3 months at the homeless shelter.
- Vincent will document his work with drawings that will be kept in a special book.
- All will go to the park together every two weeks to review Vincent's progress on his documentary, to eat lunch together, and to "play" together.

When:
- Every Saturday morning from 9 a.m. to 12 p.m. for the volunteer service.
- Every other Saturday at the park for a picnic lunch and "fun" together from 12 p.m. to 3 p.m.

Where:
- At the local homeless shelter
- At the Bicentennial park

How:
- Mom will contact the shelter to get their approval and take care of any necessary paperwork by Monday, November 9.
- Mom will take Vincent to the shelter and the park.
- Mom will provide the art supplies for the documentary done by Vincent.
- Rosa and Omar will work together on the picnic supplies.
- Wally will grill the hamburgers/hotdogs at the park.
- Cheyla will be in charge of the "play time" or family activity at the park.

Technique Highlighted: Restoring Emotional Family Bonds

TABLE 8.19 Sample Strategic Directive for an Unmet Primal Need

Mental or Physical Impairment Seed		
Unhealthy Undercurrents	**Healthy Undercurrents**	**Techniques to Inject Healthy Undercurrent**
Lack of attachment or bonding	Attachment bonds	☑ Restoring Emotional Family Bonds

Rationale

Oftentimes children or adolescents who have been exposed to extreme neglect or abuse during childhood become distrustful of others and struggle to develop healthy relationships with others. This is often seen in youth who have been removed from neglectful or abusive homes, who have parents with drug abuse issues or mental illness, who have had multiple changes in caregivers, or who even may have had a parent who was unable to bond with the child due to a parental illness requiring prolonged hospitalization. The purpose of this playbook is to inject into the family system attachment and connection by providing an opportunity for the family to come together at regularly prescribed times to engage in prescribed activities.

Procedure

The entire immediate family must be involved in this playbook, no matter the age. This sends a message to the youth that the family is united, one system, and no one is left out. The playbook in Box 8.17 can be used, adjusting the names of the family members, or can be customized for activities that are enjoyable by the particular family. Whatever activities are selected, however, consistency is a key component of this playbook and must be emphasized by the FST therapist.

Sample Wound Playbook

BOX 8.17 Playbook Example: Restoring Emotional Family Bonds

> **Restoring Emotional Family Bonds**
>
> *To Inject the Healthy Undercurrent of Attachment*
>
> As a family we will do the following to make our family stronger, improve communication, and have more fun together:
>
> WHO:
> - Mom and kids (Kathy and Mark)
>
> WHAT:
> - We will have a daily check-in and mealtime together Monday through Friday, and a bedtime ritual each day.
>
> WHEN:
> - This playbook will begin Monday, October 26.

(continued)

BOX 8.17 Playbook Example: Restoring Emotional Family Bonds (*continued*)

WHERE:
- In our home

HOW:
- We will follow the instructions below:

Daily Family Check-In

Every school day from 6:15 p.m. to 6:45 p.m., our family will sit down together in the living room and check in with one another. We will start with the high/low check-in (high = tell the best thing of the day; low = tell the worst thing of the day) and then each person will say one thing nice about another family member. We will use the "pen" technique so that everyone has a turn to talk and with no interruption. The "pen" technique simply means that whoever is holding the pen is permitted to talk. And the pen will be passed from person to person, beginning with adults. Mom will provide snacks for the check-in time.

Dinner Time

Our family will work together to make dinner. Everyone will participate in making the meal and we will all sit together in the living room. Mom will turn on the radio while we prepare dinner and she will make sure that there are plenty of places for everyone to sit. Mom will work with Catholic Charities to get a dining table for the family.

Bedtime

Mom will check on all children in their rooms before she goes to bed. She will say, "I love you" and "Goodnight" to each child. (even if he or she has had a bad day)

Mom's pledge
Mom will follow plan daily.
Mom will only drink one beer a day.
Mom will be awake when her children get home from school.

Technique Highlighted: Daily Words of Affirmation

TABLE 8.20 Sample Strategic Directive for an Unmet Primal Need

Mental or Physical Impairment Seed

Unhealthy Undercurrents	Healthy Undercurrents	Techniques to Inject Healthy Undercurrent
Lack of forgiveness/ resentment	Forgiveness, prayer	☑ Daily Words of Affirmation

Rationale

The "Daily Words of Affirmation" playbook is based on the premise that the spoken word is powerful. By the time a person reaches adulthood, he or she has likely come to realize the fallacy of the childhood statement "Sticks and stones may break my bones, but words will never hurt me." Words do have the power to hurt or to heal, to encourage or to tear down, and to teach either a positive lesson or a negative lesson. This playbook is designed for a youth and family in which the youth has received a chronic negative lesson about himself or herself from others, which, over time, has led to a deep pain in the youth's soul. The playbook in Box 8.18 aims to target that pain and inject forgiveness back into the heart of the youth. If the youth has come to believe the negative lessons heard, these words spoken consistently over him or her will begin the countering process as healing lessons are taught repeatedly.

Procedure

It is very important that the "daily words of affirmation" be consistently spoken aloud to the youth. If the parent begins to use this playbook and then stops for any reason, the damage may be irreversible. Therefore, the parent must be fully committed to speak the words of affirmation daily for the next 60 days. The playbook in Box 8.18 provides a script for the words of affirmation, but the family may choose to alter the script if desired.

Sample Wound Playbook

BOX 8.18 Playbook Example: Daily Words of Affirmation

Daily Words of Affirmation

To Inject the Healthy Undercurrent of Forgiveness

Who:
- Mom and Kathy

What:
- Mom will speak the TRUTH-Daily Words of Affirmation aloud to Kathy

When:
- Daily before Kathy goes to school for the next 2 months
- Each non-school day in the morning for the next 2 months

Where:
- At home before Kathy or Mom leave the house

How:
- Mom will say the TRUTH-Daily Words of Affirmation out loud over Kathy each day
- Kathy will listen quietly as Mom speaks the TRUTH-Daily Words of Affirmation
- Mom will give Kathy a hug after she speaks the Truth-Daily Words of Affirmation to Kathy

TRUTH-Daily Words of Affirmation

I am forgiven
I forgive others
I am valuable
I accept myself exactly as I am
I see and value my uniqueness
I will always do my best
I have learned from my past

Technique Highlighted: Connecting to God Through Service

TABLE 8.21 Sample Strategic Directive for an Unmet Primal Need

Mental or Physical Impairment Seed		
Unhealthy Undercurrents	**Healthy Undercurrents**	**Techniques to Inject Healthy Undercurrent**
Lack of connection to God or higher power	Connecting to God or higher power	☑ Connecting to God Through Service

Rationale

Research is increasingly recognizing connections between spirituality and mental health. In fact, for many people, religion and faith provide powerful help in times of crisis or trauma. The playbook in Box 8.19 is designed to inject back into the family system the healthy undercurrent of a strong connection to faith and to God that has been lost in the turmoil of their trauma (Table 8.21).

Procedure

The first step to creating the playbook "Connecting to God Through Service" is to read the story of the little boy and old woman found at the bottom of the playbook in Box 8.19. This story emphasizes that serving others is holy work and benefits the person helping just as much as, if not more than, the person receiving the help. The playbook in Box 8.19 can be customized based on the organization where the family will serve as well as the dates and time frames for service. As indicated in the playbook, however, in order for the unmet primal need of a lack of connection to God to be fully met, the family should continue finding ways to serve others after the prescription of the playbook is filled.

Sample Wound Playbook

BOX 8.19 Playbook Example: Connecting to God Through Service

Connecting to God Through Service

To Heal the Unhealthy Undercurrent of a Lack of Connection to God or Higher Power

Who:
  • Our family

What:
  • We will strengthen our connection to God by serving others by spending time with lonely people at the local Senior Citizen Home

When:
  • Each Saturday morning for the next 4 weeks we will go to the local Senior Citizen Home and spend time talking and serving the senior residents

  • Before we go to the local Senior Citizen Home, we will read together the passage in the Bible – Matthew 215:35–40 together to remind us of the greater purpose we are living out together … that is that when we serve others, we are connecting with God.

(continued)

BOX 8.19 Playbook Example: Connecting to God Through Service (*continued*)

Where:
- Memorial Homes

How:
- Dad will call Memorial Homes to schedule a time for the family to go meet with the leadership to ensure that they can come to the home for the next four Saturdays to serve the senior residents
- Dad, Mom and Sarah will spend the next four Saturdays at Memorial Homes from 10 a.m. to 12 p.m.
- After the four Saturdays are completed, we will decide as a family what our next service project will be to continue connecting with God through service

Connecting With God

"For I was hungry and you gave me something to eat, I was thirsty and you gave me something to drink, I was a stranger and you invited me in, I needed clothes and you clothed me, I was sick and you looked after me, I was in prison and you came to visit me. Then the righteous will answer him, Lord, when did we see you hungry and feed you, or thirsty and give you something to drink? When did we see you a stranger and invite you in, or needing clothes and clothe you? When did we see you sick or in prison and go to visit you? The King will reply, Truly I tell you, whatever you did for one of the least of these brothers and sisters of mine, you did for me."

—Matthew 25:35–40 New International Version

Technique Highlighted: Our Family "Life Balance" Plan

TABLE 8.22 Sample Strategic Directive for an Unmet Primal Need

Mental or Physical Impairment Seed		
Unhealthy Undercurrents	**Healthy Undercurrents**	**Techniques to Inject Healthy Undercurrent**
Mind, body, and spirit unbalanced	Restoring balance	☑ Our Family "Life Balance" Plan

Rationale

The "Life Balance" playbook is designed to bring a healthy balance in three areas: family time together, health and physical activity, and work (Table 8.22). It is not uncommon for families who have experienced trauma to try to cope with its effects by withdrawing from one another, spending excessive time at work, or stopping physical activities once enjoyed. These unhelpful coping mechanisms can quickly become a way of life without a strategic directive to break the pattern. The playbook in Box 8.20 is an example of three specific "rebalancing" activities to break this pattern and inject balance back into the family system.

Procedure

The three specific rebalancing activities in the playbook can be customized to each specific family. For example, the family may choose different family activities to be included in their playbook instead of the activities found in the playbook example's Family Home Evening (FHE) list of activities. Likewise, the meal the family commits to eating together may be a lunch or evening meal instead of a breakfast meal. Finally, if the family's location or circumstances prohibit an evening walk, another physical activity that they can participate in together may be substituted.

Sample Wound Playbook

BOX 8.20 Playbook Example: Our Family "Life Balance" Plan

Our Family "Life Balance" Plan

To Inject the Healthy Undercurrent of Balance Into the Family System

As a family, we realize that we have become out of balance in the following areas: time spent together, health and exercise, and work. As a result, we will all commit to the following activities to restore balance to our family.

Who:
- Our family (Mom, Dad, John, Cindy)

What:
- We will all commit to the following "rebalancing" activities:
  1. Family Home Evening (FHE)—everyone will stay home to do something together one night a week
  2. "Green Eggs and Ham" breakfast
  3. Evening walk

When:
- Family Home Evening will occur each Monday night
- "Green Eggs and Ham" is a special family breakfast that will occur every other Saturday or Sunday
- Our evening walk will occur 3 times a week (twice during the week and once on the weekend)

Where:
- At home and around the block (for the evening walk)

How:
- Our Family Home Evening (FHE) will include a fun family activity (selected from the list below) and is capped off with a special treat, prepared by Mom and Cindy. Everyone commits to staying home the entire evening, even after the activity has concluded. No one will go to his or her bedroom until after 9 p.m. **The FHE Activity List can be added to with parental approval*
- "Green Eggs and Ham" will be prepared by Dad and John and will either be Dad's "famous" pancakes, omelets or a surprise specialty that dad and John prepare together
- Our evening walk will include two times around the block to get some fresh air and share about the day's events

FHE Activity List
1. Play a family game
2. Play Charades
3. Make Your Own Mini Pizza Party
4. Have an Upside Down Backyard Picnic (everyone brings a whacky food item but must commit to eating their item along with the others)
5. Make a family collage

After selecting the technique in Step 1, the final step is to convert the technique selected into a customized wound playbook. This playbook will then be presented to the family at the next session during Phase III.

As outlined in Step 1, the FST therapist can either decide to keep the sample playbook from the previous session and edit it as needed and/or create a new wound playbook. In addition, based on the safety plan risk assessment from the previous session, the FST therapist may need to create a sample safety playbook (see Chapter 3 for how to create playbooks).

Step-by-Step Procedures Needed

The procedural steps needed to create a well-designed wound playbook can also be replicated to create a safety playbook. The content will be different, but the process is the same. The biggest difference is that the FST therapist selects a technique from Step 1 to convert into a wound playbook using a "who," "what," "when," "where," and "how" format. In contrast, the safety plan also clarifies roles using the same format, but it is designed to stop or eliminate specific risk factors (e.g., bullying, domestic violence, suicide threats, drug addiction).

The following four procedures outlined are used to show the reader how to create customized wound playbooks that can be replicated as needed (with some adaptations) for a safety playbook:

(a) *Select the technique or risk factor*
This first procedure is "Step 1: create own list of strategic directive strategies" of this chapter. In summary, the FST therapist would closely examine Tables 8.1, 8.10, and 8.17 and select a best-fit technique for the particular family based on the seed and healthy undercurrent targeted. If a safety plan is needed (based on the Phase II risk assessment), the specific risk factors are also identified (e.g., bullying, domestic violence, suicide threats, drug addiction).

(b) *Double-check synchronicity*
Regardless of the technique selected in Step 1, it is important to double-check that the child's problem symptom, seed, undercurrent, technique, and playbook synchronize together. For example, as Table 8.23 illustrates, the FST therapist might target the following goals of therapy: Heal John's (adolescent's) problem symptom of depression. This will be accomplished through (a) the targeted seed = unhealed wound, (b) the targeted unhealthy undercurrent = unresolved grief, and (c) the targeted healthy undercurrent = grief resolution. Therefore, within these parameters or goals of therapy, the FST therapist would closely examine Table 8.1 to choose a "best-fit" technique. However, the therapist must make sure that the technique selected will directly address "grief resolution" to heal John's depression with a laserlike focus. Table 8.23 illustrates this laserlike focus.

TABLE 8.23 Seed Unhealed Wound

Adolescent Targeted Problem Symptom	Unhealthy Undercurrents	Healthy Undercurrents	Techniques or Directives
Depression	Unresolved grief or loss	Grief education and resolution	☐ Balloon Letters of Goodbye ☐ Running the Race in Grandpa's Memory ☑ Scrapbook of Memories ☐ Opening to the Future/Reclaiming the Past ☐ Healing the Family Land & Heart ☐ Creating a Memorial

This example shows the difference between a therapist who is eclectic and hoping to find the right technique from a buffet menu of techniques and one who is integrative or connecting a specific theory or purpose to a specific technique.

In the same way, the safety playbook must also synchronize. The intervention selected must be customized and correspond with the specific area of risk. For example, one is not going to initiate a suicide watch if the targeted safety risk factor is bullying or use the technique of using a breathalyzer to monitor alcoholism to address the targeted safety factor of homelessness. Bottom line, the technique must fit the specific problem (symptom, safety factor, and set of healthy undercurrents) and not vice versa.

(c) *Remember "who," "what," "when," "where," and "how"*
As a reminder, the goal in direct trauma or wound work is *not* to heal the misuse of power seed or realign the hierarchy with behavioral contracting using rules, rewards, and consequences. Instead, the goal is to heal wounds and any associated seeds (mental or physical impairment, unmet primal needs) by clarifying everyone's roles through a clear and concrete wound playbook or safety plan to alter or change family and/or village interactions around new and healthy undercurrents.

An ideal way to accomplish this objective is to answer the questions "who," "what," "when," "where," and "how." Without typed playbooks, these questions would be typically answered through guesswork and assumptions. For example, the "what" question might be to increase nurturance between father and son (new healthy undercurrent interactional pattern) through the "how" of special outings. However, without a written playbook, critical implementation details such as the date for the outing, the time of the outing, or the type of outing itself (dinner, a movie, a hike, etc.) are left to chance. And leaving to chance is a recipe for failure even for healthy families, let alone those that are traumatized. To address this challenge, the wound playbook or safety playbook is typed around the technique or area of risk selected by answering these five questions:

1. **Who** will play a role in the playbook? (both immediate family and/or village)
2. **What** is the new task (the technique/strategic directive selected in Step 1) and/or the new dance steps (healthy undercurrents) that the playbook directs the family to begin to do?
3. **When** will the task in playbook occur? (date, time)
4. **Where** will the task in playbook take place? (location)
5. **How** will the task in the playbook be implemented? (the steps to complete the task)

The answers to each of these questions provide the content of the playbook as seen in Box 8.21. Details within each question must be outlined in writing to increase the odds for success that the child, the family, and/or the village will successfully implement the targeted healthy undercurrents.

(d) ***Customize and type the "who," "what," "when," "where," and "how"***
Once these questions are answered around the technique selected, the FST therapist will customize and type the answers to fit the particular family and problem symptom. For example, in the following playbook example, each role was clarified and customized:

Sample Wound Playbook

BOX 8.21 Playbook Example: A Scrapbook of Memories for Dad

A Scrapbook of Memories for Dad

Who:
- Everyone in the immediate family (Grandma, twin boys Rick and Anton, Luke, Jayden, Chaybree and Dad)

What:
- The twin boys, Rick and Anton, with Grandmother will research scrapbook ideas on Internet (Google "scrapbook ideas" or start at this address www.paperclipping.com/ten-scrapbook-layout-ideas-with-5-to-6-photos
- We (Rick and Anton) will come up with top ideas and present them to our entire family

When:
- Rick, Anton, and Grandmother (Sarah) will meet next Saturday at 11 a.m. to research scrapbook ideas. Or you fill in different day and time _____(day) and _____(time)
- After scrapbook idea list is completed, we will meet at therapist's office the following week _____(day) and _____(time) to present ideas to entire family, vote on top idea, and assign roles to complete scrapbook
- Date to complete our scrapbook: TBD (to be determined) _____(date)
- Date for follow-up family phone call with Dad: TBD (to be determined) _____(date)

Where:
- At home to research scrapbook ideas on Internet
- At therapist office to present top scrapbook ideas and assign teams and tasks to complete our scrapbook
- At therapist's office after Dad gets our scrapbook, we will process with him over speakerphone his thoughts and reactions (see Step #8 under "How" for proposed agenda for call)

How:
- Step #1: The twins (Rick and Anton), with grandmother's assistance will organize and type up with examples their top scrapbook ideas
- Step #2: During the next therapy session (insert date and time here), the twins will present this list with examples to entire family
- Step #3: The entire family will vote by a show of hands for their favorite scrapbook template
- Step #4: After winner announced, twins will assign teams (two per team) to work on different parts of scrapbook (early years—baby; middle years, favorite memories, funniest moments, etc.)
- Step #5: We will commit to finishing the scrapbook by this date (insert date here)
- Step #6: We will then send finished scrapbook to Dad
- Step #7: Therapist and Grandmother then arrange a date and time for us to talk to Dad via speakerphone

---

(continued)

BOX 8.21 Playbook Example: A Scrapbook of Memories for Dad (*continued*)

> • Step #8: We will all meet in the therapist's office for the phone call. Overall proposed agenda for this call: (a) Get his reaction to our scrapbook gift, and then share our reactions; (b) where do we go from here as a family in the future when Dad returns home to create new scrapbook memories? and (c) which parts of the past do we want to repeat and continue? What parts of the past do we want to leave in the past? And what do we want to do differently in the future? And who is responsible for what future changes, what do they need to get there, and how can we help them as a family?

NEXT STEPS

After editing the original sample wound playbook from Phase II or creating new playbooks or safety plans using Step 1 and Step 2, the FST therapist is now ready to move on to Phase III and present these playbooks or safety plans to the family in the next session (Phase III). These will be like the architectural blueprint drawings that the family and therapist can use to co-create a finalized plan that everyone will be proud of. As stated earlier, it is much easier for stuck families to work from a written draft than a blank piece of paper. This is why this pre-session preparation is such an important milestone in the overall success of the Family Systems Trauma (FST) model. Our hope is that combining sample wound playbooks together with a buffet menu of techniques will make the creation of customized playbooks for your traumatized families much easier and more successful.

REFERENCES

Chapman, G. D. (2004). *The 5 love languages: The secret to love that lasts.* Chicago, IL: Northfield.

Chapman, G. D., & Campbell, R. (2016). *The 5 love languages of children: The secret to loving children effectively.* Chicago, IL: Northfield.

Enright, R. D., & Coyle, C. T. (1998). Researching the process model of forgiveness within psychological interventions. In E. L. Worthington (Ed.), *Dimensions of forgiveness* (pp. 139–161). Radnor, PA: Templeton Foundation Press.

Post, S. G. (2011). *The hidden gifts of helping: How the power of giving, compassion, and hope can get us through hard times.* San Francisco, CA: Jossey-Bass.

Walsh, F. (2009). Human-animal bonds I: The relational significance of companion animals. *Family Process, 48,* 462–480. doi:10.1111/j.1545-5300.2009.01296.x

Phase III: Co-Create Playbooks

Step 1: Family and FST Therapist Present Top Strategic Directives

Step 2: FST Therapist Presents Customized Playbooks

Step 3: Family, Child, and FST Therapist Co-Create Playbooks

Step 4: Important Final Message

As the family systems trauma (FST) flowchart diagram in Chapter 3 illustrates, Phase III occurs after pre-session preparation for Phase III. The primary goals for Phase III are to (a) ask the family to present their top technique findings from their homework lead sheet; (b) show wound and/or safety playbook recommendations from pre-session preparation; (c) co-create the wound and/or safety playbook(s) together (FST therapist, child, and family); and (d) predict relapse if the family tries to implement the contract before troubleshooting and dress rehearsals are completed in the next session (Phase IV).

Unlike previous phases of treatment where there can be as many as seven (Phase I) or eight (Phase II) steps, Phase III, with only four steps, is not as complex or intensive. Therefore, the total number of sessions are often less than other FST treatment phases. Phase III has an average length of stay of one to two 2-hour sessions or two to three 1-hour sessions.

As the title of this chapter implies, the four mini-steps in this chapter will show how to co-create a finalized playbook(s) that will be ready for testing through role-plays and troubleshooting in Phase IV. There can be more than one playbook co-created depending on the family or when using a two-track process (safety and wound playbook side-by-side). However, the rule of thumb is to limit the number of playbooks and targeted child problem symptoms to only one or two at a time to avoid overwhelming the family. The timing of when and how additional playbooks are introduced into treatment is described in detail in Chapter 13, Phase V "Evaluate Progress and Relapse Prevention."

Case examples will be used to illustrate the four key steps in Phase III. The four steps are:

1. Family and FST Therapist Present Top Strategic Directives
2. FST Therapist Presents Customized Playbooks
3. Family, Child, and FST Therapist Co-Create Playbooks
4. Important Final Message

PRIOR TO THE SESSION

As a reminder, prior to the beginning of Phase III, the FST therapist should come prepared to enter the session with the following items:

☑ *Blank flipchart page with the title "Top Strategies or Techniques"*: If the family comes to the session with their homework completed, the FST therapist or another family member will write down on the flip chart the list of techniques discovered from the lead sheet for everyone to see in rank order of preference. Seeing a laundry list summary of the top picks can both inspire everyone and make it easier for the FST therapist to integrate these selections into the finalized playbooks.

☑ *Handout copies of Tables 8.1 to 8.3*: Throughout the session, the FST therapist will need to anchor any technique selections and playbook examples back to these handouts from Chapter 8 that illustrate the buffet menu of the techniques and those selected by the therapist during the pre-session preparation.

☑ *Wound or safety playbook drafts*: The FST therapist will present to the family in a handout format the wound or safety playbook drafts from pre-session preparation in Chapter 8. These will be the blueprint templates that the FST therapist and family members will use in Phase III to modify, as needed, and create a finalized plan to take into Phase IV.

☑ *Rehang feedback loops, the stress chart, and seed/tree diagram*: Big-picture anchor points are important. Therefore, prior to the session, the FST therapist should rehang the flip chart (or use PowerPoint) of these charts from past sessions (cleaned up and rewritten professionally). As with Tables 8.1 to 8.3, throughout the session, it may be important for the FST therapist to point to use these drawing to connect back to the big picture. Continuing to connect and reconnect these dots visually will answer the "Why?" (we fix the root causes of the problem) through the "How?" (we use playbooks or strategic directives to restructure the family).

STEP 1: FAMILY AND FST THERAPIST PRESENT TOP STRATEGIC DIRECTIVES

To begin Step 1, the following transition statement is recommended:

"Thank you for coming in today. I think today will be an exciting meeting for everyone. It is the day we put together our final playbook as a team like the sample one I showed you from our last session [hold it up]. The finalized playbook we create today will be like an antibiotic, used to help heal your child's wounds or problems of [restate them here]. Football teams also use playbooks during spring training to give clear direction, clarity to everybody's role, and to make sure everyone is on the same sheet of music before opening day.

In the same way, we will use our playbooks to give us clear direction on how we will work together as a team to help heal your child's problems in the here and now. [State child's name] is not alone. We can all rally together to help and be that team.

At the end of our last session, I gave you a homework lead sheet to locate any techniques or strategies on your own to help us create our playbook in today's session. In just a moment, I will ask you to share your findings. But remember what I said last week. If you were not able to do the homework, no big deal. In between our last meeting and this one, I was also able to come up with some strategies to share with you. I even made a first draft of a playbook [hold it up] (or tweaked the one I showed you last session) that I will pass out later for us to either keep as is, or tweak and fine-tune together.

Ok. let's get started. Were you able to do the homework? If 'yes' could you tell me what you found out? We will list your findings one at a time on this giant flipchart page (point to it). If not, that's ok, I will present my findings."

As already stated, if the family did not complete the homework, the therapist quickly moves to presenting the recommended technique(s) and subsequent playbook(s). However, as this transition script outlines, if the family comes to the session with homework completed, they are asked to present their findings first.

Overall Goals of This Step

The overall goals of this step are the following. First, it is always a bonus if (a) family members complete the homework assignment (this act increases both commitment and buy-in with the therapeutic process) and/or (b) the ideas or techniques presented can be incorporated or integrated into the finalized playbook. For example, as the scrapbook memories example (Chapter 8) outlines, the twin boys with grandmother were asked in their lead sheet to research scrapbook ideas on the Internet and present their ideas at the beginning of Phase III. Their ideas included adding personal letters to the scrapbook. These ideas were so well presented that the FST therapist instantly added these in real time to the finalized wound playbook:

Homework Lead Sheet

- The twin boys Rick and Anton with their grandmother will research scrapbook ideas on Internet (Google "scrapbook ideas" or start at this address www.paperclipping.com/ten-scrapbook-layout-ideas-with-5-to-6-photos)
- We (Rick and Anton) will come up with top ideas and present them to our entire family

Ideas presented by twins at beginning of Phase III session

- Passed out sample scrapbook ideas that included the use of personal letters with personal mementos such as artwork, pictures, etc.

This technique idea was then immediately incorporated into the finalized wound "family scrapbook" playbook later in the session (see italics where added in playbook section below).

What:

- Scrapbook of Memories to be created by the grandmother, aunt, and rest of the children to be hand-delivered by the grandmother to the father in prison to get him ready when he comes back home next month
- *Added to the scrapbook are the ideas presented by Rick and Anton on how to include personal notes with personal artwork or pictures. We love this idea as a family and want to use it!*

As illustrated in the preceding example, the integration of family ideas with FST therapist ideas represents what a true collaboration in FST treatment can look like. When this happens, the family usually becomes instantly energized and hopeful.

Even if the family forgets to complete the assignment, the message is clear: The FST therapist will not give up on a collaborative stance. This includes not being irritated with the family even if the homework assignment was not completed. During the ethnographic interview, when the question was asked, "*What was most helpful in today's session?*" a single-parent mom gave this answer:

You might have thought that it didn't matter much. But every time you asked my opinion or my son's opinion, it made all the difference in the world. When you grow up poor, you feel less than. The system just wears you down and you lose your voice along the way. When we have to ask or beg for help, you can just feel it in the air from people: 'You are poor and we know what's best for you or your opinion doesn't matter!' But when we come here our voice matters. And even when I was too tired to do the homework, you didn't look down on us or make us feel bad about ourselves. You didn't skip a beat. You just went on, but kept circling back with 'What do you think?' or 'What is your opinion?' You also worked hard for us in between our meetings to put these playbooks together. I appreciate that and I appreciate how you always asked my son for his ideas. It was a turning point for me. It gave us hope.

This interview quote underscores the importance of family members coming up with strategies to heal themselves in between sessions. It would be much simpler for the FST therapist to take charge, forget about pre-session preparation work, and not spend the time or effort necessary to create the homework lead sheet assignment. However, the traumatized family feels powerless to begin with. They need the opportunity to have a voice throughout the therapeutic process.

A second overall goal of this step is what we call "R&D" (research and development). If the family is shown how to find healing strategies on their own, the odds increase that this same process will be repeated long after treatment is complete. For example, the next time a crisis hits, one or more family members might say something like,

We have what it takes to handle this new crisis on our own. Remember how we looked up strategies on the Internet the last time to heal ourselves? We don't need to rush into treatment again. Let's slow down, take a moment to repeat what we did last time, and create our own lead sheets and playbooks. If necessary, we can ask for a tune-up session, but let's first try to fix the problem ourselves.

Generalizing therapeutic tools to become the new normal continues to help foster second-order change. Even if the family comes to Phase III with no homework, the process steps of how to locate healing strategies are still conveyed for use in the future.

When Family Homework Leads Are Not Used

It is important to note that the FST therapist may not choose to use the family's homework suggestions. The reasons for this decision can range from the timing not being right to the techniques selected (by the family) being too heavy-handed or the techniques not meshing well with the therapist's customized playbook. If any of these is the reason, the therapist must clarify it with the family. The therapist must stay in the role of quarterback or lead facilitator until the family obtains its metaphoric "sea legs" by demonstrating proper creation, use, and implementation of wound playbooks. In spite of this tactical decision, homework presentations are still important. The family is empowered with a voice to share their findings. They are shown the how-to process of locating healing strategies. Some of their strategies may be used later in FST treatment or on their own.

For example, it is common for the FST therapist to begin Round 1 of treatment with an intervention that is easier to execute to give the family a quick victory and momentum. A first-round customized playbook might include the technique of "simple acts of kindness" to create the healthy undercurrent of forgiveness. After the acts of kindness strategic directive is a success, the FST therapist can parlay this victory into a more difficult playbook such as "a direct apology" that the family members might have suggested during their homework presentation.

Family Presents Homework Findings

After the transition script in the preceding text is read, if the family comes to the session with homework completed, they are asked to present their findings first.

The therapist or another family member uses the flipchart page labeled "Top Strategies or Techniques" to write down the list of the techniques presented. The family is also asked to rank their top picks with rationale. During the last session (see Chapter 7) when the homework lead sheet was provided, the therapist asked the family to pick out a spokesperson for their summary report. If this did not happen, the family or therapist will ask someone during the session to assume this role. If not, chaos can erupt as everyone tries to talk about the findings all at once.

As the family delivers their findings, the FST therapist must be poised to quickly stick-and-move if the need arises. When families make their homework presentation, it is easy for them to go down unproductive bunny trails or get bogged down in the details. To counter these threats, the therapist must be poised to stick by quickly summarizing the essence of what the family is saying about the technique and then move on to refocus the family, which is getting off track. For example, the therapist might say something like:

> [Interrupts] *Let me stop you and summarize what I am hearing to see if I am tracking you. You said that you found a strategy on the Internet about how to talk differently to your child who is grieving. There are a lot of moving parts with this intervention that we can explore later if we decide to include this strategy in your first playbook. But for now, is it OK if I summarize the strategy or technique and write on the flipchart as "A Specialized Way of Communicating to Kids Who Grieve"?*

It is important to note that as the family is presenting, the FST therapist is silently asking himself or herself these two questions:

1. "Are there any techniques presented or parts of a technique that I can integrate into the technique(s) and customized playbook(s) that I am about to reveal?"
   Or
2. "Is one or more of the techniques that the family is presenting so compelling that I may need to scrap my technique and playbook altogether and start fresh with their ideas?"

Both of these questions must be answered by the therapist in real time during the session. There is no opportunity for lengthy deliberation or pre-session preparation. To help with this decision, the therapist must keep coming back to the rule of thumb of "keeping the playbook simple for the greatest chance for success" with positive changes and quick victories built in to foster confidence and momentum. During the pre-session preparation, the FST therapist should choose a technique and build a playbook with this treatment philosophy in mind.

FST Therapist Presents Homework Findings

Once the family's presentation is complete (or if they come to the session with no homework), the FST therapist begins by first passing out the handout from Tables 8.1 to 8.3 and pointing out the technique(s) indicated in the handout. This is done prior to passing out a handout of the customized playbook so as not to overwhelm family members with too much information too fast. Instead, the therapist presents the information in "bite-sized pieces."

In reviewing the handout of Tables 8.1 to 8.3, the FST therapist will provide a clear explanation as to why the FST therapist picked the technique(s) indicated over other possible picks. If the idea of "love language" is used (Chapter 8), the timing is ideal to explain how the particular technique selected matches with the child's or adolescents language of quality time, affirmation, receiving gifts, acts of service, and/or physical touch.

When the FST therapist explains the rationale for the selection, he or she can (a) verbally connect the dots by pointing to the techniques handout and/or the previous flip chart drawings (the family's stress chart, seed/tree diagram, and feedback loops); or (b) read an introductory prelude to the playbook like a great preface to a good book. The prelude contains powerful reframes and acts like rocket fuel to boost confidence in the therapist's technique choice.

Case Example

Ten-year-old Stacey was seen by both parents as the problem child and her younger 6-year-old brother Sam as the one who could do no wrong. The parents only seemed to catch Stacy doing something wrong, and this created constant fights and resulted in interactional trauma. Based on the seed pick from Phase I of unmet primal needs, the feedback loops, and this information, the therapist chose the healthy undercurrent of forming attachments and the technique of restoring emotional bonds by "catching Stacey doing something right."

To sell both parents on the technique, the therapist decided to first read aloud the introductory prelude written at the top of the customized playbook before showing the actual playbook to the family. (See prelude in Table 9.1.)

TABLE 9.1 Prelude: Introduction to the "Catching Stacey Doing Something Right" Playbook

---

Prelude: Introduction to the "Catching Stacey Doing Something Right" Playbook

Stacey's behavior right now is her best attempt to get attention and get noticed as the bright, loving, and tender girl she is so that she doesn't feel all alone.

Stacey wants to be noticed like Sam, but her creative method for negative attention has gotten her off track. Over time this has become a bad habit or a lifestyle.

It is important to note that Stacey is "wired" differently than Sam. Sam responds well to your current style of communication, but Stacey does not. You are great parents and your style of communication it not "good" vs. "bad" as others may have labeled it.

Instead, Stacey's different wiring just requires a different style of communication, just like in music. Some children may require a violin while others respond better to a trombone or drum. Sam seems to respond well to the drum whereas Stacey, with her different wiring, likely needs a violin sound.

To test this theory out, what do we have to lose by trying a 30-day experiment? The playbook or task is called Catch Stacey Doing Something Right Whenever Possible.

You, as parents, can model this strategy. I know that you are extremely flexible people and love Stacey so much that you are open to trying anything to help turn things around.

Once Stacey sees the benefits of this technique, her true self can rise to the surface as she responds to your beautiful violin playing.

To get you jump-started, I brought you a CD to play on the way home today that contains the greatest hits of violin solo artists. This music will begin this healing journey.

As illustrated in this case example, the prelude used a reframe hook to get resistant family members buy in to the technique selected. In this case, the parents loved the reframe that Stacey wanted to be noticed like her brother Sam but that she was "wired" differently, like a violin. The family was especially touched by the CD gesture. In addition, the parents' positive body language showed that they liked being called "flexible" and "open to trying new things." In reality, the parents' actions from previous sessions showed the exact opposite. But good therapy highlights areas of competency or looks beyond the surface to call up the hidden greatness in all of us.

Why Reframes or "Fake It Till You Make It" and Strategic Directive Are So Important

Stacey's family highlights two theories of change that underlines why the pairing of reframes with techniques or strategic directives are so important. First, Neil Schiff (personal Communication, November 3, 1999) stated that the secret sauce to successful directive implementation was "the buildup." If the FST therapist could "sell the technique" before it was implemented, the odds of success increased. The technique itself might be an incredible catalyst to undercurrent transformation, but without motivation, it often fails. Second, as Haley (1991, p. 56) states, "The main goal of [strategic] therapy is to get people to behave differently and so to have different subjective experiences." This means that when clients behave differently, they feel and think differently. As with Stacey's parents, if the family does not buy into the technique after a strong prelude, there is still a Plan B, the "fake it until you make it" option. This means asking the family to act their way into a new way of thinking and continue with the playbook based on their trust in the therapist.

Therefore, the FST therapist can first try insight using the handout of Tables 8.1 to 8.3. However, if the family resists or the therapist knows resistance is imminent, the FST therapist should utilize introduction preludes that contain powerful reframes and point out areas of competency. The odds of success increase by not getting locked into only one approach.

STEP 2: FST THERAPIST PRESENTS CUSTOMIZED PLAYBOOKS

To begin Step 2, the following transition statement is recommended:

> Now that I have shown you the technique(s) I picked and my rationale for choosing them, it is time for me to pass out the first draft of the wound playbook that is customized for your family. It takes the technique we just talked about and gives you the step-by-step procedures to put _____[name the technique] into action [pass out copy of the wound playbook as a handout to each person in the room].

> As you look at the playbook, please note that it is a working draft. This means that after I read each part aloud we can go back together and make adjustments or tweaks as needed. Some of the ideas in here may complement some of the ideas you laid out earlier today from your homework and some may not. And as we go through it together, when possible, we will take the ideas you gave earlier and plug them right into the template.

> [**If needed**] Because you identified the following issue _____ [name it] as a safety concern at our last session, I took the time to also draft a safety playbook. Therefore, during our time today we will also look at this playbook and make changes as needed.

> You may also like the playbook just like it is with only minor changes or none at all. Either way, please remember this is just a first step. After we make any final changes, I will take your wound playbook and type it out to give to you at the start of our next session.

At our next session, we will practice the delivery of your playbook and figure out if there are any loopholes that could derail the playbook's success. After that, you will be ready to put your playbook into effect to fix the problems you came here to fix ____[list them].

Are there any questions or comments on what I just said?

After the transition statement, the FST therapist slowly reads the wound playbook aloud line by line. For dramatic effect, using an LCD projector, the therapist can project the playbook onto the wall or screen in the family's home, during a home visit, or in the therapist's office. During the reading, the therapist can pause and make any connections or complementary fits to any homework techniques the family presented.

Playbooks Are Finalized

Playbooks are step-by-step strategies to convert techniques (strategic directives) into action. Therefore, once the FST therapist has provided a convincing explanation for the technique selection, the next step is to pass out the customized wound playbook and/or safety playbook that puts the technique into action within a "who," "what," "when," "where," and "how" framework. The playbook is customized for the specific family (name, location, steps to implement, specific details, etc.). However, the FST therapist must make it clear that the playbook handout is a "working draft" that can be tweaked or modified as needed. To make this process easy (a paint-by-number format), the steps and content of the playbook or safety plan are provided to each family and village member as a handout and, if possible, projected on a wall or television. If not, the draft will be written on a flip chart prior to the session with ample space left beneath each section for changes, additions, or modifications (see Step 3).

After final adjustments, the FST therapist will make any last-minute changes after the session. The final wound or safety playbook will then be handed out at the beginning of the next session (Phase IV). As stated earlier, the wound or safety playbook will not be handed out to use at the end of this session. Troubleshooting and dress rehearsals still have to be completed during the next session. Otherwise, the playbook will likely fail without practicing its delivery first. The exception to this rule is safety planning that cannot wait another week. For example, with safety risks such as suicidal ideation, the safety playbook must be implemented immediately. If some practice delivery is essential, based on the family, the wound playbooks may need to be delayed another week until safety is fully addressed with troubleshooting.

A "Let's Get Started" Mindset Is Essential

It is important to note that both the FST therapist and family must be committed to a "let's get started" approach. At the end of Phase III, there must be a commitment from everyone that the session will end with a finalized wound and/or safety playbook that is ready for role-play practice and troubleshooting in the next session (Phase IV). This commitment must be made to avoid "analysis paralysis" or continued delays. There is often a powerful and unseen tug that can pull both child and family to more of the same or what is called "homeostasis."

The fear of change is powerful. Hence, when there is an actual written playbook facing everyone, it amplifies this fear of change or activates what are called homeostatic maintainers (Fishman, 1988) or individuals in the family system who want to maintain the status quo. Signs to look for are when individuals within the family or village make statements such as "We need more time" (with no solid rationale); "Let's keep meeting for more discussion"; "This playbook will never work"; "We need to keep tweaking this thing"; a "Yes, but" stance; "This is too easy it won't work"; or "Our problems are much bigger than this simple playbook can solve." If any of these signs occur, the therapist must be ready with a countermove statement like the following:

> I can see by your reactions that either you want to wait, or you think the playbook is too simple for your complex problems, or one or more of you just don't agree with the plan. But here is where I am asking for your faith and trust in me as your coach or therapist. To be honest, you may be right, this playbook could fall on its face and fail. But we won't know until we try.

> And I think it is important for you to do something to move forward in order to heal the pain and the wounds both you and your child have felt for so long. Talking without any action just results in staying stuck. In the research and in my experience, trying this playbook will yield two kinds of fruit.

> The first fruit is that the playbook often works better than you think because it is a typed-up step-by-step plan and not just off-the-cuff. And when it works, we will feel hope and a sense of accomplishment. And from hope, new ideas and new possibilities can suddenly reveal themselves. So the bottom line is that I think we can use these victories and hope even if it's small.

> The second fruit is that research shows that whether the playbook succeeds or fails, the outcomes give us invaluable information on whether we should stay the course or make adjustments. Scientists call this experimentation. They perform a series of experiments and each one gives them new information and brings them one step closer to the cure. So we are being scientists. Even if this playbook is not perfect, or is too simple or maybe not even the best pick, if we try it, we get closer to helping your child heal and locating the root causes of the pain. At the end of the day, that's always a good thing.

This type of statement is powerful and hard to argue against even for the most resistant parent or child. It is also true that it is at this point in treatment that high rapport, joining, and a therapeutic alliance between the FST therapist and family pay huge dividends. Playbooks are strategic directives that require change in a stuck system and that are scary. Because of this reality, faith and trust in the therapist is sometimes necessary to get the family to try the playbook even if it is just as an experiment. In addition, if there is a battle for structure (the therapist takes a stand with "*Let's do something now*" versus the family saying "no" or "*Let's wait*"), the therapist has to have the final say. Otherwise, therapy ends here. Sometimes the only way this battle is won is when family members say something like "*At the end of day we will go forward because we trust and like you enough to do it even if we are afraid.*"

Case Example

The family initially came to therapy because the 12-year-old boy, Harry, refused to attend school. As treatment progressed and the grandparents' (who were raising their grandson without the parents in the picture) trust in the therapist increased, the family secret of living in homeless shelters and in their car was revealed. The stress of having no place to live posed a real safety issue and created a daily, chronic trauma. It, therefore, became the first problem to address, with attending school taking a close second.

As a result, the FST therapist selected the technique called "finding safety and security" to address the seed of unmet primal needs and the unhealthy undercurrent of the missing in Maslow's hierarchy of needs, lack of shelter. As the therapist read the playbook aloud, it outlined a step-by-step plan of how the therapist would act as the advocate

(continued)

Case Example (*continued*)

to contact and organize social services to find shelter. However, as the therapist read the plan, he stopped and integrated what the grandparents and Harry had stated during their homework presentation:

"As I read this plan, I almost get tears in my eyes. Against all odds you and your grandson somehow got to your local library and looked up on the Internet churches in your area and a list of the pastors. You even copied and printed the top five churches and the pastors' contact information and brought it in today. It's just amazing and awesome. I am so proud to be able to work with your family. So what I want to do is add "Contact these church pastors for help" to this playbook. You were right during your presentation. If we wait on social services it could take a while. We will still reach out to various social services, but we should also, at the same time, take your wonderful idea and contact these pastors. Later today, as we tweak this playbook, we will put our heads together as to what to say when we call these pastors and what specifically we want their help with. Thank you again for these ideas, they were wonderful and helpful. I think you guys are so good, you could do my job better than me [everyone laughs]."

In this case example, the FST therapist looked for touch points between his plan and the family's presentation. He connected the dots whenever possible in real time and looked for opportunities to highlight strengths and areas of competency. This same process can be replicated and mirrored before or after the therapist reads the customized wound playbook. The family is often too close to the problem to see clear touch points between their suggestions and the therapist's playbook. Therefore, it is part of the FST therapist's role to make these connections. After the FST therapist reads through the customized playbook and pauses to make any real-time touch points to the family's homework strategies, it is time to move to Step 3.

STEP 3: FAMILY, CHILD, AND FST THERAPIST CO-CREATE PLAYBOOKS

This step will provide the reader with how-to guidelines around the most common tactical decisions or possible scenarios that the FST therapist faces when co-creating the wound or safety playbooks:

- **How to carry over sample playbook from Phase II or keep with limited changes**
- **How to integrate new techniques outlined by the family**
- **How to scrap the playbook altogether and build a new one**

As stated earlier, this is an important decision and should be based on timing, the particular family, and a keep-it-simple framework. Whatever, the tactical decision, it is the FST therapist's job to inform the family of the decision and rationale. Each of these possible decision points are briefly outlined in the following text.

How to Carry Over Sample Playbook From Phase II or Keep With Limited Changes

If the decision is to keep the sample wound playbook from Phase II, the FST therapist may state to the family that one reason for keeping the same playbook is that the targeted healthy undercurrents did not change between sessions. If another wound playbook or safety plan is introduced, after it is read out loud, the family may state that they like it as is with no changes.

Within both scenarios, the opportunity still exists to make minor revisions or adjustments. For example, a family member may want to change the date or time of the intervention or even its location. Roles could also shift. For instance, it may be decided that a village member, such as a grandparent, play a part in the playbook or substitute for another member. The "how" steps may also need some adjustments or expansion. For example, one "how" might state, *"Grandmother will call a meeting to show us how to claim our old family traditions to reclaim our balance."* During Step 3, the grandmother may want to expand this piece to now read, *"Grandmother will call a meeting on Saturday, February 6, at 6 pm at her house to show us our old family traditions through fun storytelling, old pictures, old artifacts, and old movies. Bring you PJs, sleeping bag, and popcorn because this will be so much fun that we could go late into the evening."* In this example, the core "how" of the FST therapist's original playbook was expanded through input by the grandmother.

It is important to underscore this point. Even though the therapist does 90% or higher of the work, every time the family tweaks either the wound playbook or safety plan, it is a major victory. When this happens, the family is putting their own footprint on the playbook and taking ownership of it. Even minor changes are a big deal symbolically. The therapist also should always give all credit to the family, whether they did the heavy lifting or not. If the family perceives that the therapist did all the work, they have no ownership. As a result, the next time a crisis hits, the family will call for help. The family will think they cannot heal themselves. Over time, this can turn into "learned helplessness."

Even though the FST therapist may do most of the heavy lifting or creation of the first playbook, it can be likened to a plaster cast that a family doctor uses to reset a broken bone. The cast is temporary until the leg heals and grows stronger on its own. In the same way, the wound or safety playbook is the cast. The role-plays, the troubleshooting, and the actual implementation are owned by the family, not the therapist. As a result, when the playbook is successful, the family tends to forget about who created the original cast. The focus and ownership is now on the outcome and the healed leg, not on the cast maker.

How to Integrate New Techniques Outlined by the Family

If the decision is made to integrate the family's homework leads into the playbook, the FST therapist integrates those techniques that best fit with the customized playbook. For example, the wound playbook customized by the therapist during pre-session preparation might be "a daily hygiene plan." The family, however, during their homework lead presentation, might have suggested the technique of "proper nutrition." The therapist then is left with the decision of whether or not there is a complementary fit between the two strategies. The family and therapist would collaboratively determine touch points. In this case, there was a fit. In Table 9.2, one can see in **bold font** how this integration was done.

"Morning routines" paired nicely with "nutritional routines." In addition, "helping mental impairment with structure" integrated well with "helping feed the brain with proper nutrition." In addition, the combining of these two techniques still maintained a keep-it-simple format. However, even with a simple format, for some families, nutrition and routine might be too overwhelming at first. If that is the case, the therapist could still highlight for the family that their

---

TABLE 9.2 Daily Morning Hygiene Playbook

Daily Morning Hygiene Routine for Justin

To Inject the Healthy Undercurrents of Structure, Education and Support

Who:

- Mom, youth (Justin), Aunt Kathy, John (big brother/mentor)

What:

- Shower or take a bath using soap/body wash, shampoo and conditioner. Youth can have one "day off" per week on Saturday or Sunday.
- Brush teeth twice daily, once in the morning and once before bed. Youth will brush his teeth in front of an adult to get credit for it.
- Put on clean clothes each morning including undergarments.
- Brush hair: before school on school days; when he gets up on weekends; before he leaves the house; by 10 a.m. during summer holidays.

Integrating Your Nutritional Plan

Breakfast
- **Rotate oatmeal, eggs, or fresh juice (Justin may select his fruit for the juicer)**
- **1 liter of water**
- **Weekends (Saturday and Sunday) = cheat days—later move to only one day—start slow**

Lunch
- **Salads with a protein (fish or chicken) or sandwich with a vegetable**
- **No sugar or soda**
- **Weekends (Saturday and Sunday) = cheat days—later move to only one day—start slow**

Dinner
- **I will prepare a nutritious dinner that will vary but will include a variety of fish, chicken, vegetables, or beef**
- **Another liter of water**
- **No cheat days**

Snacks Between Meals
- **Fruit, nuts, yogurt**
- **No soda, cookies, or candy**

When:

- This morning routine must be completed EVERY DAY by times specified.
- **Breakfast meals: Monday through Friday at 7 a.m., weekends = cheat days**
- **Lunch meals" Monday through Friday at school at 12 p.m. (lunch packed by mom) and weekends at 12 p.m.**
- **Dinner: Monday through Friday 6 p.m. and also weekends on your own**

---

suggestion was great but state that it will be used later after the successful implementation of the daily hygiene playbook first. It is up to the therapist to make the final judgment call and, at the same time, be crystal clear to the family why the decision was made.

How comfortable and skillful the therapist is in taking a directive versus nondirective stance is also a key factor in the success or failure of integrating family and therapist techniques into one playbook. In the directive role, the therapist gives active advice and suggestions rather than a style of active listening and reflection. The following brief transcript illustrates a directive style contrasted with a nondirective style:

Therapist: I like your earlier technique suggestion on nutrition. It will go well together with the customize playbook we just read: Daily Morning Hygiene Routine for Justin. As you can see, I rewrote this playbook neatly on the big flip chart on the wall [or projected on the flat screen TV or LCD projector] so we can add the nutritional piece in. *Where would you like to begin and what do you want to say? Let me know, and I will write it on the flipchart or type it in.*

Or

Therapist: I like your earlier technique suggestions on nutrition. It will go well together with the customized playbook we just read together: Daily Morning Hygiene Routine for Justin. As you can see, I rewrote this playbook neatly on the big flip chart on the wall [or projected on the flat screen TV or LCD projector] so we can add in the nutritional piece. *To get us jump-started, may I suggest that we take the nutritional template that I showed you several weeks ago as our template? Let me get this out of my desk. I did not know until today we might go in this direction. As you can see, Dr. Shannon recommends these nutritional pieces for breakfast, lunch, dinner and snacks. Let's start with breakfast. Do you want to go with his suggestions? Let me start by writing underneath the "what," your breakfast ideas. Mom, let's start with you first.*

The second example represents a directive style. In graduate school, both authors were trained in a more nondirective style, so it is initially a challenge to switch gears to be directive. Believe it or not, great training on how to become more directive can be found by watching the old television series *Super Nanny* on YouTube. Jo Frost, who plays the super nanny, is very directive and her style of delivery can be mirrored in FST treatment. This directive style is a requirement when playbooks or behavioral contracts are being written in real time, with the family present. The family will get extremely anxious and become like "deer in the headlights" if their FST therapist is nondirective in this step, as well as, when role-plays and troubleshooting begin in Phase IV. Traumatized and stuck families want skills in the here and now, but they also desperately need a therapist who has a directive style of delivery.

More of this directive style is outlined in the next chapter. It is presented here because a direct style is needed when attempting to merge techniques and actively co-create a wound playbook. If the FST therapist still gets stuck, they can use the following contingency plan statement:

We have time between this session and the next one to finalize this playbook. Normally, we try to do it all in this session and all I have to do is type out what we discussed and plug and play. However, there are always exceptions to the rule.

I want to study the techniques you presented from your lead sheet in greater detail. Then, in between sessions, I will try to incorporate some of your suggestions into the playbook.

At the beginning of our next session, I will run the final version by you and unless there are major objections we can proceed immediately to role-plays and troubleshooting. I can even email it to you and get your comments or you can stop by the office on _____ [date and time]. Or I can drop it in the mail to your home. Just let me know.

This contingency statement provides a reprieve if the FST therapist feels at any time that they are overwhelmed and need a breather. It is often used more frequently in the beginning when the therapist is still learning a directive style or trying to smoothly integrate the steps one after the other in this chapter. This same contingency statement can also be used if needed within the next section.

How to Scrap the Playbook Altogether and Build a New One

If this is the decision, the FST therapist uses a directive style and together with the family, fills in the blanks of the playbook template in Table 9.3:

TABLE 9.3 Playbook Template

Playbook for [place name of seed being addressed here]:
[insert name of intervention here]

Who:

List the names of everyone who is involved with executing this intervention. Include, when applicable, extended family members or other outside villagers

- Caregiver
- Children
- Extended family
- Villagers (e.g., friends, neighbors, school counselors, local organizations)

What:

List what the intervention selected is (its name)

- Name of intervention

When:

Details of when the intervention will take place. Specificity is a must. List the actual date, day(s) of the week, and time(s). If you do not know yet, list TBD (to be determined)

- TBD or
- Date and day of the week
- Time or times

Where:

Details of where the intervention will take place (i.e., inside home, location outside the home). If you do not know yet, list TBD (to be determined)

- TBD or
- Specific location (home, at grandparents' house, outside home, etc.)

How: Clarity of Everyone's Roles

Details of everyone's role and a brief description of what each person will be doing or the steps to make the intervention work. Specificity is a must. List the name of each person involved and beside their name, what they will be doing.

- ☑ Caregiver—description of what they will be doing
- ☑ Adolescent—description of what they will be doing
- ☑ Extended family member—description of what they will be doing
- ☑ Outside organization or person—description of what they will be doing

---

The therapist and the family can look together at the techniques offered in Chapter 8 or choose one of their own. When creating a playbook from scratch in real time, the therapist must be poised and ready to use the stick and move technique when family members get off track, yell at one another, talk in long and unproductive stories, or go down a long bunny trail that leads nowhere. Also, creating a playbook from scratch in real time will likely cause the session to go over the planned hour or perhaps even a 2-hour session. This means that the therapist must inform the family that another Phase III session is needed. Some families will not like this extra session, but they will likely accept it when they understand the logic and rationale behind it.

Case Example

This case example integrates the following important concepts and principles outlined in this chapter. These include, but are not limited to (a) how to effectively use reframes and preludes to break through resistance and explain a therapist's technique selections; (b) how to incorporate family strengths; (c) how to effectively use FST treatment when a key family member is absent; and (d) how to effectively use the village whenever possible.

Twenty-year-old Denise left home soon after her father suddenly and unexpectedly died of throat cancer. She left behind her mother, Abby, and younger brother, Blake, aged 14 years. The mother came to FST treatment with the goal of reconciliation with her daughter. Denise and her mother had not spoken in more than 2 years. Along with Abby and her son, the therapist was able to recruit Abby's sister, Allison, and Allison's husband, Mack. The mom was not able to contact Denise, and neither was the therapist. Therefore, Denise was not part of any of the therapy sessions. As a result, the FST therapist had to find co-therapists in the family who could fill in key gaps of information. In this case, it was the youngest son, Blake, and Abby's sister, Allison. The mother, Abby, did the best she could, but unhealthy undercurrents blocked accurate reports.

During Phases I and II, careful questioning revealed unhealthy undercurrents that kept the mother and daughter stuck (unresolved grief, lack of unconditional love, and caustic communication). After the death of Denise's father, the mother had great difficulty showing the tenderness and empathy Denise needed. For example, Abby often used pat sayings when speaking to Denise such as "*I told you so*"; "*You just have to buckle up and deal with it*"; and "*Let go and let God, He is in control.*" These were the same communication patterns that Abby's mom and dad role-modeled when she was a child, so this is how Abby communicated in the here and now.

The paradox was that although Abby appeared harsh on the surface, her actions were almost always gracious and softhearted. Blake, her son, knew this as a fact. Therefore, when his mom talked tough or no-nonsense, he saw beneath the surface and was not impacted by this style of communication. However, according to Blake, for Denise, her belief was that the surface communication from her mother was evidence that her mother's heart was judgemental and harsh. As with Blake, the mother was also kind to Denise through actions, but Denise (unlike Blake) appeared unable to separate the person from the "pat" sayings. Based on this information, the therapist concluded that Denise likely interpreted her mother's style of communication as judgmental and toxic and Abby interpreted her style as just good old-school advice. It did not matter who was right. It was Denise's interpretation and this became her truth.

The therapist also thought that the father's unexpected and sudden death represented a negative tipping point for Denise's and her mother's relationship. After her father's death, Denise felt very alone and needed (not just wanted) soft communication from her mother more than ever before. However, Abby could not provide what she did not see as a problem in the first place.

After Denise left home, mother and daughter still maintained contact and a relationship. However, the final breaking point came when Denise fell into an emotionally abusive relationship with a boyfriend. Abby warned Denise of this boyfriend and that "*he was out to use her.*" Eventually, what Abby predicted came true. The boyfriend left her, and Denise was devastated. But instead of soft talk, the mother gave Denise another pat saying with "*See, I told you so.*" That was the last time Denise spoke to her mother.

(continued)

Case Example (*continued*)

All future phone calls, e-mails, and birthday cards went ignored by Denise. Abby knew where Denise currently lived, but she had not tried to go to her house.

At the end of Phase II, the mother, son, and village (Allison and Mack) received their homework lead sheet. Even though the lead sheet clearly tried to steer Abby toward strategies around acts of kindness or books around soft communication, these were ignored. Instead, when Abby did the homework presentation, her top pick was "Tools to Help Others Apologize."

The therapist realized that the mother was still unable to make the cognitive shift (in spite of the before and after feedback loops) on how her communication style contributed to the current breakup of the mother–daughter relationship. Instead, according to Abby, it was Denise who needed to be soft and apologize, not she. Both mother and daughter were at polar opposites on how to get unstuck. Therefore, as the FST therapist silently asked himself the following questions, he knew the answer.

1. *"Are there any techniques presented or parts of a technique that I can integrate into the technique(s) and customized playbook(s) that I am about to reveal?"*
    Or
2. *"Is one or more of the techniques that the family is presenting so compelling that I may need to scrap my technique and playbook altogether and start fresh with their ideas?"*

The therapist could not integrate Abby's #1 pick of an apology, and the other techniques presented were not compelling enough to scrap the therapist's playbook and start over. However, the real problem lay in how to sell the therapist's technique and playbook around acts of kindness and then soft talk to follow soon after. Abby was not likely to support the therapist's pick or see its value.

During pre-session preparation, the therapist picked "random acts of kindness" first and a "specialized soft talk book" second as his recommended techniques or directives (see Table 9.4). Even though Denise needed soft words, there had to be emotional warm-up action first to have the opportunity for words later. Mom knew where Denise lived, but before Denise would talk to Mom, soft words had to come from Mom through soft actions first.

TABLE 9.4 FST Therapist's Recommended Techniques

Unhealed Wound Seed		
Unhealthy Undercurrents	**Healthy Undercurrents**	**Techniques or Directives**
Lack of consistent nurturance	**Unconditional love, consistent nurturance**	☐ 30-Day Nurturing Campaign ☑ **Random Acts of Kindness** ☐ Helping Others Campaign ☑ **Specialized Soft Talk Books (second playbook)**

(continued)

Case Example (*continued*)

As stated earlier, Abby had tried acts of kindness through e-mails or Christmas cards. However, these actions were ineffective. Leaving small notes, small gifts, or Denise's favorite cookies at her actual doorstep would send a much stronger message and have a much bigger impact.

After quick victories with these acts of kindness, the groundwork would be laid for new soft talk using the book *How to Talk So Teens Will Listen and Listen So Teens Will Talk* (Faber & Mazlish, 2010). To prepare for this goal, the therapist purchased this book and preread it.

During pre-session preparation, the customized playbook (Table 9.6) was designed and typed out. However, the therapist was concerned about whether or not he could "sell" the technique to Abby and get her buy-in to try it. The therapist needed a reframe that would capitalize and integrate Abby's strengths and belief system. This needed to be written during the pre-session preparation as an introductory prelude. General McArthur once famously quoted that "every battle is won or lost before the first shot is fired." In other words, the success of this session rested on how well the pre-session preparation was done.

Within Step 1, the family and FST therapist presented their ideas for strategic directives. Then the therapist handed out and read aloud the following introduction prelude presented in Table 9.5.

TABLE 9.5 Introductory Prelude for the "Living out the Parable of the Lost Daughter" Playbook

---

Playbook for Mother (Abby) and Daughter (Denise) to Reconnect

"Living out the Parable of the Lost Daughter"

Introductory Prelude:

- Previous attempts to reconnect and repair with Denise have been through emails, phone calls, letters, and so on. These tactics (which normally work) have not worked.
- And time has not healed these wounds. Instead, further emotional distance has become entrenched.
- Therefore the playbook below represents a treatment philosophy of (a) "If what you are doing doesn't work, do something different"; and (b) we cannot change the past but we can do something different in the future. The question now is, what are we going to do in the here and now? This treatment philosophy has the advantage of showing, through actions, even greater unconditional love. In other words, physically going to the house once a week sends these powerful underlying messages:
  - Mom is not "distant" through emails or phone calls, but physically present. This sends a powerful message that Mom is serious and has intensified her efforts to reconcile in a dramatic and new way.
  - It is spiritual and fits with the Gospel. Jesus spent more time on reconciliation than most other topics. He knew that if family members or individuals were offended and stayed that way, reconciliation would be impossible.
  - As Mother Teresa said, "Do small acts of kindness with GREAT LOVE."
  - Hurting people hurt others. That is why we are to be kind to everyone we meet, because they are fighting their own battles often unseen by us.
  - And Denise is hurting and burdened with shame. (One example is being taken advantage of by a man who played her and manipulated her—one of the worst wounds a woman can receive.)
  - As a result, Denise is likely emotionally handicapped and unable or does not know how to reconcile on her own. If she could have done it on her own, it would have happened.

(continued)

Case Example (*continued*)

The message and reframes were powerful and fit the strengths of Abby. Abby was spiritual and loved God and Jesus very much. Therefore, to connect her acts of kindness to Jesus and Mother Theresa made sense to Abby. The New Testament Parable of the Prodigal Son was rewritten as the Prodigal Daughter, and the message of "doing something different" in the here and now and highlighting what was not working highly motivated this family.

The reframe that Denise was wounded to the point where she was "emotionally handicapped" and unable to make the first move was a game-changing message for Abby. Within this reframe, her defensiveness and resistance instantly melted. In addition, "hurting people hurt others" and the fact that her daughter Denise's boyfriend took advantage of Denise to create shame in her were also very helpful reframes.

With these reframes, the mother went from "Denise has to apologize and make the move" to "I now see that she is handicapped and I have to make the first move through acts of kindness that are unconditional, expecting nothing in return."

TABLE 9.6 "Living Out the Parable of the Lost Daughter"

Playbook: Living Out the Parable of the Lost Daughter

Doing Small Acts of Kindness With Great Love

Who:

- Abby, Allison, Mack, Blake, and Scott (FST therapist)

What:

- Once per week Abby and Mack (if in town) or Allison (if Mack is unavailable) will drive over to Denise's home and do small acts of kindness with great love unconditionally. (See bottom of page for several ideas of acts of kindness)
- For the first three visits "an emotional warm-up"—no physical contact with Denise will be attempted. Just notes or gifts will be left for Denise on her porch (leaving the gifts when Denise is at work)
- Fourth visit—knock on door with scrapbook gift from Mom presented in person
- Prayer before, during and after each visit—*The Power of a Praying Parent* by Stormie Omartian (2014) can be used as one tool in this process
- Read as a primer—*How to Talk So Teens Will Listen and Listen So Teens Will Talk* (Faber & Mazlish, 2010)

When:

- First three visits—need to confirm dates and time: (a) Monday, Dec 5, 10 a.m.; (b) Tuesday, Dec 13, 9:30 a.m. (c) Monday, Dec 19 at 9:30 a.m.
- Fourth visit—need to confirm date and time: Christmas Eve, Dec 24, Sat, 9:00 a.m.

Where:

- At Denise's house

How:

- **Mack (brother-in-law):** Will physically drive Abby and support her every step along the way—positive talk and no dredging up the past or assigning blame—good memories of Denise

---

(*continued*)

Case Example (*continued*)

TABLE 9.6 "Living out the Parable of the Lost Daughter" (*continued*)

- **Abby (mother):** Will put together the acts of kindness with her sister Allison's and son, Blake's, help. And everyone will pray before, during and after each visit for wisdom and the right words to speak when the time comes: "You, Abby, are the queen in the Prodigal Daughter storyline."
- **Blake (Abby's son):** Will work with Mom and aunt to come up with acts of kindness. And will encourage and cheer Mom on and tell her not to give up.
- **Allison (sister):** Will stand in for Mack if he is away on business. And will help collaboratively create acts of kindness with sister.
- **Scott (FST therapist):** Will check in with Abby during the process and help tweak the plan if needed—"We will meet for a check in two weeks into the intervention"—need date and time here—Dec 19 at time TBD

Several Ideas to Consider to Jump-Start Acts of Kindness
☐ Notes such as:

"Denise, I know this may be somewhat strange leaving a note on the door. And please pardon the intrusion. But it is the best way I know how to say and show that I am so sorry for anything I did or said that might have contributed to a break in our relationship. So I just wanted to say that I miss you so much and I will be back to keep showing you this. Love, Mom"

☐ Favorite food:

"Denise, I know this was a favorite—ingredients, flour, salt, and a cup of love

Love, Mom"

☐ A stuffed animal with note in mouth:

"Arf Arf, I am barking because I want to say I miss you, my lovely daughter. Love, Mom"

Abby and her family were now primed and prepared for the next step in Phase III, Step 2: "FST Therapist Presents Customized Wound Playbooks." The FST therapist then passed out his customized playbook as a handout (Table 9.6), giving one copy to each family member.

Abby and family loved the customized playbook draft. It translated and linked the reframes from the introduction prelude into concrete action. The plan incorporated Abby's strengths. For example, Abby loved to pray, so the book *The Power of a Praying Parent* was introduced and incorporated. The playbook also clarified everyone's role and utilized the power of the village. Mack was a strong anchor point and Abby trusted him. Therefore, it gave Abby confidence to know that she and Mack would go out together to deliver the acts of kindness. Allison's role was also key. Until this playbook, Allison had stood on the sidelines and fretted as she felt helpless not knowing how to help her sister who was wounded and in so much emotional pain. With the playbook, however, Allison had a clear role and purpose.

Finally, there was a clear segue between the first step of acts of kindness and the second step of soft talk. The family was asked in the first playbook to purchase *How to Talk So Teens Will Listen and Listen So Teens Will Talk* (Faber & Mazlish, 2010). In the follow-up playbook (not shown here), Mack was asked to take the lead and use the tools in the book to role-play with Abby again and again until her communication style began to change. And with change came a new aware-ness of how Abby's current style of communication was ineffective. Mack literally helped Abby act her way into a new way of thinking through the role–plays.

By the time the FST therapist got to Step 3, "Family, Child, and Therapist Co-create Wound Playbooks," there were little changes to make with the exception of dates and times. The FST ther-apist, however, did emphasize to Abby that her homework presentation of "How to Get Others to Apologize" was a great one, but the timing was one that could be used after the "Acts of Kindness" and "Learning How to Soft Talk" playbooks were used. Abby agreed, but appreciated the linkage back to her ideas. She and her son had worked hard on the presentation.

Because there were only minor changes needed and the therapist was experienced in FST treatment, the session was 2 hours in length and the therapist seamlessly moved from Phase III to Phase IV in one sitting. After the presentation of the playbook, the therapist still had plenty of time left to conduct role-plays and troubleshooting. The family was then ready for implementation. Therefore, Step 4: "The Important Final Message" was not used. The therapist then followed up 2 weeks later and used the steps in Phase V: "Evaluate Progress and Relapse Prevention" to determine next steps.

STEP 4: IMPORTANT FINAL MESSAGE

The last step in this session is to clearly convey the risks of implementing the wound playbook and/or safety plan (if risk factor not immediate and can wait 1 more week) prior to practicing its delivery through role-plays (dress rehearsals) and troubleshooting (Phase IV). The inherent dan-ger of early implementation is contained within this statement: "It's not what you say, but how you say it." If the delivery is poor and troubleshooting nonexistent, the playbooks will likely fail. This is another reason why we developed the PLL System of Care along with mandatory videotaped supervision. It mitigates the risk of an FST therapist who has poor delivery and poor timing. For more information on how these goals are accomplished please look at the YouTube videos on www.gopll.com or sign up for one of our webinars.

Unfortunately, the FST treatment model carries with it both inherent risks and rewards. The reward is that a well-written and customized wound playbook serves as the needed road map for both role-plays and troubleshooting. This is important because many current mental health treatment models may forgo this piece altogether. The analogy would be expecting a football team to face their opponent with no playbook or practicing plays (dress rehearsals) ahead of time. The football team would likely get slaughtered, and our families face the same risk.

However, the inherent risk is that the wound or safety playbook must be developed and co-created with the family *prior* to a Phase IV session. As this chapter illustrates, both the FST therapist and family need the opportunity to make adjustments to the playbook and take co-own-ership of the process. As a result, the wound playbook is out there, albeit not rehearsed yet and without troubleshooting. Therefore, the temptation is high for a family member to use the play-book immediately.

Statement Recommended to Prevent Premature Playbook Implementation

To counter the risk of premature playbook implementation, the FST therapist must end the ses-sion using the following clear statement:

> Before we end today, I want to say a couple of important things. First, I am asking you not to
> use any part of your wound playbook before our next session. The reason is that we have one

last step to do before using your playbook. In this last step, we will practice your delivery of the playbook and troubleshoot for any unforeseen problems that might come up. Look at it this way, you have already waited this long to solve your child's problems, what is one more week in the big picture.

Second, if you put your playbook into play without dress rehearsals or practicing your delivery, the research shows that the risk for failure is very high. It is like sending a football team out on the field with a playbook but with no actual practice of any of the plays ahead of time. The football team would not only lose the game but they would most likely get slaughtered. We do not want to come this far and do all this work only to be like this football team.

So let me go around the room to ask for your commitment to this request, one person at a time.

Asking for everyone's verbal commitment is critically important. The analogy of the football team and the statement "If you already waited this long, what is one more week" seems to help families understand the importance of waiting.

Finally, in a playful way, the therapist should collect all the playbook handouts. One playful statement might be something like the following:

The temptation to use the playbook in spite of what we just went over would be tough to follow even for me and I am a counselor. So that I can sleep easy tonight, I am going to collect all the wound playbook handouts I gave out earlier. This is just me being the worrywart!

The "it's me, not you" approach said in a playful way disarms the family and further reduces the risk of the family starting the playbook techniques prematurely, prior to Phase IV.

Exceptions to the Rule

Sometimes the family is in such crisis mode, they insist that they cannot wait another week (this is good reason to wait). Or, a key family member may be so hardheaded that he or she is convinced that he or she does not need practice, despite evidence to the contrary. If either situation happens, the therapist must predict that either the playbook will fail or its level of effectiveness will drop by 50% or more. Therefore, if either prediction comes true, it should serve not as "I told you so" but confirmation that the role-plays and troubleshooting are absolutely critical to success. In this way, the FST therapist is creatively accepting the family's resistance and using it to promote future change by predicting future fallout rather than losing a power struggle of wills. Therefore, when future fallout does happen, the therapist is seen as more of an expert and one whose advice should be followed.

As a reminder, this session represents a great transition point for an ethnographic interview (see the following questions again as a reminder). It is right before the role-plays and troubleshooting in the next phase of FST treatment. The answers for the family will consolidate the gains in this session as well as give the therapist instant feedback of what is working and what is not:

- Overall, what was most helpful in today's session?
- Overall, what was least helpful in today's session?
- What did I do or say as your therapist that was most helpful?
- What did I do or say as your therapist that was least helpful?
- What would need to happen in future sessions to make them more productive or of value to you or your family?

REFERENCES

Faber, A., & Mazlish, E. (2010). *How to talk so teens will listen and listen so teens will talk.* New York, NY: HarperCollins.

Fishman, C. H. (1988). *Treating troubled adolescents: A family therapy approach.* New York, NY: Basic Books.

Haley, J. (1991). *Problem-solving therapy* (2nd ed.). San Francisco, CA: Jossey-Bass.

Omartian, S. (2014). *The power of a praying parent.* Eugene, OR: Harvest House Publishers.

Pre-Session Preparation for Phase IV

Step 1: Type Up and Laminate Playbooks

Step 2: Create Troubleshooting Countermoves Checklist

Step 3: Ensure Key Village Members Will Be Present

As the family systems trauma (FST) flowchart illustrates, this pre-session preparation step occurs prior to Phase IV. The main goal of this preparation step is to create a first-draft troubleshooting countermoves checklist based on the finalized playbook from the previous session (Phase III). The checklist will be presented as a handout at the beginning of next session and serve as a road map to set up dress rehearsals or role-plays. For example, the FST therapist would take a finalized wound playbook such as "Building a Memorial" and create a first draft checklist with the likely "What will you do if?" scenarios for each part of the playbook (who, what, when, where, and how; see the following example):

Troubleshooting Checklist		
Name of Technique/Playbook: Building a Memorial		
Areas of the Wound Playbook to Address	**Common "What Will You Do if?" Curveballs to Derail Playbook**	**Countermove Actions or Statements**
Reprint the Parts of Your Wound Playbook Below: **Who:** *Tom, mom, grandparents, uncles, parents of teenager Bill*	• What will you do if Tom drops out or wants to quit and withdraws to his bedroom for days on end just like before?	• Uncles will come over and go into Tom's room and say "We are here for you buddy, we miss him too. Please, for your dad, yourself, and us, will you come out and not quit?"
		• If that does not work, the uncles will show unity and get sleeping bags and sleep in Tom's room or outside the door and now say anything—will let their presence speak loudly that "Tom is not alone"

As illustrated in the preceding example, the different countermove scenarios then become the road map for role-plays or spontaneous interactions called "enactments" in Phase IV. There are three pre-session mini-steps in this chapter. They are as follows:

1. Type and laminate the playbook(s).
2. Create a troubleshooting countermoves checklist.
3. Ensure key villagers will be present.

STEP 1: TYPE AND LAMINATE PLAYBOOKS

Prior to Phase IV, it is important to take any edits or additions from Phase III and type them into a finalized wound and/or safety playbook. In addition, there is something very special about handing the family a playbook that is laminated and spill-proof. As an experiment, the authors and other FST therapists started laminating the playbooks years ago. The response was overwhelmingly positive. Parents and caregivers consistently stated that the lamination was a small but important symbol that they were valued and that the wound or safety playbook was important. It is recommended that the reader perform a similar experiment to see for himself or herself the difference lamination makes; it is that important.

Finally, a laminated playbook makes it easier for the parents to tape it on their bathroom mirror to review each morning or to place it on their refrigerator. The FST therapist should make it a priority to make this request when the laminated playbook is first handed out. Treatment outcomes are much better when the parent gets into the habit or rhythm of rereading the playbook every day on the bathroom mirror while brushing teeth. When this happens, the step-by-step instructions within the playbook become ingrained in the parents' thinking to create new neurolinguistic pathways within the brain as the new normal.

STEP 2: CREATE TROUBLESHOOTING COUNTERMOVES CHECKLIST

After the wound and/or safety playbook is typed and/or laminated, the next pre-session preparation step is to create the troubleshooting countermoves checklist template to complement the wound playbook. If needed, a safety plan countermoves checklist is also created separately. A sample checklist template for wound or safety plan playbooks is presented in Table 10.1.

The FST therapist will take this template and use it as a guide to fill in the most likely curveballs and countermoves for the finalized wound playbook and/or safety plan created in Phase III. This draft is then presented to the family at the beginning of the next session in Phase IV to make any customized changes or modifications as needed. For example, a parent may object to how a particular curveball is written and want to modify it or add a countermove.

It is important to note that the FST therapist is *not* supposed to take the finalized wound or safety plan from Phase III and answer every possible "What will you do if?" scenario. Instead, the therapist should predetermine the most likely scenarios that may occur for the child and family in question. During the session itself, family members will be shown the template and asked to agree or disagree with each scenario, make adjustments as needed, and/or fill in other possible situations not listed. In this way, the FST therapist jump-starts the process with a first draft created during this step, but it is the family's responsibility to modify it accordingly in the next session.

The FST therapist customizes and completes the first draft of the troubleshooting checklist in this pre-session step for two primary reasons. First, if the therapist presents a blank troubleshooting template, the family is likely to be lost like "deer in the headlights." Families and people in general often do not recognize the implication of failing to think two steps ahead in a predetermined way. Rather, people respond to curveballs as they occur in the moment or in an "off the cuff" manner. For families or individuals not traumatized or under stress, troubleshooting in the moment may work effectively. However, for stressed or traumatized families, it is often impossible. These families are using all their mental capacity just to get through the day. Therefore, the FST therapist has to jump-start the process with concrete troubleshooting scenarios directly tied to the playbook(s) created in Phase III.

Second, it simply takes too long to start from scratch. If the family is presented with only a blank checklist, it will take an entire session just to fill in the blanks. However, with a first draft already filled in, the family can create the checklist in half the time.

TABLE 10.1 Handout Template for Troubleshooting Countermoves Checklist

Wound Playbook for _____ [name of seed being addressed by playbook]		
Name of Technique/Playbook: _____		
Areas of the Wound Playbook to Address	**Common "What Will You Do if?" Curveballs to Derail Playbook**	**Countermove Actions or Statements**
Reprint the parts of your wound playbook below:	• What will you do if an important "who" player quits suddenly?	•
Who: List the names of everyone who is involved with executing this intervention—include extended family members or other outside villagers if applicable	• What will you do if you are missing a key villager to make the playbook work better or even at all?	•
	Other possible situations not listed • ... • ...	• ... • ...
What: List what the technique or intervention selected is (the name of it)	• What will you do if the intervention is not working as you hoped or as quickly as you hoped?	•
	• What will you do if your child or another adult says, "I'm not doing this," "It's too hard to keep going," or "This plan sucks?"	•
	Other possible situations not listed • ... • ...	• ... • ...
When: Details of when the technique or intervention will take place. Specificity is necessary. List the actual date, day(s) of the week, and time(s)	• What will you do if a key person in the playbook does not show up on the date or time listed on the playbook or simply refuses?	• • •

(continued)

TABLE 10.1 Handout Template for Troubleshooting Countermoves Checklist (*continued*)

Wound Playbook for _____[name of seed being addressed by playbook]		
Name of Technique/Playbook: _____		
Areas of the Wound Playbook to Address	**Common "What Will You Do if?" Curveballs to Derail Playbook**	**Countermove Actions or Statements**
	• What will you do if the date and time on the playbook is not working as planned? And who is the go-to person to make changes?	•
	Other possible situations not listed • ... • ...	• ... • ...
Where: *Details of where the intervention will take place (i.e. inside the home, location outside the home, etc.)*	• What will you do if the location you selected is not working as planned? And who is the go-to person to make this change?	•
	Other possible situations not listed • ... • ...	• ... • ...
The How: Step-by-step instructions to complete the task with clarity of everyone's roles: *Details of everyone's role and a brief description of what steps each will take to make the technique or intervention work. Specificity is necessary* *List the name of each person involved and beside each name, list what they will be doing*	• What will you do if someone gets confused on what their role is supposed to be in the playbook?	• •
	• What will you do if the steps do not appear to be working or as well as you planned?	•
	• What will you do if your child or someone else stops doing their step(s) in the plan?	•
	Other possible situations not listed • ... • ...	• ... • ...

STEP 3: ENSURE KEY VILLAGE MEMBERS WILL BE PRESENT

At this stage in the therapy process, the FST therapist might be on autopilot. They may assume that since joining has already occurred, key village members from previous sessions will be present. However, this is not always the case. To help ensure success, as was emphasized in Chapter 6, it is essential to personally call and remind each key villager and immediate family member of the importance of their attendance.

The authors cannot overemphasize the critical point that if key village members are absent, there is a much higher risk for playbook failure. This is especially critical in Phase IV as this is the "meat and potatoes" of the FST treatment model. This is where the proverbial rubber meets the road. The therapist will actively play the role of director yelling out things like "Freeze"; "Take two"; "Let's try that again"; and "Perfect, print that" to help the family develop new undercurrent patterns (feedback loops) as the final step prior to playbook implementation.

In addition, FST treatment is a systematic approach to trauma treatment with a wraparound lens that includes the immediate family living under one roof *and* the village (extended family, friends, neighbors, and institutions) to heal wounds. It is the traumatized family, not the traumatized child. Therefore, when key people are not present to practice and troubleshoot new interactions within the playbook, confusion and a lack of coordination will result. The analogy is having a Broadway show that opens on two nights, but the supporting cast failed to show up for the final dress rehearsal. The chances of a smooth opening night are highly unlikely. Therefore, a final pre-session preparation step is to call and remind key village members and family members through phone calls, emails, and texts, if all three are available.

Case Example

Fifteen-year-old Tom was self-referred by his mother, Ann, who was raising him with the help of his maternal grandparents, Rob and Maureen. Tom's father, Ray, was killed by a drunk driver 2 years ago. The drunk driver, Bill (a 17-year-old teenager), was also killed instantly. Since the accident, Tom's depression has progressively gotten worse. At the start of FST treatment, he was so depressed that he barely came out of his room except for meals. He was on antidepressants but the side effects of weight gain and insomnia were contributing to the problem. Anytime the mother or grandparents tried to talk about his father, Tom would either cry uncontrollably or withdraw deeper and deeper into himself. To date, Tom had made one suicide attempt and, although stable at the moment, there were signs that if things remained the same, another attempt was imminent. Tom still managed to go to school, but teachers reported that he was now sleeping in class and starting to withdraw from all social activities.

In Phase I of treatment, the stressor selected by everyone was Tom's depression, with the seed of unhealed wounds and the undercurrent of unresolved grief. The decision was made by the FST therapist, with family consensus, that stabilization through behavioral or hybrid contracts was not needed prior to active and direct wound work. The rationale was that Tom's problem symptoms were the direct result of the sudden and unexpected death of his father. During Phase I, it was revealed that Tom's uncles, his father's brothers, Mike and Jim, were key supporters, but until now were on the outside

(continued)

Case Example (*continued*)

---

looking in. Therefore, the uncles were asked to join the next session in Phase II and they both became an active part of treatment from then on.

At the beginning of Phase II, the uncles were brought up to speed with everyone else through a quick review of the stress chart hanging on the wall along with the seed/tree diagram and seed and symptom picks by everyone. Throughout the first session and this one, Tom sat in a corner saying nothing and looking down at his shoes. In fact, during the stress chart discussion, the therapist had to use circular questioning by asking Mom or the grandparents questions such as "*If Tom could tell me, what would he say were his top three stressors and why?*" However, Tom's affect began to change as the feedback loops were introduced and the sample wound playbook of "building a memorial" was passed around as the same wound playbook to go along with the after feedback loop. After the feedback loops were presented, the therapist had a dramatic pause and pulled an empty chair and placed on it a picture of Tom's father (prior to the session, the therapist asked the mother to bring in a framed picture of Ray and Tom together). The therapist then summarized the feedback loop discussion with a few key reframes:

> Tom is not one to talk about his deep loss but may be a young man who needs to sweat it out through action, not words. I asked Tom's mom to bring a picture of Tom and Ray. I am placing it in this empty chair because I believe in my heart that if Tom's dad, Ray, was sitting in this empty chair next to me right now, he would probably say something like: 'Tom, I am proud of you, son, and I am so sorry that I left too soon from this earth. I know you are probably angry with me and the drunk driver, Bill, who killed me. And that's ok. Maybe one day you can forgive us both. In the meantime, your deep sadness has nowhere to go. It is stuck inside you and is paralyzing you from the inside out and killing you slowly. And I know that just talking about your pain is not helping. So let's do something completely different, let's sweat it out. My brothers will help. So as not to forget me, would you try this building a memorial idea. It's a jump-start. When it is finished, you might even consider inviting the parents of the teenager who killed me to the opening day ceremony. You don't have to decide now. It may just happen naturally as you build this memorial because I bet you these parents are paralyzed with pain as well.'

After this reframe (sweat out the pain) and use of the empty chair, there was not a dry eye in the room. Even the therapist began to weep as he told this story. But most importantly, Tom began to engage for the first time and after tears, he said "Yes, I will do this for my dad and maybe for these parents too. After all, it was their son's fault, not theirs."

At the end of this session, the therapist passed out a homework lead sheet that included websites to investigate different kinds of memorial ideas (www.usurnsonline .com/final-arrangements/memorial-service-ideas). After the sheet was passed out, the uncles and Tom decided to meet on Saturday at the library to investigate these leads and also look for other ideas. The grandfather volunteered to contact the landowner

(continued)

Case Example (*continued*)

of the spot where the car accident occurred to see if a small memorial could be placed on the edge of the land next to the road. And the grandmother and mother wanted to contact the family of the teenager who died. It would not be difficult to find these parents because their names were in the paper that reported the accident more than 2 years ago.

Self-regulation tools that were provided earlier in the session were not used because there was no therapeutic benefit for Tom to retell his wound story; it would just paralyze him further. However, safety issues were assessed, and Tom agreed to sign a "no harm" agreement while the "build the memorial" task was on full throttle. At the end of the memorial task, Tom had the choice to keep this agreement, tear it up, or put it on the memorial as a final gift to his father.

During the next session within Phase III, the homework presentation part of the session seemed to empower and energize everyone. There was a spark in Tom's eyes and a smile as he proudly showed off his top two memorial ideas. And in the process, something unexpected happened. The parents of the teenage boy, Bill, got permission from Tom to call him, and during their call, they offered to help. Old friends of his father also came out of the woodwork to help, and the landowner said he would permit the memorial. Already, Tom was starting to come out of his room and join the family again.

The therapist then showed his customized wound playbook. It was a carryover from Phase II, but more polished and detailed. The therapist used his HDMI cable to connect his laptop to the grandparents' flat-screen television for his home visit, and this allowed the family to tweak the playbook in real time. During the session, it became evident that several important parts were missing to finalize it. These items were the following: (a) What kind of memorial would be picked? (b) Who would build it, when, and where (someone's garage, etc.)? (c) What would be the target date of completion? (d) What might be a good day for the ceremony in coordination with approval from the landowner on whose property the memorial would sit? All these unanswered questions emerged naturally as the therapist and family went through the customized wound playbook draft. Time ran out in the session to do an adequate job of filling in these missing pieces. Therefore, at the end of Phase III, it was decided to wait a week and regroup for another Phase III session. This would give the family time to decide on a finalized memorial design and gather the missing information for the final draft.

The second Phase III session lasted only 30 minutes because the only thing left to do was to plug in the missing information. Tom chose a memorial design that would allow his favorite pictures of his dad to be encased within a plaster casing. However, the real challenge came at the end of Phase III. The family was itching to get the memorial built over the next 14 days and have an opening day ceremony soon thereafter. The therapist had to convince the family to wait one more week to practice playbook delivery and troubleshooting. They agreed, but only because they liked and trusted their therapist.

PRE-SESSION TROUBLESHOOTING COUNTERMOVES TEMPLATE FOR PHASE IV

Based on the information from Phases I through III and the finalized playbook itself, the FST therapist determined that the most likely future trouble spots for this family would center around the following:

- The fallout of change, meaning that as Tom got deeper into the memorial intervention, the risk increased for a flood of buried emotions to rush to the surface. As a result, the countermoves checklist had to include what the family would do if this happened as well as practicing new communication responses. The current one of "walking on eggshells" and withdrawal by the adults was not working.
- There was also the risk of unanticipated logistical challenges such as the landowner changing his mind, unanticipated costs of the memorial, disagreement over details of the memorial, and so forth.
- Finally, there was the X factor of the presence and involvement of the parents of the fallen teen, Bill, who killed the father, and its impact on Tom.

Therefore, while writing the first draft of this family's countermoves checklist (Table 10.2), these central potential curveballs or trouble spots became central themes. In the next chapter, we return to this case example to illustrate this process of turning this countermoves template into role-plays and enactments.

TABLE 10.2 Tom and His Family's Troubleshooting Countermoves Checklist

Wound Playbook for Unhealed Wounds		
Name of Technique/Playbook: Building a Memorial		
Areas of the Wound Playbook to Address	Common "What Will You Do if? Curveballs to Derail Playbook	Countermoves Actions or Statements
Reprint the parts of your wound playbook below: Who: *Tom, Mom, grandparents, uncles, parents of teenager Bill*	• What will you do if Tom drops out or wants to quit and withdraws to his bedroom for days on end just like before?	• Uncles will come over and go into Tom's room and say, "We are here for you buddy, we miss him too." Please, for your dad, yourself, and us, will you come out and not quit?
	Other possible situations not listed • If Tom continues to stay in his room despite the verbal message from his uncles	• If that does not work, the uncles will show unity and get sleeping bags and sleep in Tom's room or outside the door and now say anything—will let their presence speak loudly that "Tom is not alone"

(continued)

TABLE 10.2 Tom and His Family's Troubleshooting Countermoves Checklist (*continued*)

Wound Playbook for Unhealed Wounds		
Name of Technique/Playbook: Building a Memorial		
Areas of the Wound Playbook to Address	**Common "What Will You Do if? Curveballs to Derail Playbook**	**Countermoves Actions or Statements**
What: *Memorial for Dad placed near the spot of his accident* *Type of memorial: plaster encasement with pictures of Dad*	• What will you do if as you get into the memorial building project, there is disagreement on the design of the memorial?	• The family must decide: Does Tom have the final vote? Does majority rule? Or something else?
	Other possible situations not listed • ... • ...	• ... • ...
When: *Meet every Saturday in Tom's garage at 1 p.m. until the memorial is finished—Goal is to finish in the next 14 days or sooner* *Mom, Tom, and Grandma will meet on Sunday afternoon at 3 p.m. to look through old pictures of Dad to pick out the favorites for the memorial* *Date of ceremony—TBD*	• What will you do if someone forgets to show up on Saturday or Sunday?	• Do not just assume the worst, or immediately accuse or blame
	Other possible situations not listed • ... • ...	• ... • ...
Where: *Tom's garage to build the memorial* *Tom's home to pick out the pictures of Dad for the memorial* *End of the landowner's property on HWY 21 to place the memorial*	• What will you do if the landowner changes his mind at any point in the process?	• Do not get rattled or lose hope. Meet all together to decide other options. If you cannot think of other options, call me, your therapist
	Other possible situations not listed • ... • ...	• ... • ...

(*continued*)

TABLE 10.2 Tom and His Family's Troubleshooting Countermoves Checklist (*continued*)		
Wound Playbook for Unhealed Wounds		
Name of Technique/Playbook: Building a Memorial		
Areas of the Wound Playbook to Address	**Common "What Will You Do if? Curveballs to Derail Playbook**	**Countermoves Actions or Statements**
The How: Step-by-step instructions to complete the task with clarity of everyone's roles: *Tom, uncles and Grandfather will build the memorial on the dates and location specified* *Tom, Mom, and Grandma will pick out favorite pictures of Dad for the memorial*	• What will you do if Tom gets hit with a flood of emotions as he starts to build the memorial for his dad and he becomes even more depressed, withdraws to his room, or shuts down?	• We will practice what to do in today's session and learn new ways to talk through these emotions using new communication strategies with the self-regulation tools we learned last session. At home, if these new tools are not working and you run into problems, please call me (your therapist) for a special session if needed
Grandpa will continue to interface with Bill's parents to keep them in the loop of when the ceremony will take place	• What will you do if someone else besides Tom shuts down in the family?	• See above and also understand that Tom is not the only one in pain
Mom will contact Dad's friend to get a list of who will come to the ceremony and who might speak a few words about Tom's father	• What will you do if Bill's parents want more involvement in the project than just to show up for the ceremony?	• We will decide together in today's session
	Other possible situations not listed • ... • ...	• ... • ...

As illustrated in the case example, the FST therapist offers suggestions (within the countermoves column) that lead in to either role-plays ("*We will practice today how to talk to your son Tom if he is overcome with grief*") or problem-solving ("*If a family member forgets to show up on Saturday or Sunday, just remind him or her for next week*"). The FST therapist, beforehand as part of the troubleshooting draft, actively suggests these countermoves by going ahead and writing them on the template. Without these jump-start suggestions, the family is often lost on how to start or what to do. Or, the session can easily digress into an unproductive brainstorming session. Within Phase IV, these suggestions can always be rejected, altered, or modified by the family. However, the benefit is that it provides both the therapist and family quick footing for the next steps.

The next chapter outlines the mini-steps for Phase IV. The FST therapist with help from the child and family will locate and address any loopholes in their finalized wound playbook and then make any needed adjustments or changes in the troubleshooting countermoves checklist. This checklist will then serve as the road map for family members to practice the delivery of their wound playbook through both role-plays and enactments to try out new and healthy undercurrents to heal long-standing wounds. After Phase IV, the family will be fully ready and capable to implement their wound playbooks and after several weeks will return for the Phase V session to evaluate progress, examine next possible steps, or move to graduation from treatment with built-in tune-up sessions, if necessary, to prevent relapse.

Phase IV: Troubleshooting and Dress Rehearsals

Step 1: Present Finalized Playbooks and Locate and Close Loopholes

Step 2: Present the Troubleshooting Countermoves Checklist

Step 3: Co-Create the Troubleshooting Countermoves Checklist

Step 4: Conduct Role-Plays/Dress Rehearsals and Enactments

Step 5: Implement Playbooks

As the family systems trauma (FST) diagram in Chapter 3 illustrates, Phase IV occurs immediately following pre-session preparation for Phase IV. The main goals of Phase IV are to: (a) examine the finalized playbook(s) to identify and correct any logistical loopholes (i.e., incorrect date of intervention); (b) present the troubleshooting countermoves checklist handout prepared during pre-session preparation; (c) make any adjustments in the troubleshooting checklist as needed; (d) conduct dress rehearsals/role-plays or spontaneous enactments around targeted countermoves; (e) determine if dress rehearsals are successful or if more practice is needed; and (f) implement the playbook.

After Phase IV is complete, a 2-week or 3-week gap is recommended prior to entering Phase V. This gap provides the child and family ample time to practice the intervention and evaluate initial effectiveness. Practicing a new delivery or operating system using playbooks may also translate into additional sessions within Phase IV. This because the child and family are literally learning new feedback loops using healthy undercurrents. This often translates to a minimum increase of two to three 1-hour sessions or an additional one to two 2-hour sessions as needed. The key indicator is whether key family members (i.e. parents and/or child) are showing successful delivery within the role-plays/dress rehearsals after the first, second, or even third practice runs. If not, additional sessions are needed to help ensure successful implementation of the wound and/or safety playbook.

If a therapist's private practice or agency has a culture of the 1-hour sessions, Phase IV would be the best time to make an exception to this rule and allow for a 2-hour session. The reason is that role-plays or enactments take time to set up and execute properly. Changing family process takes more time than changing content using insight or talk therapy. Therefore, it can be counterproductive for families to get warmed up in hour one with the setup of role-plays or enactments and not immediately execute hour two. The warm-up then has to start all over again next session with the added challenge of trying to recapture the earlier momentum. Case examples are used to illustrate the five key mini-steps in Phase IV. The five mini-steps are: (a) present finalized playbooks and locate and close loopholes; (b) present the troubleshooting countermoves checklist; (c) co-create the troubleshooting countermoves checklist; (d) conduct role-plays/dress rehearsals and enactments; and (e) implement playbooks.

If troubleshooting, dress rehearsals, and enactments are done well the payoff for both the family and the FST therapist is huge. However, these parts of traditional treatment are often left out or done poorly. And this part of treatment is critical because clients have to practice new dances or positive feedback loops in front of the therapist prior to real life application. It is new for the family and they need practice.

Therefore, to lower the risk of failure, we recommend to an agency or private practice some kind of one-way mirror or direct supervision observation until mastery is achieved. To increase this kind of mastery, please view our suggestions and YouTube videos within the PLL System of Care at www.gopll.com.

THE CHANGING ROLES OF THE FST THERAPIST IN PHASE IV

The FST therapists' roles change as they move from motivator, educator, and assessor in Phases I and II, to creator and facilitator of wound or safety playbooks in Phase III. FST therapists keep all these roles but add a new one to their repertoire as they enter Phase IV with troubleshooting, dress rehearsals, and enactments.

Colapinto (1991) best describes the changing role of the therapist in this process as a "producer" who creates conditions to make change possible (i.e., troubleshooting countermoves checklist), a "stage director" or "systems irritant" who pushes the family toward healthy undercurrent patterns (i.e., dress rehearsals/role-plays), and a "narrator" or "co-author" who helps the family revise their "script" as needed (i.e., both the wound playbook and the troubleshooting countermoves checklist). In addition, as these role-plays and problem-solving activities take place, the FST therapist looks for and seizes upon opportunities for spontaneous interactions through what are called enactments (Minuchin & Fishman, 1981). Enactments are used by the therapist to convert spontaneous interactions into "new dances" or healthy undercurrents. For example, this might mean asking father and son to communicate directly for the first time without the mother's interference or even rearranging chairs and moving people around to increase or decrease emotional bonding.

Combining structured interactions through role-plays with spontaneous interactions using enactments is the perfect one–two punch. Therefore, as the reader in this chapter is being shown the logistics and timing of how to use the troubleshooting checklist as an on-ramp for role-plays (dress rehearsals) or enactments they will also receive clear guidance for a change in roles.

PRIOR TO THE SESSION

As a reminder, prior to the beginning of Phase IV, the FST therapist should come prepared to enter the session with the following items:

☑ *Finalized and typed-up wound and/or safety playbook(s):* The FST therapist should come to the session with the finalized customized wound and/or safety playbook typed up. Bring enough copies of the playbook(s) to pass out to everyone in the family. As stated earlier, if possible connect one's laptop with the playbook preloaded and use a high-definition multimedia interface (HDMI) cord to plug into the family's flat screen television if it is a home visit, or the flat screen in your office. The therapist can also use a liquid-crystal display (LCD) projector. This visual makes a "bigger than life" impact and allows edits to be made in real time.

☑ *Laminate the wound and/or safety playbook:* There is something very professional about handing the family a playbook that is laminated and spillproof. It also sends the message: This playbook is important and you are important. Laminating machines are extremely inexpensive and can be purchased online or at a local office supply store.

☑ *Troubleshooting countermoves checklist handout:* The FST therapist makes handout copies of the troubleshooting checklist draft that they completed during their pre-session preparation around the finalized wound and/or safety playbook(s). After this handout is provided, the family and FST therapist will tweak it and make adjustments as needed. As with the wound or safety playbook, it is ideal if the checklist can also be projected onto a screen. Any adjustments can then be made in real time.

STEP 1: PRESENT FINALIZED PLAYBOOKS AND LOCATE AND CLOSE LOOPHOLES

When the family arrives, the first step for the FST therapist is to hand out a copy of the typed wound and/or safety playbook. Please laminate the playbook(s) if possible. As Chapter 7 outlined, a safety playbook is only needed if a Phase II assessment revealed a risk level of **3** or higher on a scale from 1 to 5 (1 = no risk; 5 = high risk). If there are no safety risk factors or if those identified are below a 3 rating, the finalized wound playbook is the only document laminated. If, however, there was a two-track goal, both playbooks are laminated (safety plan and wound playbook).

This mini-step should only take a short time (10–15 minutes). The FST therapist will simply ask the family members to review the wound and/or safety playbooks to make sure there are no loopholes or missing information. The following transition statement will be divided into three parts: part I—request to read playbook each morning; part II—why playbook is laminated; and part III—locate and plug loopholes. The following transition statement is recommended to begin the Phase IV session:

Part I: Request to Read Playbook Each Morning

Before our meeting today, I typed up the changes we agreed to last session in a finalized version. I will now pass it out to each of you to look at.

When you get your wound and/or safety playbook, I have one simple request. Parents, would you please take your playbook(s) and as soon as you get home or before I leave (if home visit), will you tape it up on your bathroom mirror. Then each morning when you get up to brush your teeth and get ready for the day, make it a habit to read it slowly from start to finish. And teens [or kids] you are welcome to do the same thing.

Here is the reason. If you read your playbook instructions each morning, you will memorize the playbook instructions before long. Then, in the future, you will not even have to think, "Now, what did the playbook say to do?"

Instead, it will be automatic. And if this happens, your odds of success to heal your child's problems will dramatically increase. Any questions? Can I get a handshake agreement from those who agree to hang it up and read it each morning? (Get handshake.)

Part II: Why Playbook Is Laminated?

(If you laminated the wound playbook) I wanted to do something a little special and give you a small gift or token of my appreciation for all your hard work. And believe me when I say this is hard work. My small token of appreciation is that I laminated your playbook as a symbol that it is important and that you are important. And it is now spillproof! (Pass it out.)

Part III: Locate and Plug Loopholes

Now, let's take a few minutes to look for any loopholes in the actual playbook(s) itself. We will go down the list of each category of the "who," "what," "when," "where," and "how" and I will ask a few questions to see if we missed something.

If we did miss anything, I will type in any changes right in the playbook and print out a new copy before you leave or email it to you. Any questions?

Let me start with the who part of the playbook and move on from there. As I read aloud each part, stop me if you find missing information or it needs more clarity.

Use the following questions as a guide for this step in locating loopholes (these questions are the same regardless of whether it is a wound or safety playbook):

- When you look at the who part of your playbook, are we missing any last minute important people within the family or outside the family who will help? If **yes**, who are they and what is the best way to contact them?
- In the what section, did I accurately describe the intervention or technique we are going to use? Do we need a clearer description and/or did I miss anything?
- In the when section, did I get the details right regarding the date, day of the week, and time? Do we need to make any last minute adjustments?
- In the where section, did I get the details right of where the intervention will take place (inside the home, outside the home, and where, etc.)? Do we need to make any last minute adjustments?
- Finally, in the how section, was I clear enough on everyone's roles and what they will be doing or saying to make this intervention go smoothly and work well? If not, please tell me what we need to write to make things more clear.

The underlying principle for the preceding questions is that closing loopholes is an essential ingredient to successful wound or safety playbook implementation. Any loopholes left unclosed will quickly derail a playbook even before troubleshooting takes place. For example, if the "when" or date or time of a special outing intervention between parent and child is left open-ended, there is little chance that it will be successful. The same logic applies for a safety plan if the "when" is left open-ended for an alcoholic father to attend an Alcoholics Anonymous (AA) meeting. The special outing or AA strategy represents the catalyst to create the new and healthy undercurrent of nurturance (special outing) or accountability (AA). However, if the family is a stuck system, it will not take much to derail them if loopholes are left open-ended and are not closed.

Case Example

Returning to Tom's case example from Chapter 10, the family was impressed by the laminated wound playbook and the words of encouragement to begin the Phase IV session. The FST therapist used his HDMI cable to connect his laptop to the family's flat screen television and showed the wound playbook on the screen. There were currently no safety risks in this family, so there was no safety playbook to show in addition to the wound playbook (a two-track process).

The FST therapist informed the family that prior to moving onto troubleshooting, he wanted to be sure that there were no last minute loopholes in the playbook. If there were any, he could type out any recommended changes or adjustments on his laptop or the family could handwrite it right in the playbook (if using laminated playbook and no laptop, be sure to have extra paper handouts so that family members can handwrite in any loopholes found).

The therapist then went through each section using the preceding loophole questions. As this was done, the grandparents and the mother caught three important loopholes under the who and when sections of the wound playbook. The two loopholes discovered and the changes by the family are represented in larger and bold font in Table 11.1.

TABLE 11.1 Closing Loopholes in the Stark Family Playbook

The Stark Family Playbook to Help Heal Our Wounds of Grief

Intervention: Building a Memorial for Ray (Dad)

Who:

Tom, Mom, grandparents, uncles, and Bill's parents

Invite Dad's best friends to the dedication ceremony: Nick, Jerry, Stan, and Rick

What:
- Memorial for Dad placed near spot of accident
- Type of memorial: plaster encasement with pictures of Dad

When:
- ☐ Meet every Saturday in Tom's garage at 1 p.m. until memorial is finished: goal to finish in next 14 days or sooner
- ☐ Mom, Tom, and Grandma will meet on Sunday afternoon at 3 p.m. to look through old pictures of dad to pick out favorites for memorial

Some days we will have to move this date because of Mom's church commitments. If there is a conflict, we will know Saturday night. Our backup date will then be Tuesday nights after dinner from 6 p.m. to 8 p.m.

- ☐ TBD date of ceremony

(continued)

Case Example (*continued*)

TABLE 11.1 Closing Loopholes in the Stark Family Playbook (*continued*)

Where:

- Tom's garage to build memorial
- Tom's home to pick out pictures of Dad for memorial
- Edge of landowner's property on HWY 21 where accident occurred to place Memorial

How:

- Tom, uncles, and Grandfather will build memorial on dates and location specified (see the preceding text)
- Tom, Mom, and Grandmother will pick out favorite pictures of Dad for Memorial on dates and time specified (see the preceding text)
- Grandfather will continue to interface with Bill's parents to keep them in the loop of when the dedication ceremony will be
- Mom will contact Dad's friends to get a list of who will come and who might say a few words about father

Mom and Tom in consultation with rest of family will establish an agenda for the dedication ceremony when the date gets closer; otherwise, the ceremony will likely be unorganized and chaotic.

TBD, to be determined.

This mini-step of locating and closing loopholes proved invaluable for Tom's family in two ways. First, having an alternative day to Sunday was important. Otherwise, the momentum of consecutive weeks would have been disrupted. Tom was already frail to begin with and would have likely bailed from continuing the task of gathering pictures if his mom had missed a week, especially in the beginning. Second, as they thought more about the dedication ceremony, the family realized how important the agenda was to keep things organized and on track.

STEP 2: PRESENT THE TROUBLESHOOTING COUNTERMOVES CHECKLIST

After the loophole analysis of the wound and/or safety playbook, the next step is to troubleshoot each part of the playbook using the troubleshooting countermoves checklist that was drafted by the therapist during pre-session preparation. The FST therapist passes out the checklist as a handout to each family member. The following transition statement is recommended to begin Step 2:

Now that we have looked at and closed loopholes, our next step is to go through each part of your playbook using what I call a 'troubleshooting countermoves checklist.' Before today's session, after typing out your finalized playbook(s), I prepared your countermoves checklist. In this checklist, you will see all the "What will you do if …?" situations or potential challenges that I thought your family might encounter when you put your playbook (wound or safety play) into action.

After I pass out this checklist [hold it up], we will go over it together. Please note that this is a 'working draft.' This means that we will go over this checklist line-by-line together and make any changes as needed. As we make any changes, I will write them (or type if have a laptop) right into the checklist and email or print it out immediately.

OK, let me pass out a copy to everyone.

As the transition statement illustrates, it is important to make clear that the checklist is a "working draft" that will be cowritten together. As with the wound playbook, the FST therapist can jump-start the process, but if the family does not take ownership, the checklist, like the playbook, will have limited impact and effectiveness.

It is important to highlight that the FST therapist did not give the family too much information, too fast. At the end of the last session, the FST therapist did not get into a discussion about a troubleshooting checklist or details on the role-plays. This would be too much information and only cause the family to get scared or overwhelmed. Instead, the process is unpacked one-bite-sized piece or concept at a time.

Rules of Thumb on When to Include Some Family Members and Not Others

The FST therapist must decide who in the family should be physically present as they go through the checklist line-by-line and make any changes. In other words, the entire family or village may not need to be present to edit or modify the checklist. However, when practice role-plays or enactments start, certain members will need to be actively involved, others may need to be excused, others relegated to the role of observer, and still others brought in later. A good analogy is a movie director who works with the entire cast to go through each part of the script to elicit feedback and suggestions for changes. But then, depending on the scene, the director will ask certain actors to stay to enact a specific scene while others will be asked to just observe the scene, or leave the room altogether to come back later.

In the same way, prior to this session and handing out the checklist, the FST therapist should determine: (a) who in the family and village should be in the room while the editing of the countermoves checklist takes place and (b) which family or village members should stay, go, or observe while the role-plays or enactments surrounding the checklist take place. For example, if one of the playbook interventions is an apology by the parent to his or her child or adolescent for sexual or physical abuse, the FST therapist would likely meet with the parent(s) and/or key adult villagers alone first to go over the checklist itself. In addition, the therapist would also likely role-play out a practice apology with only the parent present to troubleshoot any problems prior to asking the child to come into the session for the apology.

Therefore, rules of thumb for who should stay or go can best be summed up as follows:

- *Start with the end in mind:* The FST therapist must answer two key questions: (a) What is the end goal of the checklist and the role-plays or enactments to help inject the targeted healthy undercurrents? (b) Who are "the must-have" players or family members to create these new undercurrents to heal specific unhealed wounds or targeted problem symptom.

- *Potential harm or negative implications:* The FST therapist must consider which parts of the storyboard (the checklist itself, the role-plays, and/or potential enactments) are too intense or would cause potential psychological harm to which family or village member, or even an observer, if they are part of a particular role-play or enactment.

- *Timing is everything:* The FST therapist must consider when a family member should be an active participant in a role-play and when a family member should be an observer. For example, if one role-play or enactment will be an intense forgiveness conversation between an older adolescent son and father with the promise of colorful swearing along the way, the 6-year-old brother should not be in the room to observe these metaphoric labor pains. However, once healing occurs, it may be perfectly appropriate and therapeutic for the 6-year-old to reenter the room and to hear firsthand from both father and son that there was forgiveness and that the young boy did nothing wrong to cause this wound in the first place. Then the therapist can seize the opportunity for a spontaneous interaction or enactment by nudging the father and teenager to deeply hug the little boy for 5 long minutes as he is sheltered in their loving embrace.

STEP 3: CO-CREATE THE TROUBLESHOOTING COUNTERMOVES CHECKLIST

After the troubleshooting checklist is presented in handout form, the FST therapist takes the time to slowly read each section and then pause for family input. As stated in Step 2, this is also the time to excuse certain family members from the room with a clear reason why and when they will be asked to come back. The goals of Step 3 are to: (a) accept or reject the therapist's curveball suggestions and countermoves; or (b) accept the therapist's suggestions and countermoves but with family member recommended edits or changes; or (c) family members offer additional curveball suggestions (other possible situations not listed) and/or new countermoves. The following transition statement is recommended after the checklist handout is distributed:

> Now that you have the handout, let's go through the checklist line-by-line. I will pause after each section and ask if you (a) want to accept or reject my curveball suggestions and countermoves; or (b) want to accept my suggestion and countermoves but add some of your edits or changes; or (c) if you want to make any new suggestions and/or new countermoves.
>
> Let's begin . . .

Must-Haves, Nice-to-Haves, and the Battle for Structure

As the FST therapist uses the checklist to troubleshoot each section of the wound or safety playbook, he or she should expect one of two likely outcomes. First, there will be parts of the checklist that will elicit instant agreement with no changes and only minor edits. Or, second, there will be portions of the checklist that will instantly generate intensity or conflict between family members and/or with the therapist. If the latter occurs, the therapist must be prepared to choose their battles with care and forethought.

Some of the curveballs and countermoves that the FST therapist predetermined during pre-session preparation are must-haves to jump-start a stuck undercurrent. Other curveballs and countermoves are nice-to-haves or more neutral to allow the family a wide berth to use or modify as they see fit. The decision for the FST therapist will be based on the answer to this key question:

> "Is the curveball and countermove listed in the troubleshooting checklist an essential piece of the puzzle to healing the targeted healthy undercurrent(s)?"

If the curveball and countermove are ancillary to the target undercurrent, it is still very important but more of a nice-to-have. Two examples highlighted from Tom's family illustrate this distinction:

Example of a Must-Have Curveball and Countermove

Who

Tom, Mom, grandparents, uncles, parents of teenager, Bill

What Will You Do If …? Curveballs

"What will you do if Tom drops out or wants to quit and withdraw to his bedroom for days and weeks on end as before?" (**area *central* to targeted healthy undercurrent of "grief resolution"**)

Countermove Actions or Statements

- Uncles will come over and go into Tom's room and say, "We miss him too, buddy. Please, for your Dad, us, and yourself, will you come out and not quit?" (new dance).
- If that does not work, uncles will show unity and get sleeping bags and sleep in Tom's room or outside his door and not say anything other than sending the message by their presence, "You are not alone" (new dance).

Example of a "Nice-to-Have" Curveball and Countermove

Where

- *Tom's garage to build Memorial*
- *Tom's home to pick out pictures of Dad for Memorial*
- *End of landowner's property on HWY 21 to place Memorial*

What Will You Do If? Curveballs

"What will you do if landowner changes his or her mind at any point in the process?" (***important to successful completion to the task but <u>ancillary</u> to the undercurrent of grief resolution***)

Countermove Actions or Statements

"Do not get rattled or lose hope. Meet all together and decide other options. If still stuck you can call me, your therapist" (problem-solving solution).

As outlined in the preceding example, **grief resolution** is the targeted healthy undercurrent and the centerpiece to unstick this particular family and address the unhealed wound seed. However, new feedback loops around grief resolution will initially create both stress and intensity for a homeostatic family system. And the curveball of Tom withdrawing or shutting down is normal and should be anticipated. Therefore, the countermoves for this undercurrent are a must have script for practice role-plays. If the family wants to delete this countermove from the checklist, the therapist must fight for it to be left in at all costs.

Case Example

After Tom's family was provided a handout copy of the countermoves checklist, the FST therapist reiterated that this checklist, like the wound playbook, was a working draft to jump-start the process. The therapist read through each scenario that corresponded with a particular section of the who, what, where, when, and how pieces of their playbook. Each family member was asked to closely examine each curveball and suggested countermoves. They were then asked whether or not to keep each one as is or make suggested changes or edits.

(continued)

Case Example (*continued*)

The therapist decided an hour before the session to include all the family members, including Tom, in both the co-creation of the countermoves checklist and the role-plays and/or spontaneous enactments to follow. The rationale was that there was nothing in the checklist that anyone should not hear or that would cause psychological harm to Tom or another family member. In addition, Tom and the other family members had been cooperative in earlier sessions so there was no reason to expect otherwise. Role-plays such as those to counter Tom from shutting down emotionally or talking about his grief were bound to get intense and messy. However, it was the therapist's role as stage director to keep the intensity at a workable level through both a directive style and techniques such as stick and move. If any family member started to shut down or showed an inability to handle the intensity, the therapist was poised and ready to intervene and if necessary temporarily remove individuals from the room.

Tom's family voted to keep a majority of the therapist's suggestions with some edits and additions to the template. The mom and the grandparents added some key curveball situations not originally listed. Their final checklist is illustrated in Table 11.2. The bold and larger font illustrates edits or additions to the original template.

TABLE 11.2 Tom's and His Family's Troubleshooting Countermoves Checklist

Wound Playbook for Unhealed Wounds		
Name of Technique/Playbook: Building a Memorial		
Areas of the Wound Playbook to Address	**Common "What Will You Do if ...?" Curveballs to Derail Playbook**	**Countermoves Actions or Statements**
Reprint the parts of your wound playbook in the following:	• What will you do if Tom drops out or wants to quit and withdraw to his bedroom for days on end just like before? **Voted to keep as is**	• Uncles will come over and go into Tom's room and say, "we are here for you buddy and we miss him too. Please, for your dad, yourself, and us, will you come out and not quit?" **We want to add Tom's grandfather**
Who: *Tom, Mom, grandparents, uncles, parents of teenager, Bill*	Other possible situations not listed: • If Tom continues to stay in his room despite the verbal message from his uncles	• If that does not work, the uncles will show unity and get sleeping bags and sleep in Tom's room or outside the door and not say anything but will let their presence speak loudly that "Tom is not alone." **This may be too intense for Tom but we are willing to try it since we don't have a better idea**

(*continued*)

Case Example (*continued*)

TABLE 11.2 Tom's and His Family's Troubleshooting Countermoves Checklist (*continued*)

Wound Playbook for Unhealed Wounds		
Name of Technique/Playbook: Building a Memorial		
Areas of the Wound Playbook to Address	**Common "What Will You Do if...?" Curveballs to Derail Playbook**	**Countermoves Actions or Statements**
	Other possible situations not listed: • The parents of Bill called and asked if Bill's grandparents could also attend the dedication. What should we do?	• We will take a secret ballot but will be sensitive to Tom also, so if the majority say "yes" but Tom says "no," then his vote will rule
What: *Memorial for Dad placed near the spot of his accident* *Type of memorial: plaster encasement with pictures of Dad*	• What will you do if as you get into the memorial building project, there is disagreement on the design of the memorial? **Voted to keep as is**	• The family must decide: Does Tom have the final vote? Does majority rule? Or something else? **Tom has the final vote**
	Other possible situations not listed: • None	
When: *Meet every Saturday in Tom's garage at 1 p.m. until the memorial is finished. Goal is to finish in the next 14 days or sooner*	• What will you do if someone forgets to show up on Saturday or Sunday? **Voted to keep as is**	• Do not just assume the worst, or immediately accuse or blame. **Voted to keep as is**
Mom, Tom, and Grandma will meet on Sunday afternoon at 3 p.m. to look through old pictures of Dad to pick out the favorites for the Memorial	Other possible situations not listed: • Mom has church activities on some Sundays	• Mom will look at her schedule and if there is a conflict, we will move that Sunday to Tuesday night (decided this from earlier loophole exercise)

(*continued*)

Case Example (*continued*)

TABLE 11.2 Tom's and His Family's Troubleshooting Countermoves Checklist (*continued*)

Wound Playbook for Unhealed Wounds		
Name of Technique/Playbook: Building a Memorial		
Areas of the Wound Playbook to Address	**Common "What Will You Do if...?" Curveballs to Derail Playbook**	**Countermoves Actions or Statements**
Date of ceremony: TBD	Other possible situations not listed: • **Who will be the point person to organize the dedication and put together the agenda?**	• **Mom and Tom will organize and put together the agenda (decided this from earlier loophole exercise)**
Where: *Tom's garage to build the Memorial* *Tom's home to pick out the pictures of Dad for the Memorial* *End of the landowner's property on HWY 21 to place the Memorial*	• What will you do if the landowner changes his or her mind at any point in the process? **Voted to keep as is**	• Do not get rattled or lose hope. Meet all together to decide other options. If you cannot think of other options, call me, your therapist. **Voted to keep as is**
	Other possible situations not listed: • **None**	
How: step-by-step instructions to complete the task with clarity of everyone's roles: *Tom, uncles, and grandfather will build the memorial on the dates and location specified*	• What will you do if Tom gets hit with a flood of emotions as he starts to build the memorial for his dad and he becomes even more depressed, withdraws to his room, or shuts down? **Voted to keep as is**	• We will practice what to do in today's session and learn new ways to talk through these emotions using new communication strategies with the self-regulation tools we learned last session. At home, if these new tools are not working and you run into problems, please call me (your therapist) for a special session if needed. **Voted to keep as is**

(*continued*)

Case Example (*continued*)

TABLE 11.2 Tom's and his Family's Troubleshooting Countermoves Checklist (*continued*)

Wound Playbook for Unhealed Wounds		
Name of Technique/Playbook: Building a Memorial		
Areas of the Wound Playbook to Address	**Common "What Will You Do if?" Curveballs to Derail Playbook**	**Countermoves Actions or Statements**
Tom, Mom, and Grandma will pick out favorite pictures of Dad for the Memorial	• What will you do if someone else besides Tom shuts down in the family? **Voted to keep as is**	• See the preceding text, and also understand that Tom is not the only one in pain. **Voted to keep as is**
Grandpa will continue to interface with Bill's parents to keep them in the loop of when the ceremony will take place	• What will you do if Bill's parents want more involvement in the project than just to show up for the ceremony?	• We will decide together in today's session. **We already know that they do, but will ask Tom today and be sensitive to what he has to say**
Mom will contact dad's friend to get a list of who will come to the ceremony and who might speak a few words about Tom's father	Other possible situations not listed: • **Tom writes: What about the side effects from my medication like sleeping in class, not at night, and weight gain?**	• **Reconsult with our family doctor to see if a lower dosage is possible. Also, mom will find a good nutritionist to consult**
	Other possible situations not listed: • **If Tom gets hit with a flood of emotions and shuts down, how will everyone react? Will mom, grandparents, or uncles (a) see this as a normal part of the healing process and press on; or (b) see Tom as too fragile and give up?**	• **We will practice how you might react in session**

TBD, to be determined.

The Stark Family troubleshooting checklist contains the following ideal role-play setups:

☑ *The What Part of Wound Playbook:*

- "What will you do if Tom drops out or wants to quit and withdraw to his bedroom for days on end just like before?"—**Countermoves to role-play that can also lead to spontaneous enactments**—Uncles (Grandfather added) come over and say "we are here for you buddy, we miss him too.", and/or show unity with sleepover.

- "The parents of Bill recently called and asked if Bill's grandparents could attend the dedication. What do we do?"—**Countermoves to role-play that can also lead to spontaneous enactments**—A secret ballot and emotional discussion with Tom afterward.

☑ *The How Part of the Wound Playbook:*

- "What will you do if Tom gets hit with a flood of emotions as he starts to build the Memorial for his dad and he gets even more depressed, withdraws to his room, or shuts down?"—**Countermoves to role-play that can lead to spontaneous enactments**—We will practice what to do in today's session and learn new ways to talk through these emotions using new communication strategies with the self-regulation techniques we learned last session.

- "What will you do if Bill's parents want more involvement in the project than just to show up for the ceremony?"—**Countermoves to role-play that can lead to spontaneous enactments**—For us to decide together in today's session. We already know that they want to be more involved but will ask Tom today and be sensitive to what he has to say.

- "If Tom gets hit with a flood of emotions and shuts down, how will everyone react? Will the mom, grandparents, or uncles (a) see this as a normal part of the healing process and press on; or (b) see Tom as too fragile and give up?"—**Countermoves to role-play that can lead to spontaneous enactments**—We will practice how you might react in session.

Role-plays and/or enactments can also come when problem-solving other areas in the preceding checklist. However, those listed in this checklist are the top candidates. This is because each area in the checklist is centered around actively altering the target healthy undercurrent and seed for this particular case (i.e., grief resolution and unhealed wounds). This same selection process should be replicated for therapists reading this book for their future cases.

Keep Going or Natural Break Point in the Session

If the FST therapist is only doing a 1-hour session or if Steps 1, 2, or 3 take longer than anticipated, the end of this step is a good natural break point to end the session. The next session can begin with Step 4 in the following and provide the family with extra time to role-play or conduct enactments.

As stated earlier, it is counterproductive if the therapist rushes through step 4 due to time constraints. The warm-up time is just as important as the actual role-plays or enactments themselves. The downside of ending the session after Step 3 is that the family will be literally "chomping at the bit" to go home and put their playbook into actual practice. And when the therapist says, "let's wait another week," the family may get agitated. The parent wants to see quick pain relief for their child's wounds, especially in our present day culture of **instant gratification**. Hence, when they can literally **see it** through a typed-out wound playbook and now a checklist, it is tougher to wait. However, rushing through the role-plays is not an option. The best option is still a 2-hour session for this phase of treatment or if necessary the natural break point to wait another week after Step 3.

STEP 4: CONDUCT ROLE-PLAYS/DRESS REHEARSALS AND ENACTMENTS

Treatment models that advocate for role-plays or enactments often direct the reader to "just do it" or "make it happen." This is a mistake. So much can go wrong without careful preparation and step-by-step procedures. To address this problem, beneath the umbrella of step 4, the authors provide the following eight procedural steps to successfully set up and execute both role-plays and enactments within the FST model:

- **Step 1:** Eliminate Slam Dunks From Troubleshooting Checklist
- **Step 2:** Go From Easier Role-Plays to More Challenging Ones
- **Step 3:** Role-Play Introductory Statement
- **Step 4:** Clarify Roles in Role-Play (Antagonist or Protagonist)
- **Step 5:** Sidebar Open-Ended Countermoves, if Needed
- **Step 6:** Storyboard Role-Plays With Verbal Walkthroughs
- **Step 7:** Conduct Role-Plays and Segue to Enactments, if Appropriate
- **Step 8:** Vote on Role-Play Performance Using a Scale of 1 to 5

At first glance, this may seem like a lot of procedural steps. But as one will see from the case examples, many of the steps are quick and fluid, often lasting less than 5 to 10 minutes each.

In addition, depending on the case, the role-play steps synchronize together and even overlap. For example, an enactment set to take place in step 7 following a role-play may spring up earlier in step 5 when there is a sidebar discussion of countermoves. The steps follow an ideal sequence but they should not be rigid in linear application or limit the fluidity of the FST therapist. Case examples from Tom's family are used to illustrate these procedural steps.

Role-plays and enactments are the core "meat and potatoes" of the FST treatment. The mini-steps within Phases I to III provide the FST therapist with the tools needed to "know where to tap," that is, the core unhealthy undercurrents preventing the child and family from healing their wounds on their own. However, once identified, the FST therapist must move the family system from assessment and preparation to application using role-plays and enactments. Great insight without successful application will still result in a stuck family system.

This is not an easy step for many therapists. They must be directive, assertive, and take calculated risks when asking the family to dance in their presence using new undercurrents. In addition, the stress level for the therapist will increase exponentially. Instead of having to change just one child in individual therapy, the change process is more complex because it now includes the entire family and even the village. And when the FST therapist uses role-plays or enactments to push or prod the family to dance differently, intensity in the room will dramatically increase. The therapist will literally feel knots in his or her stomach.

However, the FST therapist should take heart. Even clumsy or poorly executed role-plays or enactments can quickly unstick the family and result in healed wounds. Viktor Frankl (1959) in his famous book entitled *Man's Search for Meaning* said it best:

Suffering ceases to be suffering at the moment it finds a meaning (p. 10).

Families are extremely resilient. Therefore, when they find meaning to the suffering through even small healthy undercurrent shifts, it often triggers the activation of healing powers that are already within. As Levine (1997) writes in his classic book *Waking the Tiger; Healing Trauma*, "A healing moment ripples forward and back, out and about" (p. 38). The role-plays and enactments act as a catalyst to show the family a clear pathway to transformative change.

Step 1: Eliminate Slam Dunks From Troubleshooting Checklist

Immediately after step 3 (co-create the troubleshooting countermoves checklist), the FST therapist must locate what the authors call slam dunks. We call these slam dunks because they are the curveballs and countermoves in the checklist that can be successfully completed by the family without the need for dress rehearsals or enactments. The following transition statement is recommended after Step 3 is completed:

> Congrats everyone, we just finished going through your troubleshooting checklist to list the most likely curveballs and countermoves you will need to successfully deliver your wound playbook.
>
> Our next step is for me to quickly go through this list and place a **star** on the curveballs and countermoves that I think are clear and that you can try at home without the need for practice role-plays or dress rehearsals today. So let me put a star on the ones I think are clear and can be done on your own without much assistance from me. If you disagree with my star picks, please let me know. We can always add them to our practice delivery (role-play or dress rehearsal) list. OK, here are my choices and rationale.

This exercise should only take about 5 minutes. If a family member strongly disagrees with the FST therapist's choices, stop and ask him or her to clarify the rationale for disagreement. If the family member makes a good point, the therapist can reverse his or her decision to remove the star and include it the countermove or curveball within the series of upcoming role-plays. However, the most likely outcome is that further clarification may be needed or last minute adjustments. For example, looking at Tom's family checklist in Table 11.2, a summary of their slam dunk list would be:

- *What will you do if someone forgets to show up on Saturday or Sunday?*

  <u>Countermoves are clear and easy to implement:</u> (a) Don't blame: determine if someone simply forgot, and if "yes" simply remind him or her; and (b) Mom will look at her calendar and if there are any church activity conflicts, we will move our task to Tuesday.

- *Who will be the point person to organize the dedication and put together the agenda?*

  <u>Countermoves are clear and easy to implement:</u> Mom and Tom will put together the agenda as time gets closer. This task right now does not require immediate attention.

- *What will you do if the landowner changes his or her mind at any point in the process?*

  <u>Countermoves are clear and easy to implement:</u> Do not get rattled or lose hope. Meet all together to decide other options. If you cannot think of other options, call me, your therapist.

- *What about the side effects from my medication—like sleeping in class, not sleeping at night, and weight gain?*

Countermoves are clear and easy to implement: Reconsult with your family doctor to see if a lower dosage is possible. We liked the earlier suggested nutritional ideas and the distinction between the medicated brain and the nutritional brain. Mom will find a local nutritionist, get a customized plan for Tom, and present it for discussion in the next session.

In addition, there are time constraints to consider. The FST therapist cannot be a "jack of all trades, but a master of none." Translation: the FST therapist has to pick his or her battles and focus on the "hot spot" curveballs and countermoves most likely to alter the key undercurrents to create the most positive impact on the unhealed wounds.

Step 2: Go From Easier Role-Plays to More Challenging Ones

After the slam dunk list is complete, the FST therapist has one final tactical decision to make prior to conducting actual role-plays or enactments. The FST therapist must do a quick review of the troubleshooting scenarios still remaining. They must tactically decide which role-plays look easier to tackle first and which ones are more challenging. Role-plays are a brand new experience for families. Therefore, easier role-plays will increase the odds for successful outcomes because quick victories will build confidence and momentum for the tougher role-plays that lie ahead.

The therapist does not openly discuss this decision, but privately, in real time, he or she must prioritize the role-plays. The beginner FST therapist can begin to think about this decision as early as when the countermoves checklist is being drafted during pre-session preparation in Chapter 10 or as the family is tweaking the checklist in step 3.

Case Example

Looking at Tom's family's checklist, which of the following three scenarios are the easier role-plays and which ones are the more challenging?

☑ *The What Part of Wound Playbook:*

- "What will you do if Tom drops out or wants to quit and withdraw to his bedroom for days on end just like before?"—**Countermoves to role-play that can also lead to spontaneous enactments**—Uncles (Grandfather added) come over and say "we are here for you buddy, we miss him too," and/or show unity with sleepover.

- "The parents of Bill recently called and asked if Bill's grandparents could attend the dedication. What do we do?"—**Countermoves to role-play that can also lead to spontaneous enactments**—A secret ballot and emotional discussion with Tom afterward.

☑ *The How Part of the Wound Playbook:*

- "What will you do if Tom gets hit with a flood of emotions as he starts to build the Memorial for his dad and he becomes even more depressed, withdraws to his room, or shuts down?"—**Countermoves to role-play that can lead to spontaneous enactments**—We will practice what to do in today's session and learn new ways to talk through these emotions using new communication strategies with the self-regulation tools we learned last session.

(continued)

Case Example (*continued*)

The first scenario is the easier one. The countermove script is clearly written and the steps are laid out ahead of time. The second and third scenarios are much more open-ended and more challenging to facilitate.

In the second scenario, once the ballot is cast, the odds are great that this topic is a lightning rod for high intensity for both Tom and other family members. It will likely lead to spontaneous interactions and the opportunity for enactments. Once the ballot is cast in the therapy session, the reactions will likely be highly charged and spontaneous. There is no way to preplan or prescript these reactions as in the first scenario. As a result, the FST therapist will have to move to the role of stage director to actively facilitate the enactment by providing both wording and direction to keep the conversation away from finger-pointing and movement toward healthy undercurrents (i.e., forgiveness and grief resolution).

The third scenario is also challenging but for slightly different reasons. The countermove instructions of "using new communication strategies" have yet to be outlined or discussed with the family. Therefore, before jumping into the role-play, the FST therapist has to sidebar with the family and role-model or describe a set of concrete tools (i.e., reflective listening) that the family can use during the role-play. Therefore, in summary, the first scenario is the easiest and should be tried first and then the next two are a toss-up depending on the day and the family. For example, in Tom's case, if the first role-play was a resounding success and it put everyone in a jovial mood, the therapist might parlay this momentum into a vote and enactment discussion regarding the driver who killed Tom's dad. Or after the first role-play it might be obvious that the family was still shaky and needs additional straightforward and prescripted role-plays like the third scenario.

It is recommended that unless one has hours of experience doing enactments, the safer play is to facilitate role-plays first and then let the enactments flow out of the role-plays. Enactments are challenging because they are messy, unscripted, and require therapists to quickly "think on their feet."

Step 3: Role-Play Introduction Statement

After the slam dunk list and the FST therapist internally decides which role-play to initiate first, the following introductory statement is used to transition the child and family to their first role-plays:

> Now that we have put a star on the curveballs and countermoves you will do on your own, our next step is to practice our delivery of your wound playbook (through dress rehearsals or role-plays[1]).
>
> Actors and football teams do the same thing. Actors use dress rehearsals to practice their lines before opening night and football teams practice the plays in their playbooks over and

---

[1] *In our experience, family members and especially older children and adolescents may have an aversion to the term "role-play." They seem to dislike the term and associate it with being put on stage or made to do something. If there is no apparent aversion, role-play can be used. However, if there appears to be negativity around the term, the FST therapist can substitute the words of "practice delivery" or "dress rehearsals."*

over again before game day. In the same way, we are going to do dress rehearsals (or role-plays or practice rounds) to practice the delivery of your wound playbook so you will be ready to use it when you walk out this door.

To begin, we will look at the remaining curveballs and countermoves that we did not star and pick one curveball and set of countermoves to practice one at a time. Once we practice it and master it, we will move on down the list. We may not have time to do every single one, but we will hit the main pressure points.

After we practice our delivery (do our role-play, do our dress rehearsal), I will ask everyone to rate our performance on a scale of 1 to 5 (1 = not close to a good delivery and we need more practice and 5 = great delivery and ready to go forward). If there is a low score, we can practice a few more rounds to get it right.

Just like a director in a movie, I will yell "freeze" when I want us to stop or if we need more practice. I will also say, "that's a wrap" when everyone likes what they see and we can move on to the next curveball on the list.

Please remember that not all of you will be called on to practice at once. It will depend on the curveball and countermove we pick and if you happen to have a role in that one. Otherwise, you will be asked to be an observer.

These are important practice rounds (role-plays or dress rehearsals) because as the old saying goes "it is not what you say but how you say it."

Therefore, if you need more practice or don't get everything you want done in the time we have left, I will suggest another meeting so you can get enough practice time.

Okay, let's get started. I will go ahead and select one of the curveballs and countermove on your checklist [Pick the easiest role-play to conduct first]. We will practice it, master it, and then move on down the list.

The FST therapist may choose to condense this introductory statement or make adjustments according to his or her own personality and style. However, it is important to keep the core message points intact. It helps to provide the family with context and rationale for something brand new and strange . . . role-plays.

For example, in Tom's case, the family has to master role-plays on countermoves around the target healthy undercurrent of "grief resolution" (i.e., new communication strategies if Tom has emotional flooding, view of Tom as frail or normal but stuck in a rut, uncle and grandfather strategy if Tom withdraws to bedroom). The goal is to first pick out an easier role-play scenario to get a quick victory, move to more challenging ones next, and practice all the scenarios at least once with self-report rating at 3 or above. Short of that goal, the easiest role-play should still be picked first and then prioritized as suggested earlier if time constraints are an issue.

Step 4: Clarify Roles in Role-Play (Antagonist or Protagonist)

In the literature, an antagonist is a character that stands in opposition to the protagonist or the main character in the story. In the same way, during the initial role-plays, the FST therapist will take on the role of "antagonist" by playing the part of the family member who delivers the curveballs while the family members responsible for delivering the countermoves will play themselves in the role of main character or "protagonist." After the FST therapist makes his or her first curveball and countermove selection, clarity of roles within the role-play is communicated to the family using the following statement:

Before we get started let me clarify who is playing what role. For the first round, I, as your coach (therapist), will play _____ (person responsible for the curveball) while they observe me playing them. The person or persons delivering the countermove will play themselves. And looking at this practice scene on your checklist, that will be _____ (person or persons responsible for delivering the countermove).

You may be asking why I am playing the part of _____ and delivering the curveballs. The reason is that for the sake of time I want to serve up the right curveballs quickly like a good pitcher so the person delivering the countermove can practice his or her delivery. Then, time permitting, the person I played will take my seat, play himself or herself, and practice delivering the curveballs like he or she saw me just do to the same person who just did the countermove. That can be the final round for this curveball and we can move on down the list. Any questions?

Now, let me storyboard out the scene (or sidebar countermoves in Step 5 depending on case) with you and we will get started."

There are three reasons why the therapist insists on playing the role of antagonist. First, if the people delivering the curveball play themselves, they would not likely know what to say to get the role-play started or what unhealthy undercurrent statements to use. The role-play would then meander from topic to topic without any clear purpose or direction. In contrast, the FST therapist knows the key unhealthy undercurrents (words, statements, tone of voice, body language, etc.) causing the wounds and can get to the **heart of the matter** quickly.

Second, when the therapist is in this role it is much easier to control the flow and outcome of the role-play. The therapist can freely yell "freeze" at any point in time to highlight a key statement or action or pause to help family members who get stuck or are not sure what to do next. When the therapist yells, "freeze," he or she can also freely go to the observers and say something like, "_____ (person doing countermoves) seems to be stuck. Any suggestions of what they can say or do differently to improve when I yell 'action' again and we continue?" In this way, the FST therapist is using the observers as his or her "co-therapists" for advice to help another family member. It is much easier to do this when one is throwing the curveballs and in charge of the role-play.

Finally, it is the countermoves, in words and actions, that represent the healthy undercurrents to get the child and family unstuck to heal the wound. The curveballs represent the status quo or unhealthy undercurrents. For example, when we further dissect the following curveball and countermove example, we can see this distinction more clearly:

- **Curveball:** "What will you do if Tom drops out or wants to quit and withdraw to his bedroom for days end as before?"
- **Countermoves to role-play that can also lead to spontaneous enactments:** Uncles (Grandfather added) come over and say "we are here for you buddy, we miss him too," and/ or show unity with sleepover.

The curveball in the preceding example illustrates the homeostatic or specific unhealthy undercurrents (not all of them) that are keeping the family stuck (withdrawal, isolation, bottled-up emotions, inability to grieve). However, the countermoves represent a new feedback loop or dance with the opposite healthy undercurrents (engagement [not withdrawal], community [not isolation], openness of feelings [not bottled-up emotions], and showing grief [not inability to grieve]). Therefore, the underlying main purpose of every role-play is to demonstrate the healthy undercurrent in action as seen by the new dance by the person or persons responsible for the countermoves. The person delivering the curveballs is not expected to change his or her interactions until the countermove healthy undercurrents are in place. Therefore, it makes sense for the therapist to take the antagonist role; he or she wants to be a systems irritant to push and prod the family to use new countermoves or healthy undercurrents successfully. If he or she does, the chances of healing old and entrenched wounds increase exponentially.

The labels of antagonist and protagonist are useful terms to help the frontline FST therapist quickly define and split the roles for the upcoming role-plays. For example, prior to the role-play, the therapist can ask himself or herself, "For this particular role-play, who in the family should deliver the countermove and be the main character or protagonist(s) and who in the family will I represent as the antagonist to deliver the curveball?" In sum, the FST therapist's role as antagonist parallels the dance between a hitting coach and a rookie hitter. Initially, the hitting coach (the FST therapist) pitches curveballs (curveballs on checklist) to the rookie batter (the family members responsible for implementing the countermoves) to see if he or she can hit the "curve ball." If they struggle and their mechanics are off base, the hitting coach will yell "freeze" to show the rookie the correct stance, how to hold the bat, timing, and so on. The hitting coach then goes back to pitching move curveballs to see if there is improvement. If not, the hitting coach yells "freeze" again but this time the hitter often shows improvements from practice and may only need minor adjustments. After more pitches and freeze sequences, the hitter is no longer a rookie. They can now hit the curve ball with mastery.

Step 5: Sidebar Open-Ended Countermoves, if Needed

If the countermoves on the checklist are clearly scripted (e.g., *Uncles and Grandfather will come over and go into Tom's room and say "we miss him too buddy, etc." If that does not work, the uncles will show unity and get sleeping bags and sleep in Tom's room, etc.*), the FST therapist can skip this step and go directly to "storyboarding" with verbal walkthroughs in step 6. However, if the countermoves in question are open-ended (e.g., "for us to decide in today session"), then after roles are clarified in Step 4, the therapist must do a sidebar with the family to coach or role-model possible strategies to fill in the blanks. This step is introduced using the following statement:

> Before we move into storyboarding the next curveball and countermove on your checklist, I can see that the next one on the list is open-ended or for us to decide something here and now. It is _____ (restate what is open-ended). If we need to problem-solve something we can do it here and then practice its delivery. If the countermove requires that we talk through a tough issue, we can do that also. Or if it requires tools for things like better communication I can offer suggestions and even show you what the tool looks like. However, I left some of these things open-ended on purpose so that we can come up with your own ideas together.

> Let me get the ball rolling by starting the conversation or giving you one concrete idea and then see if you want to use this idea, tweak it, or suggest something else.

The FST therapist will have the benefit of studying every playbook and technique in this book and on our website (www.gopll.com/trauma) beforehand. Therefore, they will have an arsenal of techniques in their head to offer as suggestions in relation to the open-ended countermoves. For example, if the countermove reads, "we will use new communication strategies if our daughter starts to shut down," a common and easy strategy to demonstrate is the tool of "reflective listening." In addition, the open-ended countermove may not call for a therapeutic technique but to simply problem-solve a specific issue ("we are supposed to meet for our special outing and the other person does not show") or it may require spontaneous interactions and lead to an enactment (see the following case example).

Whatever the requirement, the therapist must be careful to strike a balance between doing it all for the family versus doing just enough to allow the family creative license to come up with their own strategies. The FST therapist does not want to create a robot family that just parrots the words or actions of the therapist. Instead, the therapist wants to be like a great director who provides the actor with lines to say or suggestions, but gives the actor freedom to ad-lib and take ownership of the scene as it unfolds in real time. The wound playbooks provide the clear step-by-step procedures for the family to follow (who, what, where, when, and how) but the actual delivery or countermoves is left open-ended at times to push the family to unstick themselves and stretch their muscles. Otherwise, the family does not take credit for the change and the new tools do not become the new normal resulting in only first-order change.

Case Example

In the case of Tom's family, looking at the checklist in Table 11.3, during the sidebar discussion the therapist chose to combine two open-ended countermoves that were interrelated: (1) *talk through Tom's emotional flooding and withdrawal using new communication strategies along with self-regulation techniques* and (2) *If Tom hits a flood of emotions and shuts down, how will everyone react? (a) see this as a normal part of the healing process and press forward; or (b) see Tom as too fragile and give up.* Both are interrelated because the mom's, grandparents', or uncles' belief system will determine their communication strategies whether they use self-regulation techniques or not. If they believe Tom is too fragile, they will continue to present their "before" feedback loops or undercurrents of giving up and letting Tom withdraw (what is happening now). However, if the adults change their belief to "Tom is normal but stuck in a rut," it will immediately open up the door to new and healthy undercurrents or "after" feedback loops.

TABLE 11.3 Two Open-Ended Countermoves That are Interrelated

Wound Playbook for Unhealed Wounds		
Name of Technique/Playbook: Building a Memorial		
Areas of the Wound Playbook to Address	Common "What Will You Do if ...? Curveballs to Derail Playbook	Countermoves Actions or Statements
How: Step-by-step instructions to complete the task with clarity of everyone's roles: *Tom, uncles, and Grandfather will build the Memorial on the dates and location specified* *Tom, Mom, and Grandma will pick out favorite pictures of dad for the Memorial*	• What will you do if Tom gets hit with a flood of emotions as he starts to build the Memorial for his dad and he becomes even more depressed, withdraws to his room, or shuts down? **Voted to keep as is**	• We will practice what to do in today's session and learn new ways to talk through these emotions using new communication strategies with the self-regulation tools we learned last session. At home, if these new tools are not working and you run into problems, please call me (your therapist) for a special session if needed. **Voted to keep as is**

(continued)

Case Example (*continued*)

<table>
<tr><td colspan="3">**TABLE 11.3** Two Open-Ended Countermoves That are Interrelated (*continued*)</td></tr>
<tr><td colspan="3">**Wound Playbook for Unhealed Wounds**</td></tr>
<tr><td colspan="3">**Name of Technique/Playbook: Building a Memorial**</td></tr>
<tr><td>**Areas of the Wound Playbook to Address**</td><td>**Common "What Will You Do if ...? Curveballs to Derail Playbook**</td><td>**Countermoves Actions or Statements**</td></tr>
<tr><td>*Grandpa will continue to interface with Bill's parents to keep them in the loop of when the ceremony will take place*

Mom will contact Dad's friend to get a list of who will come to the ceremony and who might speak a few words about Tom's father</td><td>Other possible situations not listed:

• **If Tom gets hit with a flood of emotions and shuts down, how will everyone react? Will Mom, grandparents, or uncles (a) see this as a normal part of the healing process and press on; or (b) see Tom as too fragile and give up?**</td><td>• **We will practice how you might react in session**</td></tr>
</table>

Based on this knowledge, the FST therapist can metaphorically "kick the tires" and ask each adult in the family how they see Tom and even ask Tom himself. The therapist is banking on the fact that the steps of the FST treatment up to this point have already begun to shift people's thinking from precontemplation to a contemplation stage of readiness. If this happens, a family member who has shifted into contemplation can be recruited by the therapist to be his or her cotherapist to help influence others.

In the following transcript, one will see how the FST therapist briefly veers off the role-play track to go into creating an enactment by challenging the family's worldview to move to a "normal, but stuck in a rut" mindset as a prerequisite to new communication strategies. This is a concrete example of the fluidity of the procedural role-play steps. The therapist is in Step 5 but jumps to Step 7 (conduct role-plays and segue to enactments, if appropriate), and then will return to Step 6 (storyboard role-plays with verbal walkthroughs).

The therapist does not have to get everyone on board (e.g., Grandmother) but just some of the key adult players. He or she can position it gently as an experiment or to "do something different" for everyone to see and evaluate in the future. In this case, what will it look like when the ensuing role-play will have new communication strategy dances around a new belief system performed by someone in the family who believes that Tom is normal, but stuck in a rut?

The balance move is now set in motion. Can the therapist skillfully ride the fence of being a great stage director to give enough direction in the upcoming enactment

(*continued*)

Case Example (*continued*)

to steer the family to accept a new belief system with new communication tools while allowing the family their own voice to take ownership of these new undercurrent directives?

FST therapist: Put another checkmark on your checklist. We just success- fully practiced and knocked off our list three curveballs. You all are getting better and better as we go on. Can you feel it?

It is important to consolidate gains made during the session. One suggestion is that the therapist ask the family to take their checklist handout and literally check off or strike- through with a pen each curveball and countermove completed. It gives them a sense of pride and accomplishment.

Uncle: Definitely, let's keep going.

FST therapist: I am glad to hear that because the level of difficulty is just about to go up. But from your earlier practice and success, I believe you are ready for the next challenge.

Before we move into storyboarding the next curveball and countermove on your checklist, I can see the recommended countermove for this one is open-ended and we need to decide what is meant by "new communication strategies."

Mom: (Interrupts) Yes, I agree, what do you mean by new commu- nication strategies?

FST therapist: Excellent question. I left this open-ended on purpose because how you react and communicate to your son in pain going forward is directly connected to this curveball listed. Let's read it together. *If Tom gets hit with a flood of emotions and shuts down, how will everyone react? Will Mom, grandparents, or uncles (a) see this as a normal part of the healing process and press on; or (b) see Tom as too fragile and give up?*

The FST therapist is intentionally opening the door for an enactment by directly and overtly challenging the family's worldview. This will increase the level of intensity.

Grandmother: I can't speak for everyone else but for me if this memorial thing causes my grandson Tommy more pain and it is obvi- ous to me, he might try to kill himself again. He is fragile and we will need to back way off.

(continued)

Case Example (*continued*)

FST therapist:	I appreciate the wisdom in that statement *(compliment)* especially when you consider Tom has already had one suicide attempt. Therefore, before I offer some suggestions, let's take a vote, including you, Tom. By a show of hands, going forward, if Tom gets hit with a flood of emotions and shuts down, who votes that we should see this as a normal part of the healing and who votes that we should see Tom as fragile and back off? (It's a split vote down the middle with Tom voting the fragile option.)
	To grandfather (who voted for the normal option), I don't want you to sleep on the couch tonight (joking) but you disagree with your wife, why?

The FST therapist successfully seeks out and finds a cotherapist in the grandfather.

Grandfather:	I think before we came here we did not have any tools and we never worked together as a family or had a playbook. And even though Tom went to the hospital after his suicide attempt he came back just as depressed. All I am saying is that seeing him as frail has not worked. I think Tom is stuck, but with us all together now, I think we should press forward.

The FST therapist was correct in his assumption. Earlier steps in the FST model coupled with the concrete playbook provided specific family members with confidence and in turn changed their previous belief systems. The therapist will also take the opportunity to **fan the flames** *further by connecting the dots to earlier role-play successes to further challenge the family's worldview.*

FST therapist:	The couch will have to wait. I think you are both right. I think, Grandfather, you are right in that now, you, as a family, do have a plan. And you saw in our first role-play today that Tom did respond favorably to both his uncles and grandfather pressing forward if Tom tried to close himself off in his room.
	It shows me that there is strength in numbers. This means that when Tom knows he is not alone and you treat his grief as normal and don't let him hide in the pain, he rallies. And Grandmother, you are right in that if Tom does not respond or gets worse, we have safeguards in this checklist to call me for tune-ups or to make adjustments. I think you have great wisdom as Tommy's grandmother, let's proceed but do so with caution.

(continued)

Case Example (*continued*)

As illustrated earlier, the role-play process was paused and an enactment was used (a jump from Step 5 to Step 7: segue to enactments, if appropriate) to challenge the family's worldview and connect one countermove to another. Whenever possible, it is important for the therapist to create a win–win scenario. In this case, the grandmother's beliefs were incorporated and respected (win) while at the same time setting up the entire family to shift to a new undercurrent worldview (win).

Also illustrated is how balance is achieved. The FST therapist did not use his or her expert status to ask the family to just accept his or her opinion and move on (like medical experts do). Instead, the therapist gently prodded the family toward his or her viewpoint, offering plausible explanations and safeguards. In turn, the family felt respected and took ownership of the process. They also inherently understood that all these roads lead to the same goal: To rally together to help Tom heal his wounds through "Now what?" here and now strategies and new belief systems.

In addition, when there is a therapy of action, the odds go up dramatically that undercurrents will rise to the surface. In this case, just the expectation that a role-play was coming shortly was enough to trigger tough discussions long since buried. The context was now set to return from enactment back to role-play to practice the delivery of the countermove of new communication strategies.

Step 6: Storyboard Role-Plays With Verbal Walkthroughs

In the early days of the FST model, this technique was not used. Instead, role-plays were quickly set up by the therapist and started with the word "action." The new skills and healthy undercurrents were so new that the child or family got easily stuck. Common phases we heard were things like, "Now, what were we supposed to say again?" or "We are not sure what to do next."

In response to these early challenges, we started to experiment with storyboarding combined with a verbal walkthrough. A storyboard plans out a movie in advance by previsualizing each scene using illustrations or images (Whitehead, 2004). In the same way, the FST therapist will take each curveball on the checklist and help the family previsualize each scene before it happens and actually write out their script (what they will do and say). This will increase the success of role-play outcomes before they even begin. The definition of a verbal "walk-through" is the act of going slowly through the steps of a process in order to practice doing it and to help someone learn it (Merriam-Webster, 2015).

In the same way, immediately following storyboarding, the therapist will ask the main character in the role-play to do a verbal walkthrough of the steps by prompting him or her with the words, "And then what?" After the verbal walkthrough is complete, the therapist will immediately yell "action" and go into Step 7: conduct role-plays and segue to enactments, if appropriate. Picking back up from where we left off with the transition script in Step 4, the final set of instructions prior to the role-play starting that now include the message of storyboarding and verbal walkthroughs are highlighted in **bold** in the following:

Before getting started, let me clarify who is playing what role. For the first round, I, as your coach (therapist), will play _____ (person responsible for the curveball) while they simply observe me playing them. The person or persons delivering the countermoves will play themselves. And looking at this practice scene on your checklist that will be _____ (person or persons responsible for the countermoves).

You may be asking why I am playing the part of _____ and delivering the curveballs. The reason is that for the sake of time I want to serve up the right curveballs quickly like a good pitcher so the person delivering the countermoves can practice his or her delivery. Then, time permitting, we will switch roles. The person I played will take my seat, play himself or herself, and practice delivering the curveballs like he or she saw me just do to the same person who just did the countermoves. That can be the final round for this curveball and we can move on down the list. Any questions?

If no questions, let me storyboard out the scene (or sidebar countermoves in Step 5 depending on case) **and we will get started.**

(Storyboarding)

In this first scene, let's write on our storyboard that we will be at this location, _____ at this time of day _____.

Now, if I start off with my curveball of _____,

Looking at your checklist sheet [state person's name] what do you imagine you will say or do in response: _____ Your Countermove? I will write down what you will say and do.

Then I will do _____ in response to you. Let me write down what I will do also.

(Verbal walkthrough)

Now that we have laid out the scene, let's walk it through and then begin.

If I start off with my curveball of _____ at this place and time.

Then what will you do or say next _____ ?

And then what _____ ?

And then what _____ ?

In a nutshell, storyboarding and verbal walkthroughs allow for a verbal dry run like actors running through their lines before the director yells "action" and the cameras roll. Actors need these dry runs before a scene and so will the family. Storyboarding and verbal walkthroughs parallel the feedback loops drawn in Phase II. The current role-play being executed may be different (or not) from the after feedback loop sample illustrated in Phase II, but the process is the same. The only exception is that one is drawn on paper with arrows and the other is a verbal interaction and real life. During the feedback loop drawings, the therapist states something like, "The teenager started the first dance move (a first curveball) by doing, thinking, or saying _____, then the parent made the second dance (then what) by doing, thinking, or saying _____, which then led to the third dance move by _____ (then what) and so on. During the verbal walkthrough the therapist does the exact same feedback loop process but without drawing it on paper. Instead, the therapist verbally states, "And then what?"

Case Example

In the case of Tom's family, looking at the checklist in Table 11.4, the countermove for the uncles and grandparents is already scripted and **does not** need Step 5: sidebar open-ended countermoves if needed. Therefore, after clarification of roles in Step 4: clarify

(continued)

Case Example (*continued*)

roles in role-play (antagonist or protagonist), the FST therapist was immediately ready to proceed with storyboarding and verbal walkthroughs and then to begin the first practice role-play or dress rehearsal.

TABLE 11.4 Storyboarding and Verbal Walkthroughs

Areas of the Wound Playbook to Address	Common "What Will You Do if …? Curveballs to Derail Playbook	Countermoves Actions or Statements
Reprint the parts of your wound playbook in the following: **Who:**	• What will you do if Tom drops out or wants to quit and withdraw to his bedroom for days on end just like before? **Voted to keep as is**	• Uncles will come over and go into Tom's room and say, "we are here for you buddy and we miss him too. Please, for your dad, yourself, and us, will you come out and not quit?" **We want to add Tom's grandfather**
Tom, Mom, grandparents, uncles, parents of teenager Bill	Other possible situations not listed: • If Tom continues to stay in his room despite the verbal message from his uncles	• If that does not work, the uncles will show unity and get sleeping bags and sleep in Tom's room or outside the door and not say anything but will let their presence speak loudly that "Tom is not alone."

Storyboarding

Therapist: Looking at your checklist, let's try out the situation or curveball of what you will do if Tom drops out or wants to quit and withdraw to his bedroom for days on end as before. For the first couple of practice runs, Tom, I will play you, and uncles and Grandfather, you will play yourselves. Tom, I want to tell you ahead of time, I am not the best actor, so please forgive me if I don't say it exactly like you would or do exactly what you might do. In fact, please give me pointers as we set up the scene. Will you please?

Tom: Sure.

Therapist: Okay everyone, like a director of a good movie let's storyboard out this scene. For the first round, let's do a best case scenario. [**In this first scene we will be at this location and this time of day** _____] Let's pretend, we are all together in Tom's garage working on the Memorial. And then suddenly [**If I start off with my curveball of** _____] I, as Tom, see or do something that triggers me to get really upset and sad. Next, I say something like, "I can't handle this" and suddenly leave. Tom, any suggestions here or are you okay with this description?

(*continued*)

Case Example (*continued*)

Tom:	Pretty good. I just don't think this will ever happen.
Therapist:	You're right, it may not. This is just practice in case it did ever happen. The point is that it is good practice for your family just in case you start to withdraw or your emotions of sadness or depression get overheated. So this practice is really for them, not you.

The FST therapist does a good job of sidestepping the challenge of **it will not work**.

Tom:	Okay I get it. Then if this happens, I would add me swearing to the mix.
Therapist:	Thanks for that, I will be sure to add that. Okay after I get upset, let's pretend that next I leave the garage and slam my bedroom door. You then come up and knock on my door, and what do you say, uncles and grandfather? Look at your countermoves checklist [**Looking at your checklist sheet (state person's name) what do you imagine you will say or do in response _____ Your Countermove**].
Uncle:	It says to say something like "Tom, we are here for you buddy, we miss him too. Please, for your dad, yourself, and us, will you come out and not quit?"
Therapist:	Then in response to you, best case scenario, playing Tom, I will come out and start doing the memorial again with the thought bubble over my head that says, "I am not alone, the men in my family will rally on my behalf and not let me turtle-shell in my hole and wallow in my pain. This is new for my family and I like it."

As one gets more advanced in the FST Model, it is easy to look for moments to add "that little extra something" to expand the family's range just a little bit more. In this case, it is that thought bubble like a comic strip with the cognitive thoughts in full view. Creative therapists will even have poster boards handy to quickly draw out a thought bubble, write the thought out, and hold the poster board over their head as they play the role of antagonist.

Verbal Walk-Through

Therapist:	OK, let's do a quick verbal walk-through and begin. I will start things off playing, Tom, and say something like: "The more I am involved in building the Memorial, the more it is stirring up my hurt and pain. I just want to quit and go back to my bedroom where it's safe" (goes into bedroom, slams the door).

(continued)

Case Example (*continued*)

Then what? [What will you do or say next _____?]

Uncles and grandfather: We go to his door.

Therapist: *Then what?*

Uncles and Grandfather: We knock on the door and ask to come in.

Therapist: Then, if I say "okay" and then you enter,
                              Then what?

Uncles and Grandfather: We say, "we are here for you buddy, we miss him too," and then... not sure.

Therapist: You will say, "Please for your dad, yourself, and us, will you come out and not quit?" Then I will come out with my thought bubble.

Everyone: Got it.

Therapist: Let's begin . . . action

As illustrated in the preceding example, the storyboard is a clear outline for both therapist and family members on how the countermove will be utilized. Once the storyboard process is finished, the FST therapist begins the verbal walkthrough process by using the prompt of "Then what?" to allow the different players to verbally go through the sequence of steps from the storyboard.

Step 7:- Conduct Role-Plays and Segue To Enactments if Appropriate

The role-play is conducted immediately after the storyboarding and verbal walkthrough is finished. It is critically important to prevent the role-plays from going on too long or to unravel themselves. The rule of thumb is that once the key target undercurrents or central principles are demonstrated, the therapist should be poised to yell "freeze" or "time out" to stop the role-play. In this brief example of another case where the parent is attempting to praise his daughter, the therapist yells "freeze" at the right time.

Therapist: OK, let's begin, action.

Therapist: Why are you coming to my bedroom to give me a note telling me how proud you are of me? It's a little too late [angry and disrespectful voice]. (Curveball, play part of daughter).

Dad: You're right. I have no excuse. I take full responsibility for the past, and I apologize. You do not have to forgive me if you do not want to. I have to prove it in the future with actions and maybe then you can. (Countermove healthy undercurrent of accountability and apology).

| Therapist: | This is all BS and this note, I am ripping it up. |
| Dad: | [Calmly] I understand I might do the same thing if I were in your shoes. Like I said, my kindness has to be love that's unconditional. I will keep doing acts of kindness to keep saying sorry. (Countermove: healthy undercurrent of unconditional love). I will leave now. I love you. |

Freeze

As this example illustrates, the therapist yelled "freeze" at the right time. The key undercurrents were demonstrated and to go on would have only served to unravel the goals of the role-play.

After yelling "freeze," the therapist has a tactical decision to make. The therapist can either (a) segue the role-play into an enactment; or (b) get feedback from family members on their reactions and get people's vote on a scale of 1 to 5 (see the following) to see if additional role-plays are needed due to low scores. If there was demonstrated success, it would then be time to move on to the next curveball to role-play.

There are time constraints in every session. So therapists must look at the clock and "pick their spots" with the time remaining in the session. A good rule of thumb to help with this decision is to look to see if the role-play stirred up high passion or intensity, and/or if the role-play demonstrated a must have key undercurrent. If the answer is "yes" to either one or especially both, it is a good indicator that an enactment may be in order.

Step 8: Vote on Role-Play Performance Using a Scale of 1 to 5

At the end of each role-play, the FST therapist will turn to the observers and also to the role players themselves with the question, "On a scale of 1 to 5 with **1** meaning that the parent, child, or village member lacked confidence and needs more practice and **5** meaning they demonstrate confidence and are ready to deliver the countermove, what is the first number that comes to mind?" If the overall average score is 3 or less, it often indicates that another practice round is needed. The persons receiving the ratings are only the people responsible for the countermoves unless the role-play evolves to the person delivering the curveball playing himself or herself. The therapist will ask for concrete suggestions from the raters on what the role player needs to do or say in the next role-play to raise their rating one or two points. The therapist can use the following transition statement to introduce this step.

> **Freeze:** OK, let me go around the room and evaluate the delivery. Let me start with the observers first and then ask everyone in the scene. I will be the last to go. On a scale of 1 to 5 with 1 meaning that you do not feel confident and need more practice and 5 meaning you have total confidence and you are ready to deliver the countermove, what is the first number that comes to mind? [If the therapist played the role of antagonist and served up the curveballs, only ask family members to rate the people delivering the countermoves]
>
> _____ [Call on person] what is the first number that came to mind [let them answer]? And why did you give that number?
>
> What could that person do or say in the future to go from _____ [number they gave] to a _____ [the next higher number]?
>
> (Optional) And what did they do or say to get to _____ [number they gave]? In other words, why are they not at a lower number?

After the observers answer, the therapist can direct the question to the role players themselves. To save time, the therapist can then call on one or two family members and ask them,

"What does the person you rated as _____ need to do or say in the next round to go one or two points higher?" The therapist can also ask, "Why is the number you gave not lower, what are they doing well that you saw to get to a _____." The rating scale is an invaluable strategy to empower the family to provide solution-focused suggestions to improve on the next role-play and consolidate any positive gains that were made.

For example, the parent may receive a general consensus from everyone that timing and message was perfect but the tone of voice was shaky and lacked confidence. Therefore, in round two, there would be a focus on sounding more confident and more assertive. The FST therapist may even ask the person who gave the feedback to quickly demonstrate what confidence and assertiveness look like. Finally, the ratings make it easier on the therapist to call another practice session or Phase IV session if time runs out. Low ratings on key role-plays will be evident to everyone in the room and the negative implications of going forward will be obvious.

STEP 5: IMPLEMENT PLAYBOOKS

At the end of Phase IV, the FST therapist has a tough decision to make. Does the child and family demonstrate sufficient competence in the role-plays and/or enactments to warrant playbook implementation? The rating scale scores will help guide this decision but it is still the therapist's judgment call on what he or she will recommend to the family. This decision is not an easy one. After the checklist and delivery practice runs, the family will often want to put their playbook into actual practice, whether they are ready or not. The therapist may have to use the full weight of his or her expert status and high rapport and trust with the family to convince them to wait for another practice session. Contextually, families have been entrenched in unhealthy undercurrent dances for months or years. Therefore, one session or even two of role-playing healthy undercurrents may not be enough.

However, that being said, there is therapeutic value for families to struggle with the new delivery of the playbook, even if they are not completely ready. This is because "directives [the playbook] can get people out of their ruts with *the smallest change possible*" (Gehart, 2013, p. 26). And when the directives work even a little bit, it unleashes a sudden shift in emotion, insight, and behavior. From this position of momentum and hope, the family is more likely to allow future corrections in delivery or push them to work through more difficult challenges. In addition, each succeeding session can get closer to the bull's-eye of healing the wounds permanently because the therapist is getting instant feedback on what is working or not. Adjustments to the playbook are made accordingly. For example, after 2 weeks of using the playbook, the father might say, "When I tried the special outings piece in the playbook with my son it worked great. But Saturdays are not a good day for us. And I did not expect this but now my daughter feels left out." As a result of this feedback, the playbook can then be tweaked with changing the day from Saturday to Sunday and including a special outing for the daughter. As Haley maintained, "the best task is one that uses the presenting problem [of the child] to make a structural change in the family" (Haley, 1991, p. 85). Therefore, there is wisdom in sending the family home to try out their wound playbook even if the family did not show evidence of pristine practice role-play delivery or perfect closure through enactments.

Ultimately, key determining factors are stability and safety. If there is less stability and safety is still in question, the role-plays and enactments have to be better and include more practice rounds. For example, if the adolescent has a history of violence or is cutting, the parents or village have to show competence in their role-plays because the margin for error is greater. If however, safety symptoms are currently stabilized, the therapist can move forward if the family shows some degree of role-play success. This can happen even if there was not enough time in the session to cover all the curveballs listed on the troubleshooting checklist. Enough role-plays were covered successfully to give both the family and the therapist confidence to push forward.

Next Steps If Recommending Implementation

If the decision is to recommend playbook implementation, the therapist can use the following transition statement:

> Congrats, you are now what I call battle-ready. This means that your wound playbook is well written and free of all the loopholes we could find up to this point. And you have done a good job troubleshooting or figuring out the most common curveballs or "What will you do if …?" situations if they should ever occur. Finally, you have done well with the practice dress rehearsals. By doing all this prep work ahead of time, the odds of your success have greatly increased. You are therefore ready to implement your playbook to actively start healing your wounds of _____ [fill in the blank].
>
> Let's wait a couple of weeks before we meet again to give you time to implement your playbook. Then in the next session, we will all evaluate how the playbook went on a scale of 0% to 100%. Zero percent meaning the playbook did not work well at all and 100% meaning the playbook is working without a problem. Then we will decide where to go from there.
>
> So just to be clear one last time, let me quickly go around the room with your playbook in hand and ask each one of you to tell me what you will be doing this week or your role in the playbook [go around the room]. And before you leave, let's pick a good date and time in 2 weeks for your next appointment [pick date and time].
>
> I will email you or send you via regular mail your cleaned-up playbook and countermoves checklist as two separate but interrelated documents. When you get them, please tape them to your bathroom mirror. And each morning as you brush your teeth, read and review both documents. This is no different from what generals do every morning prior to stepping on the battlefield. So if they do it to be successful, we should follow the same steps. So can I get a commitment? Will you tape it to your mirror and review daily?
>
> Have a great week. And one last thing. The research shows that it is normal to expect only 10% improvement each week. That is just how people change, about 10% improvement each week. So if you go above that 10% mark, great, but if you don't, that's normal and what to expect.

As illustrated earlier, it is important to give the family at least 2 weeks in between sessions to try out their playbooks. The exception would be if there are still safety concerns to monitor then weekly sessions make sense. The next session will be Phase V: evaluate progress and relapse prevention. This is the final phase of the FST model and will be outlined in Chapter 12. It is also important to provide the family with an upcoming preview of the goals for the next session and how the therapist will use a 0% to 100% scale to evaluate progress. The therapist also reiterates the importance of taping the playbook to the bathroom mirror and how any final edits to both the playbook and troubleshooting checklist will be emailed or mailed to them.

Finally, the 10% strategy that Jim Keim (personal communication, January 2015) uses has really been a game changer for many clients. When it is clearly communicated that only a 10% change per week is normal and expected, anxiety levels drop and it puts the family at ease. A 10% change feels achievable to the family and is a win/win for the therapist. If the child and family only achieve a 10% change that is to be expected, and if they go above this mark, it is a bonus. It is rare that a family drops below 10% change because they are equipped with a typed-up playbook and have participated in well-scripted role-plays. The 10% change also seems to have a paradoxical impact. The more the therapist says to slow down, the more the family wants to speed up. Finally, it is ideal to communicate the normality of a 10% change when the main goal is to heal wounds.

REFERENCES

Colapinto, J. (1991). Structural family therapy. In A. Gurman & D. Kniskern (Eds.), *Handbook of family therapy* (Vol. 2, pp. 310–360). New York, NY: Brunner/Mazel.

Frankl, V. (1959). *Man's search for meaning.* Beacon, MA: Beacon Press.

Gehart, D. R. (2013). *Mastering competencies in family therapy: A practical approach to theory and clinical case documentation.* Independence, KY: Cengage.

Haley, J. (1991). *Problem-Solving therapy.* San Francisco. CA: Jossey-Bass

Levine, P. A. (1997). *Waking the tiger: Healing trauma.* Berkeley, CA: North Atlantic Books.

Minuchin, S., & Fishman, H. C. (1981). *Family therapy techniques.* Cambridge, MA: Harvard University Press.

Walk-through. (2015). *Merriam-Webster's school dictionary.* Darien, CT: Federal Street Press.

Whitehead, M. (2004). *Animation: Pocket essentials series.* Harpenden, UK: Oldcastle Books.

Pre-Session Preparation for Phase V

Step 1: Type and Laminate Final Playbooks and Troubleshooting Countermoves
Checklist

Step 2: Proactively Initiate Any Midweek Check-Ins as Needed

Step 3: Create Decision Tree Handout

Step 4: Create a Red Flags Checklist Template

As the family systems trauma (FST) diagram flowchart in Chapter 3 illustrates, this pre-session preparation step occurs prior to Phase V: evaluate progress and relapse prevention. Phase V is the final phase of treatment in the FST model. There are two important core strategies within this pre-session preparation step. First, the FST therapist uses a tool developed within the FST model called the **decision tree checklist: five different options**. This tool will help the FST therapist and family determine the next treatment steps within five different options. Options range from graduation with relapse prevention strategies to a new symptom and a new wound playbook to even leaving treatment prematurely. The therapist must use pre-session preparation time in this step to carefully study each option as it relates to the particular family and be ready to adapt his or her recommendations based on new information presented by the family during Phase V. Second, the FST therapist will use another tool developed in the FST model called a red flags checklist. The checklist contains the top "red flags" or most likely early warning signs for relapse for a particular family. To accomplish these goals, there are four mini-steps. These are as follows: (a) type and laminate final playbooks and troubleshooting countermoves checklist; (b) proactively initiate any check-ins as needed; (c) create a decision tree handout; and (d) create a red flags checklist.

STEP 1: TYPE AND LAMINATE FINAL PLAYBOOKS AND TROUBLESHOOTING COUNTERMOVES CHECKLIST

Prior to Phase V, it is important to type up and laminate the final wound and/or safety playbook and troubleshooting countermoves checklist. At the end of the last session, in Phase IV, there were final changes to the playbook (loophole checks) as well as edits to the troubleshooting countermoves checklist. As stated in Chapter 11, the FST therapist either prints out in real time a new copy of the changed playbook and/or troubleshooting countermoves checklist, or sends any final edits and changes immediately after the session via email or regular postal mail. This is important because the family will be implementing their wound playbook during the next 2 weeks and must have the latest typed-out version. In addition, in the spirit of being both professional and honoring, it is still recommended to present a final laminated version of both the playbook and troubleshooting countermoves checklist to the family at the beginning of the next session.

STEP 2: PROACTIVELY INITIATE ANY MIDWEEK CHECK-INS AS NEEDED

If it was evident during the dress rehearsals that the family was still shaky on their delivery, it is wise to proactively make a few check-in phone calls during the week. Shaky is defined as a family who demonstrates enough safety and stability to proceed forward, but shows evidence that their delivery was still rough and needs improvement.

It is also our experience that the saying no news is good news does not apply with wounded families. These families will often not call if things are going poorly during the week, but instead will suffer in silence. Suffering in silence and in shame has historically been the coping strategy of wounded families. Traumatized families also do not typically have many reboots left. This means that as a computer must reboot itself if it shuts off, so must a family. And if the child or family is traumatized for a long period of time, they often do not have the energy to get back on track quickly or reboot if something goes wrong. Hence, if the playbook implementation is a failure even after all the extensive preparation, a traumatized family may not have enough gas in the tank or energy to reboot a second time. For example, in one family, the wound playbook directive was for the mother of an estranged daughter to catch the daughter at home and surprise her with a heartfelt apology. The mother went to her daughter's house three different times, but each time the daughter was not at home. Even though no one was at fault, the mother was so wounded that she simply gave up and could not reboot herself to try again.

Therefore, your proactive check-ins can make all the difference in the world. Even minor suggestions over the phone can make the difference between success and failure. As a result, if the dress rehearsals are shaky, midweek check-ins by phone or even an unplanned session should be part of your pre-session preparation. Suggested solution-focused questions that can serve as a guide when calling are:

- Just checking in . . . What is working so far? [Always start out with positive]. How do you account for the fact that _____ is working so far? What are you doing or saying differently? How will you keep it going?

- What is not working so far? [stay away from yes or no questions] What is your theory or best guess as to why it is not working? Specifically, what part of your playbook is giving you the most difficulty and why?

- Based on what you are telling me, what are one or two things that you want to be sure to hit on during our next session? And what is one thing, as your therapist, that you want from me next session to make it even more productive and helpful?

The FST therapist is not expected to use every single question provided earlier. It is simply meant to be a helpful guide when the call is made and provide clear focus from a solution-focused perspective.

STEP 3: CREATE DECISION TREE HANDOUT

Many treatment models lack this critical step of concretely reviewing with the family next possible treatment steps or options. Instead, the individual or family may accomplish the first goals of therapy, but lack clarity as to the next action steps or what the different treatment options look like. As a result, the client may end treatment without ever considering other options available, or options to prevent future relapse. In fact, comprehensive termination and proper closure are one of the least researched and understood parts of the entire therapeutic process (Schwartz & Flowers, 2010). In one study, 60% of clients felt that their therapy either lasted too long or ended too soon (Luczaj, 2008). It was concluded, that while there is widespread agreement that termination should occur naturally, with an agreement of timing, more often than not, this does not happen (Roe, Dekel, Harel, & Fennig, 2006).

To address these common problems, the FST model includes what is called a decision tree checklist: five different options. The handout in Table 12.1 should be copied by the FST therapist and handed out to each family member during the next session.

TABLE 12.1 Handout of the Decision Tree Checklist: Five Different Options

Option A: **Graduation and Red Flags Checklist:** Overall, your family and child self-report (and your therapist is in agreement) a 70% or higher wound playbook effectiveness on a 0%–100% rating scale (presented at the beginning of Phase V). It is decided between you and your therapist that your child and your family are ready for graduation and to finalize your red flags relapse prevention checklist along with scheduling the first 30-day callback with your FST therapist.

Option B: **Tweak the Current Playbook:** If your playbook is not working at a 70% or higher effectiveness (i.e., need more practice role-plays/dress rehearsals, need more clarification, need to include key missing extended family members, etc.) a predetermined number of additional sessions are negotiated with your therapist to work through any identified barriers.

Option C: **Pick a New Problem and Build Another Playbook:** You as a family agree that although the first playbook was successful, other critical wounds still linger and remain (i.e., unresolved grief is a success but still have unforgiveness). It is also agreed that you as a family do not yet feel confident or strong enough to complete and implement a second playbook on your own. A specific number of new sessions are then negotiated with your therapist.

Option D: **Additional Safety or Misuse of Power Issues Emerge:** Additional safety issues emerge or old ones resurface. Healing wounds can act as a cork on a bottle. Once the cork is removed, extreme behavioral problems may reemerge or occur for the first time with your child or teenager. They may be temporary but, you, as the parent or caregiver still need a behavioral or hybrid contract to weather the storm. A specific number of new sessions are then negotiated to help tweak an existing safety plan or behavioral contract or build a new one.

Option E: **Terminate Against Therapist's Recommendation:** The therapist and your family may disagree as to the next steps. Your therapist may advise you that critical work still needs to be done but one or more key family members refuse to go any further. At this point, termination of treatment proceeds forward against your therapist's recommendation. However, the door is left open to return at any time if relapse occurs and the family agrees to then follow the therapist's recommendations.

During pre-session preparation, the FST therapist should study this decision tree handout closely. The therapist should reexamine all the evidence up to this point and predetermine which of the five options in Table 12.1 they are going to recommend as the next step. One does not want to be thinking about such an important decision as the session unfolds. Instead, it is important to have a good idea beforehand as to what option to recommend with solid rationale. This pre-session decision may be altered depending on new information in Phase V but it is wise to have a well thought out direction beforehand. For example, at the beginning of Phase V, both the child and family could report that the wound playbook was working at 90% effectiveness. This family could also present strong and convincing evidence. Because of this new information, the FST therapist may change the initial recommendation he or she formulated earlier.

However, these kinds of shifts are rare. What the FST therapist has seen up to this point in treatment often does not change dramatically within a 2- to 3-week window in between sessions. For example, if the family struggled with playbook delivery in Phase IV, there is usually a carryover into Phase V (even if improved). The following case example illustrates an example of pre-session preparation. The FST therapist will examine the decision tree checklist and type out privately his or her top one or two most likely recommendations with rationale. In this way, the therapist is polished and prepared, yet flexible enough to alter these recommendations as needed.

Case Example

Fifteen-year-old Tonya had been referred by her mom based on a multiple problem symptoms. The most prevalent problem was clinical depression and the extreme behavior problems of daily disrespect and refusal to go to school. During Phase I, it was obvious that the biggest precipitating factors were unhealed wounds and the misuse of power seed. The wound was the direct cause of a bitter divorce between Tonya's parents, Sandra and Mike, 3 years ago. It was so bitter in fact that there was open warfare in front of Tonya nonstop. Tonya was being used as a metaphoric battering ram between her parents. When she visited her father, he openly told her to disrespect her mom and that her mom was "worthless." When Tonya was with mom, she stated basically the same thing about the dad. However, Tonya only belittled and disrespected the mother, not the father. In addition, both the father and Tonya reported little to no behavioral problems during weekend visitations with the father. It was only at the mother's home, Sunday through Friday.

The feedback loops had the look and feel of parental alienation syndrome (PAS). PAS is a term coined by Gardner (1998) to refer to what he describes as a disorder in which a child, on an ongoing basis, belittles and insults one parent without justification due to the indoctrination by the other parent. Even through PAS has received its share of criticism due to lack of scientific evidence and lack of inclusion in the *Diagnostic and Statistical Manual of Mental Disorders* (5th ed.; *DSM-5*) as an actual disorder (Warshak, 2001), the characteristics of PAS were a helpful framework to view this complex case and identify the stuck interactional family patterns (unhealthy undercurrents) in this family.

There was also evidence of rampant misuse of power with an upside down hierarchy at the mother's home. Tonya totally controlled the mood of the household. The mother could not and would not set limits. If she tried, Tonya would either blatantly ignore mom or spit in her face. The father would not come to the mother's defense. In fact, he openly indicated to both the FST therapist and Tonya that the mother deserved this kind of disrespect.

Mom and Dad could not be physically in the same room, so therapy had to be split up between a family session with Dad and then another with Mom. The dad refused to accept a PAS type hypothesis or explanation, no matter what the FST therapist tried. The mom accepted the hypothesis because it reinforced her view of the father but was still too afraid of Tonya to set any limits.

The FST therapist was then essentially stuck. He knew that whoever controls the definition of the problem, controls the therapy and way the problem is treated. Neither parent would agree with the FST therapist's definition of problem and what was keeping Tonya traumatized:

(continued)

Case Example (*continued*)

The unhealed wounds of the bitter divorce were exacerbated by the day-to-day interactional trauma (constant fighting between Mom and Dad) and an inability for Dad to see his role in the indoctrination of his daughter against the mother (**unhealthy undercurrent—bitterness or lack of forgiveness**). In addition, Mom had bitterness toward Dad and an inability to set consistent limits (**unhealthy undercurrent—lack of consistent disciple**).

As a result, the FST therapist had a battle for structure on his hands. Within this battle for structure, the therapist was left with only one option: to get both mother and father to **act their way into a new way of thinking**. Trying to get both parents to **think their way into a new way of acting** was not working no matter reframe or information was used.

As a result, the FST therapist proposed a 30-day experiment using a hybrid contract:

A behavioral contract for the extreme disrespect and school refusal that included an explicit agreement by both parents of **cease-fire**: Not talking badly about the other and supporting one another as parents.

This proposal was vetted separately because Sandra and Mike literally hated one another. Both agreed to the experiment because they agreed with the logic that nothing was working and therefore they needed to do something different. Once agreed, the FST therapist took the role of mediator in Phase III and had both parents in the same room in a tightly controlled session of constant stick and move by the therapist. Tonya was not allowed in the room for this session because of the volatility of both parents.

During Phase IV, both Dad and Mom demonstrated shaky ground with their practice delivery of the playbook. The area of greatest concern was their ability to contain their bitterness when the therapist played the role of the other parent. Phase IV was done separately with both parents in different sessions. Again, Tonya was not present for these role-plays. The rationale was to avoid exposing Tonya to further trauma until one or both parents showed success in the dress rehearsals.

Ultimately, the decision was made to try the hybrid contract based on the following rationale. It could be argued that both family systems were neither safe nor stable. However, the FST therapist had zero chance to move either father or mother from a precontemplative stage of readiness to a contemplative one unless they experientially saw and felt firsthand the impact their bitterness was having on Tonya remaining both traumatized and symptomatic (depression and defiance).

Therefore, the FST therapist took a calculated risk. He agreed to go forward with the hybrid contract on one condition. The therapist would have to be allowed to do a home visit in the role of stage director. In front of the therapist, the mom would ask Tonya to turn off her electronics before bedtime. This request would guarantee open defiance. Dad would be there to see firsthand the extreme disrespect and be coached by the therapist to back Mom (like he did in the practice role-play) for the first time ever to see its positive impact on Tonya. No part of the hybrid contract could be implemented until this practice session took place. Both parents agreed.

(continued)

Case Example (*continued*)

On the night in question, Mom did a great job and Tonya predictably was defiant. Afterward, Dad said, "You were right; I now see it with my own eyes. Tonya treats her mom with total disrespect and I am a big part of the problem." Mom then started to cry with tears of relief as Tonya then gave up her smartphone for the first time ever. The session concluded with both parents saying that they were now motivated to come to the next session with a fresh start, put aside their differences, and find a way to coparent for the sake of Tonya.

During pre-session preparation, the FST therapist typed up on the decision tree checklist in Table 12.2 the recommendations he planned to give the mom and dad with rationale. The outcome of what actually happened versus what was recommended will be revealed in Chapter 13. Stay tuned.

TABLE 12.2 Pre-Session Preparation for the Decision Tree Process

---

Option A: **Graduation and Red Flags Checklist:** Overall, your family and child self-report (and your therapist is in agreement) a 70% or higher playbook effectiveness on a 0%–100% rating scale (presented at the beginning of Phase V). It is decided between you and your therapist that your child and your family are ready for graduation and to finalize your red flags relapse prevention checklist along with scheduling the first 30-day callback with your FST therapist.

I predict that the parents will state that Option A was TBD. It was too early and premature to see if the hybrid contract would work. The parents must continue the cease-fire and coordinate more in detail what day-to-day support and backup would look like- So I think Option B is the one to recommend.

Option B: **Tweak the Current Playbook:** If your playbook is not working at a 70% or higher effectiveness (i.e., need more practice role-plays/dress rehearsals, need more clarification, need to include key missing extended family members, etc.) a predetermined number of additional sessions are negotiated with your therapist to work through any identified barriers.

This is the option I will recommend. Both parents, because of the experiment, are now in the contemplative stage of readiness. The next stage of readiness is preparation and then action. Therefore, even though we have already done our preparation (we have a typed-up contract and already did Phase IV role-plays) and are in action (Saturday, both parents actually implemented the disrespect contract with me present), we need to circle back around. The reason is that the parents for the first time are "contemplatively" ready for change because the contract helped them act their way into a new way of thinking. This was a success. So we have a written contract but have to backtrack to another Phase IV set of role-plays but this time both will now be in the same room without Tonya present. This is a huge structural shift. The directive of the contract used the presenting problem of Tonya to make this huge and significant structural shift in the family as an on-ramp to finally "peeling back the layers of the onion" to get to the "root" or unhealed wound (bitterness and unforgiveness between both parents).

Option C: **Pick a New Problem and Build Another Playbook:** You as a family agree that although the first playbook was successful, other critical wounds still linger and remain (i.e., unresolved grief is a success but still have unforgiveness). It is also agreed that you as a family do not yet feel confident or strong enough to complete and implement a second playbook on your own. A specific number of new sessions are then negotiated with your therapist.

(*continued*)

TABLE 12.2 Pre-Session Preparation for the Decision Tree Process (*continued*)

This option does not apply at this time. First things first. We have to stabilize the first problem with a hybrid two-track contract with these healthy undercurrents intact (misuse of power: consistent limits) along with parents on same page (misuse of power: same parent philosophies) and unhealed wounds (forgiveness).

Option D: **Additional Safety or Misuse of Power Issues Emerge:** Additional safety issues emerge or old ones resurface. Healing wounds can act as a cork on a bottle. Once the cork is removed, extreme behavioral problems may reemerge or occur for the first time with your child or teenager. They may be a temporary but, you, as the parent or caregiver still need a behavioral or hybrid contract to weather the storm. A specific number of new sessions are then negotiated to help tweak an existing safety plan or behavioral contract or build a new one.

None at this time; see the preceding text.

Option E: **Terminate Against Therapist's Recommendation:** The therapist and your family may disagree as to the next steps. Your therapist may advise you that critical work still needs to be done but one or more key family members refuse to go any further. At this point, termination of treatment proceeds forward against your therapist's recommendation. However, the door is left open to return at any time if relapse occurs and the family agrees to then follow the therapist's recommendations.

The hope is that this will not take place. The cease-fire, however, just like between two countries at war, is always tenuous and could break down at any time almost for any reason. The key is for the cease-fire to last long enough for some trust to be built and for the wet cement to dry.

TBD, to be determined.

As the case example in Table 12.2 illustrates, it is extremely beneficial for FST therapists to go through each option ahead of time with privately written comments that only they will see. It allows them to be fully prepared for this critical crossroads decision of next steps that both the therapist and family will face together in the session. This kind of preparation for the decision tree can make the difference between a family successfully navigating the waters into second-order change (the right decision tree option is made) or continuing first-order change (the wrong decision tree option is chosen or the family terminates treatment prematurely).

STEP 4: CREATE A RED FLAGS CHECKLIST TEMPLATE

A final pre-session preparation step is to create a red flags checklist that is customized to the particular family seen in the next session. Simply defined, the purpose of the red flags checklist is to (a) prevent relapse and (b) solidify positive gains. This is accomplished through parts I, II, III, and IV of the red flags checklist:

- *Part I: Areas of the Playbook Not Followed.* Areas within the playbook at greatest risk for relapse or compromise for that family are listed with next action steps to get back on track as quickly as possible.
- *Part II: Areas of Safety.* A reemergence of safety concerns (self-harm, running away, alcohol or drug use, aggression, etc.) and next action steps if these return.
- *Part III: Unhealthy Undercurrents or Trauma Symptoms Return.* The unhealthy undercurrents and trauma symptoms that the particular family battled to overcome with their healthy undercurrent counterparts are listed, so no one forgets. If any undercurrents or symptoms return, next action steps are listed to prevent relapse.

- *Part IV: First Callback Date.* Before the family leaves the office or home session, both therapist and parent get out their calendar to confirm a first date and time (30 days from now at 5 p.m.) in which the therapist proactively calls the parent to go over the checklist together. This callback will happen again at day 60 and day 90. This callback process and its importance are outlined in Chapter 13.

As with the troubleshooting countermoves checklist, the FST therapist will type out the first working draft of the red flags checklist. During the session, it will be modified with the family's input. The template, however, will allow the discussion to be laser focused rather than one of unfocused brainstorming and bunny trails.

The red flags checklist is used if there is a decision for graduation or if the family elects to terminate against the therapist's recommendation. It will also be used if the family wants to prevent relapse even if the other decision tree options are selected (option B, C, or D). In this case, the only part missing would be Part IV because graduation and scheduling the callback has not yet taken place. As a result, the FST therapist will still create a working draft of the red flags checklist during pre-session preparation regardless of the decision tree option selected. Box 12.1 illustrates what the working draft of the red flags checklist would look for Tonya's family. The same template can be replicated with other families.

BOX 12.1 Red Flags Checklist

Red Flags Checklist

Part I: *Areas of the Wound Playbook Not Followed*

- Tonya's mom feels that she not doing her part (being consistent) and/or Tonya is not following her part of the playbook (respect and going to school) **for three straight days**.
- Sandra (Tonya's mom) or Mike (Tonya's dad) says something negative about the other parent to Tonya or each other even one time.
- Mike is not backing up Mom around the playbook or Sandra is not backing up Mike around the playbook even one time.

  Steps to take if playbook is not working for three straight days:
  - ☑ Mom will call a "check-in" meeting with Tonya at the kitchen table to see what the barriers are and what needs to be done to get back on track.
  - ☑ After the "check-in" meeting, if not back on track, Mom will call the FST counselor.

  Steps to take if Mom and Dad are not supportive of one another or say something negative:
  - ☑ Such an important part of playbook success, one or both parents, or Tonya will call the FST therapist immediately and to determine if a tune-up is needed.

Part II: *Areas of Safety:* If Tonya ever again begins to exhibit one or more of the following safety areas:

- Spitting on Mom or anyone
- Showing aggression toward any person

(continued)

BOX 12.1 Red Flags Checklist (*continued*)

Steps to take:

- ☑ Mom and Dad agree to immediately disable Tonya's smartphone for a minimum of 4 months.
- ☑ If the aforementioned incident happens a second time, smartphone penalty is a minimum of 1 year.
- ☑ Call FST therapist to check in.

Part III: Unhealthy Undercurrents or Trauma Symptoms Return

- Mom starting to be inconsistent or use empty threats
- A return of Tonya shutting herself in her room for days on end
- Dad or Mom starting to feel resentful (beginning of bitterness) toward one another again
- Mom and Dad starting to disagree on parenting issues again
- Tonya starting to lose interest again in outside activities and life in general

Steps to take:

- ☑ Mom and Dad will remind each other of what is missing in private and if corrections are not made within 1 week, they will call the FST therapist.

Part IV: *Date for First Callback* _____

Underlying Goals of the Red Flags Checklist

There are several points in Box 12.1 to highlight. First, within "Part I: Areas of Playbook Not Followed," it is important to put specific time frames for when the "steps to take" are to occur. In Tonya's family, it is three straight days of either Mom or Tonya not following the playbook or the first time either parent goes back to old behaviors of openly criticizing the other in front of daughter and not being supportive. Any of these problems would trigger the recommended steps to occur. However, if no specific time frame is included, it is a setup for failure for a family who is still brand new to the playbook.

Second, the steps listed in the red flags checklist have to be concrete. This includes steps for the family to take (i.e., a check in meeting at the kitchen table, taking away smartphone for acts of aggression, parents reminding one another) **before** they call the FST therapist. The expectation continues to be that the family can generalize new undercurrents to different situations but with concrete actions to take if signs of relapse occur.

Third, it helps to put the previous and unhealthy undercurrents front and center within Part III: Unhealthy Undercurrents as Well as Old Trauma Symptoms Return. In the busyness of day-to-day life, families can forget the original reasons or causes of what brought them to FST treatment in the first place. To put these reasons front and center will remind the family of (a) how far they have come and (b) why they never want to go back to the way things were before. Part III functions as the tremors to listen to and stop before it degenerates and they evolve into a major earthquake.

Finally, playbooks help heal the wound, but new feedback loops or healthy undercurrents are like "wet cement" that has not dried yet. During this wet cement period, future additional stress can put the child or family system at risk for relapse. However, long-term treatment is not always the answer. It can create "learned helplessness" whereby the family becomes dependent on treatment or prevents the family from using their own muscles or undercurrents on their own.

Therefore, the FST model looks at a working smarter not harder paradigm and uses the safety nets of the red flag checklist along with the decision tree checklist, callbacks, and tune-ups. Within this context, the FST therapist can then be on the periphery to come in only as needed for tune-up sessions: one or two sessions to get the adolescent and family back on track without a return to long-term treatment. In this way, the cement can dry on new undercurrents and in the process give family members both time and confidence to weather the storm themselves.

Troubleshooting Countermoves Checklist Will Help Create Red Flags Checklist

When trying to come up with red flags or areas of relapse, a first place to start is the family's troubleshooting countermoves checklist. These two checklists synchronize nicely together. The troubleshooting countermoves checklist answers the question: What will you do if this curveball takes place? And the red flags checklist answers the question: What will you do if there is relapse in the areas of the playbook, safety, and/or a return of unhealthy undercurrents? Therefore, if the troubleshooting countermoves checklist highlighted a curveball of "the parents starting to get resentful again" (a return to an unhealthy undercurrent) the FST therapist might choose to carry over this risk to the red flags checklist under Part III: Unhealthy Undercurrents or Trauma Symptoms Return. If however, the checklist highlights the curveball of a return of the adolescent to aggression (a safety issue) then this possible relapse would best fit under Part II: Areas of Safety. The key is to look at the curveball and to determine its best fit within which category of Part I: Areas Specific to the Playbook; Part II: Safety Areas; or Part III: Undercurrents or Trauma Symptoms Return.

It is important to note that not every troubleshooting curveball should be carried over and listed as a potential relapse red flag. The rule of thumb is whether (a) the area of concern in the troubleshooting countermoves checklist is an ongoing issue; or (b) the curveball in question is a major area of concern to trigger a relapse instead of a minor problem-solving issue. If neither concern exists, there should be no carryover.

In addition, the countermove recommendations in the troubleshooting countermoves checklist can be the same or different under the Steps to Take section within the red flags checklist. For example, the step to call the therapist is often not the first countermove recommendation within the troubleshooting countermoves checklist. Instead, the countermove is a recommendation of what to do immediately in the "here and now" within the home. Likewise, the step to call the therapist on the red flags checklist may not be the first recommended step.

A first step to take if there is a warning sign of relapse might be to regroup around the kitchen table to try to get back on track, and if that does not work then call the FST therapist. The FST therapist must use sound judgment, considering the particular family, to determine which countermoves should carry over to the red flags checklist and which should not. Curveballs in the troubleshooting checklist are the equivalent of red flags or areas of potential relapse and countermoves are the equivalent of steps to take but they are not always one and the same. It is important to note that the actual unhealthy undercurrents are implied in the troubleshooting countermoves checklist but not usually overtly stated in writing. However, in the red flags checklist they are overtly stated in writing under Part III.

REFERENCES

Gardner, R. A. (1998). *The parental alienation syndrome: A guide for mental health and legal professionals.* Cresskill, NJ: Creative Therapeutics.

Luczaj, S. (2008, January 16). Research on termination of therapy: Too much or not enough? *Counselling Resource*. Retrieved from http://counsellingresource.com/features/2008/01/16/termination-therapy-research

Roe, D., Dekel, R., Harel, G., & Fennig, S. (2006). Clients' reasons for terminating psychotherapy: A quantitative and qualitative inquiry. *Psychology and Psychotherapy: Theory, Research, and Practice, 29*, 529–538.

Schwartz, B., & Flowers, J. (2010). *How therapists fail: Why too many clients drop out of therapy prematurely.* Manassas, VA: Impact Publishers.

Warshak, R. A. (2001). Current controversies regarding parental alienation syndrome. *American Journal of Forensic Psychology, 19, 3*, 29–59.

Phase V: Evaluate Progress and Relapse Prevention

Step 1: Scaling to Assess Overall Progress

Step 2: Mini-Scales to Consolidate Healthy Undercurrents

Step 3: Review Decision Tree for Next Steps

Step 4: Co-Create Red Flags Checklist

Step 5: If Graduation: Callbacks and Tune Ups

The final phase in the family systems trauma (FST) treatment model shows clear if/then decisions within the FST diagram (see Chapter 3). Looking at the diagram, there are two major decisions for the FST therapist to consider: (a) graduation from FST treatment is put into motion if the family reports an overall success rate of 70% or higher (a C grade: average) with no safety issues or other remaining major wounds; or (b) if lower than 70% (a D grade: below average or F grade: failing) or safety issues, one of the other four options from the decision tree checklistis recommended:

Option B: **Tweak the current wound playbook**

Option C: **Pick a new problem and build another playbook**

Option D: **Additional safety or misuse of powerissues emerge**

Option E: **Terminate against therapist's recommendation**

The best possible outcomes for Phase V are that the child and family are able to graduate naturally with prevention tools (red flags checklist) and tune-up sessions if needed, or that there is mutual agreement on one of the other options without the need for a battle for structure. Even the option of premature termination (Option E) may be therapeutic if done correctly (see the decision tree section in this chapter).

To accomplish these goals, there are five mini-steps. These are as follows:(a) scaling to assess overall progress; (b) mini-scales to consolidate healthy undercurrents; (c) review decision tree for next steps; (d) red flags checklist; and (e) if graduation: callbacks and tune-ups.

PRIOR TO THE SESSION

As a reminder, prior to the beginning of Phase V, the FST therapist should come prepared to enter the session with the following items:

☑ *Laminated playbook(s) and troubleshooting countermoves checklist:* The FST therapist should have already sent or emailed copies of both the finalized wound playbook and troubleshooting countermoves checklist immediately after the last session. The reason is that the family will need the finalized versions before they implement their playbook. Therefore, the only remaining item to give to each family member is the laminated versions of both the wound and/or safety playbook and the troubleshooting countermoves checklist at the beginning of this session.

☑ *Decision tree checklist:* five different options handout: Prior to the session, the FST therapist makes copies of this handout (without their private notes included) to pass out to each member of the family.

☑ *Red flags checklist:* The working draft completed during the pre-session preparation should be brought to the session as a handout. Ideally, the checklist can be projected onto a television flat screen or liquid-crystal display (LCD) projector so that changes can be updated in real time. A second option is to provide a handout and then handwrite the template onto a giant flip chart page.

STEP 1: SCALING TO ASSESS OVERALL PROGRESS

Immediately prior to the appointment, the FST therapist will draw on a giant flip chart page or dry eraser board a scale from 0% to 100%: 0% = the playbook is not working at all and 100% = the playbook is effective all the time as seen in Box 13.1.

BOX 13.1 FST Rating Scale of Playbook Effectiveness

0%	10%	20%	30%	40%	50%	60%	70%	80%	90%	100%

It is ideal to begin Phase V with the scaling technique. It acts as a laser beam to provide both the family and therapist a road map of what is working, what is not, and what is needed to improve in the future. Scaling overall progress also has a secondary benefit of providing a foundation for the subsequent steps in Phase V. For example, when the FST therapist is giving rationale for their decision tree recommendation in Step 3, they may state something like, "Earlier you presented an overall score of 80% for your playbook success. According to our decision tree options, this makes you (the family) a great candidate to graduate and to create what is called a red flags checklist to prevent future relapses." As this example illustrates, the overall scaling scores provide the perfect foundation to segue into the other mini-steps in this chapter. The following transition statement is recommended to introduce this step:

> What you see on the flip chart is somewhat similar to the stress chart that we used during our first meeting. The difference is that the first 0% to 100% scale measured your overall stress in the form of a stress chart. This time, the 0% to 100% scale is used to measure the overall progress of how well each of you personally thinks your wound playbook has worked since the last time we met over 2 or 3 weeks ago.

Your rating will be somewhere between 0% and 100%. [Point to scale] 0% means that you think that the playbook is not working at all and 100% means that it is working great 100% of the time.

Starting with the kids first, I will go around the room and ask each of you for the first score that comes to mind. I will then write your first name directly over the percentage number you select.

After everyone gives their overall score, I will circle back around, starting with the kids again first, and ask this question: If we can improve how your playbook works by just 10%, what do you or others need to do to make this happen?

Then I will this second question: What is happening now to account for the fact that the number you gave is not lower?

This information is important because it helps tell us where we go from here or our next steps.

(If any previous safety issues from Phase II were identified, ask this question: "And when we are done, just to be on the safe side, I want to check in with the safety issues we identified earlier [list them]. I want to make sure they are still at a 3.5 or above on a scale of 1 to 5, with 1 meaning not safe at all and 5 meaning very safe right now.")

As with the stress chart, it is important to ask the child or adolescent first. Otherwise, their answers will tend to be skewed by the parents or other adults in the room. If there were safety issues previously identified and addressed with a playbook, it is important to separately use the same scale but to just focus on the overall success of this plan. It would confuse the family to try to use the same scale for both playbooks at the same time. If safety issues have again destabilized, please see Step 3 in the following for more information. Further safety planning may be needed prior to recommending graduation.

After the overall stress level answer is obtained, the two follow-up questions (i.e., "What can raise the percentage by 10%?" and "What is happening now that is positive to prevent that number from being lower?") are important. They provide both the therapist and family with a road map of built-in next steps to improve the wound playbook.

Case Example

Turning back to Tom's case from Chapter 11, everyone (uncles, Mom, and grandparents), except for Tom, chose an overall rating of 80% or above (Box 13.2). Tom chose a rating of 60%.

BOX 13.2 FST Rating Scale of Wound Playbook Effectiveness for Tom and his Family

						Tom		Uncles & Mom	Grandparents	
						X		X	X	
0%	10%	20%	30%	40%	50%	60%	70%	80%	90%	100%

(continued)

Case Example (*continued*)

This kind of discrepancy rating between the child and the adults can be normal. If it happens, a common underlying reason has to do with hierarchy. The traumatized child can receive a secondary gain from the wound. In Tom's case, before the playbook, the adults walked on "eggshells" based on a worldview that he was fragile. As a result, Tom had unlimited freedom. He stayed up as late as he wanted (even on school nights) and played video games all the time. He even had a bell in his room to ring when he wanted his food brought up to him on a tray.

However, after the playbook and the role-plays and enactments were conducted, the adults had a new worldview that Tom was normal, but stuck in a rut. Consequently, they set limits and stuck by them. For example, they refused to let Tom hide out in his room for days. He now had a regular bedtime with lights out and no electronics. And Tom was expected to be present at the table for dinner. Tom, of course, did not like these sudden changes to his lifestyle. In time, this initial negative attitude will likely go away. Children want structure and consistency but it usually takes a minimum of 30 days to kick in or longer for a child to see the benefits of consistency and thereby adopt a more positive attitude.

In addition, to put things in context, since the wound playbook was first initiated, the time between Phase IV and Phase V was only 2 to 3 weeks. Therefore, when there is a discrepancy, the FST therapist must be quick to normalize this point by connecting the dots to an initial disruption in the child or adolescent's lifestyle. Otherwise, the risk is high that adult anxiety and stress levels will escalate. The parents want their child to like the playbook as they do. And if they do not, the parent may think that the treatment must not be working.

In summary, when the child or adolescent views the playbook in a much more negative light than everyone else, the therapist will want to examine possible secondary gain and not panic (along with the family). The playbook is often working even if the child does not like the chain reaction changes in lifestyle.

Therefore, after discovering the discrepancy between Tom and the rest of the family, the FST therapist stated the following, to quickly normalize these differences:

> Before we go on, let me pause here. As you can see from the chart, there is a pretty big difference between how the adults in this family see the playbook working at 80% [point to chart] efficiency or higher and how Tom sees it working at only 60%. Let me start with you, Mom. Any guesses as to why?"

> Mom: No idea, except that for Tom it is not working and maybe we need to change things around? [Grandmother is shaking her head, yes].

> Tom: Yeah, I agree.

> Before we jump the gun, let me ask Tom a question. Tom, has it been hard on you to get back to the routines of eating dinner with the family, bedtimes with lights out and no electronics, and not being allowed play video games in your room whenever you want and for as long as you want?

> Tom: "Yes, it sucks big time."

(continued)

Case Example (*continued*)

Everyone, this is normal. Tom is going through normal withdrawal. Look, it has only been a few weeks since we started the playbook. And Tom and the rest of you are still working through your grief muscles. They are still sore and out of practice. Remember, Tom had a certain routine and lifestyle for almost 2 years since the sudden death of his dad. So even though this new lifestyle will be better in the long run, in the short term it is a shock to your system and you will go through normal withdrawal. For example, I love a new pair of shoes until I get blisters. But I keep wearing them because I know that it's going to take time to break them in. In the meantime, I miss those old shoes. Does this make sense to you, Tom? And to the rest of you?

Tom: [begrudgingly] Yes, but I don't have to like it.

Tom, you hit the nail on the head. You are perfectly within your right to be grumpy right now about these new shoes. I wouldn't like the blisters either. But the good news is . . . this too shall pass. Give it about 30 days and then reassess the playbook with Tom. In the meantime, don't do any major changes to the playbook. In summary, under the circumstances, Tom's answer of 60% is normal and to be expected.

After this exchange, the follow-up questions generated interesting answers (i.e., *"What needs to happen in the future to take the percentage up 10%, from 80% to 90% for the uncles and Mom, or higher (grandparents) or from 60% to 70% for Tom? and what is happening now as to why your current ratings are not lower?"*).
Some of the answers included:

- Grandmother: "Based on what you just said Dr. Sells, a 10% raise for me would indicate I am no longer giving into my fears. As you remember from last session, I was the biggest one to worry that if we pushed Tom too hard, he might get suicidal again. It's my biggest fear, and I find myself drifting back to those 'walking on eggshells' days. Just the other day, I said to Tom's mom, 'Let Tom stay up and play videos, so he won't get mad or upset at us.' I yelled at her in fact. I need to stop doing that and let nature take its course, as you say."
- Grandfather: "For me, the 10% improvement would be me being nicer to my wife. I was the one as you recall who said we need to stop babying Tommy. And now I can see today that this is hard for my wife. I need to just be more encouraging to her and tell her she is doing a good job."

Dr. Sells stopped the session and redirected it to a short enactment after grandfather's statement. He said, "Mike (grandfather), will you hold your wife's lovely hand and tell her how proud you are of her and how sorry you are for being a little tough on her. That until now, you just didn't connect the dots." The grandmother immediately starts to cry. Mike does this well.

Dr. Sells then stated, "Lily (grandmother), you can't change the past but we can change the future. So given that truth, Mike, can you turn to your beautiful bride and ask, Lily, what can I do or say in the future to say, 'We are in this together and I am here to support you'" [Mike does this].

(continued)

Case Example (*continued*)

Lily: *"You can say that I support you every night right after the lights go off in bed."*

Dr. Sells: *"Can he hold you tightly and snuggly in his arms as he says it?"*

Lily: [Crying] *"I would like that. This whole thing with our daughter and Tom has really pulled us apart."*

The enactment is now dangerously moving into marital therapy and that is not the goal of this session. Therefore, Dr. Sells does not take this bunny trail. Instead, he quickly redirects, using the stick and move technique, to move back to the 10% question.

This enactment highlights that trauma is systemic within the entire family. Through Tom's healing, others in the family are healed as well. This enactment may also set in motion Lily and Mike calling the therapist, Dr. Sells, over the phone to initiate couple counseling because of the trust and joining that occurred through the child's therapy work. They begin to see the problem systematically on their own, without the jargon. If this happens, separate marital therapy sessions can occur, but only after the first priority of getting the child on track takes place.

- Tom: *"To go from 60% to 70% I have to first get used to these blisters. And I think I will get to 90% after the memorial ceremony takes place 2 weeks from now. I'd be lying if I did not tell you I am nervous about seeing the parents of the kid that killed my dad. But they have been super nice to me this whole time and I am glad we contacted them. It's helping more than I thought it would."*

When Tom says, *"It's helping me more than I thought it would"* the temptation is high for the FST therapist to stop the session and say to Tom, "tell me more." However, the timing is not right here. Dr. Sells can put this statement in the back of his head and pull it out later. He can even see Tom for a later individual session. In addition, an enactment was just completed with Tom's grandparents, and another one with Tom right afterward would be overload.

- Both uncles: *"I agree with Tom. The memorial ceremony will definitely bump us up to 100% because it is this playbook* [they hold up their laminated copy] *that was the thing that got us from A to B and all the way to Z."*

Dr. Sells, the FST therapist, then switched gears. Due to time constraints, he did not ask the uncles or Mom the question, "What is happening now as to why your rating of 80% is not lower like 70% or 60% . . . ?" Instead, the therapist just had to select one or two family members whom he thought would give a great answer or had become like a cotherapist in previous sessions. That person was the grandfather.

Mike, what would you point to as the major reasons why your rating of 90% is not lower, like 80% or even 70%? In other words, what are you doing right to get to that 90%?

(continued)

Case Example (*continued*)

Mike: *Three words, 'Staying the course.' It's not easy. I know we are here for Tom, but the memorial stuff is bringing up sadness about my son that I tried to bury. A couple of nights ago I told everyone that I needed to get something at the store. But honestly, I just pulled over on a side street and cried my guts out?*

Did you feel better?

Mike: *A lot better, but it's still hard.*

Mike I so appreciate your courage. By a quick show of hands, who feels like Mike at times [everyone's hands go up]? This is normal because as we asked Tom to open up, you are now opening up. This is normal. You may not know it, but you have permission to open up in front of everyone and not hide your pain in some back alley. You can ask Tom, but I bet he would say it would help him to not feel like the only one grieving if you feel safe enough to grieve out in the open and not behind closed doors like Tom did for two straight years. Tom, would you agree?

Tom: *Yes.*

And Mike, you just gave me a great idea, thank you. After we get Tom going and after the memorial ceremony, I am going to give you a referral to a local adult grief group. Mike, you and the rest of the adults in this room might want to check it out to see if it helps. You don't have to commit yet, but can I pursue it and get back to you, if you think you might be interested?

The adults: *Yes, we are interested in this option.*

Again, Dr. Sells, the FST therapist, had to make a quick decision in real time. Does he go down the road of further exploration with Mike after the bombshell he just revealed, move on, or somewhere in between? Dr. Sells, choose the latter. The scaling is solution-focused and is designed to act as a catalyst to generate solutions from the client's own perspective.

Therefore, Dr. Sells chose to normalize and then make the connection that the central overall undercurrent of grief resolution for Tom also meant grief resolution for the entire family. In addition, as stated in Chapter 1, good to great trauma treatment can be both/and, not either or. In other words, FST treatment can be a great on-ramp to a referral for individual or group trauma-informed counseling and vice versa. In this case, "the somewhere in between" was to use the FST treatment as an on-ramp to follow-up with group grief counseling for the grandfather and possibly other adults in the family. Dr. Sells also closely watched the grandfather's body language and other nonverbals to confirm that he was on track.

STEP 2: MINI-SCALES TO CONSOLIDATE HEALTHY UNDERCURRENTS

The next step in Phase V uses a tool developed for the FST model called mini-scales to spotlight the effectiveness of healthy undercurrents for that particular family. The FST therapist will draw the mini-scales in real time on a blank flip chart or a white board. The scales go from 1 to 5 (1 = no improvement in the healthy undercurrent; 5 = a lot of improvement).

The mini-scales of 1 to 5 will be used to document two different time periods, **before** FST treatment started and **after** FST treatment, that is, at the present. This **before** versus **after** context is not done with the intent of saying, "look how great FST treatment is!" Instead, it is done to serve as an anchor point to help family members see how far they have come in a relatively short time. In turn, the hope is that this will help the family take credit and pride for any key undercurrent changes and keep them going long after treatment ends. The following transition statement is recommended to introduce Step 2:

> Thank you for giving me your opinions of how well your wound playbook is working and concrete suggestions to make it work better in the future.
>
> I now want to take things a step further and take about the next 20 to 30 minutes to ask you a question around what we call mini-scales. These will be used to see how much progress we have made with each of the healthy undercurrents we targeted to help your child. So here is the question:
>
> On a scale of 1 to 5 with 1 meaning little to no improvement in_____(insert healthy under-current) before we started counseling to 5 meaning 100% positive change since counseling, where do you think you started and where are you today?
>
> Let me write out each one of your healthy undercurrents in a table format (see example in Table 13.1) and we can get your ratings one at a time. Because of time constraints, I will not be able to ask everyone. I will pick out one or two of you to answer. If I don't pick you and you want to add something, please feel free to jump in.
>
> After you answer, I will ask you, How do you account for this improvement? or What has been happening in your family to account for this improvement?
>
> Remember, these healthy undercurrents are important to look at. If we heal them, it will help heal your child's wounds long after counseling ends.

The sample in Table 13.1 illustrates how to write out these undercurrents and rate them. For example, if the family in question had the target healthy undercurrent of forgiveness within the unhealed wound seed, "accountability" around the mental or physical impairment seed, and "attachment" around the unmet primal needs seed, "before FST" and "after FST mini-scales" might look like the sample in Table 13.1.

TABLE 13.1 Sample FST Mini-Scales to Consolidate Healthy Undercurrents

Healthy Undercurrent	Before FST	After FST (Now)
Forgiveness	2 out of 5	4 out of 5
Accountability	1 out of 5	4 out of 5
Attachment	1 out of 5	3.5 out of 5

Why Are the Mini Scales Empowering?

As this example illustrates, the mini scales not only instill confidence, but also *consolidate* healthy undercurrent gains. For example, if a family member self-reports a change from a 1 on attachment to a 3.5, the follow-up question is "How do you account for this change/improvement?" This follow-up solution-focused question forces the family to openly state all the concrete changes they personally have made and/or the family has made as a whole. As a result, a family member might state something like:

> We went from a 1 to a 3.5 because we saw our playbook working. In other words, when I actually start hugging my child every day unconditionally for 2 weeks straight, I could actually feel his muscles loosen and press into me just like the playbook predicted. And then we just began to get so much closer. Without the jump-start and clear step-by-step instructions from the wound playbook, we would have remained frozen in time.

The preceding example statement illustrates consolidation in action. The family verbally states the improvement for everyone to hear. And in turn, the family members can say to themselves, "Yes, I did this." In turn, this ownership can evoke second-order change as the parent continues "hugging" as the new normal long after counseling ends. In essence the mini-scales can help a metaphoric "cauterization" take place.

By definition, cauterization takes place when a heated instrument (the healthy undercurrents within the playbook) stops the bleeding (lack of attachment), so the wound can heal. Words have power. Therefore, when a family member uses the mini-scale as an on-ramp to verbally state how he or she, or another family member, personally mastered the unhealthy undercurrent, it is life-changing to both of them and to others witnessing the change.

Finally, this kind of mini-scale solution talk is contagious and fun for the entire family. Once one family member gets excited, it ripples out to other family members who suddenly "jump on the bandwagon." They join in with their own excitement and stories as to what they have contributed. In turn, this process frees up the child to jump in and take credit for what he or she has done. Once again, the pressure is now off the child as the only one who needed to be fixed. The child is relieved when he or she sees how other family members are now openly stating what they did personally to change themselves for the benefit of everyone, including the child.

Case Example

In Tom's family, the FST therapist wanted to generate enthusiasm; so to begin this process, he changed the cadence in his voice to one of excitement. He also jumped out of his seat with joy and enthusiasm. To begin Step 2, the therapist wrote on the giant flip chart page a **before** and **after** table with the top two healthy undercurrents for Tom's family (Table 13.2).

TABLE 13.2 FST Mini-Scales for Tom's Family to Consolidate Healthy Undercurrents

Healthy Undercurrent	Before FST	After FST (Now)
Forgiveness		
Grief healing (Resolution)	0 out of 5	5 out of 5 (according to Micah [uncle])

(continued)

Case Example (*continued*)

There were of course additional auxiliary undercurrents (i.e., restoring balance, accountability, and safety), but forgiveness and grief resolution were the two core ones. After the table was written, the therapist intentionally picked the family member who would most likely continue with the enthusiasm started by the therapist with the goal of igniting others. The therapist closely examined each family member's body language as this tool was introduced and looked for the person with the most enthusiasm. One of the uncles (Micah) was literally jumping out of his chair with joy, so the therapist chose him first.

Therapist:	Micah, you look like you are about to jump out of your chair with excitement. So let's go to you first. Before FST, how would you rate your family's ability to forgive? Forgiveness toward the teenager, Bill, who killed your brother Rob and even forgiveness toward Bill's parents and grandparents. This is both for you and for Tom. And then I will ask how has that number improved after FST or since coming here? On a scale of 1 to 5. With 1 meaning there is no improvement in forgiveness to 5, which indicates a lot of improvement.
Micah (uncle):	If it's okay, can I take the grief category first?
Therapist:	Go for it!
Micah:	I am just busting with pride in Tom and his mom. They were all alone. We didn't have the slightest idea on what to do. Tom went to a counselor for his depression and the hospital for almost killing himself. But never ever were we invited to these meetings. And I just felt in here [pounds his heart] that we needed to go old school. My sister and Tom needed us. And then you actually called and personally invited us. All this to say, before you called and we got help [before FST] we were at a 0, not even on the board, and now I feel we are at a 5.
Therapist:	How do you account for this huge jump?
Micah:	Like I said, us coming together with a clear plan for what everyone is supposed to do. We are all rowing together. Like when me, my brother, and my dad did not allow Tom to go hide in his room again and be alone with his thoughts. Then, with my sister and mom coming together to get pictures for Rob. And then putting the memorial together. All of it.
Therapist:	[Mini enactment] Can you turn to your sister and Tom and tell them how proud you are?
Micah:	[Starts weeping] I can't…too choked up.
Therapist:	We will wait for you. You can cry here, it's safe. You do not have to pretend to go to the store for food like your dad said earlier today and cry alone in the car. Your tears are your prayers, for you, Micah, and your family. The Jewish culture in the Old Testament has a tradition. They cry their tears in a bottle to save them for all to see. Their tears are their prayers.

(*continued*)

Case Example (*continued*)

(Three minutes go by and everyone is still in the room as Micah sobs and everyone else starts to weep as well.)

Therapist:	Help him, Tom and Mary, sit close to him.
Tom:	[Hugs Micah as Mary scoots closer] Micah, it is okay. I know you said that I am not alone now, but neither are you buddy.
Micah:	I miss him too. And Tom, I have to thank you. Because without you, we wouldn't be here. When I was building the memorial to help you, it was actually helping me too. Your courage became my courage. For the first time, I can sleep without sleeping medicine. Thank you, buddy and thank you sis. You know you how much I look up to you.
Mom:	No.
Micah:	Well, now you know.

In this interaction, we can see the inherent strength of the FST model and more importantly the power and resiliency of families. The enactments just flows from the techniques to create a clear on-ramp for the family to metaphorically wrap their arms around the wounded child but at the same time heal themselves. With great pain, comes great opportunity for deep healing. And healing for the therapist as well. Would the reader be surprised to know that as the first author revisits this family he is weeping right at this moment as he writes these very words. But they are tears of joy because I, Scott Sells, had the privilege of being used as Mother Theresa wrote, "A pencil in God's hands." We, as authors, look forward to future stories from the readers of this book who will experience the same life-changing pencil impact.

After this enactment, the family and the therapist had to take a breather. The FST therapist modulated these intense emotions by asking the grandfather to give his opinion on the forgiveness undercurrent. This helped bring the emotional intensity back down to a workable level. And more importantly, the FST therapist did not have to ask everyone their opinions. The point was made. The family "had what it takes" to accomplish the healthy undercurrents and keep the healthy undercurrent fire burning, long after treatment ended.

STEP 3: REVIEW DECISION TREE FOR NEXT STEPS

As stated earlier, the combination of Steps 1 and 2 provide the data needed to recommend the best option for the particular child and family. The FST therapist provides each family member with a copy of the decision tree handout. The following transition statement is used to introduce Step 3:

After looking at your progress on both your overall rating scale [point to it] and your mini-scales [point to them] we are now in a great position to take this information to help us decide Where do we go from here? or What are our next steps?

To help with this decision, let me hand out what we call a decision tree with five possible options listed. I will read off each option slowly. As I read each one, privately for now, pick your top choice. Don't shout it out just yet. After I finish reading off each one, I will go around the room starting with the adults, to see what option they voted for and why? I will write your name and vote on a blank flip chart page. Then I will ask the kids for their vote.

[Usually, the therapist goes to the child first. But when there are important family decisions as a whole, hierarchy must be respected. In this case, the parent or caregiver is the pack leader (even if in reality the child still is) and must, therefore, be given the first voice.]

Finally, I will give you my vote with my reasons. And then we all have to reach agreement and pick one option together. Ok let's get started.

Please copy Table 12.1 (*Handout of the Decision Tree Checklist: Five Different Options*; Chapter 12) and provide a copy to each family member.

This step combines three central principles: (a) three rules of thumb (and exceptions) that indicate the family is ready for: Option A: graduation and red flags checklist; (b) the final battle for structure if disagreement ensures between therapist and family over which graduation option to select; and (c) if the family still decides to terminate treatment against therapist recommendations, how can it still be a potential positive outcome.

Three Rules of Thumb to Indicate Option A: Graduation and Red Flags Checklist

The following is a quick summary of three rules of thumb to look for (and exceptions to the rule) that indicate the child and family are ready for graduation from FST:

1. Seventy Percent or Higher Overall Rating: This average overall indicates that the family may be ready for graduation even if the child or adolescent has a lower rating. This is the case if there is clear evidence that the child's negative rating or attitude is correlated with a realignment of hierarchy. The family should also present compelling evidence to support their rating, and the FST therapist should agree with the evidence presented.

    Exceptions: (a) The family provides an overall 70% rating but cannot support their rating and the FST therapist concurs that this percentage is inflated based on the evidence; (b) There is stark disagreement between family members (i.e., one parent has a 75% rating and the other parent a 50% rating); (c) The FST therapist is convinced based on evidence that the family is not ready even though the family say they are; and (d) The therapist knows that there is still a juggernaut undercurrent (i.e., family secret)or problem (sexual abuse) not addressed.

2. There are no Active Safety Factors in Play: In Phase II, a safety assessment was conducted using a scale of 1 to 5 (1 = high risk and 5 = no risk). If the safety risk is still at a **3** or higher, the FST therapist has an obligation to recommend Option D: additional safety work needed. In the short term, it is normal for the playbook to act as a systems irritant and create high intensity. In turn, this high intensity may activate safety stressors. This is normal. Therefore, the therapist must watch for this cause-and-effect relationship and then normalize this direct connection with the family.

    Exceptions: (a) The FST therapist is actively working with another agency or therapist (i.e., family preservation) who is responsible for addressing the safety issues. This agency and/or therapist states that the wraparound support, therapy, and/or monitoring is sufficiently in place so that FST graduation is possible; (b) The FST therapist sees clear evidence that the family is on the cusp of stabilizing and is willing to continue to be in weekly contact with the family using red flags checklist guidelines, which includes an immediate tune-up should any safety red flag on the checklist emerge.

3. Mini-scales Indicate Positive and Forward Progress: There does not have to be significant number shifts. One is looking for at least a one- or two-point overall shift forward on each undercurrent.

    Exceptions: (a) The family is underinflating their true numbers. Occasionally, family members may be so humble or even unaware of how truly far they have come. If this happens, the therapist must jump in with multiple concrete examples to support a reality of higher ratings; (b) There is forward movement, albeit small. Some families developmentally and based on the particular wound playbook are only expected to make small changes (see the 10% rule outlined at the end of Phase IV). Small changes are where certain families are expected to be at this point in therapy. Therefore, with a good red flags checklist and careful monitoring with callbacks and tune-ups, a family's therapy that requires only small changes is ready to graduate.

The Battle for Structure

Within any of the three rules of thumb listed earlier, the FST therapist must be prepared for a final battle for structure. Even with all the evidence, the family consensus might differ from the therapist's recommendation. This disagreement does not happen frequently, but when it does, the therapist must be ready to fight for their position. At the last stage of FST treatment, winning this battle for structure is critically important. The implications are that if the FST therapist loses the fight here, termination or graduation will be messy and ineffective. For example, what happens if the therapist sees that the family desperately needs more role-play practice or further refinement of the playbook (Option B), but the parents are ready for graduation (Option A). If the family wins the battle, they will likely relapse, even with the help of a red flags checklist. In turn, the parents may mistakenly either blame the therapist or see the treatment model as flawed when they simply needed additional dress rehearsals.

When Termination against Therapist's Recommendation Can Be Therapeutic

A final core principle is what to do if the family decides **Option E: terminate against therapist's recommendation**. If this happens, please understand that some families have to fail before they are ready for change. The key is allowing that family to both "save face" and keep their pride intact.

To make these two keys happen, the FST therapist must "respectfully" predict the fallout of picking the wrong option. Respectfully means taking a one down position with specific predictions (not generalized). The clear message is that if these future predictions transpire, the therapist will never say, "I told you so," but instead will just move forward. For example, the therapist might state something like:

> "When we did the role-play on how to apologize, I, playing your teen, was able to easily push your buttons and get you off track, even after we did three different takes. The apology, as you know, is the bread and butter of your wound playbook. It is like a house of cards. If the apology fails, the rest of the cards in the playbook fall. Therefore, I predict that if we graduate too early, the apology will not work, your teen will be more resentful than ever before, and you will get tired of trying and give up. Then your teen is likely to go back to cutting on himself again and start have other problems."

When therapists are this specific in their predictions and they come true, they are seen as more of an expert. But they must be an expert in humility. The therapist must tell the family that "at the end of the day" it is not a matter of who is right or who is wrong. Instead, it is about working together as a team to help the child overcome his or her trauma or wounds.

In addition, the therapist should point out the fact that it is normal to have differences of opinion and to try out different options. It is not always a straight line from point A to B. The therapist can quote J. R. R. Tolkien (2012) in his book *The Fellowship of the Ring*: "not all who wander are lost."

The only request is if the family returns to treatment, they will agree to try the therapist's recommendation the second time around. Otherwise, therapy will continue to be more of the same. This last condition must be stated as a must-have to return to FST treatment.

Case Example

Returning back to Tonya's case in Chapter 12, the following outcome took place when they came to Phase V. The FST therapist anticipated that the breakthrough momentum from the home visit 2 weeks earlier would carry over into this session. In fact, during his pre-session preparation, he reviewed his private notes on the decision tree checklist, which stated:

> *Option B:* **Tweak the current wound playbook:** *If your wound playbook is not working at a 70% or higher effectiveness (e.g., need more practice role-plays/dress rehearsals, need more clarification, need to include key missing extended family members) a predetermined number of additional sessions is negotiated with your therapist to work through any identified barriers.*
>
> *This is the option I recommend. Because of the home visit experiment both parents are now in the "contemplative" stage of readiness. The next stage of readiness is preparation and then action. Therefore, even though we have already done our preparation (we have a typed-up contract and did Phase IV role-plays in our last session) and are now in the "action" stage of readiness (Saturday, both parents actually implemented the disrespect contract with me present) we need to circle back around and continue with additional preparation and more dress rehearsals. This means that although we have a written contract we need more Phase IV role-plays but this time with "both parents in the same room" but still without Tonya present until there is proven competency. This is a huge structural shift. If successful, it will be the breakthrough needed to finally get to the promised land of Tonya's unhealed wounds: Bitterness and unforgiveness between both parents.*

Unfortunately, however, only the mother came to the session. The first four words out of her mouth said it all:

> I am so done!
>
> I told you if I tried your way it wouldn't work and I was right. You got my hopes up and now I am even more crushed. In fact, my individual therapist agrees. I was never strong enough emotionally to handle this kind of pressure.

(continued)

Case Example (*continued*)

You actually created a monster with my ex. After our last meeting, I asked him to watch Tonya because I had a date Friday night and told him he was late with his child support. He just exploded. And then Mike said that he saw firsthand that I did not have it in me to stick to the contract. Then over the weekend, Tonya told him 'Mom can't follow through, and this contract is BS.' And then Mike told my daughter that he agreed with her and . . . .

There was more to follow, but the reader can fill in the rest. Therapy ended in failure. However, we learn from our failures. Therefore, what can we learn from this treatment failure? And how will this treatment failure connect back with the decision tree choices that the FST therapist recommended to this family? Newton's third law of motion states: "For every action, there is an equal and opposite reaction."

Translation: When the therapist recommends a playbook or implementation at the end of Phase IV, it is important to think two steps ahead. In other words, how will this decision impact the decision tree options in Phase V? For example, in the therapist's private notes given earlier, he defended his decision to go forward with the playbook because it would likely cause a positive outcome. However, within his notes under "Option E to Terminate Against Therapist's Recommendation," the therapist also considered the "equal and opposite" risk of the cease-fire not holding for 2 weeks.

*Option E: **terminate against therapist's recommendation***

The hope is that this will not take place. The cease-fire, however, just like between two countries at war, is always tenuous and could breakdown at any time almost for any reason. The key is that the cease-fire last long enough for some trust to be built and for the wet cement to dry.

In the end, Option E occurred. As a result, here are two questions to ponder:

1. What tactical mistakes did the FST therapist make? It is not a helpful framework to write off termination because family members are "resistant" or "unmotivated." This is the easy way out and releases the therapist from examining his or her part in the failure. And without self-examination, we do not learn and grow. Worse yet, we will likely repeat the same mistakes with another client. Therefore, a better definition for resistance is:
   Resistance is the best way a client has to tell us that what we are doing is not working.
2. What part of the FST model itself failed, and what knowledge and insight can we apply to future cases?

Key identifying information has been changed to protect confidentiality (all the case examples in this book follow this protocol). But with full disclosure this was the first author's (Dr. Sells') case.

Therefore, in summary, here are the mistakes I made. There may be more, but these are the highlights.

(*continued*)

Case Example (*continued*)

POSSIBLE TACTICAL MISTAKES

☑ *Batten Down the Hatches Before Sailing to Sea:* Looking back, I failed to communicate fully and clearly with the mom's personal therapist. I should have had a session with Mom and her therapist before it was decided to do the home intervention with the playbook. Mom had been emotionally abused by her ex-husband for years. Therefore, the cease-fire would be tenuous at best and there needed to be both informed consent and clear troubleshooting of "what will you do if scenarios" around the cease-fire.

  • During the session with Mom and her therapist, Dr. Sells could have posed the question, "Does anyone have a better idea?" and reexamine the treatment failures up to this point in time. From this question, all three parties could have better looked at all the possible options and their implications. At that time, the playbook intervention could also have been more clearly linked to the framework of parental alienation syndrome (PAS) for both Mom and her therapist as solid rationale for Dr. Sells' recommendation.

  • Finally, if no better idea emerged, Dr. Sells could have posed the question, "If we go forward with the home intervention, what can Mom and her therapist do in the interim to prepare for any possible fallout?" What will you do if scenarios needed to be discussed at length. Bottom line, without the mom's therapist preapproval, the playbook should not have been implemented.

☑ *Triangulation = Strangulation:* Closely related to the aforementioned tactical error are the problems inherent with triangulation. Just like a three-legged stool, when two people have instability, one or both will try to form a coalition with a third party to be that third leg on the stool. Dr. Sells did not fully take into account the implications of triangulation. Without the preapproval and blessing of the mom's therapist, the mom could easily triangulate her therapist against Dr. Sells. The daughter, Tonya, could also skillfully triangulate her father against both Mom and Dr. Sells. And the father could skillfully triangulate both Dr. Sells and the playbook against the mother. In effect, all of these triangulations took place within the space of 1 week.

☑ *Mom Without Dad:* It would have been extremely challenging, but Dr. Sells could have tried to get stabilization around disrespect and school refusal without Dad. An alternative method would be to access Mom's church community to look for the support she needed. And the village family meeting could have included Mom's therapist. Dad would still be the X-Factor in the background but possibly Dr. Sells could have neutralized Dad through more individual sessions to still get a cease-fire. And he could have tried to recruit a guy friend in Dad's circle to come to a session and help as a co-therapist. In turn, if Mom had a victory over her daughter's disrespect, her trust and confidence in both the therapy model and the therapist would increase. From this position of momentum and success, the intervention with Mom and Dad could be reexamined.

(*continued*)

Case Example (*continued*)

POSSIBLE FST MODEL FAILURES

☑ *Misapplication:* Within this book, there is solid rationale for quick victories with low-hanging fruit to build momentum **and** prior behavioral stabilization before direct trauma or wound work. In hindsight, Dr. Sells did not adhere to this key principle closely enough. Dr. Sells locked into a PAS mindset without greater consideration of stability and safety first. The mother and father were not stable enough for a cease-fire attempt even after the successful home visit. It was still too new and too fresh and too shaky. In addition, safety was not addressed adequately enough or at all with Mom's therapist. Because of these factors, Dr. Sells should have tried behavioral stabilization with Mom and her village first, and not as an afterthought. In addition, for this particular family, there was not enough trust built between Mom and Dr. Sells for such a high risk, high reward intervention.

A treatment model is only as good as the person using it. In this case, there was a misapplication of the model because of the person using it.

The good news or the silver lining is that Dr. Sells learned a lot from this treatment failure. It led to a much more refined safety approach within the FST model using the steps and techniques of self-regulation strategies, safety risk assessments using a 1 to 5 rating scale, nutritional analysis, better-informed consent, a better role-play framework with better timing, and enhanced rules of thumb of when to start small with quick undercurrent victories before tackling more challenging ones.

In addition, we also owe Dr. Figley (2009) a debt of gratitude. He was one of the first and only traumatology experts to put together six recommended core criteria or ingredients for any psychotherapy model used for traumatized families. We outlined these in Chapter 1, but it is worth repeating here:

At the very minimum, trauma-informed therapy would include (a) the establishment of safety, (b) informed consent, (c) titration of exposure-related stress and (d) client self-soothing competence during and between treatment sessions. (p. 180)

During the past 8 years that the FST model has been refined, researched, and used in over 13 states, these six core criteria have served as a lighthouse to keep returning back to when there is treatment failure.

STEP 4: CO-CREATE RED FLAGS CHECKLIST

As stated earlier, regardless of the decision tree option, the FST therapist will distribute a copy of the red flags checklist that was customized for the family during pre-session preparation. In addition, if graduation is not the decision the red flags checklist will still be distributed but without Part IV: first callback date. Part IV will be used only when graduation is the goal. The red flags checklist should be framed to the family as a proactive relapse prevention plan. Because of this fact, the checklist should be reviewed daily, especially within the first 30 days when the risk for relapse is higher.

If the FST therapist is using a flat screen television or LCD projector, they would project the red flags checklist on the screen to go through each part line by line. If no technology interface is used, the therapist should go to a blank flip chart page and handwrite each of the four parts (to save time, this can be written by the FST therapist before the session):

- Part I: Areas of the Wound Playbook Not Followed
- Part II: Areas of Safety
- Part III: Unhealthy Undercurrents or Trauma Symptoms Return
- Part IV: Date for First Call Back (only if graduation or termination)

As with the troubleshooting countermove checklist, going through each part of the working draft red flags checklist will allow the family to help co-create the final version and take ownership of the document. Without the template prepared ahead of time, this process will take too long and move into unproductive brainstorming. The following transition statement is recommended to introduce this step:

> Now that we have decided on next steps or which **option** from the decision tree handout, let's create what we call a red flags checklist together. I took the time before our session today to create a template like I did with your troubleshooting countermoves checklist. As we did with your troubleshooting checklist, this red flags checklist template is a working draft. In a moment, we will tweak it as needed. [Hand out copy of template to everyone.]
>
> As we look at this red flags checklist handout together, I listed potential red flag behaviors that could cause you or your child to relapse. Any relapse will not likely be as bad as before, but if it happens, we still want to address it quickly before it gets out of control like a brush fire. The research shows that your first 30 days puts you at the greatest risks for relapse because your playbook is still brand new.
>
> Therefore, after we create this red flags checklist together, I ask that you tape it to your bathroom mirror right next to your wound or safety playbook to review each morning as you brush your teeth. Will everyone give me a verbal agreement to review this checklist at least once a day to prevent relapse? [Get verbal agreement from each person.]
>
> OK let's begin. I will go through each part, beginning with Part I, line by line and ask everyone to either agree and vote to leave as is, tweak it, or change it. If we disagree, I will try to get a consensus. If not, I would like the final vote as your therapist so we can get the checklist completed in a timely manner. [I reproduced each line on this blank flipchart, or I will type in any changes as we go, using my laptop.]

As with the troubleshooting countermoves checklist, please be ready to use the stick-and-move technique as needed. Certain family members may try to either dominate the session or take the focus down bunny trails. In both cases, the therapist must stand ready to take charge of the session and bring the conversation back to the task at hand.

Tune-Ups Versus a Return to Full Therapy

A key underlying principle of the FST model is "working smarter, not harder." Nowhere is this principle better illustrated than in the integration or pairing of the red flags checklist with the concept of tune-ups. A "tune-up" is defined as a "general adjustment to ensure operation at peak efficiency" (Merriam-Webster, 2015). Therefore, whenever possible, the therapist must communicate to the family that once graduation is set in motion, the goal is not a full reboot or return back to full therapy. Instead, the goal is only the number of sessions needed to get back on track as quickly as possible. The ideal place to introduce the tune-up concept is within the Steps to Take section when there is a step to call the therapist for assistance. When this happens, the FST therapist can use the following transition statement:

> Within your Red Flags Checklist, you will see Steps to Take throughout the checklist. One of the possible steps might be to call me for what we call a tune-up session. A tune-up session is similar to taking your car in for service after the "service engine" light on the dashboard of your car comes on. These lights indicate the need for a tune-up. In the same way, if the red flags go off in your checklist, it is time for you to have a tune-up. A tune-up usually takes just one or two sessions to get back on track quickly. It is NOT, I repeat, not a return to full-blown therapy.
>
> **[Only if graduating]** *In a moment, I will explain how we will use what we call 30-day callbacks to also help us know when a tune-up might be needed. These 30-day callbacks work hand in hand with your checklist.*

The parallel connection between a car dashboard, the red flags checklist, and the concept of tune-ups often resonates extremely well with family members. The family is visibly relieved when they clearly understand the concept and purpose of tune-ups and how it directly connects to the red flags checklist. As a result, the checklist takes on added importance and the family is more prone to call their FST therapist should red flags occur. This is because they understand it is just a tune-up to get back on track, and not a return to full-blown therapy.

Case Example

It was decided in Tom's family to move to Option A or graduation. Tom's lower rating of 60% was explained within the context of his initial and normal reaction to a change in hierarchy and lifestyle. The adults rating of 80% or higher was well-supported. There were no safety issues and there was definitely forward movement on their mini-scales with the targeted healthy undercurrents of forgiveness and grief resolution. Finally, there were no looming juggernaut unhealthy undercurrents or behavioral issues in Tom to stabilize or restabilize. Therefore, based on the preceding information, the FST therapist recommended Option A.

During pre-session preparation, the therapist typed up an initial red flags checklist. He went back to examine Tom's troubleshooting checklist from Phase IV (Chapter 11) to get ideas to put into the red flags checklist. To choose the right curveballs, the therapist asked himself two important questions: (a) "Is the area of concern in the troubleshooting countermove checklist an ongoing issue?" or (b) "Is the curveball in question a major area of concern to trigger a relapse instead of just a minor problem-solving issue?" If the answer is "no" to both questions, there should be no carryover.

After close examination of the who, what, where, when, and how parts of the Stark family troubleshooting checklist (Chapter 11) the following areas were selected for a carryover into the red flags checklist:

(continued)

Case Example (*continued*)

"WHO" CARRYOVER

- Tom drops out or wants to quit and withdraw to his bedroom (curveball): *still an ongoing issue and an area that could trigger full-blown relapse in this family.* (**Needs to Go Under Part I on the Red Flags Checklist.**) Keep first countermove as first step to take but if going to Tom's room with the message to come back out does not work, call therapist as second step instead of going to the second countermove of using the sleeping bags.

- *The other areas of inviting the grandparents of Bill (drunk driver who killed Tom's father) to the memorial ceremony is already resolved successfully (they were invited) and friends of Dad (Nick, Jerry, Stan, and Rick) were invited. <u>Areas resolved=no carryover</u>.*

"WHAT" CARRYOVER

- <u>*Nothing to carry over*</u>. *The area of "What will we do if there is disagreement of the memorial choice?" is a nonissue. The Memorial is finished—just waiting for the day of the Memorial dedication ceremony.*

"WHEN" CARRYOVER

- <u>*Nothing to carry over*</u>. *The troubleshooting issues of forgetting to show up to build the Memorial or Mom's scheduling conflict with church are no longer an issue. The Memorial is built.*

- *Evidence of second-order change through the generalizing of healthy undercurrent steps is already beginning. The task of Mom and Tom putting together the agenda for the ceremony went smoothly on its own. Previous to the playbook, Mom and Tom could not sit in the same room together without open conflict, especially when it came to discussions around Tom's dad. Now, they are both cooperating and there was mutual respect. Most importantly, they can both talk about Rob (Tom's dad) without finger-pointing and blame. This is a concrete example of the healing ripple effect of systems theory on wounds. The FST therapist did not have to directly intervene. This area healed on its own as a by-product of healing in other areas.*

"WHERE" CARRYOVER

- <u>*Nothing to carry over*</u>. *issue of landowner already decided*

(continued)

Case Example (*continued*)

"HOW" CARRYOVER

- These three key issues still remained as possible future relapse risks:

  ☐ Tom is hit with a flood of emotions. This would not occur over building the Memorial (already built) but it could occur after the dedication ceremony coming up in 2 weeks and beyond. *Still an ongoing issue and an area that could trigger full-blown relapse in this family.* **Needs to Go Under Part I:** Keep countermoves of **reflective listening and self-regulation strategies** as is but need to add more emphasis on a tune-up if Tom starts to regress rapidly.

  ☐ "What if other family members shut down?" This is showing up with Mike (grandfather) feeling the need to pull over into a back alley and secretly weep. **Needs to Go Under Part III** as both a trauma symptom and example of unresolved grief. No countermove listed in the checklist, so will carry over what was mentioned about a referral to a grief group.

  ☐ There is still risk to drift back to a worldview that Tom is frail, fragile, and incapable of grieving properly. This is not a major risk because things are going so well presently but could be one again if Tom starts to relapse. **Needs to Go Under Part III** as an example of helpful or unhelpful worldviews around unresolved grief. No countermoves in checklist, so have to be written for the first time under Steps to Take.

TARGET UNDERCURRENTS

- Undercurrents of forgiveness and unresolved grief are not overtly stated in the troubleshooting checklist.
- Therefore, they must be overtly stated and written into the red flags checklist under Part III.

Based on the answers to these questions, the initial red flags checklist was created and then brought to the Phase V session in the form of a handout. The therapist's laptop was connected to Tom's home television through a *high-definition multimedia interface* (HDMI) cable and the checklist was brought up on the screen. Changes recommended by the family are highlighted in **bold** in the Stark family red flags checklist in Box 13.3.

(continued)

Case Example (*continued*)

BOX 13.3 The Stark Family's Red Flags Checklist

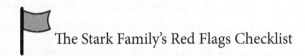

The Stark Family's Red Flags Checklist

Part I: *Areas of the Wound Playbook Not Followed*
- Tom drops out or wants to quit and withdraw to his bedroom
  Steps to take if this happens:
  - ☑ Continue countermove from the troubleshooting countermove checklist with: uncles and grandfather will come over and go into Tom's room and say, "We are here for you buddy and we miss him too. Please, for your dad, yourself, and us, will you come out and not quit?" **Voted to keep as is**
  - ☑ **Add: If the preceding step does not work the first time, call the FST therapist for a tune-up. We do not want to regress in this area.**
- Tom gets hit with a flood of emotions, not over building the memorial because it is already built, rather it is due to the approaching day for the dedication ceremony.
  Steps to take if this happens:
  - ☑ Use the countermove of **reflective listening** and self-regulation techniques. **Voted to keep as is**
  - ☑ But if Tom starts to withdraw again, has insomnia, or shows signs of depression over the course of 2–4 weeks, call the FST therapist to discuss whether a tune-up is needed. **Voted to keep as is**

Part II: *Areas of Safety:* If Tom ever again begins to exhibit one or more of the following safety areas:
- Suicidal thoughts
- Depression
- Chronic insomnia
  Steps to take:
  - ☑ Family meeting with Tom to tell him he is not alone. **Voted to keep as is**
  - ☑ Call FST therapist to check in **and we want a tune-up**

Part III: *Unhealthy Undercurrents or Trauma Symptoms Return*
- Unresolved grief comes back or is still lingering: **Like earlier today as shared by both Mike (grandfather) and Micah (uncle)**
  Steps to take:
  - ☑ **Dr. Sells will locate for the family an adult grief group. The adults (Grandfather, uncles, Grandmother, and Mom) will go to the grief group at least twice and then will reevaluate.**
  - ☑ **Mike will briefly check in with Dr. Sells after two meetings at the grief group to provide an update.**
  - ☑ **If Tom relapses (withdraws, experiences emotional flooding, etc.) we will use our steps outlined in Part 1.**

(continued)

Case Example (*continued*)

BOX 13.3 The Stark Family's Red Flags Checklist (*continued*)

> - Unforgiveness reappears
>   Steps to take:
>   - ☑ After the dedication ceremony, the FST therapist requests a tune-up session with Bill's parents and grandparents to discuss forgiveness. If not for Tom, for them. These parents did not have the benefit of the playbook. Therefore, depending on how the day goes, Mom **(we want Grandfather to do this)**, will you ask them? **Voted yes**
> - Old worldview returns: Tom is frail, incapable, and unable to grieve properly
>   Steps to take:
>   - ☑ If you see them return, Grandfather will call a family meeting with everyone to discuss without finger-pointing. **Voted yes**
>   - ☑ If family meeting does not resolve the issue, will contact FST therapist. **Voted yes**
>
> Part IV: *Date for First Callback:* 30 days from today, December 31 at 5 p.m. We will all get on your free conference call number 000-111-2222 access code 12345#.

The FST therapist subtly put into the red flags checklist under Part III the following: *Unforgiveness reappears*

STEPS TO TAKE

☑ After the dedication ceremony, the FST therapist requested a tune-up session with Bill's parents and grandparents to discuss forgiveness. If not for Tom, then for them. Bill's parents did not have the benefit of the playbook. Therefore, depending on how the day goes, Mom **(we want Grandfather to do this),** will you ask them? **Voted Yes**

The rationale was that this undercurrent still needed to be addressed in the future. However, it was not a must have juggernaut for this particular family (in other families it might be). To push Tom's family on this issue when there was so much to celebrate would be a tactical mistake. Putting it into the checklist was a great way to gently kick the tires or **chum fishing** to see if the family will bite and take ownership of the idea. Again, the idea here is to play the role of **coach** to jump-start the healthy undercurrents and set things into motion in such a way that the family takes credit for the changes and generalizes them on their own.

STEP 5: IF GRADUATION, CALLBACKS AND TUNE-UPS

This last step in the FST model is of great importance. Clients typically do not proactively call the therapist if problems reemerge. If clients do call, it is often only after the problems have raged out of control again. In addition, therapists are often onto new cases and get too busy to check in on their old clients. They may assume a no news is good news mindset or that it is up to the client to call back if they need help. The following transition script is recommended when using Step 5:

> [**If graduating**] Before you leave today, we have one final thing. At the bottom of your red flags checklist [point to it], you with see Date for First Callback. This means that once a month for the next 3 months I will briefly call to check on how things are going. Of course, you are encouraged to call me if you see signs of relapse on your red flags checklist according to the steps we outlined today. But, I will call to check in regardless. I want to do this for three reasons:
>
> 1. You have all worked so hard and it was both an honor and privilege to work with you. Therefore, I want to offer our five star service (said with a smile). I want to check in for the first 3 months to make sure the changes stick and encourage you. It is my way, through actions, not just words, to say thank you for all your hard work.
>
> 2. The research shows that the first 90 days put you at the highest risk for relapse. This is because the playbook is still so new and the cement is still drying. Therefore, if you have some relapses, it's okay. It's normal, so don't worry about it. It is why we have tune-ups.
>
> 3. If I call and things are sliding a bit, we can jump on things quickly to get back on track. It is so much easier to tweak things at the first signs of relapse rather than waiting until after a full-blown crisis.
>
> Do these three reasons make sense, and do you have any questions or comments?
>
> So let's get our calendars out and pick our first callback date and time, approximately 30 days from now.
>
> [Optional: if you have a free conference call number] For that first callback, I have a free conference call number we can use so that everyone can call in wherever you are that day.
>
> On this call, please have your red flags checklist with you, so we can use it as a guide. If you forget, I will have mine. Let's go to Part IV now and handwrite in on your red flags checklist, the date and time for this first call. At the end of this first call, we will set the date and time for the next 30-day callback.

Why Are Callbacks So Important?

It is true. There is an inherent responsibility for the family to be accountable and call if relapse occurs. However, as so often happens, either family members wait too long or get too busy. The FST therapist's callbacks once every 30 days for the next 90 days is an X-Factor. The therapist is the lifeline that can prevent real problems from gaining traction. They also can prevent the undoing of all the foundational work that was accomplished before graduation.

A great saying is that it is "easier to step on a moving train than one at a standstill." In other words, it takes much less time and energy for an FST therapist to get the family back on track when relapse is still in its infancy versus after things have completely unraveled.

The main pushback for therapist to the idea of callbacks is that callbacks are not billable or that it is not their job to callback once they graduate. Research on relapse prevention, especially in the areas of addiction, seems to indicate that the highest window of risk for relapse occurs within the first 90 days after treatment ends, with the very highest risk within the first 30 days (Brandon, Vidrine, & Litvin, 2007; Larimer & Palmer, 1999; Witkiewitz & Marlatt, 2004). Therefore, based on this research and the rationale provided, please reconsider or try the 30-, 60-, and 90-day call-back script in Table 13.3 as a personal experiment. After day 90, it is up to the therapist and family on a case-by-case basis to go further on the callbacks.

TABLE 13.3 Sample Callback Script

Opening Questions
- What has been getting better since we last met?
- How do you account for the fact that these things are better? *[Always begin with the positive]*

Questions Regarding Part I: Playbook
- How often is your child or teenager not following the playbook in each of these areas from your checklist? *[List off one at a time]*
  - Less than 50% of the time? or
  - Over 50% of the time? *[If over 50%, ask what is the specific percentage]*

Questions Regarding Part II: Safety Stressors
- From your list of safety stressors, which safety stressor has occurred and how often? *[List off each safety stressor from their checklist, making sure to ask "when did it occur" and not "did it occur"]*

Questions Regarding Part III: Unhealthy Undercurrents Return
- Go down the list and ask which unhealthy undercurrents have resurfaced
- *[If any answer is "yes"]* What is your hunch as to what is causing it to resurface?

End of Call Wrap-Up Questions
- *[If relapse is indicated]* What has gotten in the way of not calling me for a tune-up or as indicated in your Steps to Take on your red flags checklist?
- *[If tune-up is needed]* Let's go ahead and schedule a tune-up meeting to get everyone back on track and on the same page

Final Statement if Relapse Has Occurred
- You have done so much hard work *(list off examples)* and I want to remind you that relapse is very common. Don't get discouraged because, frankly, I would have been surprised if we did not have at least one relapse. So let's schedule a tune-up session to get back on track as quickly as possible.

As illustrated in the sample callback script (Table 13.3), the callback questions are open-ended, not closed-ended. For example, when the question of "When was the last time your child or teenager did not follow the playbook?" is much different than the closed-ended yes or no question of "Has your child or teenager followed the playbook?" The former will force the parent to give a more accurate and honest answer. The script also helps the FST therapist move beyond the standard "How are things going?" phone call to a specific drilldown of very real relapse possibilities. Tune-ups are also tied to the callback script, especially with the **end of the call wrap-up questions**. The script is a great on-ramp to both normalize relapse and to provide the family a safe and open door for a tune-up if needed.

Case Example

With Tom's family, once the red flags checklist was completed, the FST therapist ended the session with the benefits of using once a month callbacks every 30 days for the next 3 months to prevent relapse. Before the family left, the therapist and family got their calendars out to enter the date and time of the first callback. The therapist asked that prior to the call, the family would have their checklist in front of them because they would be using it during the call to assess progress or the need for a tune-up.

They especially liked the idea for the first callback to be a conference call with everyone using the conference call number. The grandfather stated, "We are all in this together as a family for Tom so why stop now with the callback."

After the family graduated, the following significant follow-up events occurred. First, as predicted, the Memorial ceremony was a great success. The owner of the property allowed for a small marker to be placed on his property, and it was engraved with a plaster case holding pictures of Tom and Dad together, along with other pictures.

It was particularly emotional when Bill's parents openly apologized to Tom and then the entire Stark family. Tom wept and said "thank you." Because of this event, there was no longer a need for a more formal healing therapy session between the two families. The healing of the wound occurred naturally after the wound playbook was set in motion confirming again the resiliency of families and what Viktor Frankl said "suffering ceases to be suffering at the moment it finds a meaning."

The opening day had a huge transformational catalyst impact on Tom. At the 30-day callback with the family, Tom stated that at the Memorial ceremony he found meaning in what happened. Others had suffered just as much (Bill's parents and grandparents) and that he was not alone. He also said that he was finally able to say good-bye to his dad. Tom said it was like a 1,000 pound weight lifted off his shoulders.

The grief, however, that lifted off Tom had not quite lifted off the adults. Mike described it this way,

> As long as Tom had problems, we could focus on him and stuff our pain. But now that he is better and there is no more drama, we now have to deal with our own long buried emotions.

Without being parentified, Tom moved into the role of co-therapist and actually helped his family members navigate their grief (he was now an expert in this area). Additionally, all the adults participated in the group grief counseling the FST therapist had recommended. The follow-up consisted of group grief counseling and a tune-up session with the FST therapist for the adults only.

The mom told the therapist, "Without this callback, there was no way we were going to call you on our issues. Until our call today and your clarification, we had no idea that we could focus on our adult grief for our tune-up. You might have mentioned it before but we did not understand."

This was a critical observation by both Mike and Mom.

If the adults did not heal their own grief, there would be a high risk for Tom to relapse. Children consciously or unconsciously like to protect their parents and will often sacrifice themselves. If Tom saw his mom, uncles, or grandparents start to go downhill emotionally, Tom may have started to become depressed again to help his family distract from their pain.

If the family is not graduating within Option A or terminating against the therapist's recommendations, they are within Options B, C, or D:

Option B: **Tweak the current wound playbook**

Option C: **Pick a new problem and build another playbook**

Option D: **Additional safety or misuse of power issues emerge**

If one of each of these options is the goal, the following question is asked "after" the red flags checklist is presented and completed:

"Now that you have competed your red flags checklist, let's review your decision tree one last time to answer this question before we end therapy today and schedule our next session:

'How many more (1- or 2-hour) sessions do you think we might need to successfully complete the option we picked?' AND

'What will be happening in your family and with your child that will tell you that we met our goals and it is time to end treatment within the option we picked?'

As your therapist, I will give you my opinion first with my reasons and then I would like to hear what you think?"

Therapists and treatment models do not often overtly ask the question with the client, "How will we know when therapy ends?" "In other words, what will be happening in your family and with your child that will tell you we have met our goals and it is time to end treatment"? Families like when their therapist uses Covey's (1990) 7 Habits of Highly Effective People: Habit #2—**start with the end in mind**:"Begin each day, task, or project with a clear vision of your desired direction and destination, and then continue by flexing your proactive muscles to make things happen" (p. 22).

To successfully answer the preceding two questions, the FST therapist must give their answers first. This is because they know the phases of the FST model better than the family. And the therapist will likely have a better idea of what ideal outcomes within Options B, C, and D might look like and the approximate number of sessions it will take. The set of general guidelines in Table 13.4 will serve as a road map. Depending on the family, the FST therapist may want to replicate these guidelines as a handout and pass them out to the family.

TABLE 13.4 Treatment Regime Guidelines for Decision Tree Options B, C, and D

Option B: Tweak the Current Wound Playbook

☑ *Estimated Total Number of Sessions:* one to three 2-hour sessions or three to five 1-hour sessions
  ○ Phase IV: one to two 2-hour sessions (two to four 1-hour sessions): more role-plays and enactments in Phase IV (No need to recreate the troubleshooting countermove checklist. Only need to refine the checklist and/or refine the wound playbook as needed.
  ○ Phase V: (graduation) one 1-hour session (no need to repeat the red flags checklist)

(continued)

TABLE 13.4 Treatment Regime Guidelines for Decision Tree Options B, C, and D (*continued*)

**This option has the least number of total sessions compared to Options C and D. Why? No heavy lifting is needed. No need to go back to Phases II and III to create new safety plans or additional wound playbooks. Phases II and III are skipped and the therapist goes right to Phase IV.

☑ *Phases in the FST Model for the Family to Complete:* Phases IV and V

☑ *Estimated Level of Difficulty:* Between a 2 and a 3 (lowest levels of difficulty on a scale of 1–5). Why? Already have the playbook well developed and only have to focus on better delivery or troubleshooting with minor tweaking of the playbook.

Option C: Pick a New Problem and Build Another Playbook

☑ *Estimated Total Number of Sessions:* three to four 2-hour sessions or six to eight 1-hour sessions

  ○ Repeat pre-session preparation for Phase III

  ○ Phase III: one 2-hour session (two1-hour sessions): repeat all the steps to create a new playbook

  ○ Repeat pre-session preparation for Phase IV (therapist only)

  ○ Phase IV: one to two 2-hour sessions (four 1-hour sessions): need to repeat all the steps and build a new troubleshooting countermove checklist with fresh role plays. BUT DUE TO THE FAMILY'S FAMILIARITY WITH THE PROCESS, THIS WILL TAKE LESS TIME.

  ○ Repeat pre-session preparation for Phase V (therapist only)

  ○ Phase V: (graduation) one 2-hour session (two 1-hour sessions): repeat all steps but again, due to the family's familiarity with the process, this will take less time.

**As stated for Option B, the time for these sessions may be less due to the family's familiarity with the process.

☑ *Phases in the FST Model for the Family to Complete:* Phases III–V

☑ *Estimated Level of Difficulty:* between a 3 and 4 (higher level of difficulty on a scale of 1–5). Why? Usually at this point, the therapist is helping the family co-create a wound playbook on a more challenging problem and set of undercurrents than the first round. And they are likely building this new playbook from scratch.

Option D: Additional Safety or Misuse of Power Issues Emerge

☑ *Estimated Total Number of Sessions:* five to six 2-hour sessions or 10 to 12 1-hour sessions

  ○ Repeat pre-session preparation for Phase II (Not as intense as first time around. The former feedback loops and sample playbook or contract is helpful. Therapist only).

  ○ Phase II: one 1-hour session (two 1-hour sessions): Do not repeat all the steps of Phase II. Only repeat these steps as needed: safety assessment, self-regulation techniques, feedback loops.

  ○ Phase III: one to two 2-hour session (two to four 1-hour sessions; may need more time if you need to build a behavioral contract for misuse of power): Need to repeat all steps and build a new playbook or contract. BIGGEST DIFFERENCE IS IF YOU HAVE TO GO BACK TO BEHAVIORAL STABILIZATION, AND IN THAT CASE WILL NEED A BEHAVIORAL CONTRACT AND NOT A WOUND PLAYBOOK.

  ○ Repeat pre-session preparation for Phase IV.

  ○ Phase IV: two 2-hour sessions (four 1-hour sessions): Need to repeat all steps and build a new troubleshooting countermove checklist with fresh role-plays. BUT DUE TO THE FAMILY'S FAMILIARITY WITH THE PROCESS, THIS WILL TAKE LESS TIME.

  ○ Phase V: (graduation) one 2-hour session (two 1-hour sessions): Repeat all steps but again, due to the family's familiarity with the process, this will take less time.

(*continued*)

TABLE 13.4 Treatment Regime Guidelines for Decision Tree Options B, C, and D *(continued)*

**This option is more complex and difficult due to the need to balance safety with misuse of power issues and choose the right option between playbooks, contracts, or hybrid contracts.

☑ *Phases in the FST Model for the Family to Complete:* Phases II–V

☑ *Estimated Level of Difficulty:* Between a 4 and 5 (highest level of difficulty on a scale of 1–5). Why? This high level of difficulty is because the therapist must contend with complex safety issues and/or the need for behavioral stabilization with an unstable hierarchy.

There is an old saying that states, "It is better to underpromise and overdeliver." Clients often hear what they want to hear, like we all do. Therefore, if one underestimates the time and number of sessions needed, clients will not be happy and may even resent it. As a result, it is important for the therapist to emphasize the word *estimate* and then have the parents repeat back in their own words "that it is an estimate."

Use the Family Systems Trauma (FST) Flowchart

The FST therapist must clarify the different phases with the different goals in each phase. To help with this process, we **highly** recommend that one shows the flowchart of the FST Model to the client (Figure 3.1). The flowchart is literally a road map that will calm the anxiety and stress of the family when they can see the big picture: zoom out, before zooming in.

Finally, after reviewing the guidelines in Table 13.4, there is a risk that one or more family members will say something like, "this is too big a commitment," or "this is too overwhelming." The reply from the therapist is:

Let me reemphasize, the number of total sessions is only an estimate. It might be lower. Let's just begin with the first step. This means you do not have to commit right now to everything we just went over. Just commit to the next session and see how it feels, and we can go one baby step at a time.

This is a critical message. Most people can only commit to one thing at a time to prevent being overwhelmed. And if they like this first step, then they get hooked and want to keep going. If this still does not work, do not take it personal, but move into the "terminate against therapist's recommendation" message outlined earlier in this chapter: Predict relapse but leave the door open to resume later. Also, offer to do a 30-day callback.

If the family agrees to continue with Options B, C, or D, end the session with this final message:

Thank you so much for agreeing to continue. We now have a clear focus, clear next steps, and clear estimated numbers of sessions that we will meet together. When we get back together we will start immediately at Phase _____[dependent upon selected option]. If I have any pre-session preparation to do, I will be doing it. Between now and the next time we meet, please remember three things:

- One: Don't expect any changes yet. We have not yet begun this work.

- Two: Continue with your red flags checklist and look at it each morning.

- Three: If there are any signs of relapse, follow your Steps to Take and only call me if that is the next step. If not, wait until next week and we will discuss what happened [good to set boundaries for your clients].

All right, see you next week.

FINAL THOUGHTS

We hope you enjoyed the step-by-step procedures and the multitude of case examples to bring theory to practice. Many books today provide general theory and helpful concepts but lack the step-by-step procedures to really help when one is on the frontline. Traumatized children and their families in pain emit much drama along with so much fire and smoke that it is hard for the therapist to see where to navigate. Drama equals trauma, and the interactional trauma or constant fighting and stress keeps tearing off the scab over and over again so that the child's wounds never fully heal. Over time, both the child and family start to lose hope. The good news is found within an old story told by the great Virginia Satir (Satir & Baldwin, 1983):

> After listening to the engineer's description of the problems and asking a few questions, he went to the boiler room. He looked at the maze of twisting pipes, listened to the thump of the boiler and the hiss of the escaping steam for a few minutes, and felt some pipes with his hands. Then he hummed softly to himself, reached into his overalls and took out a small hammer, and tapped a bright red valve one time. Immediately, the entire system began working perfectly, and the boilermaker went home.
>
> When the steamship owner received a bill for one thousand dollars, he became outraged and complained that the boilermaker had only been in the engine room for fifteen minutes and requested an itemized bill. So the boilermaker sent him a bill that reads as follows:
>
> For tapping the valve: $.50
>
> For knowing where to tap: $999.50
>
> TOTAL: $1,000.00 (pp. 239–240)

In the same way, we hope that we not only showed you where to tap (locating the key unhealthy undercurrents preventing the wounds from healing) but also **how to do the tapping**. Coming full circle from the beginning and end of this book, the tapping or concrete strategies answer the "Now what?" question.

> What are the tools we need in the here and now as a family and village to rally around our children to help them heal their wounds and in the process heal our own?

Once these questions are answered ("Where to tap?" and "How to tap?"), the FST therapist can quickly cut through the smoke, pain, and drama to dial into the family's beautiful music just beneath the surface. Beautiful music such as the sounds of a mother asking forgiveness of her daughter to bring healing from depression, cutting, or sexual promiscuity. Or the beautiful sounds of a young man like Tom inviting the parents of the son who killed his father to attend the dedication ceremony of a memorial he and his family constructed. Or the sounds of a mother struggling in prayer for her lost daughter and going over to her house with cookies and a note saying, "Like the prodigal son, I will wait as long as it takes." Or the sounds of a father getting on his knees weeping, with tears hitting the carpet like raindrops. And then night after night doing a body check and holding his son in his arms without saying a word. Or the sounds of a therapist being in the middle of it all and being so impacted by the wounds healing that he or she cannot speak for a full 5 minutes.

It took us, eight long years to write the pages you have read. At times, we nearly gave up. But we could not. We know our world is getting tougher. Several major indicators support this viewpoint. According to an article in Time Magazine (Schrobsdorff, 2016), anxiety and depression in our adolescents is increasing with an estimated 30% of girls and 20% of boys (6.3 million teens) having anxiety disorders and 3 million teens aged 12 to 17 having had at least one major depressive episode in 2015 alone. Technology addiction is also on the rise and is reflected in Louv's (2008) book *Last Child in the Woods* and the term "nature-deficit disorder." A term describing a trend of children and adolescents who are more likely to spend hours online or tied to their cell phones rather than passing weekends or summer days hiking, swimming, or playing outside until the street lights come on.

Since 1988, when we first started, these types of major changes are leading to more broken families, more divorce, more addiction, less connection with extended family, more isolation, more anxiety, and ultimately more trauma. In a mental health field saturated with trauma-informed books, we hope this one stands as a beacon to the benefits of using systems theory to heal the traumatized child through his or her family and community. And in the process of rallying to heal their child, they are also healing themselves. It has been our honor and privilege to go on this journey, and now we pass the baton onto you!

REFERENCES

Brandon, T. H., Vidrine, J. I., & Litvin, E. B. (2007). Relapse and relapse prevention. *Annual Review of Clinical Psychology*, 3, 257–284.

Covey, S. R. (1990). *The 7 habits of highly effective people*. New York, NY: Free Press.

Figley, C. R. (2009). An introduction to the special issue on culture and international contributions. *Traumatology*, *15*(1), 1–2.

Larimer, M. E., & Palmer, R. S. (1999). Relapse prevention: An overview of Marlatt's cognitive-behavioral model. *Alcohol Research and Health*, *23*(2), 151–160.

Louv, R. (2008). *Last child in the woods: Saving our children from nature-deficit disorder*. New York, NY: Workman Publishing.

Satir, V., & Baldwin, M. (1983). *Satir step by step: A guide to creating change in families*. Palo Alto, CA: Science and Behavior Books.

Schrobsdorff, S. (2016). Teen depression and anxiety: Why the kids are not alright. *Time Magazine*, *188*(19), 188–195.

Tolkien, J. R. R. (2012). *The fellowship of the ring*. New York, NY: Ballantine.

Tune-Up. (2015). *Merriam-Webster's school dictionary*. Darien, CT: Federal Street Press.

Witkiewitz, K., & Marlatt, G. A. (2004). Relapse prevention for alcohol and drug problems. *American Psychologist*, *59*(4), 224–235.

Index